A CASE STUDY OF
BALLOTING REGULATION

A CASE STUDY OF BALLOTING REGULATION

The Boston and Maine Recapitalizes

1948–1953

ROBERT L. MASSON

Professor of Finance

HARVARD UNIVERSITY · DIVISION OF RESEARCH
GRADUATE SCHOOL OF BUSINESS ADMINISTRATION
Boston 1956

Foreword

EARLY IN 1951 Professor Masson began a study of the voluntary stock modification plan of the Boston and Maine Railroad, which had been submitted to stockholders for their assent in July 1950. This plan was the first all-stock modification plan submitted to vote under Section 20b of the Interstate Commerce Act. The study was to probe deeply into all the factors which were relevant to a full understanding of the plan itself and the management problems involved in developing the plan and getting it adopted. The objective of the project was to develop the broad implications for the management of financial reorganizations from an intensive, carefully analyzed case study.

The lengthy challenge to the validity of the votes of assent and the balloting procedures held up the culmination of the plan for more than two years, during which time the study of the plan itself was shelved. The contest which developed raised vividly a new series of questions on balloting procedures and the administration of procedures for obtaining stockholder assents in financial reorganizations. These are the questions that are explored in this volume. They have significance far beyond this particular episode and will be relevant to all parties involved, public and private, in many other kinds of corporate contests which are brought to a stockholder vote.

This is the first of two volumes dealing with this voluntary stock modification plan. The second will appear when work is completed on the broader study.

Financial support for this project has come from the general research funds of the School. These funds were given to the School by several industrial corporations to be used in support of research projects selected at the discretion of the School.

BERTRAND FOX
Director of Research

Soldiers Field
Boston, Massachusetts
November 1955

Preface

THE Boston and Maine case challenged the validity of balloting procedures at so many points that it has taken a sizable book to consider them. In the usual case of capital readjustment the battle comes mainly on the plan itself. In the Boston and Maine case not only was there controversy on the plan at every stage but the battleground shifted to the voting procedures. The issues were so broad and deep as to engage the Department of Justice and the courts, and to carry into another round of public hearings before the Interstate Commerce Commission.

I have long believed that for real understanding of the factors bearing on any major financial problem one needs the background story not revealed in the final decision. This is particularly true of financial reorganizations. Back of the final plan lie the realities that explain it — the initial steps, the false starts, the backstage maneuvers and negotiations, the conflicts of interest, and the ultimate compromises. Oftentimes the working papers or the preliminary drafts are more revealing of a party's motive or a point of view than the finished document itself.

Those best able to describe the developments in proceedings would naturally be the participants themselves, who as eye witnesses could place the whole action in perspective. Their recollections would give added meaning to the briefs, memoranda, correspondence, and documents. They could tell of the unpublished moves, mostly lost to the outside observer.

When big events are taking place in the political scene, it is not uncommon for the participants to keep diaries of their personal impressions. These firsthand observations later give new interpretations to the final outcome. In major financial developments, such as promotions, mergers, and reorganizations, the operators are not usually so history-minded. The realities along the way are seldom preserved to explain the final document.

To supply this lack in financial writings I began looking for some likely episode where I could try my hand at reconstructing the action to get its full financial meaning. I found one at my very door. Boston and Maine Railroad had been working since early 1948 on a stock modification plan under the new section 20b of the Interstate Commerce Act. Here was a situation made to order for following the working of a new statute. I was fortunate in getting assurance from Mr. E. S. French, then president of the Railroad, that its records of the undertaking would be made available to me. This was in March 1951.

During the previous year I had prepared for class discussion the plan as presented and the official explanation of its rationale. Mr. Everett W. Smith, who as assistant to the financial vice president had been working on the plan since April 1948, not only helped to assemble the material but led one class discussion to bring to it the realities that never appear in print. The success with this short case, together with assurance of cooperation by the Railroad officials, made more extensive research on the plan appear feasible and valuable.

The recapitalization had been stalled early in 1951 by a challenge by a minority group to the validity of the stockholders' vote accepting the plan. Later the Department of Justice entered on a full-scale inquiry into the charges. The effect of these developments on my research came abruptly on September 7, when representatives of the Department of Justice appeared at the Railroad's office and requisitioned all files and records relating to the plan and the solicitation of votes. I was then at work on documents from the files; I placed a marker at the page I had reached and hoped for an early end to the interruption.

Events moved fast. It became clear that the balloting dispute ran deep. The ICC, the Railroad's officers, and all concerned with the balloting and its aftermath were giving first attention to the instant controversy. In these circumstances it would have been highly unrealistic for one interested in financial realities to take only casual interest in the all-absorbing current action. The paramount issue had shifted to the merits of the challenge to balloting procedures. It took all my time to follow the fast-moving controversy; further study of the plan itself was of necessity held in abeyance.

Hence came this book, an analytical account of balloting problems in an actual case. The primary source materials were the extensive public record, which afforded background and analysis of unusual breadth. They were supplemented by interviews with most of the participants and my attendance at the hearings and court proceedings. This personal observation throughout the succession of events provided overtones not to be caught from the printed records.

New transactions in Boston and Maine stock lately have made headlines under conditions that indicate there are still unsolved problems in the area of corporate elections and control. Proxy fights have been the order in recent years, notably in railroads. Some of the technical aspects of corporate voting, particularly for stock in "street names," still pose questions as they did in the vote on the Boston and Maine plan.

At one point or another as the case developed, three government agencies played a part, with the ICC in the major role because of its primary regulating responsibility. Access to operating files in the government agencies is not available to an outsider, however, even though his objective is known to be only a study in the public interest. Although the ICC's public dockets contain all official papers and releases, the researcher cannot explore the veritable mine of relevant material in interoffice files. Just as legislative hearings throw necessary light on the intent of Congress in a statute, so the first drafts and office memoranda would reflect meanings not fully seen in the Commission's final reports. As will appear many times throughout the book, there remain unexplained questions about the participation of the Department of Justice. Much of importance to an understanding of its administrative decisions in this case must be left to surmise. The Securities and Exchange Commission came into the case only briefly in its investigation of broker participation in the balloting. Here, also, the results are sealed to the outsider as such investigations of private matters must necessarily be until they emerge in formal charges and action. Nothing has been released by the SEC in the way of findings from its study of alleged irregularities.

A case study of this sort, holding the spotlight as it does on a prolonged dispute over procedures in a narrow area of agency regulation, carries a danger of distorting the whole picture of regulatory operations by emphasis on one aspect only. It is important to keep a clear perspective. The Boston and Maine case was one of many types on the operating agenda of the ICC at the time. There is constant pressure on the Commission to get things settled. This necessity for action within a reasonable time is reflected in its approach to the task of establishing a practicable procedure. Procedural problems must be viewed in the setting of ever-widening responsibilities of an agency with limited staff, budget, and time. The new statute, section 20b, was seized upon by many carriers as a feasible way of solving problems and it had to be applied in a variety of situations. The challenge to regulation is to determine what is needed for a workable statute. It is for Congress to provide the necessary means.

To make the study more than a mere bookish review of the printed record, it was especially important that the Commission's operations be understood. Commissioner Charles D. Mahaffie was from the start sympathetic with the project and permitted me to talk over procedural matters with officials in the Bureau of Finance — its Director, Mr. C. E. Boles, now retired; Mr. R. T. Boyden, his successor; Mr. Vernon V. Baker, Assistant Director; and Mr. Homer H. Kirby, the Hearing Examiner on the case. While the text of the study may not be construed as expressing their views, I owe much to their patience and helpfulness in responding to this extra demand on their time in connection with the case that of itself provided troubles enough.

The Railroad made available its files on the case. To these were added the personal interest of the Railroad officers who were close to the action in all stages. They gave ready attention to my many requests for explanation and interpretation. In particular, Mr. Richard Jackson, general attorney of the Railroad, read closely and commented on an entire preliminary draft of the manuscript. Mr. Everett W. Smith also discussed with me many aspects of the procedures.

Mr. Sidney V. Smith, counsel for several assenting stock-holders as interveners, was helpful especially on the matter of the settlement that took the plaintiffs out of the proceedings. Members of Old Colony Trust Company's staff read drafts of my manuscript relating to their operations. It is a pleasure to report also that all the other parties concerned with the case gave help to the extent that their positions permitted. Litigants are not generally given to *post mortems* for publica-tion, and understandably so. It has meant a great deal to my study that all showed interest in my major objective.

It has been gratifying to find widespread interest among many outside the case in helping along a study not directly bearing on their own immediate problems. Mr. Ray Garrett of the Chicago bar and Messrs. G. Clark Cummings and De Forest Billyou of the New York bar gave me the benefit of their professional experience in railroad reorganizations. I am indebted also to Mr. Roger S. Clapp, a businessman with a student's interest in corporation finance as it affects the stockholder. His familiarity with the whole proceedings, as an onlooker only, provided cogent comment on all chap-ters. Throughout the course of the research my inquiries on technical matters met willing response from many financial men, too numerous for individual mention. Among these were officers of the New York Stock Exchange.

For personal and official encouragement in the early stages of the study, I wish to thank the former Director of Research, Professor Emeritus Melvin T. Copeland. The present Di-rector, Professor Bertrand Fox, gave critical attention to the whole manuscript and made constructive suggestions on both exposition and content. Professor Emeritus Henry W. Dunn was very helpful, as always, particularly on the question of voting classes considered in Chapter VI. My colleague, Pro-fessor Arthur H. Cole, gave time in discussing the general approach to this type of research, as did Professor Louis Loss, of the Harvard Law School, on matters of SEC procedure.

Special acknowledgment is due for the invaluable assist-ance of Miss Carolyn Stubbs from the very inception of the project through the last page. In addition to her skill with the details of the source materials and their use as the manu-script evolved, she made a significant contribution as a con-

structive critic on both substance and presentation. In full
charge of the details of publication, Miss Ruth Norton, Secretary to the Division of Research, kept things moving with
quiet efficiency.

The usual affirmation is in order: the full responsibility for
exposition, interpretation, and conclusions is mine alone. In
so broad a field it is manifest that further inquiry is necessary
to find definitive answers to many questions raised. There
remain unresolved problems for the legal and financial specialists in regulation.

ROBERT L. MASSON

Soldiers Field
Boston, Massachusetts
November 1955

CONTENTS

xiii

A CASE STUDY OF
BALLOTING REGULATION

CHAPTER I

Introduction

THIS IS a case history of the balloting experience of the Boston and Maine Railroad in a voluntary stock modification under a new amendment, section 20b, of the Interstate Commerce Act. The new legislation for railroads in April 1948 first made it possible to force minorities to go along with a modification plan that a majority of 75% of each class would accept. Justice would certainly be served, it was thought, if the plans of security modification were considered "just and reasonable" by the Interstate Commerce Commission and also by so large a majority of security holders.

Among the cases under this statute, the Boston and Maine case was first in two important respects: it involved the first all-stock modification plan to be accepted by the Interstate Commerce Commission and later put in effect, and it was the first case in which there was litigation over balloting matters, which in the other situations had been largely routine.

There were two phases of this episode in recapitalization. The first was to prepare a plan that would gain acceptance by the Commission and the stockholders. One could see at a glance that the stock structure of the Railroad had grown into a complex of overlaid preferred stocks with little relation to present or prospective earning power. Preparation of the plan presented many problems of its own; as is usual in such cases, it was certain that some stockholders would object to its terms. Nevertheless, by early 1949 the Railroad had worked out a plan with every prospect of support from stockholders. The Commission held a public hearing on the plan in March of that year. On the basis of the hearing and argument, the Commission in 1950 issued an order approving the plan with some amendment and submitting it to vote.

3

The second phase of the case involved the many basic questions of voting procedure. It began in July 1950 with the submission of the plan to the stockholders for their assent and continued in the solicitation of assents by the Railroad and in the recording of assents by a depositary, a trust company approved by the Commission. As of January 1951 the vote had been taken and officially certified to the Commission and the Commission was in process of giving it effect.

Quite unexpectedly, as had never happened before at this stage in any section 20b proceeding, the same minority that had protested unfairness in the plan now started to oppose on another tack; it challenged the validity of assents and of solicitation procedure. In short, it alleged that the Railroad's certificate that the required majority vote had been obtained was invalid and the whole plan of modification was therefore a nullity.

The Commission denied the petition to reopen the proceedings; but the objectors, not easily discouraged, obtained a court order to stay the plan and promptly filed a civil suit. Their allegations of irregularity were so alarming to the Department of Justice that it took up the plaintiffs' case, conducted its own intensive investigation, and after some six months came out with a Trial Brief summing up its position on the balloting as follows:

The railroad solicitation of assents commenced after July 10, 1950, and continued until 5:05 P.M. on December 14, 1950, at which time the railroad by telegram notified the Commission that the required percentage of assents . . . had been received. . . . Subsequently, the railroad [sent to the Commission] the certificates of the depositary and of the railroad itself to the effect that the required percentage of assents had been received during the submission period. The United States will prove that these two certificates were invalid in that the depositary did not receive the required percentage of valid assents of the four classes prior to 5:05 P.M. on December 14, 1950.[1]

[1] Department of Justice, Trial Brief of Defendant, the United States, in the United States District Court for the District of Columbia, Civil Action No. 763–51, December 1951, p. 20 (mimeo.) .

The suit ended a year later with the Court's complete support of the Commission's part in the procedure. Nevertheless, the Court's decision added the strong suggestion that the Commission reopen the proceedings to investigate the charges of irregular balloting. There followed five days of public hearings on the charges. The Commission's final report was issued on April 21, 1953, finding that the minimum percentages of assented shares had been obtained in a lawful manner although it disqualified three blocks of stock. "Holders of the requisite percentages . . . ," said the Commission, "assented to the plan of modification. . . . The stockholders' assents constituting such percentages were procured in a lawful manner and in conformity with the provisions of the said order of April 19, 1950." [2] The plan was ordered effective as of May 21, 1953.

The story of the Boston and Maine stock modification is thus a composite of the normal procedures in any such situation and of extended litigation. Several previous section 20b modifications had been voted on with no such contests over validity of procedure. Objections by intervening parties are usual in such actions until they naturally subside after the final decision and order of the Commission. It is exceptional when interveners choose to undergo the additional expense of further challenge. It is still more rare when objectors can have the support of the Department of Justice in arguing their cause before a court. It took the Court's action, the Department's brief, and the subsequent public hearings and records, however, to highlight some unexpected problems of procedure, which if they remain uncorrected will open the way to similar troubles in the future.

Disputes serve to clarify basic issues. The application of a new statute is not unlike the experience with a new development in production: first a pilot plant and then adjustments for unforeseen "bugs" until smooth operation is achieved. So in procedures to implement a statute, no blueprint can show all the hidden difficulties that cases later reveal. For a variety of reasons, which will appear as the story unfolds, the problems and conflict in the Boston and Maine

2 282 I.C.C. 750, at p. 798, April 21, 1953.

case provide the setting and the material for close analysis of the administrative procedures necessary to fulfill the requirements of a new statute.[3]

WHY STUDY AN UNUSUAL SITUATION?

A situation may seem unusual because it is the first in which troubles show up; or it may be unusual in the sense that it includes features so extraordinary as not likely to be repeated. The Boston and Maine case is clearly the former. There is value in examination of a case in which disputes arose, even those without merit, because it forces study of things taken for granted. Where and why did events jump from the normal channel and move from one crisis to another, all outside the regulatory system whence they started? Unexpected troubles did show up, and they point the way to difficulties that may recur unless procedural changes are made. What appeared to be an unusual case serves as a dramatic example to force re-examination of the statute and regulations so as to forestall interruptions in orderly and dependable procedures.

There is evidence from recent "proxy fights"[4] that many features of voting procedures open the way for litigation, and there are some in which there is little or no case law for guidance. It was in anticipation of possible trouble or perhaps a protracted count at the New York Central election in May 1954 that the three inspectors of election chosen the

[3] The Interstate Commerce Commission's proceedings on the Boston and Maine Railroad Securities Modification are contained in Finance Docket No. 16250. The decisions are: Report of the Commission by Division 4, 275 I.C.C. 397 (April 19, 1950); Report of the Commission on Reconsideration, ibid., 527 (July 10, 1950); Supplemental Report of the Commission, ibid., 752 (January 23, 1951); Second Supplemental Report of the Commission, 282 I.C.C. 750 (April 21, 1953). The decision in the civil suit before the U.S. District Court for the District of Columbia — Civil Action No. 763–51 — is found in *Sakis* v. *United States,* 103 Fed. Supp. 292 (February 21, 1952).

[4] In the spring of 1954, for instance, proxy fights were prominent in the financial news; four notable ones were those of the New York Central Railroad, the New York, New Haven and Hartford Railroad, the Minneapolis and St. Louis Railroad, and the American Woolen Company. Early in 1955 a contest over control of Boston and Maine Railroad resulted in a complete overturn of management.

previous year, who had served annually for 6, 10, and 21 years, respectively, withdrew. Three law professors specializing in the corporate field were appointed in their stead to conduct this election. The margin of victory was wide, however, and there was no legal action over the vote, probably because such action even if successful would not have changed the result. A tight contest with subsequent litigation would furnish answers to many unsettled problems. Enough complications appeared, however, especially with regard to brokers' proxies, to justify thorough re-examination of procedures and possibly further regulation in this whole area.[5] In a real sense, the Boston and Maine case was a forerunner; it focused on some trouble spots in corporate voting methods that are an invitation for future challengers.

THE OBJECTIVES OF THE STUDY

The very magnitude of the troubles that plagued the voting on the Boston and Maine plan invited an over-all analysis of their nature and a search for causes and remedies. It was first necessary to draw from the voluminous record the central questions at issue. Each party, of course, could restudy its own special operations to find where things went wrong. It probably would have definite ideas of necessary changes if the balloting was to be repeated. This piecemeal approach would lack the advantage of a comprehensive review of the whole episode by one who had no part either from the regulatory side or in the operations whose validity was challenged. One outside the action gains perspective in dealing with the challenges and the answers so that the whole record can be marshaled systematically to point up the critical issues and give a basis for constructive suggestions.

The next objective was to determine how far the alleged wrongs stemmed from statute and regulations, and how far the fault lay with the operations themselves. When a judgment was reached on these points, there remained the final

---

[5] In 1955 the SEC was proposing an amendment to its proxy rules relating to the circumstances under which brokers or dealers might give proxies, consents, or authorizations for securities carried for the accounts of customers. See Release No. 5166, Securities and Exchange Commission, May 5, 1955.

step of presenting recommendations for changes in the statute and regulations and in operating procedures in order to insure dependable results.

It needs no argument that a certified total of votes must come from a provable tally of ballots and in strict accord with known rules. The Boston and Maine case has provided a dramatic example demonstrating the importance of a system for balloting that will stand up against challenges to its validity.

Although the balloting here was under rules for a special vote in a statutory recapitalization, many conclusions from the study have a broad application. Some of the issues in this case have their counterpart in the wider field of corporate voting; many of the arguments in this litigation suggest directions for further inquiry into the whole machinery of stockholder voting as it presently works.

One would expect that a study of procedures controlled by an administrative agency of the government would include observations on the strictly administrative aspects as to both policy and performance. When there is a record of prolonged disputes over operations, as in this case, it is natural to look for defects in administration. There were many instances where it seemed probable that had a different administrative policy been established at the very start, the succession of difficulties would have been halted. So-called principles of sound administration are easy to state, but the trick is to know how they apply in the particular case. Throughout the book an ancillary objective is to deal with administration at all the levels of responsibility. Some general conclusions on administration follow in the next section; others will develop from the detailed description of operations in later chapters.

It will be apparent to the specialists, particularly the lawyers, that I have not reached the bottom of every issue opened up in this episode. My intention was to go far enough to provide a firm basis for some general conclusions. The study is not a manual of technical procedures, nor are all aspects of the various topics fully explored. It will serve a proper purpose if it uncovers areas where more work is to be done, and is helpful in pointing the way.

SOME CONCLUSIONS ON ADMINISTRATION DRAWN
FROM THE STUDY

Case histories of administration in practice can furnish real opportunity to find out why some procedures work and others fail. Administration is one of those general words that need definition in terms of plans and people in order to have meaning for effective ways of doing things. In simple terms, administration starts with planning in three areas: what is to be done, what people are to do it, and how they are to do it. Then, since plans are only good as they can be carried out, good management embraces the doing as well as the planning.

The words of the section 20b statute [6] with reference to balloting embrace these aspects concisely:

> . . . the Commission shall cause the carrier, in such manner as it shall direct, to submit the proposed alteration or modification . . . to the holders of each class of its securities . . . for acceptance or rejection.

Here we have the three essentials of the administrative concept. There is the top responsibility of the Commission to accomplish a vote, presumably valid, by organizing a procedure that involves people and rules and making sure that it works.

Administrative responsibilities lie at different levels. In any complex problem in administration there is a range of decisions starting with the top policies that shape the general pattern and descending to the operating procedures for carrying them out. The sequence of decisions to carry out the major objective is not unlike that in a military campaign. Once the major decision is made in terms of alternative points of invasion, size of force, components, time, and other critical elements in the operation, there then must follow the delegation of lesser responsibilities to carry out the master plan. There are the initial policies at the top and precision operations to implement them.

In the case before us the statute laid the broad require-

[6] 62 Stat. 163 (1948), 49 U.S.C. Section 20b (1952 edition). See Appendix A.

ments, such as 75% assent by classes, official solicitation material, and no votes permitted to securities under the control of the Railroad. The Commission was the "high command" to carry out these objectives and implement them with detailed orders. Below the over-all responsibility of the Commission lay the subordinate responsibilities of the operating parties within the orbit of their own organizations — in this case the Railroad and the depositary. There were two main areas where action had to conform to rules, namely, in the solicitation of votes and in the recording of them. Solicitation was the Railroad's part in the action, controlled by the statute and any special rules laid down in the Commission's order. The depositary was the intermediary agency under the direction of the Commission to set up and operate the mechanism for accurate recording. If the voting procedure in a section 20b proceeding was different from the traditional proxy system in corporate voting, the difference should have been made clear by the Commission and understood by the depositary at the start. The Commission's concept of the limits to proper solicitation should have governed the Railroad.

How was it possible for so routine a procedure as balloting and certification of total assents to be met suddenly by challenge in many sectors, challenges apparently with enough merit to enlist the active support of the Department of Justice? The Commission itself had long supervised the voting in section 77 cases,[7] and four section 20b cases had been completed without challenge to the voting results. Old Colony Trust Company, the depositary in this case, was experienced in corporate voting, and the Railroad's own counsel was probably among the few railroad counsel thoroughly familiar with the new section 20b. He had been close to the legislative development of the new law and, with the impending Boston and Maine plan in mind, had been personally active in getting the provisions of the statute broadened to include a modification plan where only the capital stock structure was involved. Why could not these three parties, each skilled and presumably competent, bring about a result that could be

---

[7] Section 77, an amendment (1933) to the National Bankruptcy Act, applied specifically to railroads. 47 Stat. 1474 (1933), 11 U.S.C. §205.

certified with such assured authority as to discourage challenge from the start?

From the record in this case it can be assumed that when the balloting opened, the parties to the operation felt sure that the essential procedural matters were in order. When at 5:05 P.M. on December 14, 1950, the Railroad telegraphed the Commission that enough votes were in hand and the submission period was closed, it is reasonably certain that none of the parties had even a passing thought that a sequence of disputes over the validity of ballots would be touched off to continue for two and one-half years. The unexpected happened; and a minority committee was prompt to seize upon many ways of keeping the case open.

If we assume operating competence in the several parties, the troubles that developed must trace largely to a lack of coordination, essentially a problem in administration. Coordination implies direction. It is not spontaneous; it must be planned. Even perfect operation would not be insurance against the nuisance-value critic who aims to profit by threats of trouble; one can be sure, however, that proper administration would be able to deal promptly with those who bring charges of irregular procedure, whether honestly or otherwise. To spot the problem is not to solve it, but it is the necessary first step.

Although once the litigation had started the record is largely in the lawyers' briefs and answers, it is submitted that the essence of the problem from the viewpoint of causes was not legal but administrative. The litigation was the aftermath; had there been proper administration a large part of the litigation might well have been avoided. For the lawyer, the litigated parts of this episode pose several problems; his interest lies in the decisions reached in view of the facts, the statute, and the pertinent legal precedents. For the businessman and the government agency, the Boston and Maine case spells costly failure, and failure calls for search for the contributing causes.

The success of a small minority in holding up a plan on charges of invalid procedures under surveillance of our oldest government regulating agency compels a re-examination of the proper handling of the balloting in section 20b proceedings. The administrative job was not complete unless, when the depositary certified to the total assents cast, those ultimately responsible could say that the machinery was adequate for legal assents and a running surveillance during the process was maintained to assure compliance. This done, any challenge would amount to a direct charge of the Commission's incompetence or worse — hardly a move to be made lightly as a mere obstructive tactic, but only after sober reflection on its costs.

The experience of the Department of Justice in seeing its extended list of charges fade under closer analysis should cause it concern over its methods and proper role. The costs and delays of this case raise the significant question of whether protection of the minority can pass a line where it works injustice to the majority. The art of administrative law is to give the one without bringing the other.

THE RELATION OF ADMINISTRATIVE AND LEGAL PROBLEMS — THE BUSINESSMAN AND THE LAWYER

Our conclusion that the problems that made this case notorious were in considerable degree administrative must recognize that once the litigation started the legal questions became paramount. After the Commission refused to permit further delay in putting the plan into effect, and the minority group got a court order to stay the proceedings, then the lawyers for all parties took virtual command until the legal proceedings ran their course.

Indeed, from the very start of setting up the balloting mechanism there were legal decisions to make. The statutory requirements had to be followed, and they called for interpretation. To vote by classes — what is a *class?* To bar *controlled* stock from voting — what is *controlled* stock? When the statute provides that all solicitation material be passed on by the Commission, does it thereby deny the right of oral solicitation? Interpretation of the statute is for the lawyer, but the statute must be workable and fit the business realities. Further, the actual voting procedure presented legal niceties at every stage.

Recognizing, then, that a complete study of the manifold

problems plaguing this operation would include technical legal studies, I emphasize that the legal questions are left to the trained lawyer. My purpose is to treat the whole modification program as a major objective requiring the most skilled direction by responsible executives. Many legal questions were unavoidable and the lawyers were the ones to decide them, but only in their function as an adjunct to conducting the administrative process so that there would be no weakness in its legal armor. This was the relation of the businessman and the lawyer while the balloting operation was being planned and conducted. As soon as the whole matter was in litigation, the business executive as such could do little but stand by and anxiously wring his hands.

*   *   *   *   *

The parties in this case included both the judicial or quasi-judicial government agencies and those private parties who were in the role of adversaries. The result was a collection of briefs, answers, transcript records, and official opinions that almost defies orderly presentation. The difficult task for one in search of correct principles in a controversial procedure is to get at the central issues and then to sift out the relevant arguments. The problem is the same as that which impressed the ancient commentators on human action:

> *He who states his case first seems right,*
> *until the other comes and examines him.*
> The Proverbs 18:17
> (Revised Standard Version)

The proverb seems to say, "Hold your judgment until all sides are heard and examined." It carries a strong implication that *ex parte* statements — "he who states *his* case" — uniformly are self-serving; they should be tested by searching questions. The eleven chapters to follow in this book aim to do just that. They will examine the charges brought by those who held that the balloting procedures in the Boston and Maine case were defective in principle and practice.

As a basis for full understanding of the central issues, which are analyzed in Chapters V–X, necessary details are given in Chapters II–IV as to the parties in the action, the origins of the complexities in the stock structure, and the course of events throughout the balloting dispute. The parties so familiar with the action itself may consider the preliminary chapters skimpy in detail. To supply the general reader with enough descriptive facts, and in the right sequence, has posed many problems in writing.

As things turned out, the policy-makers of each of the parties, looking back on their own decisions along the way, could doubtless see errors of omission and commission. My own judgments after the event are summarized in Chapter XI — Policies in Retrospect. A final chapter then draws from the whole analysis suggestions for changes in statute, procedures, and broad administrative policies.

CHAPTER II

The Parties

THE PARTIES in this balloting dispute divide into three groups. The first comprises those directly concerned with the balloting itself as a normal operation: Boston and Maine Railroad, the Interstate Commerce Commission, Old Colony Trust Company as depositary for tabulation of the assents. With these should be included Georgeson & Co., which was employed by the Railroad to solicit assents, as is frequently done in such voting campaigns. In the second group are those who took legal action on alleged invalid voting procedures: the Sakis group of objecting stockholders and the Department of Justice. The third are those who came in as the legal proceedings progressed: a three-judge Court, L. F. Rothschild & Co. and Goldman, Sachs & Co., and other interveners and negotiators interested in speeding the effective date of the plan. Still another party, who officially reviewed the record and wrote a report after broad personal investigation in early 1953, was Mr. Robert D. L'Heureux, chief counsel for the Senate Committee on Interstate and Foreign Commerce.

PARTIES DIRECTLY CONCERNED WITH THE BALLOTING

Boston and Maine Railroad (hereinafter generally called the Railroad)

The first action in a voluntary securities modification under section 20b is taken by the applicant, the carrier. A very brief sketch of the action of the Railroad as a party will suffice here. In early 1949, after withdrawing its first plan, the Railroad prepared a revised plan and submitted to the Commission an amended application for authority to modify the various classes of its outstanding capital stock. Its most difficult work was accomplished when the plan was complete and it was prepared to defend the plan at the public hearing.

Once the formal requirements were met — application filed with the Commission and supported by testimony and briefs, depositary selected and ready, manner of submission and solicitation material prepared and approved — the part played by the management of the Railroad was mainly that of helping to locate unassented stock and keeping score on assents. The big problem of the management throughout the voting was to help in rounding up the shares of holders who had not assented to the plan. The financial officers kept a duplicate record of stockholders and corrected it each day as the reports on new assents were received from the depositary. As would be expected, inquiries about the plan came from stockholders and also some criticisms, all requiring answer. In addition, after the voting had been under way for several weeks the officers concluded that it was necessary to engage specialists in proxy solicitation to assist in locating stockholders and soliciting assents, as permitted by the Commission's order. Furthermore, although the letter of instructions on the depositary's procedure had been drawn up at the Railroad, questions arose as the voting continued that had not been anticipated by officers of either the Railroad or the depositary; these required discussion with Railroad counsel.

Two further important decisions were required of the Railroad management in connection with the modification plan. One was whether to close the submission period before the final date set by the Commission. The officers decided to close the submission period at once when the responsible officer of the depositary telephoned that the required percentage of assented shares had been reached for the last of the four classes. Consummation of the plan was held off, however, by the civil suit filed by the Sakis Committee in February 1951, which caused many months' further delay and expense as well as lengthy and tedious litigation. It is not surprising therefore that the executive committee of the Railroad took the second important decision, which was to approve in August 1952 a settlement negotiated by the Railroad and interested banking houses with the Sakis group.[1]

---

[1] Some details of the settlement are given in Chapter IV. The settlement was the subject of an investigation by the Commission under Docket No. 31257, Inquiry into Legality and Propriety of Payments by Boston & Maine

The Interstate Commerce Commission [2]

The Commission has had much experience with balloting in railroad recapitalizations since the enactment of section 77 of the Bankruptcy Act in 1933 and the later temporary chapter XV of the same act [3] to govern voluntary debt adjustments. These acts not only gave the Commission responsibility for approval of the plans of reorganization or adjustment but also put into its hands supervision of the voting on the plans by the affected security holders. The Commission itself has conducted the balloting and tabulation of the votes under these laws. Up to 1950 it had supervised balloting in some 35 such recapitalizations.

The handling of section 20b cases grew out of the experience with the cases coming under the earlier laws. In May 1948, after conferences with officials of railroads then considering modifications of securities under the new act, the Commission set up rules to govern procedure.[4] They were based in large measure on those developed under section 77 and chapter XV. The same thorough procedure of applications, hearings on the proposed plans, and reports and orders supported by full analysis is used as in previous cases.[5]

Railroad on Account of Legal Services and Expenses and of Other Activities in Connection with Proposed Modification of Securities. Public hearings were held before Commissioner Mitchell on December 28, 1953, and March 12 and June 2, 1954. The Report of the Commission is found in 294 I.C.C. 549 (March 7, 1955).

[2] The exhaustive study of the Commission is *The Interstate Commerce Commission* by I. L. Sharfman (New York, The Commonwealth Fund, Parts I and II, 1931; Part III-A, 1935; Part III-B, 1936; Part IV, 1937).

[3] Enacted as the Chandler Act, 53 Stat. 1134 (1939), effective for 1939–1940, and the McLaughlin Act, 56 Stat. 787 (1942) effective for 1942–1945.

[4] The Commission's regulations of May 25, 1948, are contained in the *Code of Federal Regulations* (1949 edition), Title 49, Section 55. The rules significant to balloting are given in Appendix B.

[5] For a description of the Commission's processes in the 1930's, see Sharfman, op. cit., Part Four, Chapter XVII. Much of the development of the procedure in reorganizations and securities modifications, however, has taken place since the publication of Sharfman's volumes. See also the U.S. Attorney General's Committee on Administrative Procedure, *Administrative Procedure in Government Agencies,* Part 11, Interstate Commerce Commission (Washington, Government Printing Office, 1941).

One major change was made, however. The Commission has put the responsibility for tabulating the assents to a section 20b plan into the hands of a depositary, a financial institution designated by the railroad and satisfactory to the Commission. It declares the plan effective on the basis of the railroad's certificate, supported by the certified report of the depositary on the total assents received. Use of a depositary was not statutory under section 20b, but was provided by a Commission regulation in order to avoid an additional burden on its staff. The thought was also to take advantage of the professional experience of large financial institutions in tabulating ballots.

Section 20b cases, unless they reach the full Commission, are the responsibility of Division 4, which functions through its operating unit, the Bureau of Finance. Three Commissioners,[6] who have responsibility for cases in financial regulation, constitute Division 4. Although an occasional important case goes directly to the full Commission for decision, in the usual situation the Commission's report and order are formulated by Division 4, and the case goes to the full Commission only if reconsideration of decisions or policies is requested.

Before an application for securities modification is made, officials of the railroad usually talk informally with officials in the Bureau of Finance on the basis of a rough draft of their plan. These conferences are mutually beneficial even though the proposed plan described in the application still has to survive the scrutiny by Division 4 or the full Commission after a public hearing and the Hearing Examiner's report based thereon.

As soon as an application is filed and assigned for hearing, the Bureau of Finance names a Hearing Examiner to preside at the hearings.[7] To insure a useful record for the Commission, much depends on the skill of the Examiner in conduct-

[6] Commissioners Mahaffie, Patterson, and Mitchell constituted Division 4 when the report of April 19, 1950, on the Boston and Maine modification was issued. Commissioner Cross took Commissioner Patterson's place in 1953.

[7] The Boston and Maine case was assigned to Hearing Examiner Homer H. Kirby, who from the nature of his function and responsibilities became the operating officer who stayed with the case throughout the proceedings.

ing the hearings.   Next, in normal procedure, from the record and from briefs by the contending parties the Examiner draws up his Proposed Report, which in turn becomes the target for exceptions and oral arguments by the parties.   The basic records, the Proposed Report, and the sheaf of ancillary briefs and exceptions then go for consideration first to the Director and Assistant Director of the Bureau, and then to Division 4 or the Commission, one of which promulgates the definitive report and the order either of denial or of submission of the plan to vote.

The order of submission governs the procedure to be followed by the railroad in obtaining assents and by the depositary in receiving assents and revocations.   In addition, the material drawn up by the railroad or stockholders for use in solicitation of assents or dissents is examined with meticulous care within the Commission; and frequently changes are requested before approval is given.

The rules of the Commission covering section 20b procedure definitely place upon itself the responsibility for giving direction ". . . (1) as to the manner in which the carrier shall submit the proposed [plan] to the holders of each class . . . for acceptance or rejection, and (2) as to the manner of proof to be made by the carrier of the percentage of assents. . . ."   On the basis of the railroad's certificate and other procedural documents the Commission issues a final order setting the date upon which the modifications provided in the plan are to become final.

There was hardly an aspect of the normal procedure for assents that escaped attack by those who challenged the validity of the certified vote in the Boston and Maine case.

Old Colony Trust Company (hereinafter called Old Colony or the depositary)

Long the transfer agent for the Railroad, Old Colony was its natural choice for depositary in the balloting process. Confirmed by the Commission in that role, Old Colony certified to a successful vote.   When the Department of Justice in the fall of 1951 undertook investigation of the assents, the resulting charges of invalid assents brought Old Colony by its very position into the vanguard of the defense.   It had to wait over two years, until the final report of the Commission in April 1953, before it was cleared of the charges that it had certified to invalid assents.

The reader will more easily understand the developments in Old Colony's part of the procedure if the setting in which it functioned is described briefly.   Old Colony, an affiliate of the First National Bank of Boston, had probably the largest transfer business in the United States except for banks in New York City.   In addition, it had had broad experience with operations involving voting by stockholders, including voting on reorganizations and capital readjustments.   Between 1928 and 1952 it had processed between 2,000,000 and 3,000,000 proxies.[8]

Certain personnel relationships between the Railroad and Old Colony were important, also, because they led the Department of Justice to question the depositary's ability to act as independent agent.   Mr. E. S. French, then president of the Railroad, was also a director of the First National Bank, the stockholders of which owned Old Colony beneficially. Mr. T. Jefferson Coolidge, one of the Railroad directors in charge of formulating the plan, was also a director of the First National Bank and of Old Colony.   These facts must have been known to the Commission, which raised no question of disqualification of Old Colony.   Although interlocking directorships are studied by the Commission with care in situations of railroad management, here they were apparently disregarded as irrelevant.

Georgeson & Co.

Georgeson & Co., a specialist in general stockholder relations, is well known as a professional solicitor of votes in corporate elections.

The place of Georgeson & Co. in the Boston and Maine case is particularly important because one of the charges brought by the Sakis group and the Department of Justice related to the operations of the paid solicitors.   The participation of the specialist in proxy solicitation [9] is common prac-

---

[8] Brief of Old Colony Trust Company, Intervenor, before the Interstate Commerce Commission, Finance Docket No. 16250, October 20, 1952, p. 5.

[9] At the time when this chapter was written, Georgeson & Co. was active in a number of campaigns, two being the two railroad situations in which

tice when contests for stockholder support are in prospect; and the hiring of paid specialists was permitted by the Commission's order in this case. Georgeson & Co. had been employed in soliciting for the Railroad's bond adjustment of 1940. In September 1950, after several weeks of voting had shown the difficulties of locating holders of the common stock and obtaining their assents, the Railroad turned again to proxy specialists, and hired Georgeson & Co. to solicit assents from common stockholders. Mr. Richard S. Nye, a partner, was in direct charge of the work, which was carried on by the company's offices and representatives in cities throughout the country.

The long-established reputation of professional solicitors is evidence enough of the value of the functions they perform and their successful methods. Their main function is the development of methods of finding the stockholders and presenting arguments to them rather than the preparation of the arguments themselves. In fact, as previously noted, section 20b requires the solicitation material to be approved by the Commission. This stated control of solicitation material at once led the Sakis group and the Department of Justice to question the legality of oral solicitation. They also stressed the danger that solicitors would make serious misrepresentations in oral solicitation.

Another problem in the Boston and Maine case was whether assents resulting from Mr. Nye's personal transactions in the Railroad's stock were controlled by the Railroad. Details and conclusions on all these matters must await development in Chapters IX and X.

PLAINTIFFS IN THE BALLOTING LITIGATION

The Sakis Group

Of the numerous interveners in the first public hearing in March 1949, the Sakis Committee and Mr. George P. Sakis were the only ones to continue active opposition after the

---

fights for control were paramount issues in 1954 — those involving the New York Central and the New Haven railroads. At the Hearing before the Examiner on September 10, 1952, in the Boston and Maine case (p. 1771), the managing partner commented that the company had handled some 175 campaigns in the past year.

Commission's report of April 19, 1950. The committee was described as a committee of stockholders of Boston and Maine Railroad, composed of Mabel Benson Sakis, Byron J. Harrill, and Robert W. Hart,[10] and with Mr. Donald S. Caruthers as counsel. In March 1949 the committee represented 533 stockholders owning 58,676 shares of various classes.[11] In the fall of 1949 it claimed proxies for over 700 stockholders and over 75,000 shares.[12] As of the reopening of the case by the Commission in February 1952 the committee claimed to represent some 800 holders of approximately 60,000 shares.[13] The Railroad, however, by a check made in December 1951 of the list of stockholders from whom the Sakis Committee held proxies, claimed that only 232 holders remained who had neither sold nor assented their shares. These 232 holders held 22,468 shares, or 2.1% of the outstanding stock.[14]

Mr. Sakis, husband of Mabel Benson Sakis, did not join the committee; he wanted to present his own calculations and amendments at the public hearing on the plan in March 1949, whereas the committee believed that it held proxies for opposing the Railroad's plan and not for proposing any new plan.[15] Counsel for Mr. Sakis was Mr. Albert C. Borghi,

10 Mr. Hart later withdrew; in January 1952 Mr. Harrill died. The petition to the Commission in February 1952 was filed in the names of a committee of stockholders composed of Mabel Benson Sakis and Byron J. Harrill (deceased) and Mabel Benson Sakis, an individual.

11 Hearing before the Examiner, March 28, 1949, p. 4. These proxies had been given in response to a letter sent by Mrs. Sakis to all stockholders on March 18, 1949.

12 275 I.C.C. 397, at 405 (1950).

13 Testimony of Mrs. Mabel Benson Sakis at the hearing on the "settlement" question before Commissioner Mitchell, June 2, 1954. She stated that most of these proxies were given in April 1949 for a two-year term. No action had been taken to renew them. Proceedings before the Interstate Commerce Commission, Docket No. 31257, June 2, 1954, pp. 200–204.

14 Record of Pre-Trial Conference in Civil Action No. 763–51, December 10–11, 1951, p. 24.

15 Hearing before the Examiner, March 31, 1949, p. 636. An interesting detail in the strategy of opposition appears in another important reason for having Mr. and Mrs. Sakis represented as two separate objecting parties by two separate lawyers of the same firm. The advantage lay in the time allotted in hearings or court proceedings to counsel when arguments were on a time basis. This seemingly small matter suggests that from the very start the strategy of intervention was thoroughly studied in these whole proceedings.

a partner of Mr. Caruthers. At the hearing Mr. and Mrs. Sakis were said to own, jointly, or as tenants in common, 200 prior preference shares and between 3,000 and 4,000 shares of various series of the first preferred stock. Each owned some stock separately.[16]

Because Mr. Sakis usually supported the committee's petitions, and because his lawyer and the committee's lawyer were partners, this study generally refers to these interveners collectively as the Sakis group.

Mr. Sakis had been interested in Boston and Maine stocks at least as early as August 1945 when he began a correspondence with a New York investment dealer [17] with regard to the speculative possibilities of the stocks, particularly the first preferred. This correspondence shows that Mr. Sakis was following the market on the stocks and had informed opinions on the plans of stock recapitalization being suggested. At one time he made the suggestion that the Railroad "purchase and retire a substantial percentage of the prior preferred stock. This will increase the equity of the junior shares to a point where a proposition can be made acceptable to the junior equity holders." The point to be emphasized here is not the merits of the suggestion but the fact that his interest in a plan was real and based on stock ownership at least three years before he became an intervener.

Events in the next two chapters show how actively the Sakis Committee entered the proceedings from the first public hearing in March 1949 until the committee's withdrawal in August 1952. Mr. Sakis also took an active part, particularly at the beginning. At the 1949 hearing he presented five exhibits on such matters as liquidation and book values, the effect of the Railroad's plan on book values and voting power, as well as a plan of his own. His counsel submitted a brief after the hearing and presented in May 1950 a petition for reconsideration of the Commission's report and order of April 19, 1950. Thereafter, Mr. Sakis generally acted with the committee in opposition to the plan.

---

[16] Ibid., pp. 634–635.

[17] Price, McNeal & Co., a firm that had been active throughout this period in urging the necessity for recapitalization and proposing plans to accomplish it.

The Department of Justice (hereinafter generally called the Department)

Like any suit challenging the provisions of a Commission order, the Sakis Committee's suit to set aside the order making the Boston and Maine modification effective was brought against the United States. The Department came into the case as the statutory defender of the United States. The usual role of the Department in such suits was to follow the proceedings, to be represented officially at all court sessions, and to leave the active defense to the agency under attack. In this instance, its first move was an answer stating its opinion that the Commission had acted legally and regularly in all respects.

After filing this answer on April 28, however, the Department entered upon an intensive investigation of its own, extending into the fall of 1951, with the assistance of field offices of the Antitrust Division and F.B.I. agents. Not being an original party, it must have dealt firsthand with the Sakis group at an early stage.[18]

The Department's investigation culminated in its Trial Brief, which challenged the validity of the tabulating methods and of certain assents and charged irregularities in the Commission's methods. This considerable document was the basis of much subsequent litigation and inquiry concerning the balloting procedures in the case, although it was never formally introduced in any hearing before either the Court or the Commission. The Trial Brief, together with the affidavits, depositions, and photostats of records and correspondence offered as supporting evidence, was apparently followed by counsel in drawing up the concrete charges of the Sakis group's brief before the Court and their later petition to the Commission. The Commission itself used the Department's evidence and Trial Brief [19] as the starting point in its subse-

[18] At the pre-trial conference on December 10–11, 1951, in Civil Action No. 763–51 (Record, p. 95), counsel for the Sakis Committee said that, after learning from SEC records that a Boston and Maine director had reported the purchase of 8,500 common shares in the last three days of the voting period, he had asked the Department to investigate.

[19] A footnote in the Commission's report of April 21, 1953 (282 I.C.C. 750

quent inquiry. Other defendants, notably the Railroad and
the depositary, were careful to meet the allegations of the
Trial Brief in their briefs and testimony before the Court
and the Commission.

The Department was unsuccessful in its attempt to get its
charges before the Court. Since the charges were not in the
record on which the Commission ordered the plan into effect
— the subject of the pending suit — the Court ruled that it
could take no cognizance of them. Thus prevented by the
Court, the Department took no further part in the proceedings, although invited to do so by the Commission; but, instead, made its depositions, affidavits, and photostats of the
depositary's records available to the Commission's Bureau of
Inquiry.

THE COURT PROCEEDINGS AND PARTIES
IN SUBSEQUENT DEVELOPMENTS

The Court (also called the three-judge Court)

At 9:20 P.M. on February 21, 1951, less than three hours
before the modification plan was to take effect, the Sakis
Committee obtained from a judge of the District Court of the
United States for the District of Columbia a temporary restraining order directing the Commission to postpone the
effective date of the order of January 23. The judge thereby
made possible the chain of events that opened up the whole
balloting procedure to analysis and appraisal.

The opinion of the Court, based on a three-day trial in
January 1952, was a major document in the proceedings. It
disposed decisively of the contentions concerning the uncon-
stitutionality of section 20b and lack of due process, and
squarely supported the Commission's findings on all issues
where there had been evidence before the Commission. The
final paragraph, however, virtually remanded the case to the
Commission for its own investigation of the affidavits and
depositions taken by the Department for fraud and irregu-

---

at 752) remarks that, although the Trial Brief was not a part of the record
before the Commission, the report would refer to it because its more elab-
orately stated charges made it a better basis for exposition than the Sakis
Committee's petition.

larities of procedure. The Commission promptly followed the Court's suggestion.

The Banking Houses

Relying upon the stockholders' favorable vote on the Railroad's plan, L. F. Rothschild & Co. and Goldman, Sachs & Co., with other firms taking lesser interests, invested large amounts in the old stocks of the Railroad, against which they sold the new stock on a when-issued basis.[20]   Goldman, Sachs & Co. alone invested $1,300,000.   This is common practice in such cases, where the issue of the definitive certificates is a matter of the completion of certain formalities.   The New York Stock Exchange had acted favorably on a listing application for the two new stocks on a when-issued basis and an active market ensued.   Since the contracts of sales were of necessity executory, contingent upon the plan's being made effective, the profits in the arbitrage were contingent upon the delivery of the new stock, which could only be made after the exchange.   Any delay locked up the bankers' funds, thereby accumulating carrying charges and threatening capital losses if the plan failed.

Counsel for the banking houses were active in the defendants' cause from the time the Department took a position similar to that of the Sakis group; they appeared at hearings and filed memoranda, motions, and petitions with the Court and the Commission.   The banking houses were also ready to agree to settlement with the Sakis group on the eve of the last public hearing, because every month's delay cost interest on their investment.   The $35,000 finally paid by the bankers would be worth while to them if the dragging events were shortened by anything over three or four months.

[20] These facts were included in the replies of a partner in Goldman, Sachs & Co. at a public hearing before Commissioner Mitchell on Docket No. 31257 in New York, March 12, 1954. A partner in L. F. Rothschild & Co. also testified on the matter of negotiations for a settlement to expedite the determination of the issues in the case. (Transcript, pp. 55–75) The Commission's second supplemental report (282 I.C.C. at p. 754) said the Rothschild company had owned 23,071 shares of various classes of stock since December 22, 1950, and Goldman, Sachs & Co. had owned 29,916 shares since January 2, 1951.

Negotiators of the Settlement

The negotiations leading to the settlement between the Railroad and the banking houses on the one hand and the Sakis group on the other were pushed to a successful conclusion by Mr. Sidney V. Smith, counsel for certain stockholders, and Mr. William F. Thompson, a New York broker. Mr. Smith's reasons for undertaking to bring about the withdrawal of the Sakis group were given in his brief to the Commission on October 20, 1952. While the plan had been in litigation, he said, the when-issued securities had depreciated several million dollars in market value and a conditional declaration of dividends of over $2,000,000 had become null and void; further delay would be highly prejudicial to the assenting stockholders. Mr. Thompson had long been interested in Boston and Maine securities. He had been an intervener in the first public hearing on the plan itself, and also through business connections knew the stockholders represented by Mr. Smith.

Special Investigation by Chief Counsel for the Senate Committee on Interstate and Foreign Commerce

An opinion [21] on the Boston and Maine case was filed on April 15, 1953, by Mr. Robert D. L'Heureux, Chief Counsel for the Senate Committee on Interstate and Foreign Commerce. Critics of the plan had explained their case to Senator Tobey, the chairman of the committee. Having no basis for judging the merits of the controversy, the chairman asked the committee's counsel to make his own investigation with recommendations as to whether the committee should hold hearings on any aspect of the case. Mr. L'Heureux, after two and a half months' study of the whole record and personal interviews with witnesses and other participants in the proceedings, including the Department of Justice, issued a 69-page report recommending no hearings. "I am convinced," he said, "that this Committee could not bring out

---

[21] Robert D. L'Heureux, Opinion of the Chief Counsel, U.S. Senate Committee on Interstate and Foreign Commerce, in re Boston and Maine Railroad Stock Modification Plan, April 15, 1953 (mimeo.), found in Finance Docket No. 16250, Vol. 1-c; referred to hereinafter as L'Heureux, Opinion.

one single item of important evidence that has not been fully explored in the Court, the I.C.C. hearings and my personal investigation. . . . To my knowledge, not over three people have contacted our Committee to complain of the Plan." [22]

Within the week, on April 21, 1953, the final report of the Commission was issued. Mr. L'Heureux then added a memorandum dated April 24, 1953, disagreeing with the Commission's disqualification of three blocks of stock, but again advising against further hearings.

The L'Heureux Opinion has particular significance in that it was an independent and objective effort, written after searching investigation by one who admittedly suspected that all relevant facts in the case had not come out. Also, under order from the chairman of the Senate Committee he could go to officials of the Department who worked on the case, and thereby gain a vantage point not open to those dependent on the public record only. References to his Opinion, which came to the same essential conclusions on many of the charges as the Commission itself did a week later, will appear at many places throughout this study.

*   *   *   *   *

The purpose of this chapter has been to enable the reader to recognize the various parties as action proceeds. The principal participants and their places in the action follow in summary.

Parties	*Part taken in the action*
1. Boston and Maine Railroad	The applicant for stock modification under section 20b. Defendant in the civil suit brought by the Sakis group. Participant in the settlement with the Sakis group and in the reopened hearing before the Commission.
2. Interstate Commerce Commission	Regulatory agency responsible for the procedures under section 20b.

[22] L'Heureux, Opinion, pp. 61–62.

Parties	*Part taken in the action*
3. Old Colony Trust Company	Depositary of assents, July–December 1950. Intervener in the civil suit and in the reopened proceedings before the Commission.
4. Georgeson & Co.	Special agent to solicit assents from common stockholders, September–December 1950.
5. The Sakis group	Interveners at the first public hearing in March 1949. Plaintiffs in the civil suit to set aside the plan. Participants in every part of the hearings and litigation until their withdrawal after their settlement with the Railroad and the banking houses, August 25, 1952.
6. Department of Justice, Antitrust Division	Represented the United States in the civil suit. Investigated for fraud and irregularities; wrote the Trial Brief; withdrew after the Court decision of February 1952.
7. United States District Court, District of Columbia	Heard the civil suit and delivered the Opinion, dated February 21, 1952.
8. The banking houses: L. F. Rothschild & Co. Goldman, Sachs & Co.	Interveners in the civil suit and in the reopened proceedings before the Commission. Participants in the settlement with the Sakis group.

Parties	*Part taken in the action*
9. Negotiators of the settlement: Sidney V. Smith William F. Thompson	Active in negotiating the settlement with the Sakis group.
10. Chief Counsel of Senate Committee on Interstate and Foreign Commerce: Robert D. L'Heureux	Investigator of the whole case, January–March 1953, and author of the report to the chairman of the Senate Committee on April 15, 1953.

CHAPTER III

The Changes in the Stock Structure

It is important for several reasons to start with a brief account of the Railroad's financial history to explain the complex stock structure as it stood in 1950. First, a main charge was that the Commission's decision to divide the securities into four classes was arbitrary and erroneous. To evaluate the charge, one must know some history of the classes. Second, to understand the relative positions of the several stocks one must go back to the recapitalizations of 1919, 1926, and 1940 for explanation of the significant provisions of the stock issues, and even of the bond indentures to the extent that they affect the stock. Again, the Sakis group, which spearheaded the attack on the fairness of the plan and continued with charges of invalid balloting, held stock principally in the so-called lettered series of first preferred stock; this fact helps to explain their continued resistance.

When all is said, the advantage of tracing the history of the Railroad's stock structure lies in the plain fact that background helps in the clearer understanding of anything. It is particularly needed for problems dealing with a hierarchy of stock issues inherited from the past and ill-fitted to the present and foreseeable future.

A history showing that the present stock structure is of patchwork origin gives a realistic touch to the problem of solicitation of votes to change the structure. Also, attitudes of the voters must have been conditioned by the circumstances in which they acquired their stock. The holder of first preferred stock Series D, for example, might have received his shares in the exchange in 1919, or bought them at 195 in 1929, or at 4 in 1949, or even at 10 after the voting started.

Even though the stock structure on the balance sheet may

remain the same, its meaning to the holders becomes different as the outlook for earnings changes. Moreover, recapitalizations run headlong into the psychological problem that arises because many stockholders believe that past values of each layer of stock retain a present validity. This fallacious concept can best be corrected by the realistic view that every thorough overhaul of a capital structure is essentially the financing of the promotion of a new company. Except for the belief of many security holders that their paper values are merely dormant and can be revived, it ought to be easier to rearrange the stock claims of a going enterprise with a long history than to set up a new promotion starting from scratch, for the reason that the operating performance of the former is a known fact and forecasts to that extent are more dependable.

STAGES IN ADDED COMPLEXITIES OF STOCK STRUCTURE

The layers of Boston and Maine stock as of 1950 reflect four broad epochs in the Railroad's financial history: the system-building of the nineteenth century; the increasing difficulties from 1900 to the major reorganization in 1919; continuing problems over the next twenty years, eased only temporarily by the voluntary recapitalization of 1926; and the most recent period of growing financial strength from the voluntary bond adjustment of 1940 to the stock modification.[1]

In 1950 the Railroad operated 1,702 miles of steam road, representing a decline of over 500 miles from the period of peak mileage around 1917. It served the four northern states of New England and an edge of eastern New York, and freight produced about 75% of its total operating revenues. By and large, the Boston and Maine system has no long hauls; it has been called a terminal railroad, distributing incoming raw materials and goods and collecting and shipping out

[1] A most useful source of information for this section was an unpublished memorandum by Mr. Richard Jackson, then General Attorney of the Railroad, tracing the Railroad's financial history up to 1926. Other principal sources were the Railroad's Annual Reports and the official statements of the various recapitalization plans.

mainly manufactured goods. This character of the business has brought about many special problems so that exceptionally competent management is required for profitable operations.

System-Building to 1900

During the nineteenth century the Boston and Maine system as an operating entity was gradually put together by the integration of many small companies.[2] The three railroads composing the early Boston and Maine were chartered in the 1830's in New Hampshire, Massachusetts, and Maine; their consolidation took place in 1843. By 1900, through the process of acquiring other railroads by purchase, lease, or merger, Boston and Maine Railroad had emerged from the intense competition of many independent railroads as the leader in northern New England. Growth was slow at first; by 1850 the Railroad operated only 80 miles, and in 1884 just over 200 miles. Expansion then followed more rapidly, principally through lease of its largest rival, until by 1900 the system as we know it was practically completed, with 1,800 miles of road, about 70% leased. The marked increase in common stock during the period typically represented exchanges in mergers, and a noncumulative preferred issue used in merger financing in 1890 stood intact until 1953.

The balance sheet of June 30, 1900, shows about $21 million funded debt, $3 million noncumulative 6% preferred stock, and $22 million common stock plus a profit and loss account of $1.5 million; but the relative size of the equity was misleading in view of the rental charges paid to the leased lines. The Railroad customarily guaranteed not only the interest on the leased lines' debt but also the dividends on their stock, usually at high rates.[3] The leases in any realistic sense were a part of the capital structure; the rent payments were as fixed as bond interest so far as the earnings position of the Boston and Maine common stock was concerned.

[2] The Railroad's Annual Report for 1949 notes that 178 separate corporations were eventually included in the system.

[3] The funded debt of the leased roads totaled nearly $25 million and the capital stock nearly $41 million in 1900.

The Second Period, 1900 to 1919, Ending in Receivership
and Subsequent Consolidation with the Principal Leased
Lines

A constant succession of financial problems was met in the years following 1900. The road and equipment needed heavy expenditures to handle increasing business and to keep step with railroad development. The drain from rentals was large. In addition, during the latter half of this period declining earnings forced the management to abandon its earlier policy of financing by stock [4] and long-term bonds and to turn to the temporary expedient of one-year notes. Furthermore, even in face of the high fixed charges the management was reluctant to pass dividends, which had been paid continuously since 1838 on the common and since 1890 on the preferred stock. Although dividends were not wholly earned in several years, they were not discontinued until 1913.[5]

By 1915–1916 it was obvious that drastic steps were required to restore the Railroad to a sound position. The capital structure was top-heavy with fixed obligations, deficits were shown in 1914 and 1915, and noteholders were requested to extend maturities. After an unsuccessful attempt to accomplish a reorganization outside the courts, the Railroad entered receivership in August 1916. Within the receivership and under federal wartime control, the management worked out a plan of reorganization involving consolidation of the Railroad with its principal leased lines. This plan met with stockholder approval, and in December 1919 the receivership ended and the consolidation took place.

This was the first of the most notable series of voluntary reorganizations ever accomplished in the history of one large railroad — four major capital readjustments outside the

[4] From 1891 to 1911 a good dividend record and apparently favorable earnings prospects had enabled the Railroad to raise large amounts by the sale of well over 200,000 shares of stock, usually to stockholders but to some extent at public auction. Prices ranged from $196\frac{1}{2}$ a share at public sale in 1901 to $105\frac{1}{4}$ at public sale in 1911. (Annual Reports for 1901 and 1911.)

[5] A letter, dated February 11, 1916, from the directors to stockholders said that for the 15 years beginning in 1900 net earnings after fixed charges averaged less than $1,250,000 a year.

courts, including the last one under section 20b. The first two — 1919, 1926 — produced a variety of preferred stocks, and in both instances the bondholders were willing to extend and modify their contracts.

In essence, the 1919 reorganization absorbed seven major leased lines by giving stockholders of the leased lines a share of a new issue of Boston and Maine first preferred stock for each share of the leased-line stock, the new share bearing the same dividend rate as the rate on the share surrendered. These differences in dividend rates brought about the division of the first preferred stock into five series, A–E, above the outstanding 6% noncumulative preferred stock. When the reorganization was completed, the stock structure totaled $81,472,800 par value, divided as shown in Exhibit 1.

EXHIBIT 1. CAPITAL STOCK STRUCTURE OF THE RAILROAD, AS OF DECEMBER 31, 1919

First Preferred A,	5%, $100 par	188,600 shares
B,	8%,	76,488
C,	7%,	79,171
D,	10%,	43,270
E,	4.5%,	650
		388,179 shares
Preferred, noncum.,	6%,	31,498
Common,		395,051

In view of the later arguments centering around these new lettered series, both as to their allocation under the 1949 modification plan and as to the way the Commission ordered them to vote, their chief provisions in addition to the dividend rates should be made clear. The first preferred series had cumulative dividend preference and were noncallable. No series of the first preferred stock had any preference over any other series.[6] Each share had one vote in ordinary cor-

[6] The agreement (actually dated November 26, 1918) embodying the reorganization plan said: "No class of the first preferred stock shall have any preference or priority over any other class and whenever any dividend is declared upon the first preferred stock less than the whole amount of accumulated dividends then remaining unpaid, such dividend shall be apportioned among all the classes of first preferred stock in proportion to the amount of preferred dividends then accumulated and unpaid on the respective classes."

porate business, the customary practice among railroads, which gave voting rights to both preferred and common stock. In liquidation all classes, preferred and common, would share alike as to claims for principal.

The 1919 reorganization provided for a five-year reduction in first preferred dividends in order to build a fund for repayment of debt and for betterments. It also improved the debt position of both the Railroad and the former leased lines; for the Federal Government took bonds in return for advances of nearly $20 million to meet overdue debt, and stood ready to advance sums necessary to pay off dissenting stockholders.

The Second Voluntary Capital Readjustment: 1926

Although the voluntary reorganization of 1919 relieved certain pressures and probably went as far as the stockholders of the several railroads were then prepared to go, it fell distinctly short of the thoroughgoing changes necessary to carry through a succession of poor years. True, the dividends previously guaranteed on the leased lines' stock were changed to the contingent dividends on the new preferred series and, in addition, the new preferred dividends were to be cut by 20% for five years. If income held up to the mark set in the year just before the Federal Government took over wartime control, the management hoped to pay both fixed and contingent charges. The consolidated company also provided a larger asset base for new mortgages to finance additions and betterments. On the other hand, the reorganization itself brought no new money and, in temporizing fashion, made no provision for heavy debt maturities in the next few years.

Profits were small in 1920 and 1922, and losses were heavy in 1921 and 1923. Dividends were discontinued after 1920. By the time earnings came back in 1924–1925 there was already need of more than palliatives to restore the Railroad's credit. The next five years would bring total debt maturities of $65 million, and the needed improvements for the period were estimated at $20–$30 million.[7] The existing financial structure was a serious obstacle to new issues of bonds or

[7] Estimate given in letter dated December 17, 1924, from the Chairman of the Executive Committee of the Railroad to the voting trustees.

stock. Another recapitalization seemed imperative and, as before, the first objective was to avoid a court proceeding.

Mindful of the failure to obtain new money in the previous reorganization, all plan-makers gave new money first importance in their plans. All proposals included extension of maturing debt and raising around $13 million in new money through an issue of 7% preference stock to be offered to the old stockholders. Early plans expressed the hope that the existing structure could be simplified by combining all series of first preferred stock into one class with a 7% rate, and by changing the noncumulative preferred into common stock. These plans for simplification were soon abandoned, however, presumably because the exchange ratios to be worked out for the various series were too intricate to gain acceptance within a reasonable time.

After much work and many changes, a voluntary committee known as the General Readjustment Committee, representing substantial holdings of all stock classes, published a plan in September 1925 calling for assents by deposit of stock. If successful, as the president commented in the 1925 annual report, this railroad reorganization would stand as the largest ever achieved in which all classes conceded something in a voluntary agreement without a court proceeding. The Committee was hopeful of general acceptance even though some unassented stock might be left outstanding if the plan was carried through outside the courts.[8]

[8] The different effects of voluntary adjustments involving bonds and stock were pointed out by counsel for Boston and Maine Railroad in a Congressional hearing in 1947, as follows:

"I want to call attention here to a sharp difference in the possibilities of rearranging debt and stock by wholly voluntary plans. . . . [Small amounts of old bonds can be carried without trouble until redeemed.] In such bond situations there may be a temporary complicating of the debt structure, but the chances are that it will not last long.

"It is true that the positions of assenters representing the vast majority are unfairly prejudiced and nonassenters end up in a better position than those agreeing to the exchange, but if a sufficient number of bondholders are willing, for the good of all, to sacrifice something with respect to their position . . . the plan will be successful.

"The same thing cannot be said of a stock reorganization by entirely voluntary action. In this case not only will nonassenters be likely to cause an increase in the number of classes of stock outstanding and a further complicat-

A voluntary readjustment was successfully achieved. The plan was declared operative as of September 1, 1926, 86.5% of the stock and 88% of the bonds having assented.[9] In very general terms the plan produced the following results: [10] Over $40 million bonds were exchanged for new refunding bonds, which extended maturities for 15 years. A new issue of prior preference stock in the amount of $13 million was sold, most of it subscribed to at par by the assenting stockholders.[11] In addition, the assenting first preferred stockholders surrendered their claim to the dividends accrued for the past five years and in return received priority in liquidation over the assenting plain preferred and common stockholders.

It is important to note that the agreement as to rights in liquidation was strictly a matter between the stockholders themselves entirely outside of their contracts with the corporation. The stock of assenting holders was stamped as assented. The stock of those refusing to assent remained unstamped and still carried its old rights. This differentiation between stamped and unstamped stock, that is, assented and unassented stock, carried into the market for shares. From 1926 until the section 20b modification plan became effective in May 1953, every class of Boston and Maine stock below the

---

ing of the capital structure, but this situation is likely to be permanent. Furthermore, dissenters must be paid their arrearages in full before any relief can be afforded any holder of stock junior to theirs. . . . If voting is by classes, a very few nonassenters may end up with control of a certain class of stock and consequently with a considerable amount of control over the corporation."

From Statement of Robert J. Fletcher, General Counsel, Boston & Maine Railroad, in *Modification of Railroad Financial Structures,* Hearings before the Committee on Interstate and Foreign Commerce, House of Representatives, 80th Congress, 1st Session, on H. R. 2298, May 19, 1947 (Government Printing Office, 1947) , pp. 56–57.

9 Notice to Assenting Stockholders and Bondholders by order of the General Readjustment Committee. Counsel for the Railroad in the hearings in 1947 on H. R. 2298, op. cit., p. 54, said that approximately 75.5% of the first preferred stock outstanding, 95% of the preferred, and 97.5% of the common assented to the plan.

10 For further detail on the plan see Appendix D.

11 In 1930–1931 the total prior preference stock outstanding was increased to $23 million as the result of conversion of about $10 million of the refunding bonds.

new prior preference stock was traded in two categories, assented and nonassented, each carrying a different price. The stamp was the origin of one of the charges brought in 1951 by the Sakis group and the Department of Justice, who argued that the Commission erred in its decision not to treat the stamped and the unstamped shares as separate classes for voting.

The readiness of stockholders to assent to the 1926 plan, with added investment in the new prior preference stock, attests to their reliance on the fairness of the Committee's recommendations. Certainly the advantage of the plan to them was not easy to demonstrate. This was an instance where much depended upon the prestige of the guiding hand with the rank and file of holders. Also, the stockholders could only be thankful that they were again permitted a period of grace by holders of the heavy debt soon to mature.

Twenty years later, in 1947, before a House Committee on the proposed Mahaffie Bill, the general counsel for the Railroad summarized the results of the 1926 readjustment as follows:

> . . . The result of this voluntary readjustment of the capital structure was highly satisfactory at the moment from a financial standpoint and showed that it was possible to obtain the cooperation of a large percentage of the security holders of the railroad.
>
> At the same time, however, it left the capital structure of the railroad in a very involved condition. After completion of the plan, there were outstanding prior preference stock, five classes of first preferred stock, preferred stock and common stock, and all of these, except the prior preference, were outstanding in stamped and unstamped form. This adds up to the astonishing total of 15 classes of stock, no two of which have precisely the same rights. This situation has existed up to the present time.[12]

Financial Record After the 1926 Readjustment

Dividends were paid continuously on the new prior preference stock through 1931, and none thereafter. They were paid in full on all first preferred series to cover the period

---

[12] Hearings in 1947 on H. R. 2298, op. cit., p. 54.

from the second half of 1925 through the first three quarters of 1931. Dividend payments on the two lowest classes had to wait until all dividend accumulations had been paid on the unassented first preferred stock, which had refused to surrender any claims in 1926. Early in 1929 these arrearages also were fully paid,[13] clearing the way for resumption of dividends on subordinate classes. The noncumulative 6% preferred stock, which had received only $4.50 since 1913, was paid full dividends in 1929 and 1930, and $4.50 in 1931. The common stock, which had received nothing between 1913 and 1930, received $4 for 1930 and $1, the last payment, on April 1, 1931. It took a payment of almost $2.7 million to the nonassenters in the 1926 plan in order to resume dividends on stock that had thirsted for nearly 20 years. By thus preparing for dividends to the two lowest classes the management showed its apparent expectation that the boom conditions of the late 1920's would continue. Yet after only $2.5 million had been paid to the lowest preferred and the common classes, payments were stopped completely on all classes of stock.

The nonassenting holders of first preferred stock profited handsomely by standing firm on their contract. Not only were their original rights intact, but they had received all arrearages in cash. From this point on, however, holders of the stamped first preferred stock held a somewhat superior position, in theory at least; they still had a claim to half the dividends they had forfeited, although these would be payable only if earnings and dividends rose to great heights; and they also had the claim to priority in liquidation against the assenting junior shares. The market prices of the stamped assented first preferred stock in all series now rose generally above the unstamped, whereas they had been lower before payment of the nonassenters' arrearages.

Following this brief spell of optimism ending in 1931 came renewed financial difficulties resulting from the depression of the 1930's and from property damage by flood and hurricane. Although fixed charges were earned except in 1936 and 1938, and good maintenance and economical operation were kept up, dividends were perforce discontinued and maturing obli-

[13] Boston and Maine Railroad, Annual Report for 1929.

gations extended. By 1940 the Railroad's borrowing capacity had been exhausted by large emergency loans for damage repairs from banks and the Reconstruction Finance Corporation. Mounting maturities of funded debt again brought the threat of bankruptcy.[14] There was no hope of public financing in the face of continued depression and impaired credit; and the RFC refused further help unless the Railroad rearranged its whole debt structure and reduced its fixed charges.

The Voluntary Bond Adjustment of 1940

The management remembered its past successes with voluntary readjustments; it would again try a voluntary plan first, and turn to reorganization under section 77 only as a last resort. Assisted by the RFC and a committee of savings banks and insurance companies holding nearly 40% of the maturing bonds, it worked out a voluntary debt adjustment plan in 1939, which was accepted by holders of 93% of the outstanding mortgage bonds as well as by the RFC and banks holding the secured notes. The plan was consummated on July 25, 1940.

In sum, the old funded debt was exchanged for about $68 million first mortgage 4% bonds due in 1960 and $48 million income mortgage $4\frac{1}{2}$% bonds due in 1970. Only some $7 million of the old funded debt, in addition to about $3.5 million of equipment obligations, remained outstanding. Fixed interest charges were thus reduced by over $2.5 million. The new mortgage indentures restricted the application of net income to contingent interest, sinking funds, and a capital fund to finance property additions and betterments. Until $25 million principal amount of funded debt had been retired, net income could not be used for any other purposes.[15]

This last provision was crucial to the dividend hopes of

[14] The balance sheet of December 31, 1939, showed funded debt outstanding as follows: $136,746,500 mortgage bonds, of which $33,392,000 were held by the Railroad for various purposes; $4,288,000 equipment trust obligations; $3,653,000 collateral notes; and $2,305,196 miscellaneous obligations. Some $36,500,000 of the mortgage bonds and practically all the other funded debt would come due before the end of 1945. Current liabilities included $16,-467,130 in loans and bills payable, representing primarily loans from the RFC.

[15] See Appendix D for further details of the 1940 plan.

stockholders. Although this was strictly a bond plan, it all but removed any possibility of dividends for the reasonably foreseeable future. With the unexpected increase in earnings during the war years after 1940, however, the specified debt retirement was soon to be accomplished. Brokers and other advisers to stockholders began weighing the alternative of payments on the heavy dividend arrearages since 1931 against some plan acceptable to the preferred classes for canceling arrearages in exchange for new stock or perhaps some mixture of cash and stock.

The New Haven Interest in Boston and Maine Stock

A wholly owned subsidiary of the New Haven railroad, the Boston Railroad Holding Company, held so large a block of Boston and Maine stock in 1948 as to give it strategic power in the formulation of a plan.

In 1907 The New York, New Haven and Hartford Railroad Company began buying a controlling interest in Boston and Maine stock. Neither the courts nor the Massachusetts legislature looked with favor on unchecked control by the New Haven. In 1909 through special legislation the Boston Railroad Holding Company was formed for the sole purpose of holding the Boston and Maine securities owned by the New Haven. The New Haven transferred these securities to the new company and took the Holding Company's common stock and bonds in return. In 1910 the Holding Company refunded its bonds with 4% preferred stock, which the New Haven management planned to sell to the public in order to recoup its investment. After about 14% of the shares had been sold, the declining earnings and dividends of Boston and Maine Railroad made further public sales unwise. The preferred stock was guaranteed by the New Haven as to dividends and as to par value in liquidation.

In response to strong protests in New England against New Haven control, the Interstate Commerce Commission conducted an investigation in 1912–1913.[16] Later, court action

16 The Commission's reports are given in 27 I.C.C. 560 (June 20, 1913), "The New England Investigation," and 31 I.C.C. 32 (July 11, 1914), "In re Financial Transactions of the New York, New Haven & Hartford Railroad Company."

was taken by the Department of Justice against the New Haven and certain affiliates and subsidiaries as parties to combinations in restraint of trade. The action was ended by a consent decree entered by the court in October 1914.[17] One of the requirements of the decree, which had the practical effect of preventing the forced sale of the Boston and Maine stock at a probable loss, was that the New Haven should turn its Holding Company stock over to trustees appointed by the court. The trustees, who also became directors of Boston and Maine Railroad, were to vote the stock wholly in the best interests of the public and the Railroad, and to sell the stock before January 1, 1917. Unable to arrange for an acceptable sale, however, the trustees obtained time extensions and were still in control at the time of the 1919 reorganization.

The 1919 reorganization made an important reduction in the percentage of the Boston and Maine voting power controlled by the New Haven railroad through the Holding Company. Whereas the New Haven had controlled 52% of the outstanding plain preferred and common stock, the new issue of first preferred stock increased the total number of Boston and Maine shares to the point where the stock owned by the New Haven had only 28% of the total vote. In 1923 the New Haven was able to obtain a court order by which it got back the stock of the Holding Company from the trustees. The court evidently concluded that the New Haven interest had ceased to be a threat because of its diminished percentage and the holdings no longer required special treatment.

No further important change took place in the situation until the New Haven railroad, which went into reorganization under section 77 in 1935, stopped dividends on the Holding Company's publicly held preferred stock in 1937. The public holders began pressing for dissolution of the Holding Company soon afterward.[18] There also was consid-

---

[17] See 220 I.C.C. 505 (April 5, 1937), "Investigation of New York, New Haven & Hartford Railroad Company."

[18] The original issue of preferred stock provided that, if dividends were defaulted, a majority of the preferred holders had the right to petition for sale of the Boston and Maine stock to satisfy their claims. The 1923 court decree directed that the publicly held preferred shares should be stamped as en-

erable public interest in the dissolution, because it was believed that the prospects of Boston and Maine Railroad
would be improved if the New Haven interest was ended.
In addition, it was thought that an independent Boston and
Maine Railroad would take more aggressive action toward
developing freight traffic for the Port of Boston. At this time
the Holding Company held 26.25% of the total outstanding
Boston and Maine stock.

A Massachusetts statute [19] in 1946 gave the Holding Company two alternatives: the first, to transfer its own common
stock to Boston and Maine Railroad on or before July 1,
1947; the second, to enter receivership leading to distribution
to its stockholders of either its portfolio or the proceeds from
sale of the portfolio. When the New Haven management
failed to transfer the stock within the time set, the public
holders petitioned for receivership.

Not until June 15, 1949, after the public hearing on the
section 20b modification plan of Boston and Maine Railroad,
was the receiver appointed to take over the Holding Company's assets, to vote the Boston and Maine stock held, and to
distribute the assets or proceeds thereof. He did not dispose
of the assets immediately; during the period of voting on the
modification plan the portfolio was still intact and was voted
in favor of the plan. Soon after the close of the voting, the
receiver took advantage of comparatively high market prices
to sell all the stock except 37,790 prior preference shares.

The Pennroad Corporation's Holdings in Boston and Maine Stock

From 1931 through 1947 The Pennroad Corporation was
the second largest holder of Boston and Maine stock, owning
almost one-fifth of the total of the various classes. Through
most of this period it also owned a large block of stock of

titled to preference over the preferred shares held by the New Haven railroad
as to principal and accrued dividends in the proceeds of any sale of assets.
The New Haven reorganization, completed in 1947, removed the guarantee of
dividends but left to the public holders their prior lien on the portfolio of
Boston and Maine stock.

[19] Acts and Resolves of the General Court of Massachusetts, 1946, Chap.
518: an Act to Dissolve Boston Railroad Holding Company, approved June 11,
1946.

the New Haven railroad. Pennroad was a holding company organized with broad investment powers in April 1929 in the interests of the Pennsylvania Railroad. Its stock was placed in a voting trust, the trustees of which were the president and two directors of the railroad, and the trust certificates were sold to the railroad's stockholders. Pennroad then invested in substantial blocks of stocks of railroads important to the Pennsylvania Railroad.[20] The bulk of its Boston and Maine holdings were acquired within its first year.

Because of litigation by stockholders, the interlocking directorships with the Pennsylvania Railroad were given up in 1941 and Pennroad continued on as an independent investment company. During 1948 and 1949 Pennroad sold 71,005 shares of its Boston and Maine holdings, but in July 1950 it still held 130,382 shares, which were voted in favor of the modification plan.[21] Its importance to this study comes from the circumstances of its assent of a large block of stock sold toward the end of the voting period. The special sale arrangement was cited in the charges of controlled assents and caused the Commission to disqualify the assent. This episode will get detailed examination in Chapter X.

PLANNING FOR STOCK MODIFICATION

With the successful recasting of the debt structure in 1940, the Boston and Maine management began to think about the next logical step in achieving a realistic capital structure. From 1915 the Railroad had been struggling with the problems imposed by leases and debt, which the recapitalizations of 1919 and 1926 had only temporarily alleviated. The adjustment of 1940 at last brought the debt down to manageable size. Meanwhile, the stock structure had grown steadily more complex. Its jerry-built characteristics bore no reasonable relation to earning power, and arrearages were heavy.

In the management's opinion the overlaid strata of stocks with large arrearages, although offering no threat of insol-

---

[20] See Arthur Stone Dewing, *The Financial Policy of Corporations* (5th ed., New York, Ronald Press, 1953), Vol. II, pp. 962–963.

[21] From Annual Reports of The Pennroad Corporation, 1947, 1948, and 1949, and Semi-Annual Report for June 30, 1950.

vency, adversely affected the Railroad's financial management and therefore its stockholders. The Railroad clearly was hampered with regard to further equity financing. Furthermore, the officers were concerned about the speculative interest in the stocks when market prices were so low and volatile; they regarded speculative trading as a threat to sound management. The return to larger earnings called for a fresh look at the problem of providing a new stock structure, one that would reflect expected earnings rather than the failures of the past and would encourage investment and responsible ownership.

Creditors of the Railroad also, even though they were not directly affected by the residual claims of the stock, were vitally interested in the status of public confidence. There was always the possibility that the huge arrearages might lead to payment of large amounts of cash, or, in the alternative, that stockholders might come to regard the situation as so hopeless that they would lose interest in the long-run stability of the Railroad.

From the stockholders' point of view, marketability and prices were impaired; in fact, stockholders themselves found it difficult to appraise the various stock issues. Confusion resulted from the existence of four major classes of stock, with different rights and preferences, from the five lettered series of first preferred stock, and from the stamped and unstamped categories. Moreover, all classes except the common, which was listed on the New York Stock Exchange, were traded mainly over-the-counter, although listed on the Boston Stock Exchange.

By 1945 war earnings had made it possible to fulfill the mortgage restrictions imposed in the 1940 bond readjustment. Available net income after interest and sinking funds could now be applied to any proper corporate purpose, subject to the restriction that no dividends could be paid and no stock could be purchased except out of earnings subsequent to December 31, 1939. Although income after fixed charges did not cover contingent interest in 1945, by 1947 net income after deductions for contingent interest and sinking funds had risen to $1.2 million.

The legal moves in 1946 to dissolve Boston Railroad Holding Company added another reason for recapitalization before the dispersion of its holdings of Boston and Maine stock could disturb further an already confused market. Although the act provided that, except for the Railroad itself, no distributee or purchaser should hold more than 5% of the total vote in the class of stock being distributed, this provision would not protect against concentrated buying in subsequent sales.

As soon as earnings had brought the goal of the $25 million debt retirement in sight, talk of recapitalization appeared in the financial news. Many suggestions for plans came in from stockholders and dealers particularly interested in the market for the stock.

In 1945 a committee of the directors began to explore methods for simplifying the capital stock structure, settling the dividend arrearages, and redistributing voting power fairly to those classes with the greatest realizable stake in the company. The committee recognized from the beginning that any recapitalization under conditions of solvency would have to be voluntary and that a small minority could stand in the way. The difficulties in the way of agreement among so many conflicting interests seemed insurmountable.

Section 20b of the Interstate Commerce Act

The event that made a voluntary modification actually feasible was the passage by Congress of the Railroad Securities Modification Act, also called the Mahaffie Act, which became law on April 9, 1948, as section 20b of the Interstate Commerce Act.[22] Such remedial legislation had been under discussion since the early postwar period. The Mahaffie bill, the first draft of which applied to bond revisions only, was

[22] For a good summary of the development of the legislation relating to voluntary adjustment plans, see Arthur Stone Dewing, op. cit., Vol. II, pp. 1402–1411. Discussions of section 20b in particular can be found in such legal articles as: "The Railroad Modification Law," by Chauncey H. Hand, Jr., and G. Clark Cummings, 48 Columbia Law Review 689 (1948); "Consensual Securities Modification," also by Hand and Cummings, 63 Harvard Law Review 957 (1950); "Funding Arrearages under Section 20b of the Interstate Commerce Act," also by Hand and Cummings, 65 Harvard Law Review 398 (1952); "Railroad Reorganization under Section 20b of the Interstate Commerce Act," by De Forest Billyou, 39 Virginia Law Review 459 (1953).

changed to include stock so as to be applicable to such situations as the Boston and Maine case.

The preamble of section 20b sums up succinctly the purpose of the act:

> . . . in order to promote the public interest in avoiding the deterioration of service and the interruption of employment which inevitably attend the threat of financial difficulties and which follow upon financial collapse and in order to promote the public interest in increased stability of values of railroad securities with resulting greater confidence therein of investors, to assure, insofar as possible, continuity of sound financial condition of common carriers subject to Part I of said Act, to enhance the marketability of railroad securities impaired by large accumulations of interest on income bonds and dividends on preferred stock and to enable said common carriers, insofar as possible, to avoid prospective financial difficulties, inability to meet debts as they mature, and insolvency. . . .

It should be noted that this is an amendment of the Interstate Commerce Act, not the Bankruptcy Act, and consequently enables a railroad to do something about an unsatisfactory financial problem so as to avoid the more serious stages that might end in insolvency.[23]

The First Boston and Maine Plan: All Common Stock

In late 1947, as soon as the passage of the Mahaffie bill appeared imminent, the special committee of directors renewed its efforts to develop a plan. After several months of study and discussions with large stockholders, a plan was drawn to reclassify all outstanding stock into a single class of $100-par common stock. Application under section 20b was filed with the Commission on August 25, 1948, and docketed as Finance Docket No. 16250. This docket was destined to carry the long record of disputes not only on the plan itself but also on balloting procedures, disputes that did not end until the final order of April 21, 1953, made the plan effective.

---

[23] Dewing characterizes the act as an effort to crystallize the social and legal tendencies growing since the amended bankruptcy legislation of 1933, with important implications for the future, in that protective clauses in securities, particularly debt instruments, can be weakened under this law in the name of the public interest. Dewing, op. cit., Vol. II, p. 1410.

The plan was no sooner out than it met strong opposition from the higher priorities, especially the topmost class, mainly because their preferred position was not recognized by a new preferred stock. The plan was promptly withdrawn. After informal conferences of Railroad officers with many interests and with the Commission, a two-stock plan was substituted in a supplemental application on January 24, 1949.

The Two-Stock Plan as Finally Voted Upon

The capital stock structure had remained practically unchanged since 1931, except for slight shifts in treasury stock.[24] As of December 31, 1948, the number of shares and dividend accumulations were as shown in Exhibit 2.

EXHIBIT 2. CAPITAL STOCK STRUCTURE OF THE RAILROAD AND DIVIDEND ACCUMULATIONS PER SHARE, AS OF DECEMBER 31, 1948

Class of Stock		Shares in Hands of Public	Shares in Treasury	Dividend Accumulations per Share
Prior Preference,	7%	229,414	1,971	$119.00
First Preferred	A, 5%	188,341	259	86.25
	B, 8%	76,488	—	138.00
	C, 7%	79,115	56	120.75
	D, 10%	43,239	31	172.50
	E, 4½%	650	—	77.625
Total First Preferred		387,833	346	
Noncumulative Preferred, 6%		31,498	—	
Common		394,728	323	
Total		1,043,473	2,640	

The essential features of the two-stock plan as it was voted upon are summarized below. Before giving its approval, the Commission had made slight changes in the allocations originally proposed by the Railroad for the first preferred series. The plan contemplated the following alterations or modifica-

[24] Long-term debt had been reduced to $90,019,900 mortgage bonds, of which $4,094,700 were held by the Railroad, and $10,813,893 equipment obligations, as of December 31, 1948.

tions: (a) the aggregate par value of the capital stock would be reduced initially from $104,347,300 to $82,238,031, which would be divided between two classes of $100-par stock as follows: $27,529,680 of new 5% preferred stock and $54,708,-351 of new common stock; (b) 481,769.4 additional shares of new common stock would be authorized in order to provide for the conversion of the new preferred stock; (c) the dividend arrearages would be canceled; and (d) the 822,-380.31 shares of new stock would be distributed to the holders of the old stock on the basis shown in Exhibit 3.

EXHIBIT 3. ALLOCATION OF NEW SECURITIES AND TOTAL NEW SECURITIES PROPOSED IN PLAN SUBMITTED TO STOCKHOLDERS

Old Stock	New Securities per Share Old	Total New Securities Preferred	Common
Prior Preference	1.2 sh. new pfd.	275,296.80	
	1.0 sh. new com.		229,414.00
First Preferred			
Series A	.65 sh. new com.		122,421.65
Series B	.85		65,014.80
Series C	.79		62,500.85
Series D	1.05		45,400.95
Series E	.60		390.00
Total to First Preferred			295,728.25
Preferred (noncumulative)	.07		2,204.86
Common	.05		19,736.40
Total new shares		275,296.80	547,083.51

The most important provisions of the new securities were these: Dividends on the preferred stock would be cumulative only to the extent earned after fixed and contingent charges, including sinking fund obligations. A small sinking fund was required for the preferred stock, also cumulative to the extent earned. Except in a few special situations affecting the preferred stock, each share in both classes would be entitled to one vote. Each share of preferred stock would be convertible into $1\frac{3}{4}$ shares of common stock, and callable in whole or in part at $100 and accrued dividends.

At a public hearing held in Boston from March 28 through April 1, 1949, before Hearing Examiner Kirby of the Commission, representatives of two committees and five holders of stock (one of whom withdrew almost immediately) intervened. The Railroad presented witnesses with prepared statements giving detailed explanation and defense of the plan. Interveners cross-examined and presented some testimony and witnesses of their own. At the conclusion of the hearing, the parties asked for an Examiner's Proposed Report.[25]

This book confines its analysis to the charges of improper solicitation and invalid balloting. The objections raised to the plan itself are relevant to the balloting issues only so far as they reflect attitudes on questions of improper solicitation. The strong opposition of the Sakis group to the plan suggests the possibility that their continued opposition to balloting procedure was a strategic move rather than one on principle; because they thought the plan was iniquitous, they would use any device to kill it. Those who later held the Sakis opposition to be only for nuisance value would certainly agree with such an interpretation.

Arguments even in the first hearing and the briefs and exceptions filed by the Sakis group in 1949, however, show that their attack on the balloting front was not an afterthought. In September 1949, for example, they took exception to the Examiner's recommendation that solicitation might be carried on by telephone and personal interview. From the beginning, also, the Sakis group stressed the importance of the number of classes to be permitted to vote. They argued that the intent of Congress clearly was that all stockholders having identical rights and privileges vote as a class, and that therefore there were 15 classes when account was taken of the stamped and unstamped categories.

The Sakis group also early laid the groundwork for later technical objections to consummation of the plan. For instance, in the 1949 hearing and by brief shortly thereafter, they questioned the accuracy of the assurances of assent re-

25 The Examiner's Proposed Report (mimeo.) was published on August 17, 1949, exceptions and replies were filed in the next two months, and Division 4 heard oral argument on October 24.

ported by the Railroad.[26] In September 1949 they urged that to prevent error in the certification of assents in the final vote the Commission should require the Railroad to submit a list of assenting stockholders with the class and number of shares each held.[27] In 1951, when the group presented petitions and complaints to keep the plan from going into effect, one of their important points was that the Commission acted arbitrarily and contrary to law in denying the Sakis request to see the original assents and revocations and a stockholders' list in order to check the depositary's certificate.[28]

A brief explanation of the formula method used by the management and accepted by the Commission for allocating the new stock among the various old classes and series is given here only because of its bearing on later charges that Railroad solicitors made a misleading statement when they called the old common stock worthless. The more complex a structure is in number of classes and in large arrearage accumulations, the more expertness is needed to understand and evaluate a proposed exchange. The complexity in this case made an ideal setting for misunderstanding. If perfect understanding by two parties, the solicited and the solicitor, is necessary when assents are asked for, one can see wide room for argument as to whether misleading statements were used.

In brief, the formula method fixed the total permissible stock capitalization and divided it between common stock and a conservative amount of preferred stock. To allocate the new stock among the old classes, the first step was to project a normal earnings figure available for dividends. This was enough for the current dividend ($7) on the prior preference stock plus an amount that would clear up all the arrears on the class in about 17 years. After 17 years the same method of figuring would permit current dividends annually on the first preferred series and enough more each year to have the arrearages fully paid by 54 years later or

[26] These assurances of assent were preliminary soundings of stockholders' opinion, provided for in the statute and taken before the formal application was filed with the Commission. The procedure of assurances raised many questions, which are discussed in Chapter V.

[27] They did not explain why they thought such a list was necessary to prevent error in certification.

[28] See Chapter IV, p. 61 f.

71 years in the future. From these calculations the present values were computed for the series of annual incomes, giving results in comparable terms of value, which could be translated into stock allocations under the plan.

The formula method was discarded in the case of the plain preferred and common classes because it seemed unrealistic to be so precise for so remote an income to those classes, starting in the year 2019. Arbitrary allocations were made to these classes, not in payment for a calculable present value but in recognition of their present voting rights, which they could not be expected to surrender voluntarily unless given something.

*   *   *   *   *

This summary sketch of the history of the financial structure of Boston and Maine Railroad has served its purpose if it provides an adequate point of reference for testing the validity of the charges brought by the Sakis group and the Department.

If one can start with the proposition that the stock structure needed simplification, that an expert body found that the proposed changes met statutory requirements in all respects, then, barring a conspiracy to defraud by illegal balloting procedures, there ought to have been a workable procedure to find out the will of the stockholders.

CHAPTER IV

The Course of Events

THIS CHAPTER traces the events that stand out along the course of the Boston and Maine dispute on balloting. Just as a playwright must make situations real and alive to carry along the theme of his play, so in analysis of this actual drama of litigation the task is to set the various acts and scenes.

To present systematically the succession of events, they are condensed below in parallel columns, on the left the normal sequence of action under section 20b and on the right the unusual developments that made this case the testing ground for procedural principles.

Events as in the Normal Section 20b Case	*Additional Events in the Boston and Maine Case*
1. Preapplication activity by the Railroad. Assurances of assent.	
2. The application to the Commission, August 25, 1948. Its preparation prescribed by Commission rules.	First application (all-common plan) withdrawn, October 15, 1948. Supplemental application (two-stock plan), January 24, 1949.
3. The matter set for public hearing before a Hearing Examiner, March 28–April 1, 1949. Appearance of interveners. Filing of briefs, May 31, 1949.	
4. The Examiner's Proposed Report based on hearing	

Events as in the Normal Section 20b Case	*Additional Events in the Boston and Maine Case*
and the docket, August 17, 1949. Exceptions filed. Arguments before the Commission, October 24, 1949.	
5. The Commission's report and order, April 19, 1950, the report approving the modifications and the order defining details of the submission of the plan to vote.	Petitions of Sakis group for reconsideration, May 18, 19, 1950. Report of Commission denying petitions and setting beginning of submission period, July 10, 1950.
6. Voting by classes of securities, July 10–December 14, 1950. Tabulation of votes by depositary.	Objections of Sakis group to parts of solicitation material and their request for inclusion of additional items; denied by Commission, August 15, 1950.
7. Certification of vote by applicant, December 27, 1950.	Petition of Sakis group, January 8, 1951, to examine balloting procedures; denied by Commission, January 23, 1951.
8. Order of Commission, January 23, 1951, making plan effective as of February 22, 1951.	Petition of Sakis group for reconsideration of order, February 20, 1951; denied by Commission, February 21. Stay granted by a district judge on petition of Sakis group, February 21, 1951. Suit brought by Sakis Committee, February 28, 1951. Entry of Department of Justice for United States, defendant. Answer filed April 27, 1951.

*Additional Events in the
Boston and Maine Case*

Investigation by Department
and F.B.I.

Amended Answer, November 2,
1951.

Trial Brief, December 8, 1951.

Court proceeding, January 21–
23, 1952.

Opinion, February 21, 1952.

Reopening of proceeding by
Commission, April 7, 1952.

Sakis appeal to Supreme Court
allowed, May 2, 1952.

Investigation by Commission's
Bureau of Inquiry.

Withdrawal of Sakis group
after settlement, August 25,
1952.

Appeal to Supreme Court withdrawn, August 25, 1952.

Hearings August 25–28 and
September 9–10, 1952, Boston — New York.

Commission's final report,
April 21, 1953.

Plan effective May 21, 1953.

Continued hearings on the settlement with Sakis group.

THE PLAINTIFFS' CASE: SIGNIFICANT EVENTS IN ITS COURSE

There are three natural divisions of the period between
the Commission's first report of April 19, 1950, and its final
order of April 21, 1953:

1. the 10 months from the Commission's approval of the plan
   and order of submission, April 1950, to the institution of
   court proceedings in February 1951;
2. the year of the court action, from February 1951 through
   the opinion of the Court issued in February 1952;
3. the final year, from the re-entry of the Commission

through its Bureau of Inquiry until its final report and order making the plan effective as of May 21, 1953.

April 1950 to February 1951

On April 19, 1950, Division 4 handed down the 58-page report of the Commission, finding the proposed plan as amended to be just and reasonable and setting forth the order, effective May 19, governing the submission of the plan to the stockholders.[1] The Railroad immediately began preparations for submitting the plan to stockholders. It filed solicitation material on April 27 for the Commission's approval; but action on the material was suspended at the request of the Sakis group, which on May 18 and 19 filed petitions for reconsideration, arguing at length against the Commission's decision.

When the full Commission had considered the petitions and the entire record, it concluded by report dated July 10, 1950,[2] that the report and order of April 19 had presented no error of fact or law, and it affirmed them in all respects. The report marked the beginning of the six-month balloting period; on July 13 the Commission approved, with some changes, the solicitation material filed in April and subsequently.

The Sakis group entered the proceedings again at this point, raising objections to parts of the material and asking the Commission to require the Railroad to include additional items. The Commission ruled that the objections were not timely and that they represented an unreasonable request for inclusion of information, ". . . including restatements of portions of petitioners' arguments with respect to the merits of the plan which have been considered and rejected by the Commission, all of which are not essential to and many of which have no proper place in the applicant's submission material."[3]

[1] 275 I.C.C. 397.

[2] 275 I.C.C. 527.

[3] I.C.C. Order, August 15, 1950. It is true also that most of the figures requested, such as book values, fixed charges, debt, betterments, retirements, and net current assets, were supplied in the solicitation kit by the financial exhibits, which the Sakis counsel may not have examined.

The Railroad's active campaign for assents began with the mailing of the solicitation material on July 26, 27, and 28 to all stockholders of record. The events of the next five months are studied in detail in the succeeding six chapters: assent procedures, the vote by classes, the solicitation of assents, the tabulation of assents and revocations, and the handling of disputed assents. There is no need to elaborate on them now.

Shortly before the close of business on December 14, 1950, the depositary notified the Railroad that the required assents had been received. The financial officers of the Railroad immediately telegraphed the Commission the decision to end the submission period as of the close of business on December 14; on December 15, by newspaper publication, the Railroad formally declared the period closed and the right to revoke assents terminated.

On December 27 the Railroad filed a formal request, supported by two affidavits, asking the Commission to set a date for the plan to become binding.[4] The first affidavit was that of the Railroad's financial vice president, certifying that unrevoked assents had been given by 198,665 shares, or 86.59% of the prior preference stock outstanding; 308,445 shares, or 79.53% of the first preferred stock; 27,674 shares, or 87.85% of the noncumulative preferred stock; and 302,430 shares, or 76.61% of the common stock. It was supported by the second affidavit, a sworn certificate executed by the proper officer of the depositary, stating for each class the number of shares for which unrevoked assents were held as of the close of the submission period.

The Railroad management hoped that the plan would become effective in time for the declaration of dividends on the new stock in February 1951. It explained that this early date was desirable as a practical matter because the mortgage indentures made declaration of dividends almost impossible except during the first 60 days of the year. After that time dividends could be declared only if the directors had determined that available net income for the current year would cover full service on interest and sinking fund account for the current year, and funds to satisfy these requirements had

4 This formal request was contained in Supplemental Applications 2 and 3.

been deposited in trust. A letter to the Commission spoke of the management's desire to declare dividends and its hope that the final order could be handed down by January 28. The Commission in reply indicated its willingness to expedite the final steps necessary to make the plan effective.

At this point, however, the Sakis group again became active. On December 29, 1950, their counsel asked the Railroad for a list of stockholders and the right to inspect several items, principally the original assents and revocations. Counsel also asked the Commission for a 30-day period in which to file objections to the Railroad's request for the plan to be made effective. The Railroad management wrote to the Commission on January 3, 1951, expressing consent to an audit of the assents by the Commission, with counsel for the interveners present, although it saw no need for an audit. On the same date the Commission, refusing the Sakis request for an extension of time, set January 8, 1951, as the deadline for formal objections. Thereupon the Sakis Committee filed its reply formally requesting the Commission to order the Railroad to make available for the committee's inspection the original assents and revocations, lists of stockholders and their addresses, and other documents, and stating that it was unjust and contrary to the intent of the statute for the Commission to make a finding solely on the basis of affidavits.

These requests were considered and denied by the Commission.[5] It said in part:

> To grant the interveners' request that they be given an opportunity to make an individual investigation and inspection such as they suggest obviously would result in further substantial delay. In the complete absence of any evidence, or even any allegation that the applicant failed to follow the prescribed method of submission, or that any irregularities occurred in the conduct of the submission, or that any errors or irregularities occurred in the certifying of the results of the submission, we must conclude that there is no justification for thus delaying the consummation of this proceeding.[6]

The Commission decided that the plan had been assented to by the required percentage of holders in each class and or-

[5] 275 I.C.C. 752 (January 23, 1951).
[6] Ibid., p. 756.

dered the modifications to become binding at 12:01 A.M. on February 22, 1951.

With the effective date of the plan so near, the Railroad applied for listing of the new stocks on the New York Stock Exchange. Trading in the new stock on a when-issued basis began in January; trading was suspended on the old issues soon afterward. Somewhat later, on February 27, just after the Sakis group had begun legal action, the Railroad conditionally declared dividends for 1951 amounting to $5.58 a share on the new preferred stock and $1 a share on the new common stock, placing in trust over $2 million in a special dividend account to await the outcome of the litigation. To anticipate for a moment in order to complete the history of this declaration of dividends, it is noted that by the terms of the dividend vote itself the dividend action was annulled toward the end of 1951 and the special account was closed.

In the meantime, on February 20, 1951, the Sakis group again petitioned the Commission, seeking to reopen the case for the introduction of new evidence, reconsideration of the supplemental report and order, an oral hearing, and a stay of the effective date of the order. The petition covered the previous arguments against the plan itself and raised questions on the accuracy of the vote, the vote by classes, the use of oral solicitation of assents, the omission of additional information from the printed solicitation material, and the failure to investigate the original assents and revocations. Congress, the petition said, intended evidence of a valid vote, not mere affidavits. The petition further alleged that undue influence had been exercised by persons soliciting assents. This petition, too, was denied promptly by the Commission — within a day.

The Year of Court Action [7]

On February 21, by the narrow time margin of three hours, the Sakis group obtained from a judge of the District Court for the District of Columbia a temporary restraining order directing the Commission to postpone the effective date of the order of January 23. On February 26, accordingly, the Commission by supplemental order did stay the effective date

[7] Civil Action No. 763–51.

until a hearing could be held on an application for an injunction.

On February 28 the Sakis group filed with the Court an amended and supplemental complaint asking that the temporary restraining order be replaced by a permanent injunction. Because this complaint presented to the Court a comprehensive summary of the Sakis case, it is worth consideration in some detail. It alleged that the Commission's reports and orders were arbitrary and unsupported by evidence and were in violation of and contrary to the intent of section 20b because of 12 procedural errors; that there was no evidence to support the Commission's findings that the proposed plan was in the public interest and in the best interest of the Railroad and each class of stockholders; and, finally, that section 20b was unconstitutional.[8] Four of the procedural errors were concerned with the fairness of the plan itself, which is no part of this study. The remaining eight errors related to balloting procedures; they were, briefly, that the Commission arbitrarily and contrary to law:

(1) failed to order the plan submitted to all classes;
(2) permitted the Railroad to use oral solicitation of assents;
(3) permitted the Railroad to use solicitation material not making a fair and proper disclosure and denied the Sakis request for the inclusion of pertinent information;
(4) permitted the Railroad to campaign without any limitations on expense;
(5) ordered the plan into effect when the requisite number of assents had not been obtained by November 19, 1950, as required by the order of April 19, 1950;
(6) permitted the Railroad to spend Railroad money to obtain assents, while denying the Committee's request for the Railroad to pay its expenses and fees in opposition to the plan;
(7) denied the Committee's request to see the assents and

---

8 The committee alleged that section 20b was an unlawful extension of the power delegated to Congress by Article I, Section 8, Clause 3, of the Constitution; that it contravened the due process clause of the Fifth Amendment; that it was an unlawful delegation of legislative power contravening Article I, Section I: that it was an unlawful exercise of judicial power contravening Article III, Section I; and that it was an unlawful exercise of powers reserved to the states by the Tenth Amendment.

revocations and a list of stockholders so as to ascertain
if the affidavits were in fact correct;
(8) made a finding of fact on the affidavits only.

The complaint invoked the entry into the proceedings of
a three-judge Court to set aside and annul the order, to declare section 20b unconstitutional, and to direct the Railroad to pay the committee's expenses and reasonable fees.   If
the order was not annulled, the complaint added, the result
would be "irreparable and immeasurable injury and damage
to the plaintiffs herein, the Boston and Maine Railroad and
the stockholders of the Boston and Maine Railroad. . . ."
The Sakis group had now succeeded in turning its running
argument with the Commission into a court action on broad
procedural issues.   The United States and the Railroad were
the named defendants.   The Commission soon became an
intervening defendant and was, of course, the agency most
concerned to defend the order.   In June 1951 the three-judge
Court was finally constituted.   The Department of Justice,
which came into the case automatically, had filed its answer,
fully supporting the Commission's order, on April 27, 1951;
and pleadings had also been filed by the other parties.

The Department of Justice Becomes Active in the Proceedings

In a typical suit against the United States involving a government agency, the Department of Justice is represented
officially but leaves active participation to the agency.   In the
Boston and Maine case, however, the Department adopted a
different policy.   In the late summer of 1951 it began an extensive investigation of the original assents and revocations
and the records of the Railroad and the depositary.   It went
on to take affidavits and depositions from stockholders in
various parts of the country, from officers and employees of
the depositary, and from others in connection with specific
blocks of stock it held to be improperly voted.
If the Department of Justice had not become an active par-
ticipant with the plaintiffs, it is questionable how much
longer the Sakis group would have continued.   The specific
charges of invalid balloting might then never have reached

the documentary form of the Department's Trial Brief. The reasons for the Department's unusually active part remain the enigma of the case, and can be cleared up only by inquiry not open to an outsider.[9] The point here is that the Department's attitude and methods were its own decision; they were not established to fulfill a prescribed responsibility, like the Commission's moves in the case.[10]

In the latter half of 1951 the Securities and Exchange Commission investigated the phases of the case that concerned the activities of brokers in solicitation and balloting.

During the fall of 1951 pretrial conferences were held in an effort to narrow the issues and to set a date for a hearing; they were adjourned without a date when the Department asked for more time to complete its investigation. On November 2 the Department filed its Amended Answer, supporting the constitutionality of section 20b but challenging certain of the Commission's findings and conclusions [11] in the case and supporting certain of the plaintiffs' contentions that

[9] The Commission's then Associate Chief Counsel, Edward M. Reidy, commented at a pretrial conference that this was the first case in which the Department had gone beyond a confession of error and made an independent investigation, developing new evidence never presented to the Commission. (Record of Pre-Trial Conference in Civil Action No. 763-51, December 10-11, 1951, pp. 34-35.)

[10] The Department's explanation of its participation was as follows: "Under the provisions of 28 U.S.C. 2321 and 2322, when a suit is filed challenging the provisions of an Interstate [Commerce] Commission Order, the suit must be brought against the United States. As the primary defendant in this cause, the United States filed a *pro forma* answer which generally upheld the order of the Interstate Commerce Commission. The issues involved are of first impression. The statute under which the Commission proceeded (49 U.S.C. 20b) was enacted on April 9, 1948, and this action is the first to reach the courts on the merits. Recognizing the broad public interest involved in this litigation, the United States indicated to counsel, at the time of filing its *pro forma* answer, that it desired to investigate carefully the plaintiffs' charges of irregularities in the Commission proceedings, and to file an amended answer if investigation should indicate the desirability of this course in the public interest." (Footnote omitted.) Trial Brief, pp. 1-2.

Note: At the time the Answer was filed there was no suggestion that it was merely *pro forma*.

[11] In particular, that assents should be secured from only four classes of securities, and that the required number of valid assents had been received within the submission period.

there was lack of due process in the proceedings before the Commission. The Sakis group also formally filed by adopting the Department's answer as their own.

At a final pretrial hearing before the full Court on December 10 and 11, the Department distributed its Trial Brief to all parties. The Brief explained that the United States did not challenge the Commission's administrative judgment in finding the plan to be in the public interest and it would support the Commission's arguments on the constitutionality of section 20b. It argued, however, that because important conditions in submission procedure prescribed by the statute were not fulfilled, the Commission had no authority to enter its final order. First, the brief alleged, the Commission did not order the plan submitted to each class. A second category of charges questioned the validity of certain assents — principally assents obtained by alleged misrepresentation in personal solicitation and assents alleged to be controlled by the Railroad. A third charge was that the assents and revocations were not tabulated correctly by the depositary and the depositary did not meet all the requirements for valid assents. The brief described some 29 affidavits and depositions offered in support of its charges.

On January 11, 1952, after consideration of briefs and arguments on the subject by several of the parties,[12] the Court held that its jurisdiction extended only to the existing record when it entered the case. It refused to receive the affidavits and depositions collected and would not hear arguments on the procedures and methods. Nevertheless, the Department filed 19 affidavits with the Court.

---

[12] Counsel for the Commission, for instance, in a Supplemental Brief of the Interstate Commerce Commission in reply to Amended Answer of the United States, quoted extensive authority to show that review of Commission orders was not a trial *de novo,* where testimony never presented to the Commission would be admissible. The brief also stated that, never having been served with copies of the depositions, the Commission did not know what they contained; but that it was expected that the Railroad would attempt to explain them away by counter depositions and evidence. The Commission, said the brief, had no desire to prevent full development of all facts; it did strongly urge that, if the Court saw reasonable merit to the complaint in the light of all evidence, the evidence should be transmitted to the Commission for its consideration and report.

The case came to trial on January 21–23, 1952. Despite the Court's previous ruling that the Department's new evidence from its investigation of the balloting had no relevance to the issue before it, the Department continued its active support of the plaintiffs' charges in the suit, and was forceful enough to cause the Court to take special note of the excluded new evidence in its Opinion. As one looked around the courtroom, one saw new parties appearing as interveners. Counsel for the two banking houses, L. F. Rothschild & Co. and Goldman, Sachs & Co., took a strong position for the validity of the Commission's procedures, and later submitted a brief. Counsel for Old Colony and for The Pennroad Corporation were present, as was Mr. Sidney V. Smith, counsel for three assenting stockholders.[13]

The opposition of the Sakis group was on a much broader basis than a simple challenge to the validity of the balloting. Their brief put the case on five major issues, indexed as follows:

a. Statutory Authority Exceeded by Denial of a Hearing.
b. Statutory Authority Exceeded by Failure to Request the Carrier to Submit the Plan to all Classes of its Stock Affected.
c. Statutory Authority Exceeded by the Commission in Permitting the Solicitation of Assents through Unapproved Communications.
d. There is no Evidence to Support the Commission's Findings that the Plan of Security Modification or Alteration Approved by the Interstate Commerce Commission is Just and Reasonable or in the Best Interest of each Class of Stockholders, the Carrier or the Public.
e. Title 49, U.S.C., Section 20b is Unconstitutional, and the Order of the Interstate Commerce Commission Directing the Applicant to Put the Proposed Plan of Security Alteration or Modification into Effect is Null and Void.

Only two of these issues, (b) and (c), were concerned with alleged errors in balloting procedures; they are discussed in Chapters VI and IX following. As in their argument at the first hearing on the plan, the Sakis group reiterated in charge (d) their objections to the plan as not "just and rea-

[13] See Chapter II, p. 27.

sonable. . . ." Charge (a) protested the refusal of the Commission to grant the Sakis request for a hearing and the right to challenge the affidavits filed by the Railroad to certify the vote.

The challenge of charge (e) to the constitutionality of section 20b is a legal issue outside the subject of this book. Two of the Sakis arguments on constitutionality, however, do touch the voting area. The brief alleged that the statute deprived the parties of property without due process in that (a) the Commission denied a hearing on the questions of invalid assents, and (b) seventy-five per cent of each class was given power to deprive twenty-five per cent of their contract rights.

The Court's opinion,[14] dated February 21, 1952, upheld the constitutionality of section 20b, affirmed the Commission's conclusions on the plan and the order of January 23, 1951, and dissolved the restraining order of February 26, 1951. The Court held that the Commission's findings in its reasoning on number of classes were proper and warranted. It pointedly denied the Sakis request for a hearing on the certificates of the vote, concluding that "Section 20b (2) . . . sets out those matters which will be determined only after a hearing. . . . the question of the number of assents is not among them." [15]   Taking up the arguments as to constitutionality, the Court held that neither the statute nor the Administrative Procedure Act requires a hearing on a matter in which there is no "substantial or tangible charge that an irregularity exists." [16] As regards due process when contract rights are changed by majority vote, the Court said: "Legislation of the character represented by Section 20b is designed to modify or alter contract rights — not capriciously, but in order that the relationship between the security holder and his fellows, and between the security holder and the corporation, may be stated in terms of present day realities rather than in terms that are so remote from reality as to be misleading." [17]

14 *Sakis* v. *United States,* 103 Fed. Supp. 292 (1952).

15 Ibid., p. 309.

16 Ibid., p. 311.

17 Ibid., p. 312.

Although the Court declined to consider the additional evidence on improper solicitation and invalid balloting tendered by the Department, it concluded its opinion with a paragraph that in no uncertain terms placed the charges in the hands of the Commission as the proper agency to "sift, hear, evaluate and act upon" these matters.[18]

Thus the events in this notable case moved through a complete circle from December 1950 to February 1952. The Sakis group at the earlier date asked to audit the assents; subsequent petitions asserted that all was not right "upon information and belief." The Commission was satisfied with the certificates that the required vote was in. Fourteen months later, the Department had gathered independently what it held to be supporting evidence to the charges of invalid procedures in solicitation and balloting. The Commission was now invited by the Court to see where the truth lay.

The Final Year: February 1952–April 1953

The Sakis group immediately adopted two courses of action. They appealed the decision to the Supreme Court of the United States,[19] and they also filed a petition to take the case back to the Commission. After it had become clear that the three-judge Court would not hear the evidence on assents, they had made a motion for remand to the Commission to complete the evidence on record. Immediately upon this Court's adverse opinion, they petitioned the Commission to reopen the proceeding for the introduction of the Department's new evidence and to stay the effective date of the order of January 23, 1951, pending final determination of the issues raised. On February 27 the Commission did stay the effective date, and on April 7 it reopened the proceedings. It ordered further public hearings on evidence strictly upon the limited issues of whether the required percentages of stockholders had assented within the submission period and whether the assents had been procured lawfully and in conformity with the order of submission.

With the hope of making acceptable stipulations to save

18 Ibid., p. 314. This paragraph is quoted more fully in the next chapter.
19 Appeal No. 251, October Term, 1952.

time, the parties held a prehearing conference on April 29, 1952, in place of a scheduled hearing. The results were disappointing; the parties could agree to accept only one deposition and eight affidavits, in order to avoid calling these affiants as witnesses. Further efforts of the Sakis group to postpone the hearing until their counsel had made a search of the depositary's records were denied by the Commission, which pointed out that the committee might subpoena material as provided in the Commission's rules of practice.

To those interested in a speedy end to the proceedings, the most direct and practical approach now seemed to be a settlement with the plaintiffs.[20]   Negotiations for some sort of settlement were pushed forward in the spring of 1952 by Mr. Sidney V. Smith, counsel for certain assenting stockholders, and Mr. William F. Thompson.

From the time of the first public hearing in March 1949, the Sakis group had repeatedly asked for reimbursement by the Railroad for expenses and reasonable attorneys' fees.[21] Their argument was to the effect that section 20b, although silent on the subject of fees, gave the Commission broad powers to impose terms and conditions and to make such amendments to a plan as were just and reasonable, and that an allowance of interveners' costs and fees was thereby cov-

[20] The Railroad Brief of October 20, 1952 (pp. 6–8) described the reasons for the decision to pay for the Sakis withdrawal as follows:

"The procedural history of this instant case indicates abundantly the varied weapons for delay that lie to hand for a determined opposition; and the Railroad, judging from the prior activity of the plaintiffs, assumed that they could and would seek every possible means to delay. . . .

[there followed two paragraphs of steps presumably open to the plaintiffs, procedurally, as evidenced by their past actions and successes in the case]

"A recital of the above procedural steps must make it evident that the Railroad faced upwards of 18 months or 2 years of further struggle. . . .

". . . On the basis of the record in this proceeding, moreover, it is clear that the plaintiffs neither could nor would shed further light upon the issues framed in this reopened proceeding. Plaintiffs never indicated the existence of any evidence other than the data collected by the Department and if the tone of the Trial Brief permits any inference at all, it is that if any evidence existed which told adversely to the interests of Old Colony or of the Railroad, it would certainly have been brought forward and exhaustively discussed in the Trial Brief."

[21] A statement dated October 24, 1949, listed their expenses as $2,840.18, not including fees.

ered. They contended also that expenses of interveners in opposition were as justifiable expenses to the Railroad as solicitation expenses paid by the Railroad to brokers and agents. One might add that if payment of expenses had to be justified by some contribution toward the plan, the Sakis group could point to a change made by the Commission itself, in line with their arguments, in the allocation of new stock among the first preferred series.[22] The Commission, however, denied the requests in the report of April 19, 1950, citing its previous decision in the Lehigh Valley Railroad's modification, and stating that section 20b made no provision for the Commission to authorize payment by a railroad of compensation or reimbursement of expenses to parties in the proceedings.[23] Section 77 had specifically provided for payment of fees. Although the Sakis group consistently continued to protest the decision, urging that the denial would encourage other railroads to freeze objecting stockholders out, neither the Commission nor the Court made any change.

In this setting, in June 1952, the negotiators conferred several times with Mr. Caruthers, counsel for the Sakis Committee. Negotiations soon centered around a settlement sum of $125,000 to reimburse the committee's expenses and fees and, in addition, a proposal involving a purchase by the Railroad of 40,000 shares of the then outstanding prior preference stock and a commitment to pay a dividend on the new common stock after consummation of the plan.[24] The settlement sum would be paid by the Railroad and L. F. Rothschild & Co. and Goldman, Sachs & Co., which, as previously noted, had heavy positions in the old Boston and Maine stock. Messrs. Smith and Caruthers, and Mr. Robert J. Fletcher, counsel for the Railroad, apprised various officials in the Commission of these proposals, fully realizing that the Commission had no jurisdiction over such negotiations. Eventually, however, the Railroad officers, although they were under pressure from stockholders to end the litigation, became convinced that any such binding agreement to retire

[22] See testimony of Mr. Fletcher, Proceedings before the Interstate Commerce Commission, Docket No. 31257, June 2, 1954, pp. 185–186.

[23] 275 I.C.C. 397 at 407–408.

[24] 294 I.C.C. 549 at 555.

stock would be held to result in a different plan from that
voted on. Mr. Caruthers was informed, accordingly, that the
settlement in the form then being discussed was out of the
question.

Nevertheless, Messrs. Smith and Thompson continued
their negotiations. On August 15, only 10 days before the
scheduled opening of the public hearing before the Examiner
on the charges of invalid balloting, they reported a more
promising outlook for settlement. They indicated to Mr.
Caruthers that the banking houses would join in the settlement to the extent of $35,000 and talked of the Railroad's
payment in terms of some $65,000. The matter of the Rail-
road's purchase of preferred stock was to be made conditional.

Partners of both banking houses later [25] stressed the point
that they had insisted on the Commission's being kept fully
informed, and also that they had been assured by counsel that
the settlement terms could not be construed as a modification
of the plan. They explained that their attorneys were instructed to arrange no settlement unless the Commission had
opportunity to express objections in principle. Since the objective of the bankers was to get the plan through, any agreement that could be held to change the plan would not accomplish their purpose.

The settlement negotiations were successfully closed at a
meeting in New York on August 21, 1952, and an informal
report was made to the Commission and the Department the
next day. The terms of the final agreement provided that
the Sakis Committee and also Mr. George P. Sakis [26] would

[25] Proceedings before the Interstate Commerce Commission, Docket No.
31257, March 12, 1954, pp. 57, 64, 71, 74.

[26] His withdrawal could be only a technical matter. His individual status
as an intervener was in part to achieve a technical advantage (see footnote 15,
Chapter II, p. 22). The action of Mr. Borghi, his counsel, was always identical with that of Mr. Caruthers; they were partners in the same law office. It
was correct that Mr. Sakis received no *direct* payment from the Railroad in
the settlement, but he stated in the Proceedings before the Commission,
Docket No. 31257, June 2, 1954 (Transcript, pp. 161–167) that he expected to
receive a fee as associate counsel to Mr. Caruthers. He had received $37\frac{1}{2}\%$,
minus $3,000, of the amount already paid, and was to get the same percentage
of the remaining amounts.

withdraw in return for payment of $65,000 by the Railroad and $35,000 by the bankers in full settlement of the committee's expenses and legal fees. The Railroad further agreed to apply up to $2 million for purchase and retirement of the new preferred stock, probably by calling for tenders of stock, within a year after the consummation of the plan, if such use of funds was found possible and proper, and subject to the directors' judgment as to feasibility and to stockholder approval.[27] The Railroad was to pay half of the $65,000 when a motion to dismiss the Supreme Court appeal was filed; the rest of the money, including the bankers' $35,000, was to be paid when the plan went into effect.

The final public hearing on balloting procedures took place on August 25–28, 1952, in Boston and September 9–10 in New York. Extensive evidence was introduced by the Commission's Bureau of Inquiry, the Railroad, and Old Colony, through both records and testimony and cross-examination of witnesses. The withdrawal of the Sakis group from the proceedings before the Commission and also their withdrawal of the appeal to the Supreme Court were announced at the very opening of the hearing in Boston. The Department did not appear in the case after the Court's decision in February, and took no further action except to make its photostats of original assents and other records available to the Commission.

At the close of the hearing the parties waived an Examiner's Proposed Report, which would have called for formal answers. The case came before the Commission on the record, including briefs filed on October 20, 1952, and oral argument held on March 23, 1953.

THE COMMISSION'S FINAL REPORT, APRIL 21, 1953

This report finished the job that the Commission thought had been completed on January 23, 1951. The only unre-

[27] Since this part of the agreement was consistent with the preference of the board of directors from the beginning for an all-common stock structure, its inclusion contingent on feasibility was not looked on by the directors as a concession to the Sakis group. The stock was never bought in, however, because the Railroad's earnings after consummation of the plan were "very disappointing" (see 294 I.C.C. 549 at 559).

solved questions after the Court's opinion lay in the area of balloting, which the Commission disposed of by stating four primary conclusions, as follows: [28]

(A) Holders of the requisite percentages of each class of stock of the Boston and Maine Railroad, within the submission period, assented to the plan of modification authorized to be submitted to the railroad's stockholders by division 4's report and order of April 19, 1950.

(B) The stockholders' assents constituting such percentages were procured in a lawful manner and in conformity with the provisions of the said order of April 19, 1950.

(C) The Commission's order of January 23, 1951, approving and authorizing the alterations and modifications and directing that the plan be put into effect 30 days thereafter, should not be vacated and set aside, but, on the contrary, the Commission's stay orders of February 26, 1951, and February 27, 1952, should be vacated and dissolved, and the aforesaid order of January 23, 1951, should be made effective from and after 30 days from the date of our order herein.

(D) The Boston and Maine Railroad should make no further payment to the Sakis committee or its counsel pending further investigation of the railroad's settlement with that committee, or until permitted to do so by further order of this Commission.

This favorable outcome for the plan came in spite of the disqualification of three blocks of stock on the grounds that the Commission found control over them to reside in the Railroad. In addition, the Commission suggested improvements with regard to certain practices, which, although not contrary to existing law, it considered to be inconsistent with the public interest and likely to give rise to future evils.

Not only did the Commission stop further payments by the Railroad under the settlement with the Sakis group; on May 1, 1953, it ordered an investigation under sections 12 and 20b of the Interstate Commerce Act. Various petitions and denials delayed any hearing on the matter until December 28. A brief hearing in Boston at that time was followed by a second in New York on March 12, 1954, and a third in Washington, D.C., on June 2, 1954.

[28] 282 I.C.C. 750 at 798–799 (1953).

In March 1955 the Commission issued its report on the inquiry.[29]   With Chairman Mitchell and Commissioner Johnson dissenting, the Commission found that it had no general supervisory power to control expenditures by a railroad except in some circumstances where the public interest was involved; that the facts of record here did not warrant a finding that such a public interest problem was involved; and that the evidence did not support a conclusion that the settlement affected the plan of modification.   It found also that there was no basis for a finding of any illegality, although certain events, in its opinion, did not "altogether comport with a high standard of ethical conduct or an objective concept of public interest."   Its action, however, was not to be construed as constituting approval of the settlement or the payments.   The Commission then ordered the inquiry discontinued and the restraint on the Railroad against making further payments dissolved.

The modification plan became effective on May 21, 1953, and the exchange of new stock certificates for old began at once.[30]

*   *   *   *   *

These last three chapters have been written to set in a general way the pattern of the action that forced a broad reexamination of balloting procedures.   It now remains to see what the statute demanded, how the Commission regulated, how far charges of invalid procedures were sustainable, and where changes are indicated.

[29] 294 I.C.C. 549 (March 7, 1955).

[30] As of the close of 1953, the Railroad had issued in exchange of stock 268,165 shares of the new 5% preferred stock, or 97.4% of the total to be exchanged, and 515,747 shares of new common stock, or 94.3% of the total.   On December 30, 1953, a dividend of $6.45 a share was paid on the new preferred stock, covering accumulations from January 1, 1949, to January 1, 1953.   (Boston and Maine Railroad, Annual Report for 1953.)

CHAPTER V

Assent Procedures under Section 20b

> . . . the Commission shall cause the carrier, in such manner as it shall direct, to submit the proposed alteration or modification . . . to the holders of each class of its securities affected thereby, for acceptance or rejection.   (Sec. 20b (2))

THE PROCEDURES adopted to give effect to this provision of the statute became the main salient of attack by the Sakis group and the Department.   This importance placed on mere procedural matters, previously unchallenged, raises fundamental questions.   Did the statute and regulations give leeway for loose procedure?   Was administration by any party lax or inept?   Were the charges of invalid assents well-founded in terms of accepted business practice?   Answers to these questions are the subject matter of the next five chapters.   In this chapter the statute itself and the Commission's regulations will be considered.

At first reading, it is hard to see how any questions of principle could possibly arise under such a concise directive.   The objective is plain: to present, as in any referendum, a proposal to be accepted or rejected by a qualified electorate. The statute implies that the manner of presentation for vote might well vary; thus latitude is given in the manner of submission to vote.   Administratively, the problems could center on

- (a)   the manner of submission;
- (b)   the qualifications of voters;
- (c)   the determination of classes;
- (d)   the requirements for acceptance or rejection.

It should be noted that the *"Commission shall cause"* the balloting to meet the statutory requirements.   This primary responsibility must be kept in mind.   The responsibility, as in any administrative action, cannot be fully discharged by a preliminary and single decision by the Commission. The balloting procedure involves other parties, two principal ones in the Railroad and the official depositary, and also the usual operatives in such arrangements — brokers and special solicitors. Therefore, after the precise manner of voting is decided and the process gets under way, the Commission cannot avoid a close follow-through to correct promptly any unforeseen difficulty. Just as formulation of the balloting procedure should be participated in and thoroughly understood by all the parties who are to operate it, so it follows that interim decisions on unforeseen developments should be made with the full knowledge of all parties.

This maxim of sound administration is here put in dogmatic form to serve as a point of reference throughout the next five chapters. We shall try to find why a simple procedure like balloting, under the responsibility of an experienced Commission, became a storm center of acrimonious litigation and made the Boston and Maine case the starting point for new thinking on balloting procedures in section 20b proceedings. As we follow closely the action of two years centering on balloting problems, the reader can see how the above generalizations on sound administration developed from the record of events.

The final paragraph of the opinion of February 1952 of the three-judge Court, in the civil action brought by the Sakis group, climaxed a startling turn in the proceedings. Indirectly, but with unmistakable intent, the Court handed a virtual directive to the Commission to proceed at once with its own investigation of charges of illegality and fraud in obtaining assents. In the words of the Court:

> The affidavits and depositions submitted by the Justice Department as a result of its investigation after the issuance of the temporary restraining order by this Court contain serious charges of irregularity and fraud on the part of the Railroad, its officers, agents and employees in the obtaining of assents to the modification plan and of the depository, the Old Colony Trust Co. These documents offer evidence which if credible and true charge that a grave and serious fraud has been perpetrated upon the Interstate Commerce Commission. If the

facts alleged in these documents were established by competent evidence and were not explained and dissolved by other competent evidence, the gravity of the perpetrated fraud would shock the conscience of a Court or Commission. This Court does not believe, however, that it is the function of a statutory three-judge court to take and weigh evidence of this kind at this stage of this type case. The Court believes that the Commission is the proper forum to sift, hear, evaluate and act upon the matters charged by the Justice Department. There is no reason for the Court to feel that the Commission will not give consideration to an appropriate motion filed by the plaintiffs upon the basis of the documents tendered by the Justice Department which, in effect, constitute a claim of new evidence before the Commission.[1]

The Boston and Maine proceedings, unique in so many ways among the section 20b cases, became the first case in the history of railroad reorganization in which the whole balloting procedure was challenged. In any study of procedure in the usual 20b case, as in the section 77 cases, the voting matters could be quickly passed over as mere mechanical operations to carry out a prescribed routine. The big decisions would have been made in the formulation of the plan itself — the amount of the new capitalization and the allocation of new securities to fulfill the statutory requirements. This was the work of top-level management with Commission review and approval. The final act of submitting the plan to the vote of security classes was procedural detail much like the proxy procedures in customary corporate practice, the work of a supervised clerical staff operating under the established rules. There was no reason to expect that any special problem would arise in balloting on the Boston and Maine plan that an experienced depositary, in this case Old Colony, could not work out under the supervision of the Commission.

Here is an instance when supposedly little things, traditionally routine, unexpectedly became the dominant issues. The paramount questions then become: what went wrong? how should future proceedings be changed?

[1] 103 Fed. Supp. 292 (1952), pp. 313–314.

THE STATUTE'S REQUIREMENTS

The preamble of section 20b explained that ". . . it is deemed necessary to provide means, in the manner and with the safeguards herein provided, for the alteration and modification, without the assent of every holder thereof, of the provisions of such classes of securities. . . ." Under the law as it stood before this amendment, unless the security contracts were in default and legal action on them taken, the minority holder could stand on his contract rights. Section 20b provides a way to force him to accede to a plan supported by majorities of 75% of each class of security affected.[2]

It is important to note that section 20b (2) deals with assents of security holders at two different stages of the procedure. The first is the application stage, where it is provided that when application is made the Commission

> may, in its discretion, but need not, as a condition precedent to further consideration, require the applicant to secure assurances of assent to such alteration or modification by holders of such percentage of the aggregate principal amount or number of shares outstanding of the securities affected . . . as the Commission shall in its discretion determine.

In the final stage, after the public hearing and the Commission's acceptance of a plan, the counting of assents becomes crucial. The statute reads:

> . . . the Commission shall cause the carrier, in such manner as it shall direct, to submit the proposed alteration . . . to the holders of each class . . . for acceptance or rejection. . . . If the Commission shall find that as a result of such submission the proposed alteration or modification has been assented to by the holders of at least 75 per centum of

---

[2] A letter, dated May 9, 1947, from the Legislative Committee of the Commission to the chairman of the House Committee on Interstate and Foreign Commerce pointed out that H. R. 2298, which later became law as section 20b, had eliminated a provision contained in an earlier bill which would have permitted approval by the Commission upon assents by less than 75%, but not less than 51%, of any particular class. This provision was regarded as "representing an inadvisable reduction in the assents required for approval of such form of relief." *Modification of Railroad Financial Structures*, Hearings on H. R. 2298, May 19, 1947, op. cit., p. 6.

the aggregate principal amount or number of shares outstanding of each class of securities affected thereby (or in any
case where 75 per centum thereof is held by fewer than
twenty-five holders, such larger percentage, if any, as the
Commission may determine to be just and reasonable and in
the public interest), the Commission shall enter an order approving and authorizing the proposed alteration or modification upon the terms and conditions and with the amendments, if any, so determined to be just and reasonable. . . .

Section 20b (3), relating to the classes of securities to
which a modification plan is to be submitted, includes the
following provision:

. . . For the purposes of this section a security or an evidence
of indebtedness shall not be deemed to be outstanding if in
the determination of the Commission the assent of the holder
thereof to any proposed alteration or modification is within
the control of the carrier or of any person or persons controlling the carrier.

The various provisions with regard to assents at two different stages of the recapitalization procedure require close
examination from the standpoint of the intent of the statute,
the regulations of the Commission to enforce it, and the administrative problems for the railroads and others concerned
with the assent procedures. Inasmuch as interveners at the
public hearing in March 1949 [3] showed some misunderstanding of the assurances of assent obtained in the application
stage, and raised questions as to irregular procedures in getting such assurances, it is important to look at the requirements in this regard. Also, since consummation of the plan
was held up for over two years because of charges of irregular procedure in the final voting, the basic questions of voting
procedure must be fully analyzed. The long experience with
proxies and voting practices in the history of corporate management makes it the more surprising that so much of the
trouble, delay, and litigation in the Boston and Maine case
should center on the details of balloting. One could expect
such arrangements to have settled down into routine pat-

[3] Hearings before the Examiner, March 1949, pp. 57–58, 106–107, 159–160,
351–358, 546–556, 596–597, 600–601.

terns, especially under an experienced agency like the Commission and with an institutional trustee of the standing of Old Colony acting as depositary of assents. Nevertheless, the Department of Justice based much of its opposition on matters related to the validity of assents.

The procedures of getting assents, both at the time of the original application (assurances of assent) and at the final stage when the plan is submitted to security holders, raise many questions not apparent in the language of the statute. Certain key problems are common to both stages, while some are less important in the first and become crucial in the final voting on the plan.

ASSURANCES OF ASSENT AT THE TIME OF APPLICATION

The statute does not require assurances of assent, but leaves them to the discretion of the Commission.[4] Its purpose clearly seems to be to give the Commission a means for determining at the start that a proposed plan of modification is a realistic proposal worked out with the parties at interest. The device of "assurances of assent" would thus insure a plan offered in good faith and after effective interchange of ideas by conflicting interests so that general acceptance could be hoped for. This requirement would protect the Commission against half-baked schemes of modification, and would practically require management to bring security holders into the plan-making process. The language of the Act, moreover, implies more than an informal acquiescence: "may . . .

[4] A Comment in *The Yale Law Journal,* July 1949 (58 Yale L. J. 1291), entitled "Streamlined Capital Readjustment under Section 20b of the Interstate Commerce Act," remarked as follows on assurances of assent (p. 1303): "This provision of the Act was thought necessary to avoid burdening the Commission with dubious plans unlikely of eventual assent, but in view of the estoppel-like pressure which advance assents may exert on the Commission to approve of a plan, this discretion may well be exercised infrequently." (Footnote omitted.)

It should be noted, however, that in the regulations adopted by the Commission to prescribe the application procedure the facts as to assurances were required. Therefore a show of substantial acceptance of the proposed plan might appear at this stage whether or not the Commission followed up by requiring a certain percentage of assurances.

require the applicant to secure assurances of assent to such alteration or modification. . . ." "To secure" implies an approach by the officers of the railroad, and "assurances" certainly implies more than a casual expression of interest with a possibility of favorable consideration at a later time.[5]

The Commission's Regulations

In May 1948 the Commission adopted regulations to govern applications under section 20b.[6] The only rule on assurances of assent requires that the original application show

> The outstanding principal amount, or the number of shares and par value per share, of each class of security . . . and the percentage, if any, of the total of such principal amount and total number of shares for each such class as to which assurances of assent have been obtained from the holders, with a statement of the method of determining such percentage.

With this information at hand, the Commission can then decide whether it wants more evidence that the plan has a reasonable chance to gain support from 75% of each class. There has been no case under section 20b, however, where the Commission has called for more assurances than first reported; and no regulations have been set up to govern the procedure of obtaining such assents.[7] Presumably in such a situation the Commission would call for more formal procedures than typically have been used to obtain the percentages shown in the application.

Administratively, to fulfill the regulatory requirements a railroad must clearly present a plan of modification to stockholders and be assured of their intention to support it. It is not prescribed that the assurances be in writing, and in fact

[5] The dictionary defines an "assurance" as a "declaration tending to inspire full confidence." It would seem to imply a willingness to go on record as favoring a plan.

[6] See Appendix B.

[7] The Examiner in the Boston and Maine case said that before setting an application for hearing, the Commission gives consideration to the matter of directing the applicant to secure assurances. The provision is not ignored. Hearing before the Examiner, March 30, 1949, p. 351.

the Boston and Maine officers did not so interpret the requirement. Apparently they had no thought of formalizing the procedure at the application stage; on the contrary, they intentionally avoided all written requests in order to keep the Railroad's action out of the category of solicitation. Inquiry was not made of the Commission as to proper procedure on this point. It would certainly have strengthened the Railroad's answer to interveners if at the hearings the officers could have stated that they had carried on the assurance procedure after explicit direction from the Commission.

The regulations also require the applicant to state the method of determining the percentage of assurances reported. The Boston and Maine officers interpreted this strictly as requiring only a statement of the percentage of assurances to the outstanding amount of the securities in each class. Was it the intention of the regulation to include in the "method" a statement of the precise nature of the assurance — that is, whether it was obtained by a stockholders' meeting and vote, by conferences with large holders who had indicated support, or by some other method? It would seem that there would be no point to requiring a percentage of assurances unless there was some indication as to the nature of the evidence that the assurances were given after serious study and that the plan had substantial support.

Communication with Security Holders During the Preapplication Stage

When the law states that the Commission can insist on assurance that the proposed plan is a serious effort with substantial support, the implication is that the management has been in touch with a large cross-section of the holders during the development of the plan and that the dominant interests, if any, will go along. It is in the application stage that the most direct relationship with the security holder is necessary so that the management can be sure of adequate support when the final plan emerges with the Commission's acceptance and order for a vote.

In paragraph (1) of the first Boston and Maine application submitted in August 1948, the Railroad reported on assurances of assent as follows:

The percentage of the total number of shares for each class of securities to be affected, as to which assurances of assent have been obtained from the holders, is set forth below in tabular form:

Prior Preference	21.14%
First Preferred A	28.70
B	32.79
C	35.17
D	35.28
E	2.92
Preferred (Non-Cum.)	47.90
Common	.73

The percentages have been arrived at by computations based on the stock listing of record on July 31, 1948.

The second application,[8] submitted in January 1949, included the following computation of assurances of assent based on the stock listing of record on December 31, 1948:

Prior Preference	76.46%
First Preferred	43.68
Preferred (Non-Cum.)	68.77
Common	56.30

It was an obvious decision of the management to talk directly with officers of The Pennroad Corporation [9] and also of the New Haven railroad, owner of 91% of the stock of Boston Railroad Holding Company, each having a veto power over any plan.[10] It was testified that the president of Pennroad had said at all times that he would go along with any reasonably good and proper plan.[11] In fact, the percentages of assurances of assent reported in the application for the all-common plan evidently represented the Pennroad holdings and very few others. Mr. Everett W. Smith, then assistant to the financial vice president, testified that he included the Pennroad holdings in computing the assurances of

[8] Supplemental Application No. 1.

[9] Pennroad Corporation owned 16.66% of all Boston and Maine stock, including 29.54% of the first preferred and 47.52% of the plain preferred.

[10] Hearings before the Examiner, March 1949, pp. 256–259, 342–348.

[11] Ibid., March 28, 1949, p. 106.

assent for the revised plan.[12]   The officers also included the
Railroad Holding Company stock in the percentages of assurances for the revised plan.[13]   Presumably this stock was not
included in the earlier computation because the case testing
the constitutionality of the Massachusetts Act dissolving the
holding company was not decided until October 4, 1948.   In
view of the pending dissolution, although the case was appealed to the Supreme Court of the United States and a receiver was not appointed until June 15, 1949, it is likely that
the New Haven officers were willing to accept the judgment
of the Boston and Maine officers as to a fair plan.

The Railroad officers had also to consider who further
should be advised with and how to reach them.   Their relation with brokers over the years had shown their interest in
getting the opinion and support of those whose business it
was to handle and promote trading in the Railroad's stocks.
As a practical matter, the financial men in the market could
also be useful as effective solicitors because their zeal would
be stimulated by a direct profit motive.   Whereas the all-
common plan, apparently, had been developed without much
consultation with brokers, the revised plan was based upon an
extensive exchange of views with them.

The assurances of assent for the revised plan also included
several large holders of prior preference stock, who had objected to the all-common plan and had been drawn into a
more active part in the formulation of the second plan.

To carry discussion of managerial policy in these matters a
step further, the question may be raised as to whether it is
within the fiduciary responsibility of management to keep all
security holders equally well informed on the areas of discussion in a proposed recapitalization.   Should it be the Railroad's responsibility to keep a holder of 10 shares of common
stock in a remote town in Maine as well informed as the
largest holders, for example, the Railroad Holding Company
with its holdings of 273,873 shares of all classes?   Should all
security holders be supplied with material — directly or
through brokers — to keep them posted on the progress of
the thinking on the general shape of the plan?

[12] Ibid., March 31, 1949, pp. 549–550.
[13] Ibid., March 30 and 31, 1949, pp. 548–549.

This aspect of relations with stockholders is a policy matter of real importance, and one treated in widely different fashions. The program of Western Maryland Railway Company in its section 20b application of 1950, later withdrawn, called for a maximum effort through special meetings of stockholders, group meetings, and other devices to get the active participation of all classes in shaping a feasible plan. For the modification plan approved by the Commission in 1954, Western Maryland Railway did not make any general effort to obtain assurances of assent but consulted with a number of stockholders or their representatives in formulating the plan. It informally submitted the general terms of the proposed plan to certain stockholders and received assurances from holders of at least 0.12% of first preferred stock, 13.03% of second preferred stock, and 7.06% of common stock.[14]

In connection with preparations for a stock modification plan in 1952 the management of Missouri-Kansas-Texas Railroad Company provided for formal vote to test the backing it had from stockholders before it placed its application with the Commission. The notoriety of the Boston and Maine difficulties with procedure was doubtless a contributing cause to this show of caution by the M–K–T management. The M–K–T officers spent two days in Boston in October 1952, canvassing the whole procedure with Boston and Maine officers. A four-page letter then went out in November to all stockholders, including a short abstract of the modification plan approved by the Board and comments on the guiding principles in its formulation. Attached was a card with the caption *Preliminary Assent Solicited by the Management,* with places for checking an Assenting or Not Assenting vote, and with the explanation that "It is understood this preliminary expression is not a commitment to either accept or reject any final plan when and if presented for formal vote. . . ."[15]

[14] 290 I.C.C. 445, at 452 (October 14, 1954).

[15] On the other hand, the subject was covered in the Lehigh Valley Railroad Company's application with a statement to the effect that the plan had been formulated in conferences with representatives of large holdings of the securities affected and submitted in draft form to other large holders, whose reactions were entirely favorable (271 I.C.C. 553, at 577). Officers of Bangor & Aroostook Railroad Company discussed the plan with the R.F.C., owner of

One might ask if a broader approach to the various stockholder groups in the Boston and Maine case could have forestalled the submission of the one-stock plan of August 1948,
which drew instant fire and was so hastily withdrawn; and
if it could have reduced objections expressed at the public
hearing in March 1949 toward the two-stock plan. A special
stockholders' meeting to discuss the two-stock plan before the
hearing might have had useful results. It might have allayed
the apparent fear of several interveners that other stockholders had been given additional information. If substantial support was shown for the plan, the interveners might
have abandoned their efforts to prevent approval of the plan.
On the other hand, wide canvassing of stockholders could
have given strength to the opposition by revealing the lethargy of a large group, or the existence of many half-formed
objections.

Although section 20b plans dealing with stocks have many
problems of procedure analogous to those of bond plans, including plans under section 77, there are important differences calling for close examination of whether the method or
approach in one will fit the other. This is particularly true
as to relations with security holders.

In section 77 plans, and even in section 20b plans where
the major interests are with bonds, the different groups are
usually represented by formal committees of dominant holders, which are aggressively working under capable leadership and counsel to protect their interests. In the all-stock
plans, however, such as the Boston and Maine plan, the initiative is necessarily with the management; and the extent to
which it enlists the active participation of stockholders in the
plan-making process is largely a matter of its own choosing.
In section 77 proceedings the management is really on the
defensive, as it is to a large degree in section 20b plans deal-

---

some of the bonds; and consulted with a substantial number of public holders, with dealers whose customers owned bonds, and with objective advisers
(275 I.C.C. 369, at 378). Maryland & Pennsylvania Railroad Company made
no effort to obtain general assurances. Its plan was formulated in conference with holders of large amounts of securities, and it offered evidence only
of informal acceptances (275 I.C.C. 695, at 708). Both the Lehigh and the
Maryland railroads reported that an interested banker in each case would advise acceptance.

ing mainly with bonds.   In these the management learns
early that it faces a bargaining proposition.   In the all-stock
modification plans, since the management initiates them and
usually has large numbers of scattered holdings to deal with,
the need for explicit relations with stockholders is less apparent.   It is precisely here, however, that management
should take special care to make stockholders feel they are
participating in a necessary reconstruction job on which they
will ultimately vote.

The problem of how and when to educate the stockholder
in the complexities of a recapitalization is one of the key considerations.   This was particularly true in the Boston and
Maine case, since no dividends had been paid for the past 18
years and the market for the stock was highly speculative and
volatile.   The Railroad's management evidently considered
that active efforts to inform all stockholders would be more
fruitful after the plan had been approved by the Commission.   It had assurances of assent from important groups and
could reasonably expect that the revised plan would prove
acceptable to many other informed holders.

The Commission's Control of Solicitation During the Pre-application Stage

When the decision has been made as to what stockholders
to advise with, another key problem arises with respect to
laying tentative plans before them.   Although the statute
explicitly retains the Commission's supervision over solicitation procedure, a further question remains: Does this approval of solicitation materials apply only to voting by security
holders after the plan has been accepted by the Commission,
or does it apply equally to obtaining assurances of assent?
The statute is not clear on this point.   Nevertheless, the
place of the language in the text of the statute seems to justify the conclusion that it refers only to solicitation for the
final vote on the plan.   It is the next sentence after reference
to the findings of the Commission on the plan, the amendments, if any, and the order that the plan be submitted to
the holders "affected thereby" for acceptance or rejection.

That there was uncertainty on this problem is shown by the
care taken by the Railroad to handle its communications with

stockholders entirely on an informal basis in the preapplication period. It is shown also by the amount of time spent by interveners in questioning the Railroad's officers as to whether they went after assurances of assent, in other words solicited them, or whether they received assents voluntarily given on the stockholders' initiative. These points of view are illustrated in an exchange at the first public hearing in March 1949.

Mr. Fletcher [counsel for the Railroad]: In connection with Mr. French's testimony there was quite a bit of cross examination, Mr. Examiner, about the stockholders' meetings or so-called meetings. I think I should make a brief statement of our position on that.

It is our interpretation that the Act did not necessarily require any stockholders' approval before the filing of the plan with the Commission, although I think that we all take it it was desirable to get a considerable amount of informal approval. That being so, we did not consider it necessary to have any formal proceedings of any nature. We consulted and discussed gladly with any stockholder who approached us [on] the problem, but did not have a meeting or anything in the nature of a stockholders' meeting and did not so intend until after Commission approval.

Even then, I might add, we don't contemplate a meeting. We contemplate getting letters of assent.

Mr. Caruthers: May the record show that I am in accord with Mr. Fletcher's understanding of the provisions of the Act and that is why I am somewhat at a loss to understand why the application shows assents of the plan prior to its approval by the Interstate Commerce Commission.

Mr. Fletcher: You will find that the regulations of the Interstate Commerce Commission with respect to the application require that information.

Exam. Kirby: Requires a showing as to any assents.

Mr. Fletcher: Yes, which may have been obtained although none are actually required.

Exam. Kirby: It has been done in other cases. It is not unusual. I don't know about the circumstances of this case, but the fact that it has been done is not unusual.[16]

Early in the hearing Mr. Caruthers asked whether the stockholders listed as assenting had had any material other

[16] Hearing before the Examiner, March 28, 1949, pp. 159–160.

than the 1948 annual report to stockholders. Mr. French replied that it was his understanding that no solicitation material could be given and to the best of his knowledge none was.[17] Later Mr. Caruthers remarked: ". . . but I do think this is a most important representation that has been made in this application, and it should be clearly brought out by the evidence just how they obtained the assurances. . . ."[18]

The Railroad's position was summarized as follows in its brief submitted after the public hearing in March 1949: [19]

It may not be out of place at this point to discuss the matter of assurances of assent as reported in the Supplemental Application and to clarify somewhat an apparent misunderstanding as to the meaning of that phrase as interpreted by the Applicant on the one hand and by certain intervenors on the other. It would appear from questions and arguments made on the record that intervenors took the phrase to indicate the result of solicitation activity on behalf of the Applicant whereby the holders of the stock computed as making up the assenters were besought their assurance; that they evidenced such assurance in writing and that the assurances were considered binding (R. 351 *et seq.*). Nothing of the sort was done or contemplated by the Applicant. A much more informal operation took place. No one was solicited (R. 58, 353), but if stockholders with whom the management had been in communication voluntarily indicated their support, whether orally, in writing, or — in the case of directors — by failure to disapprove when their responsibilities were such as to require active steps to disapprove, they were considered as giving assurance of assent (R. 547 *et seq.*). At no time was it felt necessary — or indeed proper — to go beyond that point in view of the solicitation provisions of Section 20b of the Act (R. 57); and never have such assurances been deemed binding (R. 354).

On the basis of the extended discussion in the hearing and the briefs, the Commission concluded: ". . . there may be room for a legitimate difference of opinion as to the propriety of including certain assents in the calculation and therefore

17 Ibid., March 28, 1949, p. 57.
18 Ibid., March 30, 1949, p. 357.
19 Brief on Behalf of Applicant before the Interstate Commerce Commission, Finance Docket No. 16250, May 31, 1949, p. 19.

as to the accuracy of the percentages, but the record does not afford justification for the allegation that there has been a misrepresentation of material facts." [20]

Even this opinion was not adequate to settle the matter, however, and nearly two years later we find the interveners questioning the validity of the final assents on the grounds that the assurances of assent in the preapplication stage had been handled by such slipshod methods as to make any representation of the management undependable.[21]

There is still another omission in the statute, which causes some confusion on the solicitation matter. It relates to the interim between filing the application and submitting the plan to the stockholders. The plan outlined in the application is not in final form and indeed may differ materially from what finally gets Commission approval. When the general tenor of the proposed plan first appears without argument in the formal application, opposition may be fanned into a blaze by the work of an aggressive minority. An opposition committee, or even individuals on their own initiative, may run a substantial campaign and use many devices to enlist support. The statute makes no mention of solicitation at this stage of the proceedings, and the discussions in the Boston and Maine case showed considerable confusion on the point.[22]

[20] 275 I.C.C. 397, at 423 (April 19, 1950).

[21] Mr. Caruthers: ". . . when we got to the hearing and interrogated Mr. Trowbridge [the financial vice president] about these assurances of assents, we found that they were just verbal, that they included directors without consulting them, and it was impossible to determine from his testimony where he got all of this information to make exact and precise computations. He got that secondhand, from hearsay, in many cases, he admitted.

"Now, we argued strongly before the Commission that that was an unfair representation to make on the strength of the testimony of an official of the railroad, and so, when this affidavit comes in saying we now have the assents, and our challenge comes in, that we wanted to see the evidence." Transcript of Proceedings before a Three-Judge Court, Civil Action No. 763–51, January 22, 1952, p. 130.

[22] The Examiner at the first public hearing evidently assumed that solicitation material at all stages must be approved by the Commission, as shown by the following discussion relating to the pre-hearing activities of the Sakis Committee.

Exam. Kirby: In that connection I should like to clear up one feature of your committee's activity that has given me a little concern. You say, Mr.

Conclusions

For the preapplication period and the interim period between the application to the Commission and the time the plan is submitted to vote, the conclusion can be drawn that there is at present no statutory control over the material used to influence holders of securities either for or against the plan. This early period may be more important in forming the lines of support or attack than the more formal campaign during the submission period. The statute and the regulations might well extend the time of the Commission's control over solicitation so as to cover the entire period between the formulation of the plan and the conclusion of the balloting period.

We can conclude also that the purpose of the "assurances of assent" in the application stage is accomplished with less formality than in the final vote on a definitive plan, and there is less need of rigid mechanics to establish valid support. Assent at the application stage is not formalized by documents and a depositary, and is certainly not binding as a vote for the final plan.

ASSENT PROCEDURES IN THE FINAL VOTING ON THE PLAN

The procedures followed in the final balloting on the Boston and Maine plan of modification introduced many

Caruthers, that the committee was soliciting opposition to the plan. Is that right?

Mr. Caruthers: The committee has proxies which authorize Mrs. Sakis to form a committee and vote those proxies in the committee to oppose the plan as presented by the Company.

Exam. Kirby: You are aware, of course, are you not, of the provisions of Paragraph 2 of Section 20b, which requires that all material used or to be used in the soliciting of the assents or the opposition of holders to a proposed alteration or modification shall, before being so used, be submitted to the Commission for its approval as to correctness and sufficiency of material facts stated there?   (Record, March 31, 1949, pp. 636–637.)

A week or so earlier, however, the Commission's Bureau of Finance had examined Mrs. Sakis' letter to stockholders and concluded that it did not seem to be such solicitation of assents or opposition to a plan as required approval by the Commission. The Commission, the Bureau said, had no jurisdiction over the formation of protective committees under the statute. (Letter dated March 24, 1949, from the Bureau to the Railroad's attorney.)

serious and unexpected problems. The next several pages go no further than to set forth the Commission's requirements governing the voting in this case. With this background the chapters to follow examine the history of the actual balloting and the subsequent developments before Court and Commission.

Regulations Governing Assent Procedures in the Boston and Maine Balloting

The problem here was to set up a balloting procedure that would accurately register the percentage of assents to a plan. Both the statute and the Commission's regulations set the requirements for final voting in more specific terms than those relating to assurances of assent; but the statute still leaves the details to be carried out as the Commission directs. The Commission has left the initiative in method to the railroad applying for modification.

The Railroad's application for the all-common plan (August 1948) and the supplemental application for the two-stock plan (January 1949) proposed the following procedure of assent:

> (i) Assenting stockholders will deposit their securities with a depositary satisfactory to the Commission. The depositary will issue certificates of deposit for the securities deposited with it. If the Plan is approved by the Commission, and if 75% of the holders of each class assent thereto, the applicant will issue and transmit to the depositary, (who will distribute) new securities outlined hereinabove. . . . The said certificates of deposit will be transferable only on the books of the depositary. . . .

*   *   *   *   *

> (s) Applicant proposes to obtain the assent of the security holders affected by the proposed modifications by having them deposit their securities with the depositary together with a Letter of Transmittal which shall signify their assent to the same. The depositary will be responsible for reporting and certifying directly to the Commission the percentage of assents received for each class of stock. . . .

In addition to the foregoing, a meeting of stockholders to

vote upon the proposed Plan may be held if such action is deemed necessary or desirable by the officers of or counsel for the applicant.

This is the traditional "deposit certificate" plan long used in reorganization procedure. If a holder assents, he deposits his stock certificate and gets back a deposit certificate with a legend on its face describing where the original certificate is deposited and for what purpose. Each subsequent sale transfers the receipt for the deposited share certificate, and the purchaser is thus put on notice that he holds only a receipt to the certificate still on deposit. This mechanism does not insure that every subsequent holder would agree to the plan, for he might not go to the trouble of recalling the deposited certificate. It does serve notice, however, that a specific certificate number has been voted and the affirmative vote still stands.

In the period between the supplemental application and the hearing, January 1949 to March 28, 1949, the Railroad's financial officers and counsel concluded that the certificate of deposit method of assent procedure was wholly impractical in their case and would jeopardize the success of the plan.[23] They were impressed by an evident stockholder lethargy, which would severely limit voting if stockholders had to do even so much as locate the certificates and deposit them. No dividends on any stock had been paid since January 1, 1932, and the low market values, especially of the junior classes of the stock, would work against any mechanism requiring effort and expense.

In the Railroad's formal testimony entered at the hearing,

23 Mr. Everett W. Smith testified as follows at the Hearing before the Examiner in Boston on August 27, 1952 (p. 1324):
. . . I had talked to a good many people in the financial district, brokers, and so forth, and it became, at least to me, and I think the other officers of the Railroad, pretty certain that a deposit operation was impractical from the standpoint of a modification at this time. Generally speaking, a deposit operation is used where bonds are involved, and most corporate bonds are in so-called bearer form. They are not held in any registered name. Therefore, to tabulate a voting involving a bond issue it is necessary to have the bonds deposited in order to know who the owner is and how he is voting them. We felt that this was impractical from our operations, because our plan involved only stock, and of course we had a record of our stockholders.

therefore, a statement of method of obtaining assents was presented to amend the Supplemental Application:[24]

> If the Plan is approved by the Commission, assenting stockholders will be requested to send a Letter of Assent, in form approved by the Commission, to a depositary who will from time to time advise the applicant of the assents so received. The assents will be revocable at any time up to the time of declaration of irrevocability as hereinafter provided, but until notice of revocation is received by the depositary the assents will bind the holder of the stock assenting to the Plan and his heirs, successors, representatives and assigns. Upon receipt by the depositary of Letters of Assent from the holders of 75% of the number of shares of stock of each class outstanding, the depositary will immediately advise the applicant, and applicant's president may thereupon declare that the Letters of Assent shall be irrevocable and shall immediately cause notice to that effect to be published in newspapers of general circulation in the cities of Boston, Massachusetts, and New York, New York.

This procedure raises the point that the statute does not state whether 75% of each class must be in favor of the plan at the moment the submission period is declared over. This, in a close vote, may not be so. An assented stock certificate may be sold to a buyer who knows nothing of the plan; but the stock is still assented. If the plan were brought to the new buyer's attention, he might want to revoke the assents. As of a given instant one cannot be sure that all shares are in the hands of those who presently assent, except on the technical point that stock once assented stays assented until revoked. The deposit certificate arrangement would have gone far to correct this difficulty by serving more explicit notice on a subsequent buyer that a plan was afoot and his definitive certificate was on deposit in support of it. Perhaps the problem could have been solved by a stamp on assented certificates. If the assents were revoked, the stamp could be canceled. Such a procedure would introduce clerical complications in any situation, however; and it would have been especially difficult in the Boston and Maine case, both be-

[24] This became Exhibit H–13. Hearing before the Examiner, March 30, 1949, pp. 456–458.

cause of the lethargy of the stockholders and because most of the stock certificates were already stamped for the 1926 agreement.

The Commission accepted, without argument, the Railroad's suggested change in method of obtaining assents. In fact, the proposed method followed customary procedure in 20b cases. The Order for submission of the proposed modification was issued on April 19, 1950. The main provisions relevant to the problems covered in this study are summarized below:[25]

> The classes affected by the plan were (1) the prior preference stock, (2) the first preferred stock, consisting of series A, B, C, D, and E, (3) the noncumulative preferred stock, and (4) the common stock.
>
> The submission was to be made by mailing to the stockholders one copy each of the order, the Commission's report, and the plan as amended, a form of letter of assent, and a letter of transmittal requesting assents.
>
> The plan, all letters, circulars, advertisements, and other communications, including written or printed instructions to solicitors, as well as all financial and statistical statements to be used by any party in soliciting acceptance or rejection, were to be submitted to the Commission for approval as to the correctness and sufficiency of the material facts stated therein.
>
> The directors, officers, and regular employees of the Railroad would be permitted to solicit assents, and the Railroad might hire one or more firms or persons specializing in such work to assist in solicitation, with reasonable provision for compensation; and such solicitation might be carried on by personal interview, mail, advertising, telephone, and telegraph.
>
> A stockholder was to assent by sending his executed vote of assent to Old Colony within the designated time. Failure of any stockholder to act would constitute a vote of rejection without execution of any ballot or return of the form of assent. An assent would be revocable up to the declaration by the applicant of its irrevocability, but until notice of revocation was received by the depositary, an assent once given would bind the holder, his heirs, successors, and assigns. Revocation could be made only by the execution and deliv-

[25] For the complete text of the Order see Appendix C.

ery to the depositary of a letter of revocation in a form to be approved by the Commission.

Assents should be made within six months after the effective date of the order or such further time as the Commission might later designate, provided that, if at an earlier time unrevoked assents had been received from the required percentages of the classes of securities, the Railroad might declare the submission period closed. The required percentages were 75% of the outstanding shares of each of the prior preference, first preferred, and common classes, and 87% of the noncumulative preferred class.

Within 60 days after the closing of the submission period, the Railroad was to submit to the Commission a certificate of the total number of outstanding shares in each class, the number of assented shares in each class, and the percentage of these to the total in each class. The certificate was to be based on and supported by the depositary's certificate as to the number of assented shares of each class.

The Depositary's Function

The depositary had to set up its procedure for receiving and tabulating assents so as to be sure that all assents counted were valid and also that all valid assents were counted. What procedures will assure this and what are the earmarks of a valid assent?

When Old Colony was designated depositary, its officers considered the mechanism as essentially a proxy procedure, in which Old Colony had had wide experience for many years.[26] Assents, like proxies, could be given only by holders of record; they were to be given by sending the executed vote of assent within a specified time to the designated depositary; they were revocable at any time up to the declaration of irrevocability. Old Colony set up its control records along the lines of a typical proxy procedure. It had nothing to do with the solicitation material as such, nor with the form letters of assent and revocation that were sent to stockholders of record. These were prepared by the Railroad and authorized by the Commission after examination.

There was, however, a notable difference between the Boston and Maine procedure and the normal proxy operation,

[26] Mr. John Coulson so testified in the Hearing before the Examiner, August 25, 1952, p. 887.

where the voters are holders of record of a specific day even though they are allowed a period of some weeks in which to vote. The submission-period procedure in the Boston and Maine balloting gave all holders of record within the period the right to assent and to revoke, and transferees until they revoked were bound by a preceding assent of the transferred stock. Close tab had to be kept on transferred stock already assented in case the new holder sent in a revocation or a duplicate assent for the same shares.

The depositary had to be assured of five things with regard to each letter of assent: that the signer of the letter was a holder of record; that authority was shown by those signing in a fiduciary or representative capacity; that the number of shares assented was covered by the shares recorded on the stockholder's ledger card; that there was no record of previous assents for the same shares; and that the letter was sent prior to termination of the submission period. A significant note was printed at the bottom of the letter: "In all cases in which the Letter of Assent is executed by an officer of a corporation, administrator, executor, trustee, guardian, agent, attorney or others acting in a fiduciary or representative capacity, proper evidence of authority to act in such capacity must be furnished." This note is emphasized because the depositary and the Railroad agreed not to require that such evidence of authority accompany the letter, and the Sakis group and the Department later pointed to this decision as one of the responsibilities and duties in which the depositary failed "To conform to the requirements of the Commission's orders." [27]

Preview of the Department's Charges

The main charges of the Department were leveled at the three parties carrying joint responsibility for correct balloting: the Commission, with prime responsibility, Old Colony as the designated depositary, and the Railroad, which solicited assents to the plan.

[27] Amended Answer of United States of America, November 2, 1951, p. 4. Civil Action No. 763–51 in the United States District Court for the District of Columbia.

The direct charge against the Commission was that its decision that there were four classes of stock not only had no basis in principle but was not consistent with its own allocation of stock among eight distinct classes. Chapter VI is given over to analysis of the problem of determination of security classes, since the problem took on great significance in this case and received exhaustive and perhaps definitive treatment. The chapter is concerned also with some broader questions implicit in the assumption that the assents from any particular class represent the homogeneous interest of that class. We shall see that some crucial decisions on balloting matters rest on the theory that holders of the stock of a class vote the interests of that class. What happens to this theory when the facts in the Boston and Maine case show it to be quite usual for a holder to own stock of two or more classes? The hierarchy of stock issues in the Boston and Maine structure raised more problems than usual in this area.

As for the depositary, which was described repeatedly by the Department's Trial Brief as an independent fiduciary required to certify to an exact total of valid assents, the charges referred first to basic weaknesses in its system of recording assents. These weaknesses were alleged to make inaccuracies unavoidable. A most troublesome problem came out of the regulation that, until revoked, assents carried through to subsequent holders of assented shares. Some aspects of this problem are considered toward the end of this chapter, but the implications for accuracy in recording are left to Chapter VII. The charges most threatening to the depositary's reputation centered upon the alleged failure to obey the clear instructions on the letter of assent requiring evidence of authority from those acting in a fiduciary or representative capacity. A stronger word than "laxity" was used; the charge was that the depositary "ignored" the Commission's directive and in so doing failed to assert its independence of the Railroad.

The seriousness of such charges against a fiduciary institution demands in all fairness a prompt analysis and opinion at this point, lest the reader carry over even for a moment charges that in the end were not sustained. Any harm of delay in analysis can be substantially offset by the statement that the final opinion of the Commission left no taint on the reputation of Old Colony.[28]

The charges against the Railroad related to alleged improper solicitation methods and to three situations where assents were given by holders said to be within the control of the Railroad. The Commission found no basis for the first charge, but found technical violation of the statutory ban in the three control situations. Chapters IX and X are wholly concerned with the charges in these two areas.

The Higher Percentage of Assents Imposed on the Noncumulative Preferred Stock

The statute provided an exception to the requirement of assents from 75% of the principal amount of a class by giving discretionary authority to the Commission to raise the percentage [29] "in any case where 75 per centum thereof is held by fewer than twenty-five holders . . . as the Commission may determine to be just and reasonable and in the public interest." This leeway for exceptions was the basis in the Boston and Maine case for the requirement of assents from 87% of the noncumulative preferred stock.

The ownership of this stock stood as follows in April 1949: of the 31,498 shares outstanding, 75% were in fewer than 25 hands; 14,968 shares were held by Pennroad and 6,543 by Boston Railroad Holding Company; thus 68.3% were in two hands.[30] Pennroad clearly could block any plan, if 75% as-

[28] Mr. L'Heureux, after thorough review of all the record and his own personal investigation of Old Colony's performance, concluded that ". . . the proof conclusively shows that Old Colony Trust acted with the greatest efficiency and according to the highest standards and traditions of the great financial institution which it unquestionably is." (Opinion, April 15, 1953, p. 59.)

[29] The requirement of a hearing in connection with this finding, as proposed in an earlier draft, was eliminated in the final statute. *Modification of Railroad Financial Structures*, Hearings on H. R. 2298 May 19, 1947, p. 6.

[30] When the Railroad made its application for the two-stock plan, it reported that there was no class where less than 25 holders held 75% of the stock. The stockholders list drawn up for the annual meeting in April 1949 showed such changes in the ownership of the noncumulative preferred stock as to bring that class under the provision for exceptions. (Letter from W. S. Trowbridge, financial vice president of the Railroad, to the Commission, April 11, 1949.)

sent was required; and the Railroad Holding Company could also, if it could get help from 1,332 more shares, possibly through market purchases.

What is the basis for the exception granted at the discretion of the Commission? The general principle of voting laid down in the statute is on the basis of the principal amount or number of shares outstanding, not the number of holders. If three-fourths of the principal in each class assents, the plan is adopted. This percentage does not vary as the classes are arrayed from top to bottom in order of investment value. A fraction over 25% of the principal amount of the Boston and Maine common stock would have as much to say about the plan's being adopted as a fraction over 25% of the prior preference stock, which admittedly had the bulk of the real investment value remaining at the time of voting.[31] This paradox carries the logics of financial theory that apply in prosperous concerns into situations where large segments of the nominal equity maintain their percentage of vote in the face of substantial, if not total, loss of their real equity. In the Boston and Maine situation in 1948, the common stock was in such poor market repute as to sell for a total of around $700,000 at the low ($1\frac{3}{4}$ a share), whereas the prior preference stock sold, roughly, at $7,341,000 at the low ($32 a share). To take the lowest preferred class, the lowest market price ($1\frac{7}{8}$) of the noncumulative preferred stock valued the total issue of 31,498 shares at about $59,000.

On the basis of these figures, the statutory voting percentage of 75% of each class to affirm the plan would permit about $15,000 worth of the noncumulative preferred stock

---

By April 1950, Pennroad had sold all its holdings of noncumulative preferred stock. Amoskeag Company held 14,968 shares of that class in 1950. (From annual reports of those companies.)

[31] The bankruptcy statutes, Section 77 and the Chandler Act, both recognized this injustice in the extreme case by taking the vote away from any class in which the valuation of the going enterprise left them no equity. The law provides no gradations between full vote and no vote; if there is still equity but not much, the required vote of each class, no matter how much their relative equities have changed on the new valuation, is necessary to adopt the plan.

to have the same veto power on a "fair" plan as $1,835,000 of the prior preference stock.[32]

This is not to say that a just allocation of voting power requires that votes be proportionate to dollars invested. Dollars invested in the securities of a corporation buy different packages of rights: bonds with no votes but with less risk and first claim on income; preferred stocks ahead of the common stocks in these regards but behind the bonds. If a company so capitalized comes to hard times, however, but not hard enough to bring the bonds into control because of contractual defaults, the common stockholders may still stand dominant in management through voting power. Although in the Boston and Maine case the preferred stocks carried per share voting equality, the arrearages, averaging over $100 a share, shifted values heavily toward the two highest preferred classes but left voting strength undisturbed. With equity all but vanished in the two lowest classes, the ghosts of dollar values once residing in them retained full vigor as voters. This was the chronic state of the Boston and Maine Railroad during and after the depression of the 1930's.[33]

A second principle deduced from the language of the statute is that concentrated ownership in a class is suspect in itself and might conduce to oppression of the minority. If three holders, for example, hold 75% of the noncumulative preferred stock and agree to assent, that decision should not be accepted unless some part of the remaining 25% also assent. This is an exception to the general rule that the per-

[32] Someone has said, with regard to equalizing burdens of taxation through progressive income taxes, that there is nothing more unequal than the equal treatment of unequals. So here, a 75% assent total of outstanding shares in each class gives unwarranted power to a marginal, or lower, class to force an inequitable concession from those classes that have considerable equity left to them.

[33] One could argue that nobody can complain of injustice in these situations because each security holder in the hierarchy of claims holds precisely those rights he contracted for; that the mistake was made when the contracts did not provide for increased voting power to meet marked deterioration in income. Either the troublous times of low income and mounting arrearages are not clearly envisaged, or other reasons explain the failure of preferred contracts to provide automatically for voting power to be transferred from stocks with decreasing equity. Section 20b was devised to do for railroads what could not be done without such a statute to correct archaic capital structures.

centage of principal held is the criterion of voting strength rather than the number of holders.

The fact that the authority is discretionary implies that the Commission examines the facts in each special case to see if an exception should be made. What is the test for an exception? Suppose the stock is held by 24 people in substantially equal amounts. Would not a vote of 18 holders be as indicative of overwhelming acceptance as 30 out of 40 or 75 out of 100 holders of the same stock? There is no reason to conclude otherwise. The test must be that there are relatively few large holders holding the 75%, with the remainder held by a much larger number of small holders. Take the case, for example, where three holders control 75% of the vote. To maintain that such a case may call for an exception is to assume that the three who control may have an adverse interest to the rest. Can that be assumed?

The Examiner's report on the Boston and Maine situation made no recommendation of any exception to the 75% requirement for each class. The Commission's Report of April 19, 1950, said:

> Pursuant to such provision [that in such a situation the Commission may in its discretion require a larger than 75% affirmative vote] and in view of the fact that . . . 68.29 percent of the total number of shares of noncumulative preferred stock outstanding are held [by Pennroad and Boston R.R. Holding Co.], thus accounting for the major portion of the 75-percent ownership by less than 25 holders, we believe a larger percentage of assents for this class of stock is warranted. Accordingly, we find that it will be just and reasonable and in the public interest to require that such percentage should represent a total vote which will reflect the possible combined favorable vote of these two holdings plus approximately 75 percent of the difference between the larger of the holdings and the total number of shares outstanding. Thus, the resulting required number of assenting shares will be 27,403, or 87 percent of the total number of shares outstanding of this class.[34]

The Commission did not fully develop its reasons for demanding 87% vote of the noncumulative stock. The mere

[34] 275 I.C.C. 397 at 423–424.

fact of heavy concentration of over two-thirds of the class in the hands of two holders was given as the sole reason for increasing the percentage of required assents for the class.

It might be argued that because Pennroad and the Railroad Holding Company held, between them, 38.5% of the total prior preference stock outstanding, they would vote for the plan because of their larger dollar investment in the prior preference, even though they also held 68% of the plain preferred stock; whereas the remaining holders would lean toward the opposition because of the relatively small equity given them by the plan. If there were no such adverse interest, the small minority should consider themselves fortunate that so large an assent total was likely from the two holders of the dominant interest in the class.

If a plan is based on "fair" principles, however, and the two lowest layers of stock — plain preferred and common — have been more liberally treated than can be justified other than on grounds of expediency to get their vote,[35] it is hard to see any logic in being especially concerned about the voting power of the scattered holdings against the two holders of the majority of the plain preferred. If the plan is fair, and even by intention more than fair to the plain preferred and common classes, why should a larger vote margin be demanded in the noncumulative class just because two large holders both consider the plan to their interest? Even on the assumption that the two large holders were voting their major interests as prior preference holders, and would vote the same way even if the plain preferred stock got still less than the plan offered them, there is no warrant for so increasing the percentage as to give the remaining holders a powerful weapon to wreck a plan that the Commission itself supports as liberally favorable to them.[36]

[35] The Commission had found the plan just and reasonable and in the public interest, and also made the statement that:

"Thus, for all practical purposes, . . . both the plain preferred and the common stocks are worthless, since they represent no more than a call upon future earning power many years hence — approximately 75 years under the applicant's estimate . . . In our opinion, the relative treatment accorded these two classes of stock is justified." 275 I.C.C. at 446 (April 19, 1950).

[36] In the face of the Commission's finding that the equity remaining to the plain preferred was so tenuous as to have substantially no present value,

It is important, however, to consider the principle in relation to an actual situation. For a group making a real sacrifice, the Commission's requirement would be reasonable. In this case, for instance, if the class in question were the prior preference stock, the requirement could be justified on the grounds, say, that two big holders might vote for an undue sacrifice from the class in order to put the plan through. Big holders might have reasons for action that would not apply to the small scattered minority.

The decision of the Commission also assumes that the smaller holders were voting strictly as noncumulative preferred stockholders and had no divided interests, as did Pennroad, to play the lesser interest in favor of the greater. Hence, the Commission may have reasoned, it would insist on a vote in good faith, dominated by an unmixed noncumulative interest; it would require a 75% majority outside of Pennroad's holdings, or 87% over-all. This conclusion apparently was not based on any study of the cross-holdings of the small holders. Exhibit 5 in Chapter VI summarizes an analysis of the cross-holding of classes of stock in the Railroad. It shows that at the end of the voting period perhaps 10% of the noncumulative preferred stock was held by those whose interest lay solely in this class of stock. Furthermore, the data on which this exhibit was based show that most of the holders included in the nearly 90% of cross-holding held important amounts of the senior securities; very few holdings were concentrated in the noncumulative and common stock categories. Under these circumstances not even the requirement of an 87% affirmative vote resulted in a clear expression of the interest of the noncumulative preferred stock. Even if the small group holding only this class of stock had refused to assent to the plan, they would have been outweighed by the votes of those whose real interests lay in other classes. Study of the actual holdings leads to the conclusion that practically all the votes in this class would be influenced by other interests, in many combinations, and that a clearcut expression of the interests of this class would be impossible to obtain. The Commission might have reasonably concluded,

---

to raise the percentage vote required of the class was to say, "You have no equity, really, but you should have increased power to scuttle the plan!"

therefore, that no useful objective would be attained by raising the percentage from the required 75%.

This decision of the Commission, based on a principle that
simon-pure noncumulative holders should not be dominated
by two large holders who were really voting as prior preference holders, brought on practical difficulties that threatened
to defeat the plan. It certainly increased the nuisance value
of a small minority — just over 13% — which might easily
be achieved by speculators intent on buying a threat with
little cash.[37] The decision assumed that the two large holders
were voting against the interest of the noncumulative preferred stock just because they held large blocks of the prior
preference stock. In this case, and by the Commission's own
analysis, the prior preference holders really conceded something to the lower classes of stock; and hence those with large
prior preference holdings were paying a handsome price for
the cooperation of the two lower classes to put through a plan
characterized by the Commission as "just and reasonable . . .
in the public interest . . . in the best interests of the applicant, of each class of its stockholders. . . ."[38]

In another section 20b proceeding, the Maryland & Pennsylvania Railroad Company Securities Modification,[39] the
Commission studied two classes of securities in each of which
75% of the securities were held by fewer than 25 holders. In
one issue of bonds the ownership facts were exceptional in
that only $10,000 out of $900,000 of the bonds remained un-
pledged and these were held by only seven persons. The
$890,000 of bonds were pledged under another issue of bonds

[37] At the highest market price in 1950, $2 a share, the entire issue of non-
cumulative preferred stock had a market value of approximately $63,000.
Holders of just over 13%, with an investment of about $8,200, could block the
vote. This chance of wrecking a plan dealing with $180 million of new valua-
tion with so little at stake raises serious question about the merits of the Commission's exception to the 75% assent requirement. That this is not purely
academic is shown by the market activity of the noncumulative class during
the period. Also, when the facts of stock ownership showed that at least 10%
of the more speculative classes could not be located, the 13% was reduced to
perhaps 3% or less, which made the problem of rounding up votes in this
class extremely critical.

[38] 275 I.C.C. at 454 (April 19, 1950).

[39] Finance Docket No. 17035, 275 I.C.C. 695 (December 20, 1950).

and hence had no vote.   The Commission concluded that
". . . the number of holders [is] so small that any such increase [above the required 75% assent] would emphasize the
already large power of this class to defeat the plan." [40]   In the
other situation in the same case $837,000 principal amount of
bonds was outstanding, $500,000 of which was pledged back
of a loan from the Mercantile Trust Company; 76.4% of the
total outstanding was held by 11 holders.   On these facts, if
the requirement of 75% assents was retained, rejections by
more than 62% of the total outside of the pledged amount
would be necessary to defeat the plan.   The Commission explained that "In view of the other interests of the noteholder
in the plan, we conclude and find that the assents of the holders of 80 percent of the consolidated bonds should be required
for approval.   This will require the assents of the holders of
50.3 percent of the outstanding bonds, in addition to the
assent of the Mercantile Trust Co." [41]

It appears that the Commission was really saying here that
the Mercantile Trust Company had an interest that might be
adverse to that of the other holders.   It therefore decided to
offset somewhat the dominance of the Mercantile bank by increasing the percentage required for assent by five points,
from 75% to 80%.   Although there is nothing in the statute
directing the Commission to test its decision by the existence
of another and possibly adverse interest, the decision to raise
the assent percentage for one issue and not the other suggests
that the test of "adverse interest" played the decisive part.
Thus, in the Boston and Maine case, too, presumably the adverse interests indicated by the heavy holdings of Pennroad
and the Railroad Holding Company in the other classes of
stock were the explanation for the increase of the required
percentage from 75%.

The Commission apparently thought that the Mercantile
bank would assent; otherwise the plan was doomed.   It was
virtually saying that if the bank did not assent its bonds in
this issue, there was nothing that the Commission could do,
even though the bank was influenced by an adverse interest;
but that if the bank did assent, as the Commission thought it

[40] Ibid., pp. 719–720.
[41] Ibid., p. 720.

would, then the minority's right of independent judgment was not adequately protected unless they were given a larger say. This interpretation of the law gives the large holder a deciding voice without restriction in voting No, but limits his influence in voting Yes, even on a plan that the Commission has already judged to be fair.

These decisions appear to give special consideration to the small holder as against the large, on the presumption that the large holder is likely to be biased through a special interest, but with no facts to show whether or not the small holders also are biased. As was pointed out in the discussion of cross-holdings in the Boston and Maine noncumulative preferred stock, any cross-holdings of stock are likely to indicate conflicting interests. It does not appear that in the case of the second issue of Maryland & Pennsylvania bonds the Commission checked to find out whether holders other than the bank also had an adverse interest, or whether their votes would express the opinion of that class alone.

From these examples we may conclude that when the Commission finds that holdings in a class are relatively concentrated, it should examine them to determine whether the assent percentage should be raised; but the percentage should not be raised unless the Commission has reason to believe that a higher percentage would get nearer to the real opinion of the class than 75% would.

Another aspect of the voting problem when there are concentrated holdings in a class is that the situation presumably calling for the increased percentage of assents may change during the submission period. For example, the Commission's ruling on the percentage of assents in the Maryland & Pennsylvania case was based on the situation at the time of the decision, but the voting would extend over a period with changing conditions. The effect of the requirement of 80% assents was to require assents from $41,850 more bonds than would have been required under the 75% rule. If the bank concerned had an adverse interest powerful enough to warrant the requirement of 80% assents from the class, it probably would find worthwhile the temporary investment of the amount necessary to buy 42 bonds on the market in order to vote them.

In other cases, the opposite trend might occur in the market; large holdings might be sold and become more widely distributed. Market action carries on throughout the submission period, and a rule laid down by the Commission before voting begins may be made entirely inappropriate by changes in holdings during the voting period. In such a situation should the decision stand throughout the period if circumstances change? It is not fair to other holders of securities that a rule becomes arbitrary during the pendency of proceedings and the Commission does not have the means of detecting changes or the power to revise the rule. The feasibility of making the statute cover the contingency of such a change is a problem for the administrative lawyer.

An administrative agency, under the law, should have powers to keep its administration adjusted to different circumstances, if feasible. This is in no way administration by men and not by law, which is anathema to a just government. It is quite the opposite; it protects against arbitrary laws no longer applicable. To take the example of the Boston and Maine noncumulative preferred stock, assume that the rule of 87% was justified under the circumstances at the time of the Order for voting, but was not justified when voting started or as it continued. Who could be injured if a report of facts permitted the Commission to change its order in the light of them? The change would remove a rule that had become arbitrary in its effects.

QUESTIONS OF PRINCIPLE INVOLVED IN THE RULE THAT ASSENTS CARRY THROUGH TRANSFERS UNTIL REVOKED

Section 20b and the regulations clearly are drawn to give the security holder all the facts he needs to vote intelligently. The Commission's control over solicitation material and methods serves to this end. Procedures are measured in terms of their effects on getting an informed opinion of security holders. Furthermore, one has only to review the development of devices to insure full disclosure in prospectuses and in the security markets to see the importance this objective has attained in all financial regulation.

Against this background of meticulous care over prospectuses and solicitation material, we have the Commission accepting the proposal of the Railroad that the stockholder need not deposit his stock on voting but need only assent by a form letter, *which assent binds the transferee.* This was the procedure followed also in the three or four earlier cases of securities modification where stockholders had balloted as well as bondholders. It serves to obscure an essential fact from the purchaser of stock, *that the stock has been assented;* or at least the fact of assent is not flaunted in his face as it would be if stock once voted by deposit were thereafter marketed in the form of a deposit certificate, which carries the full explanation on its face, or if the original stock certificate were stamped to indicate assent.

It seems incongruous to devise a balloting procedure under government regulation that works so as to obscure the voting status of the stock in the event of transfer and forces the transferee to seek out information as to the assent status of his stock. True, there was "constructive" [42] notice here that stock once assented remained so even to transferees, until revoked; but the purchaser might have no knowledge of what the plan did for him, and might have received no solicitation material directly. Only if unassented shares were transferred to individuals as holders of record did the depositary in the Boston and Maine voting send solicitation material to new holders.[43] The new stock in a recapitalization is in a real sense a new stock, and the purchaser should know as much as he can about its position in the new capital structure. A purchaser of Boston and Maine common stock might really be purchasing, if the plan went through, $\frac{1}{20}$ of a share of *new* Boston and Maine common stock. When neither the deposit certificate system nor a stamp is used, an assent once given is more likely to stay put because market dealings do not flag the facts that balloting is in progress and the shares being purchased are already assented.

[42] The opinion and order of the Commission of April 19, 1950, which fully described the assent procedures, were included in the solicitation material sent to record holders at the start of the submission period.

[43] Testimony by Cecil Covert, given during the Deposition of John Coulson, October 18, 1951, p. 8.

We have a basic question of policy here.   Admittedly, the
Letter of Assent system was adopted because it recognized
the inertia of stockholders in two ways: signing the letter of
assent was simpler for the stockholders than deposit of certificates, or even presentation of certificates for stamping;
and the question of assent was not even raised with subsequent holders of assented shares.   The system was a concession to those who held that any tighter balloting method, requiring substantial effort and some expense, simply would
not get the statutory percentage of favorable votes.   Query:
Should regulations be written to make it easier for the Railroad to conserve assents by not reminding a purchaser that
his shares are already recorded as assenting?   Or to put it
another way, why should not the same care as regards full disclosure be given to protect a second holder of stock as was
accorded the first?   On principle it would seem clear that no
difference should be made.   The carry-over of assents to
transferees without explicit notice is a procedure that sacrifices principle to expediency.   There is a reversion to the "let
the buyer beware" policy, which the SEC has turned largely
to "let the seller beware" in the issue of securities.

Suppose the Railroad had asked the Commission for permission to announce that all stock would be considered as
assented unless "dissents" were received within a reasonable
period.   One can anticipate the answer that such procedure
would be considered as not conducive to an accurate expression of stockholder opinion; that voting implies a positive expression of opinion, not the absence of a negative expression.

On analysis, the carrying of an assent through to the transferee is precisely on the first principle proposed in the preceding paragraph.   It is a partial departure from the principle that all balloting is a positive action.   In the Boston
and Maine procedure, when the balloting ended the total of
assents were of two groups: one group of holders had taken
the positive step to assent, the other *had not taken the positive step to revoke*.   Would a strictly logical position be that
if this last group of assents reflected stockholder opinion as
accurately as the first group, then it would have been fair to
go the whole distance, and consider all outstanding stock as
assented unless dissents were sent in?

We have come head on into the dilemma that faces the administrator in any field: when should exceptions be made to a principle adopted as sound? When the statute reads, "has been assented to by the holders of at least 75 per centum of the aggregate principal amount or number of shares outstanding of each class," the meaning would seem to be that each holder has expressed his assent. The statute is general in its terms, necessarily, and the Commission's responsibility is to make the conforming rules. When can it be said that 75% of the holders assent?

At 5 P.M. December 14, 1950, the voting was closed on the Boston and Maine modification plan, and the record of assented shares in each class was certified as of that hour. But one of those assents was sent in by stockholder A, say, in August and A's stock was later transferred to B with the assent, by rule, still standing. Can it be said that as of December 14 stockholder B assented, unless one assumes that he has full knowledge of the assent status of his stock? [44] It is not realistic to assume that he has. He has not had the solicitation material that was sent to the first holders when the voting period began. Why should the vote of a holder on August 1 bind a new holder in December who has not the information the first holder had and has no direct notice of his voting rights? There is no apparent reason other than to improve the chance of saving a vote already obtained, without the necessity of further effort. Clearly, the acquiescence of the Commission in the plan of the Railroad to conserve

[44] The assumption of full knowledge of the terms and limitations in contractual documents runs through all business. How many holders of insurance policies on property know the precise limits on the protection bought? It is assumed the holder reads and understands, and that obviously is the answer of the insurance company. But the new holder of assented Boston and Maine stock did not have the information in his hands. The information was on the last pages of the Commission's Report of April 19, 1950, which he had never seen.

A feasible gesture to inform him would be to require the transfer agent to enclose a note with the new certificate to say, substantially, "This stock has already been assented to the proposed plan of recapitalization, and will continue to be unless the assent is revoked." This device would be a position between having the assent die with the transfer and the one finally adopted. It would be more clearly an effort to apprise new purchasers of their rights.

assents once given is a recognition of the practical difficulties in getting an adequate percentage of assents.

These troublesome questions illustrate conflicts of principle, which are the bane of all regulatory bodies. The problem of whether principles of action are to be carried through inflexibly to their logical conclusions, especially when to do so would defeat the major objective to be achieved, is found in a broader area than presented here. Every general principle of administrative action sooner or later comes face to face with an exception to be made.[45] Does granting the exception nullify the principle; or, in the regulatory field, does keeping the principle intact make the whole procedure unworkable?

SUMMARY AND CONCLUSIONS

Whatever one's opinion as to the motives [46] and the part played in the Boston and Maine case by the Sakis group and the Department of Justice, it is a reasonable conclusion that without the zeal of these two objectors most of the problems pointed out in this chapter would never have arisen. Laws and regulations are written, interpreted, and modified because of cases that arise under them. Not everything can be foreseen in the first draft of a statute or in the regulations to implement it. In this instance it took dogged tenacity of interveners and timely assistance by the Department, exasperating at times to the other parties, to keep the issues alive until the three-judge Court invited official re-examination.

Even in this introductory chapter some general conclusions as to policies and effective administration may be stated, to be further tested against the experiences described in the chapters following. Most significant are these:

[45] For provocative discussion of these questions, the reader is referred to A. Lawrence Lowell's small volume *Conflicts of Principle* (Cambridge, Harvard University Press, 1932) ; also to various lectures by Lord Macmillan in a volume called *Law & Other Things,* particularly the lecture on "Two Ways of Thinking," p. 76 (Cambridge, England, The University Press, 1938) .

[46] This study is concerned only with the charges themselves and an objective approach in determining their merit. Those interested in speculation on the motives of those who brought charges in this case can turn to pp. 8–22 of Mr. L'Heureux's Opinion, the section on "The Justice Department's Role."

(a) Neither the statute nor the regulations under it were wholly clear as to the procedural requirements, particularly as to assent procedure at the two stages, the definition of valid ballots, and the limitations on solicitation and control of assents by the Railroad.

(b) The Commission, having full responsibility, did not supervise the procedure so as to insure prompt and complete follow-through with the three parties directly concerned — the Railroad, the depositary, and the Commission.

(c) The depositary's officers assumed from the start that the voting procedure was just another proxy count; every new development was therefore interpreted in the light of previous proxy experience. Lack of communication with the Commission permitted unilateral decisions by the other parties to go unchallenged until the petitions by interveners raised doubts as to the legality of the final certificate of the favorable vote.

This suggests that if the depositary, and indeed all three parties, had seen the necessity for thinking through the procedural aspects of balloting under a new statute, points would have been detected and dealt with that later were used by interveners as illustrations of invalid assents.

(d) The Commission's fixing the percentage of assents by the plain preferred class at 87% rather than 75% raised a fundamental question of principle. In view of the extensive cross-holdings between classes, further factual analysis was required in this instance before such decision was warranted.

CHAPTER VI

Problems in the Determination of Classes

THE Department of Justice had no doubt about how the Railroad's stock should be classified for voting purposes:

> . . . The philosophy of Section 20b, as spelled out by Congress, will not support the Commission's findings that there were only four classes of stock in this proceeding. The evidence established that there were and are eight classes of stock affected by the plan. There is no evidence to the contrary, and the Commission acted arbitrarily, erroneously and contrary to law in finding otherwise.[1]

This positive statement invites careful analysis of the facts to see why the Commission decided there were four rather than eight classes, and why the Department holds that the decision was so wrong. Also, if the philosophy of section 20b was clearly spelled out by Congress, what caused such sharp difference of opinion as to what the philosophy really is? The purpose of this chapter is to find answers to these questions.

A simple graph at the outset, Exhibit 4, will provide a useful background for the discussion that follows.

There are some striking facts in this stock structure. The Boston and Maine plan was drawn up on the finding that on a going concern basis there was practically no equity remaining to the 6% noncumulative preferred and the common stocks. Yet one common share was as big as a prior preference share in voting power. The market's appraisal placed the total value of the common at about one eighth of the total value of the prior preference, although there were 165,000 more votes in the common shares. No one would buy or hold any of the classes for income but for sheer speculation; no dividends had been paid since 1932. The invest-

---

[1] Department of Justice, Trial Brief, p. 18.

EXHIBIT 4. CAPITAL STOCK STRUCTURE OF BOSTON AND MAINE
RAILROAD, 1950: GRAPH SHOWING NUMBER OF OUTSTANDING
SHARES AND AGGREGATE MARKET VALUES FOR EACH CLASS AND
SERIES OF STOCK

(Relative Percentages on Vertical Scale)

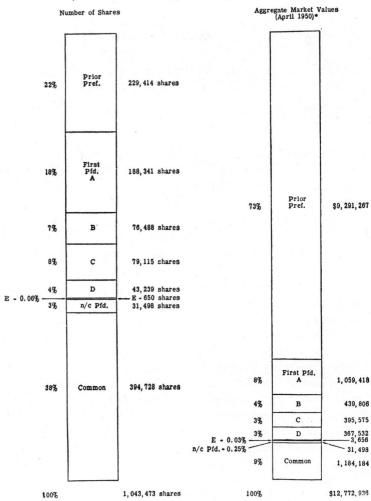

* Highest sale price for stamped or unstamped stock on the Boston Stock
Exchange: April 1950 for prior preference, A and D preferred, and common;
March 1950 for B and C preferred; May 1950 for noncumulative preferred; bid
price in May 1950 for E preferred.

ment value of the common and the 6% preferred stocks was practically gone. In fact, over 40% of the total vote was in the hands of the two lowest layers, judged by the Commission itself to have no measurable value. In our governmental voting procedures, voting rights pass with death; in finance, as already noted, the stockholder's right to vote continues to survive the death of the investment value until changed by formal capital readjustments.

Another important fact illustrated in this stock structure is the disproportionate power that might be given to the small classes in the vote on a modification plan under section 20b. Under the statute anything over 25% of the outstanding shares of a class can veto a plan. In the Boston and Maine case, if the holders of first preferred E stock were to vote separately as a class, only 163 shares (25+%) would be necessary to block a plan that the overwhelming majority of all stockholders might feel fair. Was little "E" a class or only a splinter of the larger class of $A + B + C + D + E$? In such situations objectors to the plan, whether with honest conviction or with the ethics of the highwayman, hold a potent veto power. This strategic power of the few explains the importance of determination of voting classes and why clear principles for the decision must be drawn.

VOTING BY CLASSES OF STOCK: WHAT IS A CLASS?

Section 20b specifies that voting shall be by classes when the Commission orders the plan to be submitted to stockholders for acceptance or rejection. It should be noted that in the application stage the statute makes no mention of classes but refers only to assurances "by holders of such percentage of the aggregate principal amount or number of shares outstanding of the securities affected." Even for assurances, however, the Commission's regulations go further and ask that the application report them by classes. Boston and Maine Railroad so reported assurances of assent in both of its applications.

It is clear why the question of classes was so important and became a matter of dispute between the Railroad and the interveners. The more the classes were subdivided, the easier it would be to block the plan by 25+ % of any one class. The statute does not define the word "class," nor do the Commission's regulations. As would be expected, the Sakis group in their efforts to press every objection that could be raised to discredit the plan or to impede its acceptance kept up a sustained attack on the position finally taken by the Railroad that there were four classes. The Department supported them in its Trial Brief.

The Railroad's Change of View from Eight to Four Classes

The Railroad itself changed its position on the question of classes between its first and second applications. The first application of August 25, 1948, presenting a plan "to create a single class of Capital Stock in place of the eight classes presently outstanding," reported assurances of assent for each of eight classes, including five of first preferred.

Five months later the second application, which presented the two-stock plan, dropped the word "eight," but one has to read almost through the document before there is any indication that the applicant had settled upon four classes only. In fact, in its outline of the plan, there is no mention of "classes" at all and the table giving the allocation of the new stock in eight categories is identical in form with that in the first application. The significant change from eight to four classes is still not made explicit; for below the table giving the eight categories of stock, each treated differently in the proposed plan, the document explains that "The reason for making the alterations and modifications is to create two classes of Capital Stock in place of the classes presently outstanding." This is in the identical words of the first application with the exception that the number of classes presently outstanding is not specified (stated as eight in the first application), although four classes had been decided upon. Eight pages later, where assurances of assent are tabulated, the first preferred is not broken down into classes, as in the previous application. The second application shows only by implication that the Railroad's officers had decided on four classes in all rather than eight.

It would seem better policy for a change of this importance to be fully explained. Then those disposed to attack the plan would have no basis for inferring that the change to four classes by lumping the five lettered preferred series was just a strategic move to limit the power of "splinter classes" and was not based on principle.[2] If at the time of the second application the Railroad had as clear a defense for four classes as it gave later in the proceedings, a clearcut statement in its supplemental application would have put it in a stronger position when the matter of classes became a real issue.

The Examiner's Summary and Recommendations on Number of Classes; the Commission's Conclusions

In his Proposed Report [3] to the Commission, the Examiner in the case summarized arguments on both sides of the disputed question of classes, together with his reasons for making eight classes, as follows:

> The question [of whether the lettered series comprise one class or five classes] arises primarily from the fact that the five series of applicant's first preferred (lettered) stock bear different dividend rates and have accumulated different

[2] Mr. Richard Jackson, general attorney for the Railroad, explained the change in counsel's opinion as follows at the hearing in March 1949: "Recently, as you know, as has been testified to, we have considered the problem under the Mahaffie Act, and it has been a touch and go situation. It is still a close question, there is no denying that. As Mr. Fletcher brought out by his question, we did advise our financial people, much against their will — because they had felt differently — that there were eight classes. We have recently revised that opinion, on more mature reflection, for legal reasons that we can develop on brief.

"The factual reason, which was one of the important motivating factors, was the promulgation of the ICC order in the Lehigh case and in the C & J [C.N.J.] case, where we had analogous situations to our first preferred situation. It made us believe that the ICC would agree with us in our view that there were but four classes.

"Now, Mr. Caruthers with very commendable zeal, I think, has presented to this hearing a letter from Mr. Trowbridge wherein Mr. Trowbridge talks of eight classes of stock. That of course was the result of his counsel, at that time. Mr. Caruthers could also discover that counsel themselves had made a serious admission against interest, if you will, by the first application in this case, where there is at least an implicit admission, if you will — let us not use the word 'admission' — there is an implicit legal interpretation that there are eight classes." Hearing before the Examiner, March 31, 1949, pp. 533–534.

[3] Report Proposed by Homer H. Kirby, Examiner, August 17, 1949 (mimeo.), pp. 12–16.

amounts of unpaid dividends per share, although in all other respects they have identical characteristics. . . .

The first preferred stock was issued in share-for-share exchange for stocks of the applicant's major lessor lines at the time of the applicant's 1919 reorganization, each series of such stock bearing a dividend rate equal to the rate theretofore guaranteed by the applicant on the stocks of the lessor lines. The consolidation agreement of November 26, 1918, provided that the original issued capital stock . . . "shall be divided into classes having different rights and preferences and bearing different rates of dividend," and designated those "classes" as first preferred, class A, class B, class C, class D, class E, as well as the noncumulative preferred and the common stocks, and in the provisions relating to dividends referred to the "different classes of first preferred stock." It was also provided that, "No class of first preferred stock shall have any preference or priority over any other class" of such stock.

Generally, the applicant's officers and witnesses . . . consider that there are four classes of stock, although they are not unanimous in this view. While conceding that it is a close question, counsel for the applicant are now of the view, and so testified, that, for the purpose of this proceeding, there are only four classes. This represents a revision of a former opinion of the same counsel. . . . Counsel also concede the obvious fact that a finding that there are 8 classes instead of 4, would make it more difficult . . . to obtain the required percentage of assents.

The applicant, on brief, contends that if the order of precedence of preferred stocks with respect to claims against corporate assets or earnings be the same within a group, that is, if one member of a given group of stockholders may not exclude his fellow from sharing ratably with him in such corporate assets or earnings, even though the former's share may be larger than the latter's, the group itself is properly designated as a class. . . .

* * * * *

The situation with respect to classification of applicant's stocks is further complicated by the fact that all classes, except the prior preference, appear in the market as stamped or unstamped to reflect the fact that the holder or his predecessor either agreed or did not agree to the applicant's stock readjustment plan in 1926. That plan, for the adoption of which the several series of first preferred stock voted as separate classes, and pursuant to which the prior preference stock was issued, provided for the assent of certain stockholders to the surrender and assignment to the railroad of their rights, in the event of liquidation, to receive and have paid certain cumulative dividends and in exchange for such assent such stockholders were granted certain rights and privileges over the nonassenting stockholders of their class. Thus, there were assenting and nonassenting stockholders, the stock being referred to as stamped and unstamped, respectively, for the first preferred, A, B, C, D, and E, the noncumulative preferred, and the common.[4]

The Sakis committee and the intervener George P. Sakis urge that this situation creates 15 classes of stock, composed of 2 each (stamped and unstamped) for 5 classes of first preferred, the noncumulative preferred, and the common, in addition to one class for the prior preference. These interveners contend that there has been created in the mind of the investing public a distinction between the stamped and the unstamped stock, since they are so differentiated in market transactions and quotations, and that these 2 types of stock in fact possess different rights and privileges.

The applicant contends that the existence or nonexistence of the stamp is immaterial so far as intrinsic value is concerned and asserts that the difference in rights, if any, between the stamped and the unstamped stock lies only in the amounts of their liquidation claims, which do not constitute a factor in the applicant's method of evaluating the several classes of existing stock for the purpose of determin-

[4] Under the stock readjustment agreement dated August 25, 1926, assenting stockholders (who received stamped certificates) agreed, among other things, that in the event of liquidation all sums payable to them with respect to their shares should be paid not to them but to the trustee named in the said stock-readjustment agreement, who should distribute said sums in the following order: (1) To the assenting first preferred, the full amount of dividends accumulated and unpaid; (2) to the assenting first preferred, $100 per share for all shares then held by them; (3) to the assenting preferred, the amount per share, if any, distributed in liquidation by way of dividends in excess of the amount per share distributed in liquidation to the holders of common stock; and (4) to the assenting preferred and common, the balance remaining with the trustee without preference of either class over the other. Nonassenting stockholders (whose certificates were unstamped) retained their then present status. (See *Boston & Maine Readjustment,* 111 I.C.C. 457, 460.)

ing the proper basis of allocation of the proposed new stock issues, since this is not a liquidation proceeding.

Officers of and other witnesses for the applicant expressed the view that, so far as value is concerned, any distinction between the stamped and the unstamped stocks has long since disappeared and that the provision is now worthless. The applicant's vice president in charge of finance and accounting, under whose supervision the plan of modification was formulated, also testified that, although the stamped certificate holders do have a right, on liquidation, to accumulated dividends plus par, while the unstamped certificate holders do not have such preference, he does not consider that this constitutes two classes of stock for the purpose of this proceeding. He stated that, while the stamped certificate holders gave up their dividends for a certain period, such period expired, and they were then entitled to and did thereafter receive dividends on a parity with the unstamped certificate holders who did not waive their dividends, and that dividend arrearages at the present time on both types of stock are in the same amount. It appears that the applicant does not have any present record of the number of shares of stock of the several classes affected by this feature.

On the basis of the evidence, the Commission should find that there is not now such distinction between the rights and privileges of the stamped and the unstamped stocks as to create two different classes in that respect for the purpose of this proceeding.

The Examiner concluded that the Commission should find that there were eight classes

. . . in view of the past history and the construction by applicant's counsel and officers up to a very recent date regarding the nature of the first preferred stock, indicating that the several series thereof had always been regarded as separate classes, in addition to the fact that each series carries not only a different dividend rate but also different amounts of accumulated dividends per share, which differential has been reflected in the applicant's proposed basis of exchange. . . .

We can be sure the Examiner was fully aware that his decision in favor of eight classes, if accepted by the Commission, might well make it impossible to obtain the required assents for each of the lettered series, particularly for "E" with its

650 shares.   It would be an open invitation to a hold-out.
Apparently he made his finding on principle without considering how it affected the assent problem.   One might
speculate as to whether he would decide the same way if there
were one holder of 163 shares of E stock, who would have the
power with his few dollars of market value, if E were a separate class, to dictate terms in a modification plan involving
over $82,000,000 of new stock capitalization.

The Examiner's reasons for finding eight classes are of differing degrees of significance.   He noted that the lettered
series had been called "classes" in the past, but he advanced
no argument why the Commission should give weight to
mere customary terminology.   His more significant point
was that the proposed modification plan gave the lettered
series different terms of exchange for new stock.   Certainly,
it might be argued, securities in one class should be given the
same terms.[5]   Perhaps the Examiner concluded that logical
analysis called for eight classes, and whether logic should be
overruled by the judgment factor permitted under the statute was a policy question for the Commission.

The Sakis group struck hard on these questions of classification.[6]   Their basic theory was that "every group of stockholders having 'different' rights from any other group should
be considered as a separate class." [7]

The Commission agreed with the Examiner in finding no
merit in the contention that stamped and unstamped stocks

[5] This line of argument was the one emphasized over a year later in the
Trial Brief submitted for the Department of Justice.

[6] These arguments were summed up finally in the Brief for Plaintiffs in
Civil Action No. 763–51.   In support of the contention that there were 15
classes, the brief argued that the trust agreement was still in effect, that the
transfer agent still issued certificates with the stamp, that both stamped and
unstamped shares were sold in the securities markets and at different prices,
and that delivery of one did not constitute good delivery for the other.

The Railroad's reply to such contentions had been given in a Memorandum of May 26, 1950, on the Sakis petitions for reconsideration of the report
and order of April 19, 1950: The right of the stamped stock to dividends surrendered in 1926 was so remote that it could not be valued.   Market values
were irrational and erratic, offering no proof.   The benefits to the stamped
stock in liquidation were the only ones of any significance, and this was not a
liquidation.

[7] 275 I.C.C. 397 at 420 (April 19, 1950).

constituted separate classes. It accepted the Railroad's position that the difference between the stamped and the unstamped certificates had lost all significance except for contingent benefits in liquidation; and concluded that the distinction ". . . is not of such a character as to . . . justify the creation of separate classifications for the purposes of this proceeding." [8]

Going further, after a long analysis of the problem, the Commission concluded that there were four classes of stock outstanding, to wit, prior preference, first preferred, noncumulative preferred, and common. The Commission's reasoning will be developed in the discussion that follows.

PROBLEMS CAUSED BY CROSS-HOLDINGS OF STOCK

The arguments over what constitutes a "class" for voting purposes point to some basic considerations in voting theory and technique that are likely to be overlooked.

First, if a class is defined as securities identical in their terms (or substantially identical so that the differences are minor), the implication is that the holders would have a common interest and might be expected generally to make identical response to a plan of exchange, provided they had the same information to act upon. Indeed, the art of drawing up a plan is to appraise the reaction of the holders of each class, thus defined, so that the necessary majority will respond affirmatively.

Actual cases, however, do not show entirely separable groups of holders for each class. As corporations become larger and older, the likelihood of cross-holdings between classes increases. In a closely held company with unlisted stocks a family might hold all the common stock and the public hold all the preferred. In a large corporation like Boston and Maine Railroad, with a complex array of stock issues on the market for thirty years, the most likely pattern of stock ownership is that although some holders own shares in only one class of stock, there will be some who own shares in two different classes, some in three, and some in all four classes and

[8] Ibid., p. 421.

more than one series of the lettered preferred stock, in different amounts of each.[9]

In this last case, which is the real situation in Boston and Maine Railroad, one cannot say that there exists even an approach to unanimity in the attitude of each separate class toward its own interest. How can one expect the total vote of one class, say the common, to represent what all common stockholders, as *common stockholders,* think about the plan? To make this point clear, assume the following facts of stock ownership [10] for three holders:

	Holder A	% Total	Holder B	% Total	Holder C
Prior Preference	44,304 sh.	19.31	43,990 sh.	19.17	—
First Preferred	114,550	29.54	4,151	1.07	20 sh.
Noncum. Pfd.	14,968	47.52	6,543	20.77	50
Common	—	—	219,189	55.53	1,000

Are the holders of common stock, for example, all voting to express the opinion of *common stockholders* on the merits

[9] The problem of cross-holdings as shown in this case is only one form of the broader question of conflicting interests, which so often appears when capital readjustments are being presented to security holders.

Plans designed to eliminate arrearages of accumulated dividends, even when the capital structure has only a single preferred issue, frequently involve the conflicting interests of the managements, when they have large holdings of the stock. The significant facts in such a case are the relative holdings of the management in the preferred and the common stocks. That the management may have holdings in both affords no guarantee of fairness to the stockholders of both. When arrearages are eliminated under a simple two-stock capitalization, the dividend and asset sacrifices of the preferred bring an offsetting advantage to the common. The essential problem is to find the facts on the relative percentages of the stock held by management, not just the relative number of preferred and common shares.

This again emphasizes the absolute necessity of finding out who the holders are so that the motives behind a proposed plan can be studied.

For an extended study of these problems in plans to eliminate arrearages on preferred stock see Part VII, Management Plans Without Aid of Committees, in the *Report on the Study and Investigation of the Work, Activities, Personnel and Functions of Protective and Reorganization Committees,* Securities and Exchange Commission (Washington, Government Printing Office, 1938).

[10] The holders "A" and "B" are actually Pennroad and Boston R.R. Holding Company at the time the Railroad presented its revised plan. Holder "C" is an assumption, but not an unreal one.

of the plan, that is, not on an abstract question of financial theory but on how the plan affects them as holders of common stock? Quite clearly, no. The cross-holdings of different classes shown here inject a diversity of interest; for example, votes will be recorded as *noncumulative preferred* by holders who are really voting as *prior preference* holders.

The tacit assumption in most of the documents submitted in this case, and indeed in the statute itself, is that the holders in each class are a crowd with like interests and behave as "regular party men" in their allegiance. We find many instances [11] in the legal briefs and answers that carry the implication that common stockholders will vote *as* common stockholders and the "B" holders *as* "B" holders. Nothing can be more unrealistic, especially in a complicated structure such as existed in the Railroad. To take the "B" holders as an example, when it is known that a large percentage of that stock was held by persons holding shares in other groups also, and a relatively small percentage was held by simon-pure "B" holders, an entirely new factor becomes significant in the phrase "voting by classes." [12]

[11] Phrases can be found in almost every document in the record of the case to show this unrealistic assumption that classes of stock are held by people who have a common interest arising from their particular place in the capital structure. Two such statements will suffice:

". . . the basic problem is to arrive at a plan which can be approved by the Commission and which is also satisfactory to each class of stockholders." Report of the Commission, April 19, 1950, 275 I.C.C. at 418.

"In other words, if the voters of an affected class will probably, in their own interest, oppose the treatment which they receive under the plan, . . ." Department of Justice, Trial Brief, p. 16.

[12] This question of whose views are really represented by the votes of a particular class has also been raised in section 77 proceedings. In the Chicago and North Western Railway reorganization (U.S. District Court, Northern District of Illinois, Eastern Division, No. 60448, Vol. 8, p. 5383 (1941)) the Debtor petitioned the Court for an order rejecting the certification of the vote, its objections being based on several points, one being explained as follows:

"The acceptances of many of the creditors were procured by means forbidden by law in that . . . the Life Insurance Group Committee members voted all their holdings to accept the plan *even as to those holdings which were discriminated against in said plan, namely, Class 16* . . . [emphasis supplied] and one of the members of said Committee . . . passed a single resolution to vote all its holdings in favor of said plan, which holdings included [holdings

Reflection on these facts makes such expressions as "how 'D' or 'E' holders will view the plan" entirely meaningless. A share may be technically voted as "E," but by a holder who also holds a more valuable stock. "Where your treasure is, there will your heart be also," aptly describes voting motives in these situations. Furthermore, even if these cross-holdings were identical for all stockholders (a wholly unrealistic situation in the usual case, especially with large corporations) one would not find an identity of attitude toward a plan. Different stockholders would have different conclusions as to prospects of the business and their effects on security values; and some would be so baffled by the whole affair as to have no conclusions at all.[13]

The Facts on Cross-Holdings of Boston and Maine Stock

A realistic approach to the problem compelled research into the facts of cross-ownership between classes of stock in the Boston and Maine structure. The results are tabulated in Exhibits 5 and 6. These exhibits show, as of the end of the voting period in December 1950, the holdings of stockholders of record whose holdings in one or more classes when combined amounted to at least 100 shares. This comprised roughly 90% of the total outstanding stock.

Two factors combined to make the tabulations only approximate at best, but the significant conclusions do not depend on absolute accuracy. First, the tabulation for each

---

by amount in 9 classes, including $750,000 in Class 16 allegedly discriminated against]."

There was no argument advanced by the petitioner, and the answer by the Trustee and the Order denying the petition made no reference to the particular charge. The inference raised is that the votes of Class 16 were not a homogeneous lot, but were mixed by holders who voted their "16" interests in favor of their interests in other classes.

13 These problems of voting when there are various classes of stocks, with many holders with securities in more than one class, have an analogy in the political field. A voter might find himself, in November 1952, leaning to one party because he was a laborer, or a farmer, or a retired citizen, but he might vote for the other party on the sole issue of foreign policy. Votes are the results of composite issues not unmixed with heritage and emotion; so in finance it is not simple to predict the outcome of a "class" vote, even if there are no cross-holdings. The problem becomes increasingly complex as cross-holdings increase.

holder of a few shares would have been costly. Second, in the case of brokers it was necessary to use only the "street names" in the record and not look back of them to the beneficial owners themselves.

To deal with the first factor, holders of less than 100 shares were assumed to hold in only one class or series of stock.

EXHIBIT 5.   A STUDY IN CROSS-HOLDINGS AMONG THE FOUR CLASSES OF BOSTON AND MAINE STOCK, AS OF DECEMBER 1950*

	Prior Preference	First Preferred	Noncum. Preferred	Common
Number of shares whose holders held shares in one or more other classes	147,237	223,093	28,192	280,880
Number of shares whose holders did not hold shares in any other class	54,825	133,266	1,758	101,627
Small holdings, assumed to represent no cross-holdings†	27,352	31,474	1,548	12,221
Total outstanding shares in class	229,414	387,833	31,498	394,728
Percentage of shares representing some cross-holdings to total	64.18%	57.52%	89.50%	71.15%

 * Data are for holders of record, taken as of the end of the voting period. Data were tabulated only for stockholders who held in one or more classes of stock, when combined, at least 100 shares. All smaller holdings were assumed to include no cross-holdings; from a quick survey of the records for smaller holders this appears to be true for the majority, but not all. In a few cases, where stockholders clearly appeared to be members of one family, their holdings were combined, but it was impossible to identify many of the situations where one person would influence the decisions of more than one stockholder.

 † This is a residual figure in each class, arrived at by subtraction of the first two items from the total shares in the class.

EXHIBIT 6.   FURTHER BREAKDOWN TO SHOW CROSS-HOLDINGS WITHIN THE FIRST PREFERRED CLASS, AS OF DECEMBER 1950*

	Series				
	A	B	C	D	E
Number of shares whose holders held shares in one or more other first preferred series	106,912	55,842	56,788	34,944	472
Number of shares whose holders did not hold shares in any other first preferred series	66,555	14,625	15,899	4,319	3
Small holdings, assumed to represent no cross-holdings†	14,874	6,021	6,428	3,976	175
Total outstanding shares	188,341	76,488	79,115	43,239	650
Percentage of shares representing some cross-holdings within first preferred class to total‡	56.77%	73.01%	71.78%	80.82%	72.62%

* Data are for holders of record, taken as of the end of the voting period. Data were tabulated only for stockholders who held in one or more classes of stock, when combined, at least 100 shares. All smaller holdings were assumed to include no cross-holdings; from a quick survey of the records for smaller holders this appears to be true for the majority, but not all. In a few cases, where stockholders clearly appeared to be members of one family, their holdings were combined, but it was impossible to identify many of the situations where one person would influence the decisions of more than one stockholder.

† This is a residual figure in each series, arrived at by subtraction of the first two items from the total shares in the series.

‡ Shares whose holders held stock in other series and/or other classes constituted even larger percentages of the series, as follows:

Series A	62.39%		Series D	86.08%
Series B	75.00%		Series E	73.08%
Series C	78.20%			

The assumption doubtless understated the actual amount of cross-holding; but since less than 10% of the total stock was held in small lots, any error here is relatively unimportant.

Holdings in street names, the second factor, presented the same difficult problem in this analysis that they did in the correct recording of assents, a subject to be discussed in the next chapter. A broker's record with the depositary (here also the transfer agent) would show how the shares held in his name were distributed among the various classes. It would not show, however, how many of the several beneficial owners represented by the broker held more than one class of stock. The basic data being unavailable for the holdings of these beneficial owners, it was assumed that the holdings of each of the broker's customers were as dispersed over all classes as were the shares in the broker's name. To the extent that any beneficial owners held only one class, and there must have been many, by so much the assumption was in error. For example, if a broker held 1,000 shares for 10 beneficiaries, each with 100 shares in a distinct class, there would be no cross-holdings by any beneficiary; but the broker's record would show the total 1,000 in the several classes and they would be included in the table as evidence of cross-holding.

Still another immeasurable factor bears on the dependability of the figures for brokers' holdings. If the broker advised his customers how to vote, either on his own initiative or at their request, and they voted accordingly, the result is the same so far as the accuracy of the tabulation is concerned as if he held and voted the diverse holdings for his own account. Inquiry on this point from some brokers who held substantial amounts for beneficial owners shows that advice was given when asked and that assents were actively solicited.

The point to be emphasized is that Exhibits 5 and 6 have too wide a margin of error to serve as a basis for precise calculations from their data. However, even a rough showing that cross-holdings were quite the general rule and not the exception serves to refute the argument that holders in any particular class were unfairly treated when they were not allowed to vote separately. This became a particularly weak argument in the case of series D of the first preferred stock in whose behalf the Sakis group, with their large holdings in D, were urging separate classification.

It is true that the totals for cross-holdings were swelled by the shares of the two largest stockholders, The Pennroad Corporation and Boston Railroad Holding Company; but the amount of cross-holdings among the other stockholders still remained significant. Exhibit 7 shows cross-holdings after deduction of the stock owned by these two large holders, using for this purpose the Pennroad holdings in April 1949.

Exhibit 5 shows clearly that holders interested in only one

EXHIBIT 7. EXTENT OF CROSS-HOLDINGS AMONG THE FOUR CLASSES AFTER EXCLUSION OF THE TWO LARGEST STOCKHOLDERS — BOSTON RAILROAD HOLDING COMPANY AND THE PENNROAD CORPORATION

	Prior Preference	First Preferred	Noncum. Preferred	Common
Total outstanding shares in class	229,414	387,833	31,498	394,728
Less:				
Shares held by Boston R.R. Holding Company	43,990	4,151	6,543	219,189
Shares held by Pennroad	44,304	114,550	14,968	—
(a) Shares held by all other stockholders	141,120	269,132	9,987	175,539
Shares in class representing some cross-holdings (from Exhibit 5*)	147,237	223,093	28,192	280,880
Less:				
Shares held by Holding Company and Pennroad	88,294	118,701	21,511	219,189
(b) Shares of all other stockholders representing some cross-holdings	58,943	104,392	6,681	61,691
Percentage of the shares held by all other stockholders representing some cross-holdings to the total shares held by these stockholders (i.e. the percentage of (b) to (a))	41.77%	38.79%	66.90%	35.14%

* See Exhibit 5 for explanation of data.

class held relatively small percentages of the total vote. For every class, well over half of the qualified votes would represent a divided interest of one sort or another.[14] According to the exhibit, not more than about 36% of the prior preference votes, 42% of the first preferred, 10% of the noncumulative preferred, and 29% of the common would represent votes of holders who held no stock in any other class.

Cross-holding was particularly heavy in the five series of lettered first preferred stock. Only about 38% of the votes in series A, 25% in series B, 22% in series C, 14% in series D, and 27% in series E would be uninfluenced by the effect of the plan on any other class or series. In addition, there was a considerable amount of cross-holding within the first preferred class.[15] Nearly 57% of series A was held by stockholders who also held stock in at least one other first preferred series. About 73% of series B, 72% of series C, 81% of series D, and 73% of series E also represented some cross-holding within the first preferred stock. In contrast, only about 58% of the first preferred class as a whole was held by stockholders with interests in other classes.

The Bearing of Cross-Holdings on the Problem of Classes

These data have an important bearing on the arguments raised against the merging of the lettered preferred into one class, principally by the Sakis group and the Department. The underlying assumption of those who argued, for example, that those in series D should have the chance to express their independent interest was that those who held D had an independent interest. The facts as to series D are that approximately 86% of those holding series D held other classes or series also. Only 14% were series D holders and

14 A rough check made by Railroad officers at the time of the voting indicated that 25% to 30% of the stockholders held more than one class. For this study the number of votes seemed more significant than the number of holders.

15 Common usage among stockholders and brokers, as well as management, seemed to regard the first preferred stock as one class. At the March 1949 hearing, the Brunner Committee was called officially the Committee for First Preferred Lettered Stock. Several interveners spoke of themselves as representing holders of the lettered preferred stocks, and each one represented two or more of the series.

nothing else. These facts take the force out of the argument that D holders should vote as a separate class in order to preserve their independent rights. The same can be said of the four other lettered series, but the D series was a shade more of a mixture of interests than the others.

The major contribution of this statistical study of cross-holdings is that it completely breaks down the claims of those who would support five distinct classes of the first preferred stock on the ground that otherwise the independent will of each class would be thwarted. It seems evident that submission of the plan separately to the holders of the five lettered series would not have resulted in the independent expression of the interest of each group.[16]

After the Commission has made its decision as to separate classes, it must make a further decision as to raising the percentage of assents for any particular class of which 75% is held by fewer than 25 holders. This decision requires special study of the facts. An important factor in this discretionary judgment is the pattern of cross-holdings affecting the particular class in question. If the objective in raising the percentage of assents over 75% is to be sure that the opinion of the whole class is not dominated by the concentrated holdings, then it is important to be sure that the *opinions* of the small holders are in fact those of the separate class. Otherwise the Commission's decision can only be blind and, in effect, arbitrary.

SOME PRECEDENTS IN CLASSIFICATION FOR VOTING

As precedents for classifying the five lettered series as one class, the Railroad cited instances in proceedings under section 77, where various series of bonds, issued under the same indenture but each with different interest rates, were put in

[16] One can picture the dilemma faced by many stockholders, particularly those less informed, as they tried to figure out the *net* advantage of the plan to them in view of their own cross section of interests in the various stocks. Presumably, if the net advantage was favorable, a stockholder would vote all holdings as *assents,* even though he might perhaps vote a series D holding *No* if it were held alone. In the actual voting, there were some instances of "split personalities" — voters who assented some of their holdings and not others. This was not always an oversight.

one class for voting purposes, although they were treated differently in the plan.[17]   It further pointed out similar precedents in some recent proceedings under section 20b.[18]

The Commission made special reference in its Report of April 19, 1950, to this argument from analogy and concluded that the section 20b cases cited by the Railroad were not parallel.[19] The Commission's orders in these two cases did not specify whether the submission of the plan should be on the basis of the combined issues of bonds secured by the same mortgage or on the basis of separate classes, each having a different interest rate. This matter was never presented as an issue by the parties in either case. Therefore, the Commission concluded that there was no precedent here for the classification of the lettered series as one class in the Boston and Maine case.

The question remains, however, whether the Commission can so readily dismiss the way bonds in series were classified in other section 20b cases as being entirely irrelevant to the Boston and Maine proceeding. Several bond issues were ac-

[17] It cited as examples (Brief of May 31, 1949, page 47) : Chicago & North Western Railway Company Reorganization (Finance Docket No. 10881) , 236 I.C.C. 575; In re Chicago & North Western Railway Co. 126 Fed. (2d) 351.

The following quotation is of interest in this connection:

"As originally enacted, Section 77 was thought to be defective in that it elevated dissenting groups to a position of undeserved strength. It required a division of creditors and stockholders into separate classes according to the nature of their respective interests (Section 77c (5)). This provision was interpreted by the courts in such a way as to encourage proliferation of classes, which naturally resulted in an undue strengthening of minority groups. The opportunities of such groups for quick and aggressive opposition were greater where individual classes consisted of a single or perhaps a few creditors, than would have been true if they had been submerged in the membership of a large class. The amended statute was designed to discourage such over-classification." [footnote omitted] (Warner Fuller, "The Background and Techniques of Equity and Bankruptcy Railroad Reorganizations — a Survey," in *Law and Contemporary Problems,* Vol. VII, No. 3, Summer 1940, pp. 390–391) .

[18] Lehigh Valley Railroad Company Securities Modification (Finance Docket No. 16184) , decided February 7, 1949, 271 I.C.C. 553; Central Railroad Company of New Jersey Securities Modification (Finance Docket No. 16211) decided February 28, 1949, 271 I.C.C. 501.

[19] 275 I.C.C. 397 at 416.

tually combined into one class in the Lehigh case, and the Commission validated the vote by putting the plan into effect. It would seem that the Commission's action was thereby tantamount to approval of the classification procedure. The acceptance of a certified vote would appear to be an implied stamp of approval on the method of classification adopted, even though the procedure was never in dispute in the proceedings.

As for the Railroad's reference to the section 77 cases as precedents for proper classification, the Commission's report emphasized points of difference between section 20b and section 77 that reflect a "basic difference in character and purpose of the two statutes." [20] Section 77 is much more specific in its treatment of classes.[21] The report pointed out that under section 20b procedure an adverse vote in any class is fatal to the plan, whereas under section 77 the "cram-down" provision permits a plan to be consummated even if a class votes against it.[22] When it is recalled that under section 20b a 75% majority of the *principal amount outstanding* in each class is required to assent, whereas under a section 77 proceeding only two-thirds *of the amount held by those voting* in a class is required, the importance of a careful definition of classes is manifest. The point the Commission stresses is that section 77 was less protective to minorities' rights in its provisions than section 20b. These differences between the two laws are taken to increase the Commission's responsibility under

[20] Ibid., p. 417.

[21] Section 77, subsection (c) (7), specifically directs the reorganization court to determine "the division of creditors and stockholders into classes according to the nature of their respective claims and interests." The statute also provides: "Such division shall not provide for separate classification unless there be substantial differences in priorities, claims, or interests." 275 I.C.C. 397 at 416.

[22] The requirement of section 77 on the "cram-down" provision is as follows (U.S. Code, 1952 edition, Title 11.205 Section 77 (e)): "[if after voting by classes] the plan has not been so accepted . . . the judge may nevertheless confirm the plan if he is satisfied and finds, after hearing, that it makes adequate provision for fair and equitable treatment for the interests or claims of those rejecting it; that such rejection is not reasonably justified in the light of the respective rights and interests of those rejecting it and all the relevant facts; . . ."

section 20b for scrutinizing carefully the differences in the terms of securities to see whether there is sufficient reason for making separate classes.

In the words of the Commission, the difference between the two statutes "makes it even more necessary that the rights of separate classes in a section 20b proceeding be safeguarded through adoption of a method of classification that will fairly reflect any 'substantial differences in priorities, claims, or interests.' " [23]   But, as the Commission also pointed out, section 20b already goes to great lengths to protect minority interests. The Commission's finding in favor of four classes in the Boston and Maine case can be taken to put the burden of proof on those who urge that minorities need further protection by the creation of separate classes wherever there are differences in terms.

The Commission's principle of action would seem to be: it is difficult enough to get plans through because of the 75% assent rule; we should be careful not to insist on separate small voting classes unless the division is clearly indicated by substantial differences; otherwise there is danger of making a perfectly good statute unworkable. This interpretation is supported by the wording of the Commission's finding: "We also conclude and find that, as among the different series of the first-preferred stock, there are not such substantial differences in priorities, claims or interests as to justify their being separately classified . . ." [24]

The power of hold-outs and "strikers" in reorganization procedure has long been a troublesome phase in working out plans known to express the will of the overwhelming majority. The procedure of voting by classes should not be set up so as to endanger acceptance by subdivision of classes on purely technical points. The burden of proof should be on subdivision, which obviously would make an acceptance vote harder to achieve.[25]

[23] 275 I.C.C. 397 at 417.

[24] Ibid., p. 421.   In February 1952 the three-judge Court came to the same conclusion: "Considering the testimony before the Commission and the significant facts concerning the contractual rights of the holders of first preferred stock, the Court believes that the finding of the Commission was proper." 103 Fed. Supp. 292 at 300.

[25] In 77B cases, also, frequently there are several bank loans, each differing

THE BRIEF OF THE DEPARTMENT OF JUSTICE
AGAINST FOUR CLASSES

The Department's argument against the Commission's finding of four classes can be put briefly as follows:

1. The statute required that the plan be submitted to each class of securities *affected thereby:*
    a. The Boston and Maine plan affected five classes of first preferred "directly and differently." [26]
    b. The Commission lumped these five classes into one for voting purposes, even though it made slight changes in the allocation between the five classes that was proposed by the Examiner. This was inconsistent and therefore wrong.
2. There was evidence that there were five classes of lettered preferred:
    a. Each class had its own price in the market.
    b. The Railroad's original application spoke of eight classes (five lettered preferred).
    c. The Examiner's Proposed Report found eight classes in all.

The points raised in (2) above have no significance in testing the validity of the Commission's finding of four classes. In the first place, nothing in the statute requires a separate class if a security has its own market price. If this were the test, the classification problem would be purely mechanical. Second, the Railroad's reference to eight classes in its first application could not be taken as proof that there were eight classes for the purposes of the statute. Finally, the Examiner's opinion was after all an opinion only, not proof that the Commission erred. The Examiner only proposes; it is the Commission that disposes, for reasons stated in its report.

---

from the others in terms, interest rate, and special conditions imposed in the loan agreement. These are all put in one class for voting purposes and called commercial debt. Such classification does not preclude full recognition of the differences in the instruments in their treatment under the reorganization plan.

[26] See the description of the plan in Chapter III.

A Critique of the Department's Interpretation of the Statute

The Department's argument that there were eight classes rested primarily on the fact that the proposed stock modification plan allocated stock in different amounts to each of the lettered series. "The statute," the brief said, "in plain terminology prescribes that the . . . plan be submitted to the holders of each class of the railroad's securities *affected thereby*." As each of the five classes of first preferred stock was "directly and differently affected by the . . . plan," the Commission itself did not treat the lettered stocks as an entity, and hence recognized them as separate classes. "This is the decisive test." [27]

But what makes it the decisive test? The question really comes down to what section 20b means by "class" of security, and by classes "affected" by a plan. In omitting a definition, the framers of the statute either implied that its meaning was clearly understood, or left the decision to the judgment of the Commission in each special case. There is nothing in the statute to support the Department in holding that if a plan gives series A more than series B, it follows that each is a class, which must vote separately.

This matter of *different* treatment of the lettered series raises a basic question that the Department's brief did not deal with: did the allocation of different amounts of stock to each of the lettered series necessarily mean *different* treatment? May not the five series be considered as treated alike if the plan applied the same principle fairly to each and protected their respective rights so that they were left in the same position *relative* to one another? When the Trial Brief says, "Each of these five classes . . . are directly and differently affected by the . . . plan" (and therefore should vote as separate classes), it implies a fact that still remains to be proved, namely, that the different treatment of A, B, etc., disturbed the relative positions of A, B, etc., to *one another as measured by their existing contract rights*.

The unusual complexity of the Boston and Maine stock structure presented this difficult question in aggravated form. It was agreed by all parties that the *only* difference between

27 Department of Justice, Trial Brief, pp. 15–16.

the lettered series of first preferred stock lay in the different dividend rates and consequently the different amounts of accumulated dividends on each.   All five series were subordinate to the prior preference class and stood ahead of the two lowest classes.   In this position it would be expected that the five lettered series would be concerned with their relative position in two directions: first, as a group against the prior preference, and second, as separate series, each to be fairly treated under the plan as compared with the other series. They would make common cause against the prior preference, but jealously protect their own special rights, each against the others.

For example, a series D holder with his 10% dividend rate and $172.50 a share in accumulated unpaid dividends would compare himself with a series A holder, whose stock bore 5% and had only $86.25 in unpaid dividends.   The D holder had a common interest with the A holder against the prior preference, and would view a proposed plan in the same way as the A holder, *provided* his 10% dividend and his larger accumulations of accruals were fairly recognized.   If the plan scrupulously observed the relative rights of the lettered series as between themselves, then for voting purposes A and D belonged in the same class.   The purpose of voting on a plan is to protect one's interest; if a fair allocation was made to give D equal relative treatment as against A, then there would remain only a common interest between them, which could be fully expressed by voting as a class.

In this analysis it is important to consider the order in which the Commission must make its decisions.   First comes the question of whether the plan is just and reasonable and in the public interest and the best interests of the applicant and each class of security holders affected; that is, does it accord to each security the proper value of its rights?   When this is determined, then to what classes shall the plan be submitted for acceptance or rejection?   If the statute means that after a plan has been worked out as fair, each group no matter how small would vote separately if it had a different allocation of the new securities under the plan, the statute could say so directly.   Then the mechanics of the statute would be clear even if the whole of the first preferred group were splintered into fragments so that E stock with its 650 shares would vote separately, as the Department's Trial Brief advocated. It is significant in this connection to recall that this question of voting classes has been a matter of the judge's decision under section 77 and of the Commission in cases under section 20b, and no such definition of a "class" as is given in the Department's brief has ever been discussed or advanced.

In this matter, as in other aspects of this case, the Department set its own interpretation of the statute and technical procedures against that of the Commission with its long experience with reorganization problems. In view of Commissioner Mahaffie's sponsorship of the bill, and the fact that the Commission operates under both the section 20b and section 77 statutes, it is reasonable to conclude that the philosophy of voting under section 77 applies, in the absence of specific provisions, to the general phraseology of the 20b statute.

At the very outset of the argument, the Trial Brief emphasized what it called the plain words of the statute, that the Commission must submit the plan "to the holders of each class . . . *affected thereby*." The Department's argument was based on its own definition of a class as consisting of a group of securities that are given identical allocations of new securities under a recapitalization. This leaves the obvious question — when is a class "affected" by a plan? This is the same language used in the section 77 statute, where under the procedures certain groups of securities are not eligible to vote, either because their interests are fully protected under the proposed plan, or because the railroad is found insolvent and the stock thereby excluded from voting. If these two groups are disregarded, there remains the body of security holders "affected" by the plan. The words do not mean, as the Trial Brief implies, "identically treated," but simply that the plan as proposed makes provision for them. The point here is that in the absence of specific provisions in section 20b, it is reasonable to conclude that the interpretation of the "affected thereby" phrase would follow the meaning expressed in the earlier statute, since both are under the regulatory responsibility of the Commission.

The separation of those securities affected by the plan from those not so affected, can be presented graphically as follows:

A Typical Section 77 Case

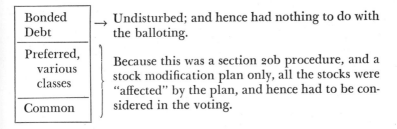

| Bonds | Undisturbed or paid in cash ⟶ "Not affected" |

| Bonds, various classes | Adjusted under the plan on some basis of exchange → | The statute calls these securities "affected" by the Plan. Nothing is said or implied about the treatment within each "class" being identical. |

| Preferred Stock | | Insolvency, if found, removes all the equity from consideration; hence all classes of stock are "not affected" by the plan, and may not vote. |

| Common Stock | | |

If this same type of graph is applied to the capital structure of Boston and Maine Railroad, there being no insolvency and the total bond structure remaining outside the plan and undisturbed, it would show as follows:

| Bonded Debt | → Undisturbed; and hence had nothing to do with the balloting. |

| Preferred, various classes | Because this was a section 20b procedure, and a stock modification plan only, all the stocks were "affected" by the plan, and hence had to be considered in the voting. |

| Common | |

It is seen that the phrase, "affected by the plan," emphasized in the Trial Brief as the basis for the charge that the Commission erred as to voting classes, has really no significance for the classification problem itself. It is a general phrase to set apart the broad section of the capital structure to which the plan applies. The first major question facing the Commission was: What Boston and Maine securities are affected by the modification plan? Answer: all the stocks and none of the debt. The next question was: How do we divide these various stocks into classes for voting purposes? Here is the crucial decision and it is not a simple one.

Nowhere in the statute is it stated or implied that, once the decision is made to classify certain securities together, then identical treatment must be given to all in the class. In fact, the statute implies the opposite: that differences not recognized as substantial can be disregarded in deciding the make-up of a class for *voting purposes,* but in justice the differences must be taken account of in treatment of the securities under the plan. The objective of classification is not the allocation of new securities, but the voting of the old.

In effect, the Department's argument ran directly counter to the concept of fairness in the allocation of new securities. Certainly no statute would permit the Commission to place securities in one class when the differences are not substantial, and then deny it the power to allocate fairly within that class in accordance with the differences that existed, but that the Commission saw fit to ignore for voting purposes.

The attitude taken by the Department on the matter of voting classes is noteworthy for two reasons. It challenged the Commission's judgment in a technical area of regulation in which the Commission's expert staff makes decisions against a background of long experience. It followed with an unprecedented attack on a sister agency by implying improper purpose in the Commission's administration of the classification provision of the statute. We can evaluate the evidence adduced by the Department in its charges of error; the Trial Brief did not state its basis for implying a sinister motive in making the error.[28]

[28] The statement in the Trial Brief on this point will bear full quotation: "By grouping the classes of first preferred stock into one class, the Commission permitted the votes of the first preferred classes to be tabulated only in the aggregate and denied to the owners of each of the five classes of first preferred stock the right to register their approval or disapproval with respect to the treatment which each class separately received under the plan. The Commission pointed out the following: 'Counsel (for the railroad) also conceded the obvious fact that a finding that there are eight classes instead of four would make it more difficult for the applicant to obtain the required percentage of assents.' (P. 15 of Commission's Report of April 19, 1950.) In other words, if the voters of an affected class will probably, in their own interest, oppose the treatment which they receive under the plan, they should not be permitted to cast their votes and have them counted by class. This is strange reasoning, indeed. Even if Congress may have reserved to itself the power to gerrymander, Congress has not in Section 20b delegated any aspect

THE RAILROAD'S ARGUMENT FOR FOUR CLASSES

The explanation by the Railroad for holding that there were four classes, rather than the eight listed in its original application, followed in the main the line of criticism offered above to the Department's argument for eight classes. The Railroad's counsel called the explanation the two-levels-of-distribution theory,[29] which sharply divides the differences in security groups into two areas — those that are not susceptible to precise mathematical measurement and those that are. When a plan gives different treatment to take account of the various factors that give value to the stocks, then a judgment factor is introduced which throws the plan into an area for bargaining among the opposing interests. Such was the case, counsel said, with the four groups in the Boston and Maine stock structure. Next and quite apart from this bargaining field, "after these initial bargainers have concluded their negotiations," [30] then the respective rights of subclasses within the first preferred bargaining group could be settled by a formula that measured accurately the differences in the lettered series. The results of this method, counsel explained, were mathematically demonstrable in absolute figures. ". . . at the secondary level there is no room for the exercise of discretion. . . . there is no need for a vote where bargaining cannot be a factor. . . ." [31]   In fact, the argument concluded, a vote would give power to an obstructive minor-

---

of this power to the Interstate Commerce Commission."   Department of Justice, Trial Brief, p. 16.

The dictionary definition (Webster's New International, 1951) of gerrymandering is "to divide . . . into election districts . . . in an unnatural and unfair way . . . to give a political party advantage . . . or for some other improper purpose."   Granted the Department had the facts to impugn the Commission's judgment, did it have the facts to impugn the Commission's honest purpose? If so, the record does not show.

The relation between the Department and the Commission throughout this case presents a challenging opportunity for a piece of constructive research in administrative law.

[29] Exceptions of Applicant to the Report Proposed by the Examiner, September 23, 1949, pp. 2–9.

[30] Report of the Commission, April 19, 1950, 275 I.C.C. 397 at 418.

[31] Ibid.

ity to block the will of the group, which it is the objective of section 20b to aid and protect.

This conclusion is the same as that arrived at by our own analysis of the Department's brief, but by a slightly different route. The analyses are the same in emphasizing the common purpose of the five series of first preferred stock, once their different rights *inter se* are measured and met under the distribution of new stock. This is the essential point in establishing the validity of the four-class decision.

There are implications, however, in the Railroad's brief at this point that relate to the principles of stock allocation, which are beyond the scope of this particular study. For example, the statement of Railroad counsel that there is no room for discretion in fixing the distribution of the new stock to the five lettered series implies a finality and an absolute standard of justice which would permit no difference of opinion. Yet the Commission saw fit to make slight changes in the distribution of shares by the plan to the lettered series, and there is plenty of evidence of divided opinion as to the basic theory used in the plan's allocation among the first preferred series.

Another line of argument in favor of consideration of the first preferred stock as a single class might be taken from the origin of the rate differences at the time of the consolidation in 1919. The "A" leased railroad had a guaranteed rate of 5%, the "D" a guaranteed rate of 10%. This difference could have been equated by giving more first preferred stock to the "D" road stockholders, but it probably was thought that the plan would be more favorably received if a former holder of 10% stock in the "D" road would get in exchange a new 10% first preferred share. If he had been given twice the number of shares of a 5% stock, he would have the same income. This would not equate the liquidation and voting rights, however, which in the consolidation plan were left the same for all the lettered series despite the differences in rate maintained. As the Railroad argued in 1949, the lettered series arose out of a transaction that was trying to equate the former status of stockholders in various leased roads, and current income based on rental payments was to remain unchanged as the old holders exchanged for new stock. The stockholders in the railroads coming into the Boston and Maine system were treated alike in that they were all given the same access to the earnings stream — first after the bonds. The only difference was in the amount of earnings each share could take out currently or cumulatively. The very title "first preferred" signified a broad class entitled to preference as one group, not as five, ahead of the two lower classes, the plain preferred and the common.

CONCLUSIONS

The first conclusion from this chapter must be that the simple phrase "voting by classes" presents in some cases complexities that almost defy analysis. Section 20b does not define a class. The decision is thus left in each case to the judgment of the Commission in accordance with precedents under section 77 of the Bankruptcy Act, which permits groups of securities to be thrown together for voting purposes if their differences in contract rights are not substantial. The Commission's first responsibility is to see that the plan fulfills the statute; second, it must then divide the securities into classes for voting purposes in order to provide a check upon its judgment. The Commission's expert knowledge and long experience are as essential in dealing with this second problem as with the first. Much hangs on the division into classes. Too few classes would submerge minority opinion; on the other hand, to recognize minor differences by making separate classes for voting would give unwarranted power to obstructive minorities. The principle upon which it was decided to vote in four classes in the Boston and Maine case is a thoroughly sound approach to a complex situation.

There is an implication in both section 20b and the documents relating to these proceedings that the holders of securities in a class have a common view as to their interests. In the Boston and Maine proceedings some stockholders objected to the combination of their security groups with others for voting purposes, even when the differences were small, on the grounds that they were thus prevented from expressing their opinion strictly from the standpoint of their own group. The argument ran from the mistaken notion that the holders of each group would think alike in deciding where their interests lay under a proposed plan.

The cause of the misapprehension probably rests with treatment of the classes as categories of legal contracts (securities) rather than as contracts held by people. The securities do not vote; the people who hold them vote. Therefore the basic facts relate to the ownership of the different securities by holders. The motives that determine the decisions on voting are never so simply analyzed as to be attached to classes *unless* the holders of one class are a wholly different group from the holders of another class. If the 100 holders of preferred stock in a company are entirely separate people from the 100 holders of the common stock, then it is proper to speak of the *holders* of the common stock voting their interests as against the *holders* of the preferred stock, and only then.

The Boston and Maine case presents an unusual, not to say fantastic, complexity in its capital structure. The question of proper classification for voting cannot logically be approached without a study of the cross-holdings of stock by all the stockholders of record. One should not be solicitous for series D holders, for example, until he has determined how many would vote their D stock to support a larger interest in some other class.

To judge by Exhibit 5 in this chapter, it would seem a hopeless piece of research in many situations to try to disentangle the maze of interclass stock ownership. We do not advise that the Commission make a meticulous study of cross-holdings down to the last single share held. Administrators should use this statistical approach only in special situations, and then only with enough detail to give the general pattern of holdings. The regulations of the Commission in section 20b proceedings might well include a reasonable requirement for a railroad itself to supply data that would reveal the extent of cross-holdings. In many cases the results of such an analysis would not be important to the decision on classes; in others, like the Boston and Maine case, they might become a determining consideration.

Even a limited examination of cross-holdings as shown in

Exhibits 5 and 6 gives a basis for an effective reply to interveners who complain of injustice when their particular group is merged with a larger group because the differences in the securities are not substantial. Furthermore, a cross-holding study is essential to a sound decision when the Commission applies its discretionary authority in raising the required proportion of assents above 75% for a particular class. The statute gives this discretion when less than 25 holders hold 75% of the outstanding stock in a class, but this fact is not enough in itself. How many of those holding stock in class "X" do not vote as "X"? An administrative decision should not be made until the facts are obtained as to how far the holders of the remaining 25% of the class represent the interests of that class alone.

CHAPTER VII

The Depositary: The System for Recording Assents

THE Department made a definitive statement of charges against the depositary:

> . . . The United States will prove that these two certificates [that the required percentage of assents had been received during the submission period] were invalid in that the depositary did not receive the required percentage of valid assents of the four classes prior to 5.05 P.M. on December 14, 1950.
>
> To support this contention, the United States will show:
>
> *   *   *   *   *
>
> 3. That the independent depositary did not function independently of the railroad, did not verify and accurately record the receipts of assents and revocations, and did not conform to the requirements of the Commission's orders.[1]

One notes that the charge was expressed with conviction. It contained no limiting phrase, such as "in some instances"; the implication is that the whole performance of the depositary was notably weak. At least, if the intention was to avoid any such implication, the statement could have been carefully worded to do so. Moreover, when this charge is read as one of four, with such language as "solicitors were very active in obtaining *invalid* assents" and "the railroad acquired control . . . through connivance," the whole government case against the depositary takes on a coloration of intrigue and malfeasance. Perhaps this is what brought Mr. L'Heureux to say in his report on the case two years later:

---

[1] Department of Justice, Trial Brief, pp. 20–21.

. . . At the beginning of this case, I looked at every aspect of it with a jaundiced eye in view of the very serious charges made by the Justice Department. I looked for fraud and irregularity at every corner, but I failed to find it. Finally, in sheer desperation, I went to the Justice Department to see if they had other evidence to bolster their case. I found out that the Department had thrown everything it had into the case.[2]

Mr. L'Heureux, it will be recalled, had been assigned to study and to recommend whether the affair should be given still another round of public hearings, this time before the Senate Committee on Interstate and Foreign Commerce. Apparently even Mr. L'Heureux, the lawyer, first viewed the Department's brief as the summary findings of a government agency reporting objectively as its role demanded, and not as that of an advocate presenting his client's case. When a government department has placed on the public record charges that fade out so completely under closer examination, two mistakes clearly have been made: the investigation was not thorough, and publicity was given to charges before a reasonable certainty existed. When an advocate pleads his client's cause, he is performing a professional duty to present his case in the best light possible. The Department here was not trying a case; it was presumably an advocate for nothing but the public interest. It was rightly concerned only about testing the truth of some serious allegations by a minority group that the statute and regulations had not been complied with.

Throughout this chapter and the three following it is important to keep in mind the function and methods of the Department of Justice. The Department came into the case to defend the United States against the Sakis Committee's suit, and some months later began an independent investigation of the charges. Granted that from various sources it found reason for investigation, no action was called for except that of conducting a thoroughly objective study. If the charges turned out to be true, they would reflect serious failure of the Commission to fulfill its responsibility, as well as reveal a trust institution as a bungler or worse. This possible outcome should not have deterred the Department from

2 L'Heureux, Opinion, p. 60.

thorough investigation, but rather should have increased its care to avoid injustice until justice was determined.

In this view, it was necessary for the Department to study the whole balloting procedure from statute and regulations to the last detail of the depositary's system, including the Commission's experience and its place in the procedure. What the next step should then have been is for the responsible administrator to decide. By implication from the Court's opinion of February 1952,[3] the Department should have turned over to the Commission a fully documented report. Since such a report would have been directed only to the Commission, it could have been framed accordingly, perhaps even sharpened to urge that body into action. At this stage the report would have been essentially an interoffice memorandum. For the public record, however, a Department of Justice would certainly guard against loose and inaccurate charges, especially those that imply intentional wrongdoing.[4]

It is as a public document that we are considering the Department's Trial Brief, which measures performance of the depositary against its responsibility as follows:

> . . . It is manifest that the depositary device was adopted by the Commission for the sole and worthy purpose of providing a reliable, independent and efficient method to secure for the Commission an accurate count of assents to the plan, recorded in a manner susceptible of ready examination, and reported in conformance with the standards set down by the

[3] The final paragraph of the opinion said: "The Court believes that the Commission is the proper forum to sift, hear, evaluate and act upon the matters charged by the Justice Department. There is no reason for the Court to feel that the Commission will not give consideration to an appropriate motion filed by the plaintiffs upon the basis of the documents tendered by the Justice Department which, in effect, constitute a claim of new evidence before the Commission." 103 Fed. Supp. 292 at 314.

[4] We leave it to the legal profession to define the standards of professional ethics. Whatever lawyers may do in trying cases for their clients, and even government lawyers when appearing for the United States, the point made here is that when the Department filed its Trial Brief it was primarily an investigator and not an advocate. Certainly at this stage objectivity was its byword, and the zeal of the advocate should have been spent in finding the truth. Words should have been assayed for their truth value and not for power to impress.

Commission. In each of these respects Old Colony proved to be wanting, so much so that the certificate filed by Old Colony with the Commission is inaccurate and unreliable. (footnote omitted) [5]

THE IMPORTANCE OF THE CHARGES TO THE DEPOSITARY

The charges struck the depositary with telling force. Its whole reputation as a fiduciary institution was placed in jeopardy; its future business depended on unshakable faith in its integrity. Its officers felt it to be the innocent victim of the Department's sudden attack, whose effect could only be distrust in the quality of the depositary's one product, trustworthy service. The concluding paragraph of the depositary's brief, after the public hearings in 1952, characterizes the Department's charges as follows:

> For the past year Old Colony's competence and standing in the business world and the honesty and integrity of its officers and employees have been subjected to attack by innuendo and indirection. It was not until the hearings just concluded that Old Colony was provided an opportunity to meet the charges made. . . .[6]

One could expect that those responsible for the Department's brief would have realized these effects and meticulously tested each sentence for unintended meaning and innuendo.

In comparison with the charges against the depositary, those against the Railroad were for the most part technical in character and depended in some part on interpretation of the statute. Being largely technical, the charges against the Railroad did not reflect on professional competence as did those against the depositary. People would patronize the Railroad even if a few technical charges had been leveled at its management and with respect to a plan that not many understood anyway. Although the Department's case carried the implication that the Commission was not fulfilling its responsibility in regulation, nevertheless the Commission was an autonomous agency and presumably could take care of

[5] Department of Justice, Trial Brief, p. 32.
[6] Old Colony Brief, October 20, 1952, p. 52.

itself.   After all, it could say, the Department was dealing with administrative matters outside its special field.

The depositary was paid $2,500 for its work.   It is preposterous to think that its officers would traffic in the institution's prestige for such a pittance, or even for its pay as the Railroad's transfer agent.   When one considers that four of its experienced staff worked directly with the procedures, checking and cross-checking, the implication of malfeasance becomes almost fantastic because it would involve collusion to an unbelievable degree and with no apparent motivation.

The charges that most directly concerned the depositary's reputation were that it failed to verify and record accurately the assents and revocations and that it ignored the fiduciary note on the letter of assent.   The brief submitted for Old Colony before the Commission in October 1952 was devoted almost entirely to repelling them.   The briefs of the Railroad and the banking houses also hit hard at the plaintiffs' challenge to the validity of assents when evidence of fiduciary authority did not accompany the executed assents.

THE SYSTEM FOR RECORDING ASSENTS

We start with two observations, poles apart:

". . . the testimony of Old Colony personnel is replete with instances which illustrate the utter inadequacies of its system and even the obvious insufficiency of its records covering its conduct as the depositary of assents. . . ."

Trial Brief, p. 44

"The foregoing description of the procedure adopted by Old Colony demonstrates how simple, and at the same time complete, this procedure was.   It was well designed to insure the accuracy of Old Colony's count of the assents received."

Old Colony Brief, p. 17

The extremes in these positions, on the same set of facts, present a challenge to anyone trying to use the Boston and Maine case as a proving ground for correct procedure under the statute and the Commission's orders.

The charge that various inaccuracies were possible, even probable, under the depositary's system for recording assents and revocations was crucial because absolute accuracy had to be assured. The depositary had first to determine what it was to certify to at the end of the submission period. Then the recording process had to be reduced to a routine that left no question about the validity of an assent or a revocation.

At this point it should be emphasized that accuracy does not permit a category of assents, even if apparently not needed, to be left out of the count because there is doubt concerning them. If there is doubt whether an assent or a revocation is countable under the regulations, the question should be resolved before the certificate is made. It is not enough to be able to say, "We certify that *at least* 75% of the common stock assented." A later contest over the validity of a block of assents would jeopardize the plan if there were not a margin over the 75% to offset those that might be thrown out. There should be no decision to ignore certain assents or to count certain revocations on the basis that it is "leaning backwards" to count only simon-pure assents. If there is question whether an assent or revocation is countable under the rule, the rule should be clarified. This sounds more simple than it is; accuracy requires careful definition of "a holder," "an executed assent," "when a revocation is effected," "when fiduciary authority is established," and the like. The importance, and the difficulties, of these precise definitions will appear in what follows.

What the Depositary Was Required to Certify to

The Commission's order of April 19, 1950, read:

> That the applicant . . . shall submit to the Commission . . . a certificate as to the total number of shares outstanding in each class . . . the number of shares of each class of affected securities held by parties assenting . . . and the percentage thereof with respect to the total number of shares outstanding in the particular class. Such certificate shall be based upon and supported by certification by the depositary, as to the number of shares of each class . . . held by the parties assenting to the plan. . . .

The cut-off time for marking the close of the polls was defined as:

> . . . if at any time prior to the expiration of [the six-months voting period] or extension thereof, assents shall be received and remain unrevoked from the holders of 75 percent of the outstanding shares of each class [87% for the plain preferred] . . . the applicant may declare the submission period closed as of such time, in which event it shall forthwith give notice thereof, and of the termination of the right of revocation. . . .

All this seems so clear that one wonders how any problems could arise. As balloting progresses, cumulative totals are kept of assents minus revocations, so that it is known when the critical percentage is getting near and the instant it is reached. Then there is nothing to do but certify the results when the Railroad declares the period ended. But problems did arise, and to understand them, as well as the criticisms leveled by the Sakis group and later by the Department, it is necessary to analyze the procedure in terms of the certificate required by the Commission's order.

Old Colony's Records for Receiving and Counting Assents

The most concise description of the procedure in this case is found in the Old Colony brief, written after the public hearings on the Department's charges.[7] The essentials in the operation are condensed in the next few pages.

Old Colony was selected as depositary because it had long been the Railroad's transfer agent. As transfer agent it had a ledger card for each stockholder, giving the number of shares held and their certificate numbers corrected daily to show the latest transfers.[8] The executive in charge of the depositary's function was the vice president in charge of the transfer department. He had been in the department since 1928, and its head since 1937. Under him was an operating supervisor, one who had worked for 20 years with such records as those involved here, and had intimate acquaintance with authorized signatures, including those of many brokers

[7] Old Colony Brief, pp. 3–24.

[8] Guaranty Trust Company of New York had been co-transfer agent on the common stock since 1927 and on all classes since August 1950. Data on transfers through it came to Old Colony by mail, customarily on the day following the transfer in New York.

in Boston, New York, and elsewhere.   Furthermore, Old Colony files contained the documentary evidence of authority to vote stock in most instances where such authority was necessary.   These facts assumed particular significance as some of the alleged deficiencies of the system were tested in the litigation to follow.

The general procedure for handling assents was worked out in conference with the Railroad's officers six months before voting started, and was confirmed by a letter from the Railroad to the depositary on December 27, 1949.[9]   Detailed procedures were worked out after discussions among a number of officers and operatives of the depositary.   When the balloting actually started in July 1950, there was no indication but that the plan of procedure was acceptable and workable.

The deposit of the actual certificates having been discarded as impractical and unnecessary,[10] the Commission had agreed and ordered that voting be done by letters of assent returned to the depositary.   Since a stockholder was to give his assent by "sending his executed vote of assent . . . to [the depositary]," the balloting was viewed by the Railroad and the depositary as essentially a proxy operation, except that dissenting votes did not appear in tabulations.   An important difference from the customary proxy operation soon presented a major problem; under the Order an assent once given was binding on transferees until formally revoked.   Transfers had to be carefully followed to prevent counting subsequent and duplicate assents for the same shares and to give effect to revocations.

---

[9] The phraseology of the letter indicates that the Railroad looked upon Old Colony as its agent in all depositary matters.   "As this entire procedure," it read, "is bound to be a lengthy one, I have not tried to be too specific about the details of each step; however, we will be careful to give you specific instructions as each phase develops."   Letter from Mr. W. S. Trowbridge to Mr. John Coulson, December 27, 1949.   Exhibit H–27 in the Hearings before the Examiner, August–September 1952.

[10] Deposit of securities was proposed in the Montana, Wyoming & Southern Railroad Company modification, involving bonds (271 I.C.C. 779, 1949), and in the unsuccessful applications of Maine Central Railroad Company (275 I.C.C. 261, 1950) and Lackawanna & Wyoming Valley Railroad Company (in 275 I.C.C. 345, 1950, as a section 77 case).

The basic data were on the ledger cards for each stockholder. As records of stock transfers accumulated, they were made up in a daily transfer sheet with full information from the certificates themselves — names of the old and the new holders, number of shares, and old and new certificate numbers. Both the ledger cards and the transfer sheets were permanent records of Old Colony as transfer agent.

The depositary added a special filing arrangement to the foregoing records to tabulate the assents as they came in. A new file was prepared which duplicated the regular ledger cards for each stockholder. This complete file was designated as "unassented" at the beginning of the submission period.

There were three key operatives in the actual processing of assents. The operating supervisor directly under the executive in charge received all assent material first, some with fiduciary papers and many over signatures he had come to recognize. He was thus able to examine papers, identify signatures, and check possible irregularities before turning the assents over to his assistant, who was principally responsible for the actual paper work. This operator, a senior examiner who had been employed by Old Colony for 30 years, handled the assents and prepared a daily report of them. Her work was finally cross-checked by a senior supervisor who had been in Old Colony's employ for over 20 years.[11]

The senior examiner's daily duty in this operation was to change the special stockholder ledger cards to reflect all transfers of the previous days, and then to check the incoming assents against the cards. If the assent squared with the number of shares shown to be held on the stockholder's card, she would record the assent and transfer the card to an "assented" file. As in any record-keeping with replies by mail from thousands of holders, troublesome variances showed up. The letter of assent sometimes stated a number of shares different from the number shown on the card. If the assent was for more than the card showed, the number assented was reduced; if for less, cards for the stockholder were then placed

[11] In addition to the daily cross-check, a comprehensive recheck of the tabulation of all assents received was made on December 6, and a final recheck of totals was made by the operating supervisor on December 14.

in both files — one in the unassented file for his shares still unassented, and the other in the assented file for the shares assented.

A daily report, which covered all assents received up through the first morning mail, was sent to the Railroad around noon each day. From this, the responsible officers of both the depositary and the Railroad knew the cumulative total of assented shares by classes each day.

For December 14, 1950, which became the last day of the submission period by the Railroad's decision, two reports were prepared. One was the regular daily report finished by noon. The second was a new report covering all other assents received on December 14; this was sent to the Railroad on December 15. According to strict instructions, no assents received after December 14 were counted.[12]

This description, concise in comparison with the pages of record transcript given over to these routines, is necessary to give the reader the background for the problems that arose subsequently. One can believe that if the Department of Justice had used in careful study of the procedure the three days that it spent in taking depositions from the depositary's officers, two years of time and expensive litigation might have been saved. The indispensable first step in solving a problem is to define the problem. The solution comes second, and criticism is meaningless without full understanding of these first two steps.

It was natural for the depositary to look to its long experience in proxy matters as a prototype for this case. If a review after the event disclosed places where past proxy methods did not fit, it would seem sounder and more constructive to start with the assumption that mistakes were honest rather than a planned swindle, or even careless. Many forms of business practice seem loose and slipshod to the uninitiated. The nod of a broker on the floor of the exchange signifies acceptance of a transaction for thousands of dollars; a casual agreement indeed it appears to one used to a formal receipt for the smallest payment.

The Old Colony brief appraises the method in positive language:

12 Deposition of John Coulson, October 16, 1951, p. 84.

The foregoing description of the procedure . . . demonstrates how simple, and at the same time complete, this procedure was. It was well designed to insure . . . accuracy. . . . The efficacy of this procedure is shown by the fact that, with regard to 80 assents, the total shares shown on each were reduced because . . . check . . . disclosed an insufficient number of unassented shares standing in the name of the assenting stockholder. Furthermore, an additional 80 assents were not counted at all, either because the person assenting had ceased to be a stockholder prior to the time his assent was received [13] or because he had no more unassented shares standing in his name. These reductions and rejections resulted in the disallowance of assents on account of over 26,000 shares.[14]

Problems That Came up During the Submission Period

Two major problems in accurate recording of assents came up during the submission period. One, cited by the Department as an instance where the depositary ignored a Commission order, was concerned with fiduciary assents not accompanied by formal documentary evidence of authority to sign. This is discussed in the next chapter.

Another difficulty arose when a holder assented for less than the total unassented shares in his name, and later sold part of his holdings. This problem related mainly to assents by brokers, where often the broker held blocks of stock in its own name and the authorized assents by the beneficial interests in the block were less than the broker's total holdings of such stock. The Commission's order did not require identification of assented shares by certificate numbers.[15]

[13] This seems to imply that the time of receipt of assents was the crucial time in counting assents, whereas another part of the brief (pp. 45, 46) states categorically that the time of mailing was the time the assent was legally acceptable.

[14] Old Colony Brief, p. 17.

[15] Some Commission orders in section 20b cases did call for identifying numbers of securities on letters of assent: for instance, in the cases of Central Railroad Company of New Jersey (271 I.C.C. 501, at 528 (1949)); Atlantic & Danville Railway Company (271 I.C.C. 605, at 647 (1949)); Montana, Wyoming & Southern Railroad Company (271 I.C.C. 779, at 793 (1949)); and Bangor and Aroostook Railroad Company (275 I.C.C. 369, at 393 (1950)). The Maryland & Pennsylvania Railroad Company (275 I.C.C. 695, at 708

Officers of the depositary and the Railroad had not fully anticipated the troublesome problems that would arise because so much of the stock was held in the street names of brokers but for their customers as beneficial owners. The large brokerage interest, of course, had been known over the years, particularly since the early 1940's when it became apparent that something might be done to simplify the capital structure. Over a period of three or four years scores of recapitalization plans had been submitted by brokerage houses interested in stirring up speculative activity in the various issues. When it came to the point of sending out solicitation material to stockholders, the Railroad asked the brokers who were holders of record to state how many beneficial holders they represented, so that the Railroad could supply enough copies of the material to be sent out by the brokers at the Railroad's expense.[16]

The first problem, one primarily for the Railroad, was to get action by the real owner of the stock in assenting through his broker. The rules of the New York Stock Exchange [17] required member firms to transmit solicitation material to beneficial owners when the soliciting company furnished an adequate number of copies and reimbursed the brokers for out-of-pocket expenses. Nevertheless, the Railroad was highly dependent on the brokers' interest in cooperating and in

---

(1950)) also proposed to have the serial numbers of bonds inserted on the assents.

The Old Colony Brief pointed out that no other type of corporate voting called for certificate numbers (p. 19).

16 The extent of brokers' names on the stockholder list of the Missouri-Kansas-Texas Railroad Company was recognized and emphasized in a letter sent to the stockholders with respect to a recapitalization plan. The president's letter of November 19, 1952, said, "I wish it were possible to contact each of you personally so that we could explain the concept of our plan. . . . Of course, it is humanly impossible for us to do this because there are over 6,000 stockholders and, too, more than 60% of the company's stock is now issued in the names of brokerage houses, the beneficial owners of which are not known to us."

The M–K–T used the brokers early when getting stockholder opinion while the plan was in the application stage, and agreed to reimburse immediately for postage and clerical expense involved.

17 Rule 871, Rules of the New York Stock Exchange, section on Proxies.

keeping the beneficial owners informed as to their rights to vote.

A second group of problems, of particular significance to the depositary, had to do with the tests of validity to apply to an assent received from a broker for beneficial holders. Did the broker have to show its authority from the beneficial owners? Should it be required to report assents by certificate numbers? When it sold stock held for the account of a client, must it specify by certificate number the shares sold as assented or unassented so that the depositary could trace assents accurately to transferees? [18]

The depositary's records would show a typical situation like this: Doe & Company — 1,000 shares of common stock registered in the name of the firm, on the ledger card by certificate numbers; 500 shares assented, certificate numbers not given because not required and their insertion would be a troublesome chore for the brokers; 300 shares later sold. Query: Were the sold shares all assented, all unassented, or some mixture of both? What record was the depositary to make in this situation? In order to anticipate action by the transferee of the 300 shares, the depositary's officers had to make a decision as to the status of the 300 transferred shares with regard to assents.

[18] The complexities of the problem raised by failure to require certificate numbers can be seen best if we start from an unreal assumption. If all stock were in certificates of one share each, which could not be changed in the stock ledger, then it would be possible to keep original certificate numbers alive and to follow transfers by the same number through the entire life of the stock issue in question. For example, the Railroad would have outstanding 394,728 numbered certificates of common stock with, say, holder A owning 100 shares numbered 1–100, holder B 10 shares numbered 101–110, and so on. Purchase and sale of these definite certificates representing one share each would be cumbersome, but in a balloting arrangement such as was prescribed in the Boston and Maine case a particular number could be reported and recorded as assented and that particular certificate could be followed by number through subsequent transfers and identified.

In the actual situation of the Boston and Maine balloting, transfers by individual holders of record presented little difficulty for accurate recording, even when an assented certificate was sold and divided into two or more new certificates. By means of the ledger cards the depositary could follow the split-up of the assented shares into the hands of new holders by certificate number. But in the case of brokers, the complexities multiplied.

With the cooperation of brokers, a situation like that described for Doe & Company could have been kept accurately in the records. When they reported assents, the brokers knew not only how many shares were assented but also by whom; for the rules of the New York Stock Exchange required them to get authorizations for the assents they reported.

Under usual conditions, however, brokers did not identify specific stock certificates with the assents. For instance, Doe & Company's over-all position with the beneficial owners could look essentially like this:

Doe & Company

Accounts in Boston and Maine Common Stock

Holder of record of the following certificates	Customer's beneficial interests
No. —, 100 shares	A — 80 shares unassented
" —, 100 "	B — 120 shares unassented
" —, 100 "	C — 300 shares unassented
" —, 100 "	D — 400 shares assented
" —, 100 "	E — 63 shares assented
" —, 100 "	F — 37 shares assented
" —, 100 "	
" —, 100 "	
" —, 100 "	
" —, 100 "	

It would have been possible for brokers to adopt a new procedure at the beginning of the submission period for the purpose of keeping beneficial owners' assents and sales earmarked with certificate numbers. Doe & Company, for instance, could have gone through its whole list of beneficial owners of Boston and Maine stock and broken up enough certificates to permit assigning specific certificates to each owner. In the example given, this would have involved delivering two 100-share certificates to the transfer agent and getting back four, for 80, 20, 37, and 63 shares, respectively. Then all assents, as well as sales, during the voting period could have been reported by certificate number.

Some effort could have been saved if the broker had assigned specific certificates only to the owners who assented, in order to include certificate numbers on the letters of assent. Then, if neither A, B, nor C assented during the period, no special action would have been necessary with respect to their holdings.

For an adequate system of identification of certificates with assenters and nonassenters, a broker would not need to do anything until a sale took place; at that time specific certificate numbers would have to be connected with the shares sold by each assenting beneficial owner. This system would require the broker to keep a record of its customers' assents. For instance, if the 300 shares sold by Doe & Company during the submission period were sold for customer D's account, the certificates sold could be reported as assented and would so stand in the assented file under the purchaser's name. If, instead, D sold 200, B 20, and A 80, the broker would simply report assents for the two 100-share certificates sold for D. The customers' records would show that D still owned 200 assented shares and B 100 unassented. If A and E ordered their stock sold, the broker would be obliged before sale to exchange two 100-share certificates for three — one for 63 shares, which would be reported as assented, one for 80 shares and one for 57 shares, which would remain in the broker's hands.

It is obvious that any such scheme for identifying brokers' assents by certificate numbers would impose a clerical burden on the brokers. In many cases, also, the system would interfere with the brokers' customary practice of trading in 100-share lots and of pooling certificates. Identification would really require brokers to give gratuitous service through the depositary in order to insure correct balloting results in a statutory recapitalization.

The ordinary proxy procedures do not raise such problems because the votes come from stockholders of record on a stated day. Since the assent procedure in this case was looked upon as proxy operation, the problem exposed by the foregoing analysis did not occur at the beginning to officers of either the depositary or the Railroad. The procedure provided carefully for the stockholder who assented only part of his shares, but it failed to recognize the necessity for certificate numbers. When letters of assent without certificate numbers began coming to the depositary from brokers, the operating supervisor asked several brokers to identify their stock. Some replied that the task would be impossible and others refused; most brokers continued to send letters of assent without certificate numbers. It was apparent that the Commission's order had not anticipated the typical situation of the broker who commingled the shares of beneficial owners. In such cases, the order, "until notice of revocation is received by the depositary, an assent, once given, will bind the assenting holder, his heirs, successors, and assigns," could not be carried out. An assent necessarily was given by a holder for specific shares, and an assent to follow to a transferee had to follow the specific shares transferred.

If the Commission had ever encountered such problems before, the depositary was not so advised. Voting had already started; such prestudy as was given to procedures had not raised this particular question. Faced with some decision, the depositary's officers concluded that circumstances forced them to make assumptions with respect to assents on stock sold by brokers as holders of record. When the broker held both assented and unassented stock, the depositary could assume that the stock sold was assented, or that it was unassented, or that it was assented and unassented in the same proportions as the total holdings. Obviously, none of these alternative methods would be sure to give results precisely in accord with the facts; the task was to select the one that would most nearly approximate the facts.

After advising with Railroad officers, the depositary officers decided to "presume that the shares sold [in such instances] consisted of unassented stock and the shares retained of assented stock." [19] This seemed to be a practical and reasonable solution, supported by the logical assumption that stockholders who assented to the plan were more likely to retain their shares and those who disapproved and refused to assent were more likely to dispose of theirs.[20] Further-

[19] Old Colony Brief, pp. 18–19.
[20] Ibid. See also Hearings before the Examiner, August 25, 1952, p. 909.

more, at the time approximately 80% of the stock held by brokers was still unassented.[21]   Another reason, later developed in the Railroad brief, was the feeling that this solution was actually "prejudicial to the Railroad, since it required a greater sales effort than would have been required had the presumption been made that stock transferred by a broker was assented." [22]   From the point of view of new purchasers, the depositary's method contributed to the purity of the assent file, discussed in Chapter V; for no purchaser of stock sold from such a broker's account would be bound by a previous assent.

There are flaws in these arguments.   As the Railroad brief points out, the assumption that shares sold were unassented does not apply to the "speculator who is in and out of a stock picture for reasons which bear little relation to the reasons which motivate an investor." [23]   Furthermore, far from being prejudicial to the Railroad, there would be situations in which the solution would be definitely helpful.   For instance, suppose Doe & Company's customer D, an assenter, sells 200 shares.   At first glance the important factor appears to be that assented stock has been returned to the unassented file.   But the total number of assents counted in the broker's name has not been reduced.   Doe & Company are now recorded as holding 800 shares, 500 assented and 300 unassented.   The number of assents (500) recorded for Doe & Company stands the same; the Railroad has not lost any votes, and instead is bettered by having a new and perhaps more amenable prospect to solicit.   The system enlarges the fair game in the field where the Railroad is hunting for votes.   To use another metaphor, it amounts to restocking the fish pond.   If the purchaser of D's stock can be induced to assent, the over-all effect has been either that those particular shares have been assented twice or that D's

21 Statement by Everett W. Smith, July 29, 1952, in the Railroad's files.

22 Brief of Applicant on Further Hearing before the Interstate Commerce Commission, October 20, 1952, p. 13.   The brief for the bankers also referred to this argument, saying, "This practical solution did not favor the Railroad, but on the other hand compelled it to seek an assent from B, a new stockholder."   Brief of L. F. Rothschild & Co. and Goldman, Sachs & Co. before the Interstate Commerce Commission, October 17, 1952, p. 15.

23 Railroad Brief, October 20, 1952, p. 13, footnote 1.

assent has been pinned on the shares still held by Doe & Company for nonassenters, A, B, or C. If these nonassenters have studied the plan and positively refused to assent, their refusal is really nullified through no action of theirs.

Under the solution adopted, also, a revocation might not be effective, as for instance in the case where the purchaser of D's stock feels strongly opposed to the plan and sends in a revocation to make sure that the stock he now holds is not assented. The stock came to him unassented by fiat of the "solution"; he really bought assented stock (D's), but the number of assents still stands as first reported in spite of the revocation.

On the other hand, if a nonassenter, A, B, or C, sells his stock, the system would reflect the situation accurately, and the fact was that the proportion of unassented to assented shares registered in brokers' names was far higher than the proportion in the entire body of record holders. Furthermore, no other solution to the problem would present a truer picture of the facts.[24]

The depositary's brief argued later that the question of how to classify shares sold by brokers became important only if an assent or a revocation came in from a transferee. In fact, only four revocations were received altogether, and all those received before the end of the period were counted. No error with respect to revocations could have resulted from the treatment of brokers' sales. The brief adds that no specific instance of double counting of assents was ever charged in the record.[25] The facts of double counting would

[24] Suppose that the depositary recorded brokers' sales as assented. Then customer D's sale would be recorded accurately. In addition, revocations by succeeding purchasers would be effective. But if B, a nonassenter, sells his 120 shares and the stock is classified as assented, then the new holder is prevented from assenting B's unassented shares, and B's refusal to assent is left permanently on Doe & Company's record. Doe & Company is now recorded as holding 880 shares, of which only 380 are recorded as assented although the original 500 assents actually remain unchanged. In a situation where the purchaser of B's stock favors the plan, all the valid assents cannot be counted. Solutions between the two extremes would be subject to the same criticisms. In addition, it would have been impossible for the depositary to apply the proportions of a broker's assented and unassented shares to all its sales.

[25] Old Colony Brief, pp. 21–22.

be very hard to ferret out, however. Wherever a broker with mixed holdings made a sale of stock that had actually been assented, then an assent of that stock by any subsequent holder might have resulted in double counting, as we have seen.[26]

The upshot of this whole analysis is that although the margin of error in the course chosen by the depositary must have been small, the only way to provide absolute accuracy would have been to attach certificate numbers to all assented shares transferred. The officers of the depositary and the Railroad did not visualize their problem when they were setting up the procedure, when there was still time to have the order amended or to get instructions from the Commission. The Commission itself failed to make its order clear and precise in this first case of a section 20b recapitalization where stock interests alone were concerned. If the problem had been foreseen by a careful projection of operating conditions before voting started, probably some answer could have been found.

The Trial Brief of the Department raised a significant objection to the procedure when it said:

> . . . under their system of operations there was no possible way to identify with certainty which exact stock certificates had been assented in an instance where only part of an owner's stockholdings had been included in a letter of assent. . . . Thus the railroad management would receive a fresh crack at a new investor. Such a disposition was made unilaterally by the railroad and Old Colony without even exposing the problem to the Commission.[27]   (footnote omitted)

We can agree that here is an area where more precise control of balloting techniques was needed. The answer to the problem is not to lay the entire blame on the Railroad and the depositary for taking the reasonable alternative, but to use the difficulty as a basis for making the procedure foolproof. It does not seem reasonable to suggest that after the

[26] It is Mr. L'Heureux's opinion that the only ones who could complain with any right were the stockbrokers or the beneficial owners, if they were not satisfied with the system, and there is no evidence of a single objection. L'Heureux, Opinion, p. 50.

[27] Department of Justice, Trial Brief, pp. 35–36.

voting had started the depositary should have rejected brokers' assents not identified by certificate numbers.

In a subsequent section 20b case, the Western Maryland Railway securities modification, the Commission adopted explicitly the solution used by Old Colony for handling brokers' assents and transfers.[28] The order has the merit of making the procedure clear to the depositary but it does not guarantee an accurate count. Our analysis has shown that although the margin for error may be very small, this solution still leaves the possibility of a double counting of assents.

The importance of certificate numbers for accurate counting of assents, as illustrated in the broker situation, suggests that some fee arrangement with broker-dealers might be worked out, sanctioned by the Commission as an expense to the recapitalizing company. The stock exchanges themselves might be interested in requiring their registered brokers to cooperate in such important matters of public interest as major recapitalizations. Or the SEC, by its supervision of the exchanges, might include a requirement in its regulations in view of the public interest involved. The fact is that correct records could be kept only with full broker co-operation.

The foregoing analysis presents a formidable list of obstacles to accurate recording in this case. There can be no compromise with accuracy if litigation is to be avoided. Some tightening procedures could meet the lesser problems

[28] The order said:

". . . In those cases where less than all the stock in the name of a particular stockholder has been assented without designation of specific certificate number or numbers applicable to the shares assented, or the certificate number or numbers designated represent shares in excess of those assented, and, subsequently, a portion of the shares in the name of that stockholder is transferred, it shall be deemed that such assent applies first to the shares retained, and such number of shares assented as are in excess of the number of shares retained shall apply to the shares transferred, unless the transferor before or at the time of the transfer, by written instrument delivered to the depositary, gives different instructions as to which shares the assent is intended to apply, in which event such instructions shall govern; provided, however, that this requirement shall not be construed to restrict the right of a transferee of assented shares to revoke an assent given with respect thereto. . . ."
Finance Docket No. 18103, Western Maryland Railway Company Securities Modification, October 14, 1954, 290 I.C.C. 445 at 473–474.

but the central difficulty, which is inherent in a system that keeps assents binding on transferees until revoked, cannot be met without complete reporting of assents by certificate numbers. Either a way must be found to get such details from brokers, a costly procedure, or the constant change of the voters' list throughout a submission period must be avoided altogether. It has been suggested that assents be canceled when shares are transferred. This proposal has merit but still would require reports by certificate numbers.

It is my conclusion that the answer lies in an established voters' list as of a record day. This change is considered further in the final chapter.

SPECIAL CASES OF ALLEGED INVALID ASSENTS

Two cases should be taken up, which were given lengthy treatment in the Trial Brief as examples of the improper assenting possible under the depositary's recording system. In each of these instances the affidavits taken from the parties signing the assents were used by the Department in presenting its argument that invalid assents had been certified.

The Bianco Assent

This block of 900 common shares was allegedly voted by the owner, Dr. Peter B. Bianco, after it was transferred. The owner's affidavit, taken by the Department on October 2, 1951, was to the effect that he signed a letter of assent November 10, 1950, but did not mail it until December 12, 1950. The New York transfer agent's records show the stock transfer was made on December 11.[29] The depositary's records show the assent was received on December 13.

The Department stressed two points in its argument that the assent was invalid. In the first place, it said, the stockholder was not a holder of record when the assent was received by the depositary. Under the depositary's system the

---

[29] In the case of one assent the Department argued that even the transfer record was not enough to establish the right to assent. It said (Trial Brief, p. 60): ". . . no stock is valid until countersigned by the transfer agent and *registered by the registrar.*" This position does not separate two questions: What makes a certificate a valid instrument? and when is a stock *transfer* accomplished?

assent should not have been counted if the stockholder's card did not show any unassented shares. It would seem that a transfer made on December 11 should have been reflected on the card by December 13. In the second place, said the Department, the system was wrong in not using the time of mailing as the test of validity.[30] According to the affidavit, Dr. Bianco was not a stockholder of record even when he mailed the assent.

Note that the Department's second point relied on the interpretation of the Commission's order that an assent was executed when mailed, not when received. The Department, however, did not raise the issue in the case of any other assent. When it argued at length for a date stamp on assents, it referred only to the date of receipt and not to the date of mailing, the postmark. Nor did the Department's brief follow through consistently with regard to assents mailed but not received within the period. It found no error that these latter were not counted.

The case became a critical salient in the depositary's defense, so critical in fact as to bring the stockholder and his banker adviser from Illinois as witnesses at the public hearing in Boston. The testimony of both was that the affidavit was in error; the assent was mailed late in November, before the stock was sold.[31] This change from an affidavit, which had been signed almost a year nearer the event, naturally raised a question of credibility. Cross-examination brought out the explanation that the mailing date given in the affidavit was furnished by the Department.[32] Additional facts

[30] Here the Trial Brief shows close analysis of a point that was not carried through as a test to all assents even if received after the closing date. As our analysis proceeds, there will be other instances noted where the Department's brief makes a significant start toward constructive criticism, but then turns to loose statement and innuendo. The regrettable aspect of the case is that the possibilities of constructive criticism by the Department were shunted for some unexplained reason into channels that pitted one government agency against another rather than merged their efforts to straighten out the workings of a new procedure under a new statute.

[31] Hearing before the Examiner, August 27, 1952, p. 1312.

[32] The implications as to the Department's methods in building its case, at least in this instance, would seem enough to arouse its policy-making officers to a searching inquiry into the facts of this particular episode.

The Department was not represented at the public hearing before the Examiner in 1952, having decided soon after the three-judge trial to let the

in the testimony were that the stock was sold on the New York Stock Exchange by a Chicago broker on November 30, and on December 4 the certificates were sent to the broker for forwarding to the transfer agent.[33]

The Commission's final report of April 1953 finds this assent valid because "the evidence of record establishes that the assent in question was mailed prior to December 1, 1950, while Bianco still had possession of the stock certificates and was a stockholder of record. . . ." [34] The Commission here is explicit in calling the mailing date the crucial date, whereas throughout the hearing the testimony of the depositary's staff was to the effect that the date of receipt was the one checked against the ledger cards to validate the ownership. If the mailing date was decisive in this case, what can be said of a system that takes no account of it in any other case?

There remain some puzzling questions about this assent. The incident highlights the need for rules that identify valid assents with precision.

The Zucker Assent

All the facts of the Zucker transaction, involving assent and sale of 5,000 shares of Boston and Maine common stock, have never been clearly established. The Commission called them the most controversial in the whole proceeding, including in all their confused ramifications "questions of conflict of evidence, inherent inconsistency in testimony, and credibility of witnesses." [35] Nine witnesses testified with respect to various phases of the case. It is not necessary for our purpose, however, to puzzle over the reasons for the contradictory versions of the story.

Only a small part of the charges involved the depositary,

Commission carry the case alone. In the usual case, even when it does not participate actively, it keeps in close touch through an observer at all proceedings. An observer at this public hearing would certainly have noted the testimony as to the mailing date and could have been expected to establish the correctness of the Department's procedure with reference to the affidavit.

[33] Hearing before the Examiner, August 27, 1952, pp. 1275–1276.

[34] 282 I.C.C. 750 at 771.

[35] Ibid. at 774.

those relating to the date of the assent and to a revocation. The other charges, which bore more heavily on the Railroad, were concerned with improper solicitation and, more importantly, the relation of this block of stock to the Coolidge purchases, which were charged with resulting in invalid assents controlled by the Railroad.[36]

The controversy over the assent arose from the fact that Mr. Harry Zucker, in an affidavit in the fall of 1951, said that he had signed an assent for 5,000 shares on December 15, 1950, the day after the close of the submission period, but had predated it December 12. Since the assent was included in the tabulation of votes received by the depositary on December 14, the Department concluded that the depositary had wrongfully counted a predated assent not received within the period.[37]

By the end of the public hearing in 1952, it was clear that there were, in fact, two assents. The evidence was conclusive that the stockholder had signed an assent dated December 12, 1950, for 5,000 common shares and that this assent had been received by the depositary on December 14 and counted in the final tabulation sent to the Railroad on December 15. Furthermore, the number of assented shares had been reduced by 700 when the depositary found that 700 of these shares had been assented by a previous owner; and it had been reduced again by an additional 1,300 shares when Mr. Zucker's revocation for that amount was honored. The signed revocation, dated December 14, was not received by the depositary until December 15, after the close of the period; but notification that the revocation was in the mail had been telephoned to the depositary on December 14. After consulting with Railroad officers, the depositary honored the revocation.

Witnesses at the hearing in 1952 agreed that an assent also had been signed on December 15. On the afternoon of that day Mr. Zucker met Mr. Greer, a special solicitor of assents

---

[36] These situations are discussed in Chapters IX and X.

[37] This incident produces an interesting question as to the interpretation of facts. The Department alleges the wrong count of an assent said to have been received on December 15 but predated as of December 12; it apparently sees no wrong worth mentioning in the predating itself.

for the Railroad, at a bank in Bridgeport, Connecticut, to
complete a transaction arranged by a broker for the purchase
of the stock at a price above the market. A signed assent for
the 5,000 shares was a condition of the sale. The transaction
was witnessed by a vice president of the bank, who was to see
that the papers when passed were in proper order. The
banker, a key witness at the 1952 hearing, testified that he
was sure the assent was dated December 15; his training always made the date on an instrument a matter for special
attention.[38] The solicitor testified that he himself destroyed
the second assent, dated December 15, "because it was of no
value at all." [39]

A striking part of the Department's action in regard to this
assent is the apparent readiness to accept at face value the
affidavits of the stockholder and his lawyer in spite of important contradictions between their testimony and that of
others who had a part in the affair. One cannot avoid asking
why the Department did not carry its own investigation
further before including the confused story in its brief.[40] It
is unfortunate, for instance, that the Department did not
take more of the banker's testimony in the course of its original investigation; he was as available for his views on critical
facts as was the stockholder. They were both in Bridgeport,
Connecticut.

The other matter relating to the depositary's procedure in

[38] Hearing before the Examiner, September 10, 1952, p. 1787.

[39] Ibid., August 26, 1952, p. 1080.

[40] A notable instance of prejudgment on part of the facts may be cited.
The solicitor, Mr. Greer, said that Mr. Zucker had sent an assent on his stock
prior to the end of the period. The Trial Brief says (p. 53): ". . . Zucker
testified that he had never at any previous time signed an assent for the
stock. . . . Greer's version is that Zucker had previously sent that assent into
the railroad or to Old Colony. . . . All of the corroborative documentary
evidence substantiates Zucker's version. . . . Greer, in an attempt to give some
color of credibility to his version, said . . ."

It is now accepted by investigators that at the time this brief was written
the depositary's records showed the disputed assent as received on December
14. If the Department had checked more thoroughly with the depositary on
the details of the transaction, it would have learned the facts that were finally
brought out almost a year later. "All of the corroborative documentary evidence substantiates Zucker's version," stated the Trial Brief — but not including the assent itself in the depositary's files.

this affair concerned the revocation. A telephone message from the stockholder's lawyer to the depositary on December 14 advised that a letter of revocation for 1,300 common shares was on its way.[41] At about the same time the Railroad received a telegram from the same lawyer to the effect that a revocation for 1,000 shares was coming from Mr. Zucker's brother-in-law. A telephone call from the depositary to the Railroad to ask advice on the revocation was misunderstood, the officer at the Railroad thinking of the 1,000-share revocation, and the depositary's officer having the other revocation in mind. The Railroad authorized honoring the revocation, intending to honor the one for 1,000 shares, but the depositary honored the revocation for 1,300 shares instead. Neither party realized that there were two revocations until the two letters arrived on December 15. Then the depositary treated the revocation for 1,000 shares as invalid according to the Commission's order. Two further documents in this proceeding, which were given to Mr. Greer on December 15, were letters from each of the stockholders revoking the rescinding of their assents.

The Commission's final report stated its finding on these revocations as follows: "In our opinion, if there was any inconsistency in the treatment of these two revocations, the circumstances do not justify a finding that the [1,000-share] revocation should have been honored." [42] Evidently the Commission considered that the circumstances did not demand that the Zucker revocation be disallowed and the 1,300 shares added back to the valid assent column. Its finding, however, still leaves us in search of a principle for handling revocations.

This whole incident lays bare a sordid type of transaction that frequently occurs in a recapitalization, particularly when highly speculative stocks at low prices are involved. The setting described when the Trial Brief introduces Mr. Zuck-

41 The question may well be raised why the revocation covered only 1,300 of the 5,000 shares assented on December 12. The answer appears to be that the lawyer was ignorant of Mr. Zucker's assent. He drew up the revocation only to cover the shares bought during the submission period, having in mind the contingency that the shares might have been assented by a previous owner. Hearing before the Examiner, September 9, 1952, p. 1619.

42 282 I.C.C. 750 at 780 (April 21, 1953).

er's interest as a stock owner is significant: "Zucker owned 5,000 shares of Boston and Maine common stock. . . . Zucker was opposed to the stock modification plan and refused to assent." [43]   So far we have him depicted as an investor who reasoned that the proposed plan was wrong on its merits.   But as the story unfolds we learn that his assent had a price tag.   He and his lawyer came to Boston early in December to negotiate a premium for the stock, with the deal falling through because the asking price was too high.   Then in the final transaction on December 15, he sold at $3\frac{1}{4}$ when the market was at $2\frac{1}{2}$.   His opposition to the plan turned out to be: "I refuse to permit an assent except at my price."

The transaction seems to be a plain traffic in votes, which in a political election would be called a scandal.   There is a difference, however.   A voter in a ward election who sells his vote for a price acts in a way that is repugnant to the very concept of citizenship and the right to vote.   There are no proxies in a political election.   Purity of the ballot requires that citizens vote their own minds.   When a stockholder sells his stock, however, he sells the right to vote with it; and the law cannot go back to the motives behind the sale of the stock.   The election official in a corporate election is not concerned with motives but only with the legal right of the stockholder to vote.

This stockholder showed that he had no deep convictions on the plan of recapitalization.   He was against it, said the Trial Brief, but he was admittedly trying, with his lawyer, for the last cent of premium from anybody who would pay it. Assents and subsequent revocations, by telephone and telegram, were handled as strategy matters only.   This was particularly true as the deadline for assents approached.   We have here a situation that called for extreme caution in forming conclusions until all the evidence was in.   The Department publicized a conclusion in its Trial Brief that later was disproved by the witness from the bank and the depositary's records.

This premature conclusion from contradictory facts, published by a government agency, was left to its insidious effects

[43] Department of Justice, Trial Brief, p. 52.

for over a year and a half before the Commission's final report of April 1953 found the depositary correctly to have counted Mr. Zucker's one valid assent.

The other aspects of this affair, bearing on the charges of improper solicitation and of assents controlled by the Railroad, are taken up in later chapters.

IS THERE A TOLERANCE LIMIT IN CERTIFYING THE ASSENT TOTAL?

The order covering certification by the depositary read as follows: ". . . certification by the depositary, as to the number of shares of each class of affected securities held by the parties assenting to the plan. : . ." This would seem clearly to require the inclusion of every legal assent. Every assenting stockholder is entitled to have his vote counted. If any method makes it impossible to say at the end of the period, "The total assents are such a number, no more, no less," then that method is not accurate. In section 20b cases, if 75% of each affected class has assented and *there is no possibility of contested ballots,* obviously it makes no practical difference whether a margin above the 75% is reported or not. But where a contest is possible, a stockholder who casts a legal ballot is prejudiced if, when later a ballot is disqualified, a surplus of valid ballots is not available to offset the shrinkage.

There is evidence in this case that all legal ballots were not included in the certified total. The order read: ". . . the assent to the plan . . . by any holder . . . shall be given by sending his executed vote of assent, within the time specified [the submission period]. . . ." The crucial fact in an executed assent thus would seem to be the time of sending it. This fact was recognized by both the Department Brief and the depositary in connection with one assent, the Bianco assent, but in that one instance only. The depositary's brief emphasized that "An assent became effective . . . when it was mailed," [44] in contrast to a revocation, which had to be

44 Old Colony Brief, p. 45.

delivered to count. The Commission itself found that the Bianco assent was valid because it had been mailed while Dr. Bianco was still a stockholder.[45]

If this is a correct definition of an executed assent, i.e., valid when mailed within the submission period by a holder of record at the time of mailing,[46] the evidence adduced in the depositary's own brief shows that the order was not followed. The regular procedure was to count assents only when they had been processed and found to be good as of the time they were received.[47] The voting period could not be ended until enough valid assents were held. There is reason, however, to hold that the final count should include all assents mailed within the period and later found to be good although received and processed after the close of the period. The submission period in this case was ended by the Railroad as of 5:05 P.M. on December 14, 1950. At that time the executive in charge instructed the operating supervisor that no more assents were to be counted.[48] The presumption is that he was following that part of the Commission's order that made termination of the period dependent on the number of assents *held* by the depositary.

There is other evidence that the depositary's officers throughout the balloting did not interpret an executed assent in the same way that its counsel did in the later proceedings with reference to the Bianco assent. For example, testimony at the public hearing referred to a situation, and a common one, when checking an assent against the sender's ledger card revealed no unassented shares. "This might arise because of a transfer prior to the time the assent was received," said the brief.[49] If an assent was executed by mailing, the crucial question was the time the assent was mailed. If the assent was mailed November 1, the stock transfer completed November 3 and so recorded on the ledger card, and the assent received by the depositary November 4, then the

---

[45] 282 I.C.C. 750 at 771 (April 21, 1953).

[46] The form of letter of assent read: "The undersigned is the holder of record of shares . . . as follows:"

[47] Hearing before the Examiner, August 25, 1952, p. 1031.

[48] Old Colony Brief, p. 24.

[49] Ibid., p. 15.

card would show no unassented shares in the holder's name. "If the person signing the assent had no unassented shares in his name, his assent was not counted at all." [50]   But the real question was: Did he have the right to assent when he did so? There is nothing in the description of the recording procedure with regard to verification of this right of the holder to vote *at the time he mailed his assent.*

The depositary was consistent throughout in counting assents when received. Only when the special Bianco case was in dispute was the literal statement of the order invoked by counsel. This raises the question of whether an assent can be validated in one case as of the date of sending, and the same principle not hold in all cases, even on the final day of the submission period.[51]

The confusion on what constitutes a countable assent re-

[50] Ibid., p. 15.

[51] The investigators for the Department moved even further away than the depositary from the idea that the mailing date should govern validity. The depositary's officers had taken the position that all valid assents received through the final day of the submission period should be counted. To achieve this purpose, they changed the recording procedure on December 14, when they felt fairly sure that the cut-off of voting was close at hand. For instance, all assents received on December 14 were counted, even though they were not processed by the regular routine until December 15. Again, the supervisor took a more active part than usual in the processing, notably in the case of an assent for 2,000 common shares from a New York broker. When that assent came in on December 14, the stockholder's card showed no unassented shares. The supervisor, however, as was reasonable under the circumstances, ascertained by a telephone call to the New York transfer agent that 2,000 shares had been transferred into the broker's name on the morning of December 14. Therefore, he authorized the counting of the assent.

The Department's investigators did not accept the testimony of the depositary's officers and employees that no assent received after December 14 was counted, and looked for objective confirmation in the records. The search became confused in the changed procedure of the final day. Questioning at length the assents reported to the Railroad on December 15, the investigators found themselves, perhaps unintentionally, leaning toward the view that only assents actually processed and reported on December 14 were valid. The mailing date was lost in the confusion.

It should be noted, nevertheless, that the Department raised a significant point in connection with the broker's assent just described. It turned out that this was the only case in which the depositary's employees had not waited for the New York transfer sheets to arrive by mail, a half to a full day after the transfer.

quires us to examine closely the Commission's order.   An assent is executed by *sending* the vote within the submission period.   On the other hand, the order required a revocation to be *delivered* to the depositary before the notice was published of the termination of the submission period, "which publication shall be made only at a time when unrevoked assents of holders of 75 percent or more . . . of each class . . . [87% for the plain preferred] are held by the depositary." Note that this said nothing of how assents were to be counted, or in any way changed the Commission's previous reference to an assent as executed by *sending*.

The next paragraph of the order read that "such assents shall be made on or before 6 months after the effective date of this order [or extension thereof], provided that, if at any time prior . . . assents shall be received and remain unrevoked from the holders of 75 percent of the outstanding shares . . . [87% for the plain preferred] the applicant may declare the submission period closed as of such time. . . ." The directive referred here only to the time when the Railroad might close the polls; it did not say that assents mailed but not received during the period should not be counted in the final and complete tabulation.   In fact, since the Railroad was given 60 days after the closing to submit its certificate, the time was more than ample to include letters of assent received after the close but mailed before it.

The apparent conflict between the order and the failure of the depositary to take account of mailing dates directed our research to other section 20b cases to see if the orders for balloting in such cases were more carefully drawn.   The same confusion appeared in all.   No order in any of the seven cases examined was clear as to whether the Commission meant the mailing date to be crucial, and if so, whether the assents mailed on the last day of the period were to be counted in the certified total.   The orders in the cases of Lehigh Valley Railroad [52] and Central Railroad of New Jersey [53] gave no criterion of a properly executed assent.   The Macon, Dublin & Savannah order [54] said that assents were to

[52] 271 I.C.C. 553 (1949).
[53] 271 I.C.C. 501 (1949).
[54] 271 I.C.C. 376 at 388 (1948).

be given by execution *and delivery* to the depositary within the submission period; this would seem to say that mere mailing was not enough. Atlantic & Danville Railway [55] required assents to be made by executing and mailing a vote of assent within the specified time. The Montana, Wyoming & Southern [56] order required the holder to mail or deliver the vote in the time specified. The Bangor & Aroostook [57] order required assents to be made by mailing or delivering within the time specified. Certainly no pattern appears in this series of orders that would precisely define validity in terms of the time factor in assents.[58]

The orders regarding revocations, however, are consistent and explicit: they must be executed *and* delivered.[59] The definiteness of a countable revocation implies a difference from the assents, but the language does not spell out the difference and depositaries have not been careful to note the mailing date of assents as significant.[60]

The Commission's order in the Western Maryland Railway modification in 1954 [61] still leaves open the question of whether the date of mailing is of any importance, despite the language that assents were to be given "by delivering or mail-

[55] 271 I.C.C. 605 at 647 (1949).

[56] 271 I.C.C. 779 at 793 (1949).

[57] 275 I.C.C. 369 at 393 (1950).

[58] The instructions for voting given to security holders in section 77 cases have given notice that ballots bearing the postmark of the last day of the period were countable. The voting instructions in the Wisconsin Central Railway Company reorganization (Finance Docket No. 14720; letter of June 25, 1953) read:

"To be effective as a vote, the ballot must be filled out . . . and filed with the Commission on or before August 4, 1953, or the envelope containing the ballot must bear postmark showing it was placed in the mails on or before that date."

[59] This was the clear understanding in the letter of Mr. Trowbridge to Mr. Coulson giving directions on procedure.

[60] I inquired of some depositaries on the matter of recording postmarks so as to validate assents as of the date of mailing. Postmarks were not recorded, and the explanation was made that the percentage of assents received was well over the statutory 75%, in one case much ahead of the expiration date. This, of course, does not meet the point raised in the text. An assent that is valid according to official orders should be counted regardless of the status of the total vote.

[61] 290 I.C.C. 445 at 472–474 (October 14, 1954).

ing an executed vote of assent." The confusion comes from the requirement that the depositary "cause the date of receipt to be endorsed (by rubber stamp or other appropriate means) upon each assent and revocation received by it." Where does this leave the assent mailed a short time before the submission period was officially closed but received, say, two days after?

Old Colony's decision to count assents as of the date of their receipt had the effect, if any, of lowering the total reported assents.[62] The policy had the effect of leaning backwards. It made the certificate really mean, with respect to common stock for instance: "We report that 76.61% assented in this class. There were really some more because we did not count any assents received after December 14. Furthermore, if a holder's card showed no shares to assent when we received the letter of assent, we did not count his vote even though he was still a holder of record when he mailed the assent."

To keep records of the mailing dates would have required close scrutiny of postmarks to compare with transfer dates and the final day of the submission period. This seems to be an unnecessary refinement. However, should not a stockholder be protected in his legal assent in case of a later dispute over votes? Should disqualification of enough votes to block the plan be allowed to stand, when his assent was not counted and the evidence (postmark) of its being a timely assent was destroyed?

This seems a case where the rules need to be clarified and consistently applied. The depositary should not be criticized for following to the letter the reference of the order to the assents *held* on December 14, except that if it had a doubt it could have cleared the matter with the Commission. If the Commission means that mailing sets the effective date *except* on the closing date, when assents must be in hand to be counted, it should state so directly. There is no logical reason, however, why mailing dates for assents should not be held throughout, and the method of recording set up

[62] Assents were received after December 14 for 1,438 prior preference, 8,743 first preferred, and 1,556 common shares. (Hearing before the Examiner, September 10, 1952, pp. 1692–1693.)

to count on that basis. Why the exception on the closing date? [63] Moreover, the mailing date was important in checking whether an assent received was mailed before a former holder had transferred his stock.

We return to the principle stated in the first part of this section. When the ballots go "over the top" of the 75% requirement, there is still no reason for not counting every legal assent. Precision in recording means precision on the high side as well as on the 75% minimum. This principle has long been recognized by governmental units in counting votes, and in ordinary proxy counts. Why make a section 20b case an exception?

The order on revocations, referred to above, and the handling of the revocations in connection with the Zucker assent raise questions about the application of the rule. The declaration of the intention of these two stockholders to revoke came by telephone and telegram on December 14, before the submission period closed; only the completed forms were not on hand until later.

In general, the order's emphasis on *delivery* of revocations is essential. A railroad could never be sure of its position in terminating a submission period if an unknown number of revocations still in the mail were countable. These two revocations, however, suggest a feasible modification of the rigid requirement of actual delivery. It can be argued that a timely notice by telephone or telegraph, confirmed by a signed form [64] mailed before the end of the period, would

[63] Checking postmarks is a quarterly routine in income tax payments. This case would seem to be a minor operation as compared with the income tax remittances four times a year. The postmark record would have caused some complications in the depositary's department handling incoming mail. If assents came in the envelopes furnished, the envelopes could have been readily identified and saved. But not infrequently an assent form came along with other papers; then the envelope was taken off and the papers sent to the different departments concerned. The clerks for incoming mail would have to be warned to keep all envelopes until the material inside was checked for the letter of assent. If one was found, then the envelope would be kept as evidence of mailing time.

[64] Forms in themselves have no significance except as they facilitate procedure. Even the order as it stands — "a letter of revocation in a form to be approved . . ." would not preclude a handwritten, intelligible letter over the signature of a registered stockholder and plainly interpretable as an intention

meet the same tests of a valid revocation as one actually delivered within the period. The real purpose certainly is not the form but the proper recording of the intentions of the stockholder within the submission period. The railroad would have adequate basis for declaring the period over if it had sufficient assents after allowance for the telegraphic revocation. Then if the form did not come postmarked as of a date within the period, the final total would exclude these shares and the official margin over the required percentage would be greater by so much.

In fact, as we have seen, the Railroad authorized the honoring of one of the questioned revocations and would undoubtedly have honored them both if there had been no misunderstanding of the facts. This course was taken in spite of strict instructions drawn up early in the proceedings to follow the letter of the order and count only revocations delivered within the submission period.

---

to revoke a previous assent. Note that the definition of a proper revocation does not read *"on the form"* approved.

Would the Commission or the Department hold that the depositary should not count an assent or a revocation scribbled on the back of an old envelope if it was sure of the validity of the signature and if the required information was given? A bank would honor a check written in like form as long as the signature was recognized as genuine. Old Colony did, in fact, honor three assents and one revocation, where the intentions of the holders were clear although the prescribed forms were not used.

CHAPTER VIII

The Depositary: Limits of Responsibility

RESPONSIBLE action, when applied to the functions of a depositary in balloting procedure, means punctilious observance of the rules of voting. Responsibility to an exacting degree is decisive in establishing leadership in the variety of financial services performed by a trust institution like Old Colony. The usual services of a trust institution embrace responsibilities in two broad areas, each of a different sort. In the one, judgment is involved as in the management of a securities portfolio under a trust. Here responsible action means that the managing officials as investment specialists use all available means for arriving at sound judgments. In another broad area, the one of interest in this case, the test of responsibility is knowledge of accepted procedures and an organization for accurate record-keeping as, for example, with trust accounts, transfer records, proxy counts and special votes, and dividend disbursements. In these matters, the emphasis must be on knowing what has to be done and then organizing to do it with strict accuracy. There may be no "right" answers to the institution's investment problems — only its best informed judgment; but there must be correct recording for stock transfers, proxies, and similar financial transactions.

In the performance of the usual financial services, the responsibilities of Old Colony were laid out in the instruments defining its duties, and by long-established business custom fortified by legal interpretation. Court cases over the years have established the niceties of almost every conceivable question related to rights of security holders. Procedures in the corporate trust department were set up to conform to accepted practice and the law. With this wide experience, to become the transfer agent for an additional corporation did not require study of new procedural problems, but merely the extension of an existing routine.

In these circumstances it was quite natural for Old Colony to take in stride the request that it serve as depositary in the Boston and Maine balloting. Not until the submission period was under way were the unique features of the balloting noted. It was, first of all, not a record-day procedure. How could assents be traced through to transferees when assented stock was not identified by certificate number? Still another problem arose: a Note at the bottom of the assent form apparently required evidence of authority to be furnished when the signers were fiduciaries or representatives of the real owners. Did the Note impose on the depositary any more responsibility than was required under proxy procedure?

Thus what was undertaken as just another job on customary lines suddenly turned into something new with unexpected complications and no ready answers. It was natural for the officers to turn to the source of their instructions, the Railroad. And, as new problems arose, it is clear why the officers interpreted their responsibility in terms of the established practices of their proxy experience.

This chapter is given over to an analysis of the two major charges made by the Department in putting its case that the depositary did not fulfill its responsibility: that it did not comply with the Commission's mandate in the Note on the letter of assent, and that it did not act independently as demanded in its position of trust.

THE NOTE ON THE LETTER OF ASSENT

A note at the bottom of the form letter of assent, which was approved by the Commission, read as follows:

> Note: In all cases in which the Letter of Assent is executed by an officer of a corporation, administrator, executor, trustee, guardian, agent, attorney or others acting in a fiduciary or representative capacity, proper evidence of authority to act in such capacity must be furnished.

The Facts

How did the Note get on the letter of assent form? Some such note had been placed on forms of assent used in the other section 20b cases. Mr. Everett W. Smith of the Railroad testified that the Note was taken from the form of assent used in the Lehigh Valley case.[1] He knew that the material sent to security holders in the Lehigh case had been passed on by the Commission. He testified also [2] that he looked upon the Note as a protection to the Railroad, in case questions were raised about the validity of votes. As is usual practice with counsel in drafting the forms used in financial matters, a document known to have been used in a similar case was used as a model with such adaptations as seemed necessary. Here it was taken without change, certainly with no apprehension that it would create a major issue in litigation.

Treatment of the Note during the submission period was described in the Old Colony brief [3] as follows:

The effect of this note was thoroughly considered by Old Colony and the Railroad early in the submission period when assents from executors, trustees and other fiduciaries began to come in. Although as to many of these assents Mr. McIntire knew that Old Colony had evidence of authority in its files or that he had himself seen evidence of authority, he was not certain how to treat assents of this kind. Consequently, he took the problem to Mr. Coulson, and was instructed to get the views of the Railroad on this question (Coulson, 912; McIntire, 1012). Accordingly, he called Everett Smith. Smith was aware that there were quite a few stockholders who were trustees and that, in view of the fact that no dividends had been paid on the stock, such persons generally took the position that they were perfectly willing to assent to the plan because they thought it was a good thing but they were not going to go to the expense or trouble of furnishing formal papers with the assent. He also knew that Old Colony, being the largest transfer agent in Boston, had in its files or had seen documentary evidence of the authority of a great majority of the well-known trustees. Accordingly, he suggested to Mr. McIntire that it was not necessary to request such evidences of authority from fiduciaries who did not send them with their assents (Smith, 1336).

[1] Hearing before the Examiner, August 27, 1952, p. 1337.
[2] Ibid., p. 1399.
[3] Old Colony Brief, October 20, 1952, pp. 25–27. Mr. Coulson was the executive in charge, and Mr. McIntire was the operating supervisor.

Mr. McIntire again talked to Mr. Coulson and was instructed to find out from Mr. Smith if the Railroad counsel concurred in this suggestion. Mr. McIntire did so and was informed that counsel did so concur and that, if any assent which was not accompanied by documentary evidence of authority were challenged, the Railroad would obtain the additional evidence of authority, if needed (Coulson, 913, 317; McIntire, 1012; Smith, 1337).

Mr. McIntire conveyed this information to Mr. Coulson and the latter decided that the Railroad's suggestion was a good one and would be followed. He felt, first of all, that in many cases to require formal evidence of authority would be redundant since Old Colony already had examined such documents when the stock was transferred into the name of the fiduciary concerned. As transfer agent, Old Colony had for many years required that, when stock was presented to be transferred into the name of an executor, for example, the documentary evidence of that person's authority had to be exhibited to the personnel of the transfer department (Coulson, 913, 917). Furthermore, Mr. Coulson was also aware that the stock had not paid dividends for over twenty years and sold at very low prices.

In these circumstances, it seemed to him that fiduciaries would be very reluctant to go to the bother of obtaining formal documents. He knew that in all his experience with corporate elections — it must be remembered that this operation was essentially a proxy operation and so considered by Old Colony and the Railroad — such formal evidence of authority had never been required (Coulson, 918). For these reasons, among others, it was Mr. Coulson's decision not to make any special effort to obtain documentary evidence of authority, but to adhere to the normal practice in such cases where such evidence did not accompany the assent (Coulson, 918, 919).

The Department's Charge that the Note Was Ignored

In view of later analysis it is important to note certain points in the excerpt above. The first sentence tells us that slight consideration, if indeed any at all, was given before the voting began to what the Note required. Thorough consideration, it said, started after assents began to come in. The decision was promptly reached, without consultation with the Commission, that evidence of authority need not accompany the assents. The brief further emphasized that both the depositary and the Railroad considered this assent procedure essentially a proxy operation, in which formal evidence of authority had never been required; hence, the decision was made "not to make any special effort to obtain documentary evidence of authority, but to adhere to the normal practice. . . ." The Department's charges with respect to the Note should be considered in this setting.

The Department held that because the letter of assent had been approved by the Commission, the Note was required, and for the depositary to ignore the Note, even with advice from the Railroad, was as illegal as would be sending out a piece of solicitation literature not passed on by the Commission. Here was an instance, the charge ran, where an institution responsible for being on the lookout for irregularity deliberately skipped an essential step for assuring absolute regularity, a step that was required by the Commission.

So much of the aftermath of controversy over the depositary's performance in this case centered on the charge of ignoring a mandate of the Commission that the Note can be viewed as the crux of the Department's case against Old Colony. The charge was stated as follows:

> In the course of its duties as a depositary Old Colony was confronted with a question relating to assents received from persons acting in a fiduciary or representative capacity — specifically Old Colony did not know how to act upon such assents where evidence of authority to act in such capacity did not accompany the assent. Despite the presence of a provision in the form of letter of assent approved by the Commission to the effect that proper evidence of authority "must" be submitted in such instances, Old Colony consulted the management of the railroad who advised the depositary to ignore this basic requirement. As a result, Old Colony proceeded to honor as valid any such assent in the absence of the required proper evidence.[4]   (footnotes omitted)

The Trial Brief presented a revised count of assents, which appeared to be based on the theory that all the assents received from fiduciaries were invalid. Three classes out of

[4] Department of Justice, Trial Brief, pp. 32–33.

four given in its table of results were under the required percentage, two by substantial margins. Furthermore, the column headed "Shares Voted by Fiduciaries" was explained as
reflecting "merely some of the assents received from securities
broker-dealers, who, the principal executive officer of Old
Colony stated in his testimony, acted in a representative or
fiduciary capacity. . . . Should all the instances of this departure from the Commission's requirements be tabulated, it
is beyond doubt that the deficiency figures in the table above
would be increased substantially." [5]

The Department here made a broadside charge; it attempted no analysis or precise definition of the parties acting
in "fiduciary or representative capacity" and assumed that
broker-dealers were so classified. It made no attempt to
clarify the basic issues relating to the purpose of the Note —
what constituted evidence of authority, when it must be furnished, and why broker-dealers came under the requirement.
The charge also carried the implication that the depositary's
action was not the result of its own judgment on the full
meaning of the Note; rather it followed advice by the Railroad management "to ignore this basic requirement."

In this, as in other parts of the Department's case, it is important to observe how far investigation of the procedures
was carried before the charge was formalized. The Brief
shows no evidence that the Department did more than assert its own interpretation and measure the depositary's duty
by it. Although the Department emphasized that the Note
was a requirement of the Commission, yet at no time did it
check with Division 4 of the Commission to find what was
required for full compliance. Presumably the Commission,
which authorized the requirement and had had experience
with it in its own ballot counts and in other section 20b cases,
would know its real purpose. The allegation of deliberate
departure from the Commission's "basic requirement," without preliminary inquiry of the Commission itself, again raises
the question of interagency cooperation. Granted that the
Department in its first review of the facts came to the quick
conclusion that the depositary had been remiss in not following the Note to the letter, it could readily have checked its

[5] Ibid., p. 34 (footnotes omitted) .

judgment with the Commission.   Also, the Department could have learned much from the experience of the SEC in the control of proxy machinery.

It doubtless could have learned enough to conclude that there was no basis for the serious charge that the depositary had deliberately flouted a prescribed procedure.   We can believe that such inquiry would have dissipated the charge that the depositary abused a trust, and thus have prevented the aftermath of delay, expense, and unsavory publicity.   Later analysis, in public hearing and in the reports of the Commission and Mr. L'Heureux, found the procedure followed to be reasonable and adequate for the purpose.

To answer the attack on its "competence and standing in the business world and the honesty and integrity of its officers and employees," [6] the depositary's counsel gave nearly half of their 53-page brief to this charge.   An early paragraph said:

> In the various stages of this proceeding there have been perhaps more assertions and charges based upon misinformation and misunderstanding of this subject than with respect to any other aspect of this matter.   An examination of the facts and the law will demonstrate conclusively that there is no basis for questioning Old Colony's conduct with respect to proof of authority.[7]

The issue was here clearly joined.   The Department asserted that the depositary ignored an important requirement, with the result that assents for thousands of shares were improperly counted.   The defense held that the Note, reasonably interpreted and in normal practice, was complied with in every respect.   The next sections deal with this clash of views and the findings in the Commission's final report.

Responsibility of Depositary in the Absence of a Note

The depositary's brief presented a carefully documented argument that in the absence of the Note the assents themselves constituted sufficient evidence to justify their being counted.   It was well established, said the brief, that a proxy

[6] Old Colony Brief, p. 52.

[7] Ibid., p. 25.

apparently executed by a stockholder and having the appearance of *prima facie* authenticity might be properly counted, and indeed could not be refused by election inspectors. The same principles applied to assents executed by persons purporting to be agents or representatives for stockholders of record. It was an established rule of the law of agency that if the agent was in fact authorized to act, it was immaterial whether the fact of his authority was made known to the person with whom he dealt. The presumption was that proxies were properly given in the absence of contrary evidence. The signature of one of several executors or trustees, signing on behalf of all without proof of authority, would fall into the category of signatures by representatives. In such case, proxies submitted by corporate officers or others signing on behalf of corporations, which were the stockholders of record, would be considered valid without further evidence of authority. A person signing an assent in a representative capacity impliedly represented by the very act of signing that he was authorized to act; and this representation ordinarily constituted sufficient evidence of a valid vote. Furthermore, the brief said, in reorganization cases under section 77B of the Bankruptcy Act and in cases of stockholder votes generally, the courts invariably have held that the signature on the consent or proxy of a person acting in a representative capacity constituted sufficient evidence in itself of his authority to warrant election officials in counting his vote.[8]

[8] Old Colony Brief, pp. 34–37. Cases cited were *In re Cecil*, 36 How. Pr. 477 (N.Y. 1869) ; *Atterbury* v. *Consolidated Coppermines Corp.*, 20 A (2d) 743 (Del. Ch. 1941) ; *Gow* v. *Consolidated Coppermines Corp.*, 19 Del. Ch. 172, 165 A 136 (1933) ; *In re Clark & Willow Streets Corp.*, 21 F. Supp. 43 (E.D. N.Y. 1937) ; *In re Baldwin Locomotive Works*, 21 F. Supp. 94 (E.D. Pa. 1937) ; and *In re Pressed Steel Car Co. of New Jersey*, 16 F. Supp. 329 (W.D. Pa. 1936) .

The brief referred also to two articles by Leonard H. Axe on "Corporate Proxies" (41 *Michigan Law Review* 38 and 225 (1942)), which treat the whole question of proof of authority in corporate elections and the acceptance of proxies signed by representatives. At one point (p. 61) the article comments: "Where proxies are accepted and acted upon as regular by the inspectors, and no objection is made as to the form, execution or validity, the courts have held that the proxies are entitled to be taken as regularly executed and given by persons entitled to vote. Since such evidence is sufficient to satisfy the courts that the person signing as agent had the necessary authority so to

The depositary also argued, referring especially to assents by brokers, that established business practice did not require an election judge to discover undisclosed beneficial interests represented by a stockholder of record. A record holder was entitled to vote stock registered in his name. A broker was required by exchange rules to obtain the right to vote for beneficial interests, and it could be assumed that he observed the rules.[9]

The conclusion of the brief was that accepted proxy law left no doubt that the depositary had fulfilled its responsibility in checking on valid assents.

The Purpose Served by the Note in Section 20b Situations

The question remained: did the Note require anything more than the usual proxy procedure? How did it happen that this unusual requirement of evidence of authority had become attached to section 20b balloting?

The statute makes no mention of fiduciaries or representatives or evidence of authority, but leaves the supervision of balloting to the Commission "in such manner as it shall direct." The Commission itself did not touch the subject in its general regulations.

It is when we come to the Commission's orders in specific section 20b cases that we find the first requirements concerning verification of signatures, particularly with regard to votes by bondholders. The order in the Central Railroad Company of New Jersey case, for instance, said that the form of assent might provide for verification by requiring the bonds to be identified and the signature to be guaranteed by a bank, trust company, or registered security dealer or broker.[10] The orders in the securities modifications of Montana, Wyoming & Southern Railroad Company [11] and Bangor and Aroostook Railroad Company [12] provided that the letter

---

sign, it would seem that the inspectors would be justified in drawing the inference that the person signing as agent for the stockholder had the authority or power so to sign." (footnote omitted)

9 Old Colony Brief, pp. 31, 32. Assents by brokers are discussed more fully later in this chapter.

10 271 I.C.C. 501 at 529 (1949).

11 271 I.C.C. 779 at 793 (1949).

12 275 I.C.C. 369 at 393 (1950).

of assent should contain a certificate by a bank, trust company, safe deposit company, or registered dealer or broker that it had identified the bonds and guaranteed the signature. No certificates were required, however, for bonds owned or held by insurance companies, banks, trust companies, safe deposit companies, registered dealers or brokers, or educational or charitable institutions. In other words, the verification insisted upon was as to the signatures of individual bondholders rather than as to authority of fiduciaries to act as such.

The order in the Boston and Maine case is silent on the subject of evidence of fiduciary authority. Counsel for the depositary in arguing the meaning of the Note, considered this a significant fact. Ordinarily, said the depositary's brief, there would be no occasion for the Commission to concern itself with a requirement of this sort unless it intended to depart from the normal practice in corporate elections. If the Commission intended to set up a stringent requirement, it could be expected to do so expressly and not by implication. As a practical matter, the brief continued, a requirement of formal documentary evidence would have been unduly burdensome for the Boston and Maine stock, with its record of no dividends and low market prices. The depositary urged that the Note only put signers in specified categories on notice that they might be required to furnish evidence of their authority to act.[13]

Mr. L'Heureux also held that if the Commission had intended to make conformity with the Note necessary for valid assents, it could have called special attention to this rigid requirement, or have adopted a special regulation.[14] The omission of any such directions suggested, he thought, that the Commission felt no need for unusual precautions in this situation.

The fiduciary note appears customarily in section 20b cases, as it did in this case, on the form letter of assent included with the solicitation material sent to security holders when

---

[13] Old Colony Brief, p. 30. The brief of the banking houses presented a similar argument. Brief of L. F. Rothschild & Co. and Goldman, Sachs & Co., October 17, 1952, p. 4.

[14] L'Heureux, Opinion, p. 46.

balloting starts. Although the wording may vary slightly from case to case, the typical form letter from the beginning has called for evidence of authority. Whether or not it has supervised the drafting of the forms, the Commission has always insisted upon their inclusion in the material submitted for approval. What, then, does the Commission's approval of the form of letter of assent imply?

The statute covers succinctly the matter of the Commission's approval of solicitation material:

> . . . All letters, circulars, advertisements, and other communications, and all financial and statistical statements, or summaries thereof, to be used in soliciting the assents or the opposition of such holders shall, before being so used, be submitted to the Commission for its approval as to correctness and sufficiency of the material facts stated therein. . . .

The reasonable interpretation of this sentence is that it refers solely to statements and supporting data intended to convince the stockholder that he should assent or oppose. Only solicitation material in the strict sense is what the Commission must approve. It must be sure that the stockholder has all he needs to know, without distortion, for reaching an informed decision. The statute was concerned with how a railroad put its case before the stockholder, not with the mechanics of tabulation of the vote.[15] The note directing fiduciary authority to be furnished certainly would not be included in the material facts submitted to give adequate basis for the stockholder's decision.

The Commission's order in this case follows the statute closely. Its letter of July 13, 1950, approving the material submitted by the Railroad, states that "it has approved as to the correctness and sufficiency of the material facts stated therein the proposed documents enumerated in the first paragraph of this letter." [16] The forms of letters of assent and revocation were in no sense a part of the material to help the stockholder to reach his decision. They were included obvi-

---

[15] The S.E.C. has given special attention to proxy solicitation, with the result that Regulation X–14 controls in meticulous detail the use of proxies. In all its concern in such matters there is no attention paid to the mechanics of counting that the Department holds that the I.C.C. was so insistent upon.

[16] Quoted from Old Colony Brief, p. 30.

ously to make it easy for him to register his opinion, and were presumably approved as such when all the material in the case was approved.

From language used in other section 20b cases calling for submission of forms of letters, the inference seems justified that examination for approval need not be so meticulous as it is for solicitation material. For instance, the order in the securities modification of the Lehigh Valley Railroad Company refers to "a copy of a form of letter of assent for bonds or for stockholders as the case may be, in substantially the form submitted with the supplement to the application." [17]

Our analysis so far supports the defense of the depositary that "the note on the bottom of the assent form does not state a requirement of the Commission." Whether one argues, as did the depositary, that the care to be exercised by the Commission applies only to approval of the correctness and sufficiency of the material facts (obviously not the Note) or whether one puts emphasis on the point that the letter of assent is not solicitation material, it is still debatable whether the Commission intended to insist upon literal compliance with the Note.

Counsel for the banking houses pushed the subject even further in denying that the Note required anything more than the usual proxy procedure. They presented a highly technical legal argument to deny the right to anybody, even including the Commission, to challenge the authority of one signing in a fiduciary or representative capacity, unless the objection be made "by the beneficial owner of the stock and then only if the objection is timely made." [18] By a series of quotations from legal treatises, state laws, and court decisions, counsel stated their unqualified conclusion that

> . . . If anyone suffers because of what the "fiduciary" does or fails to do without authority, it is the beneficiary of the trust. Only the beneficiary can claim injury because of the trustee's misfeasance or nonfeasance, and so only the beneficiary can sue to enjoin the fiduciary or obtain redress. Third parties, as a consequence, have no standing whatsoever to raise the issue of the fiduciary's lack of authority.[19]

[17] 271 I.C.C. 553 at 598 (1949).
[18] L. F. Rothschild & Co., and Goldman, Sachs & Co., Brief, p. 8.
[19] Ibid., p. 10.

Counsel further argued that the Note requiring evidence of fiduciary authority was not a rule of procedure laid down by the Commission, and concluded:

> Old Colony and the Railroad were, therefore, completely justified in treating the legend as being for the protection of the Railroad in case a beneficial owner challenged the assent executed by his record holder.[20]

This line of argument is far from convincing. First, it is palpably wrong in a recapitalization proceeding to say that the beneficiary of a particular trust is the *only* one to suffer if his trustee exceeds his authority in voting on the plan. *All* security holders, whether individual holders or beneficiaries under a trust, have an interest in having only valid assents counted. It would work a rank injustice for a plan to go through when some fiduciaries had voted without authority but challenge was prevented by a legal technicality that objections were not made by the beneficiaries under trust agreements. The conclusion reached by counsel for the bankers would even preclude the Commission from raising the issue of the fiduciary's lack of authority, it being a third party and having "no standing whatsoever."

To follow this line of argument is to place the Commission in an impotent position in fulfilling its responsibility. Suppose the beneficiaries do not bestir themselves to protest, is the Commission obliged to remain blind to balloting without authority? Does the statute charge the Commission with a responsibility that it cannot legally fulfill? If the fiduciary votes without authority and a beneficial owner does not challenge, what then? The conclusion from the brief seems to be that the Commission would have no interest in a breach of fiduciary power if the beneficial owner was not alert enough to challenge it. This interpretation, based upon a technical point in trust law, implies an attitude of the Commission blind to the public interest.

Counsel further states that "If the Commission had meant to require the furnishing of evidence of authority — an unusual and burdensome requirement . . . it should have done so by a specific provision. . . ."[21] Presumably only in

[20] Ibid.
[21] Ibid., p. 4.

the event of a specific requirement in the order would they admit the right of the Commission to question the validity of a fiduciary's assent.

The brief for the banking houses stretches a technical rule of law to the breaking point. It is one thing to say that the Note was ambiguous as to the time factor and the type of evidence required, and that its real purpose could be fulfilled without the presentation of formal documents along with the letter of assent. It is quite another to say that *nobody* could legally challenge an improper fiduciary assent but the beneficiary of the trust served by the fiduciary. Although the Commission approves an official depositary in section 20b cases, there is no basis for concluding that it would ignore the need for fiduciaries to show authority, and place itself in the position of saying to beneficiaries: "You watch your own interest; if you don't complain when the trustee exceeds his authority, we can do nothing."

Some such reasoning as this undoubtedly underlies the Commission's unwillingness to accept the argument that normal proxy procedures are adequate to protect the rights of all parties in balloting on recapitalization in section 20b cases. The Commission regards these votes as so important to the public interest that special care must be exercised by fiduciaries and representatives in furnishing evidence of their authority to sign. The note on the form letter of assent underscores the need for care.

In the Boston and Maine case, therefore, after study of the briefs submitted in October 1952, the Commission stated that the Note was intended to mean something more than accepted proxy practice. At the same time, the Commission concluded that the depositary had, in fact, made substantial compliance with the Note. Although this finding does not furnish the firm direction for future cases that we should like to see, it furnishes a basis for clarification of the rule in future cases. The Commission said, in its final report of April 21, 1953:

> The material transmitted by the carrier to the Commission included, among other things, the form of assent upon which was the paragraph requiring that proper evidence of author-

ity to act be furnished in certain instances. The submission of such material evidenced the carrier's intention to submit the plan in the manner set forth by the documents, and such was the manner of submission approved by the letter of July 13, 1950. The order of April 19, 1950, specified clearly that the submission should be made by mailing, among other things, "a form of letter of assent." We believe the foregoing evidences a clear intention that in connection with the voting on the plan, "proper evidence of authority to act" should be furnished by the security holders of the nature specified, and that such a manner of submission was directed by the April 19, 1950, order.

*   *   *   *   *

While, undoubtedly, these propositions [Old Colony's propositions concerning normal proxy procedure] are true as general principles applicable to the use of proxies in the conduct of ordinary corporate elections, we are unable to agree that they may be extended without reservation to govern the situation with which Old Colony was confronted under the circumstances of this case. In our opinion, it was incumbent on Old Colony to have or to procure "proper evidence of authority" in those instances where it was apparent or there was reason to believe that a letter of assent was executed and submitted by a person acting in a representative capacity.[22]

The Meaning of "Fiduciary or Representative"

Before we examine the arguments as to whether the depositary did fulfill its responsibilities, it is essential to develop precise meanings so that the parties to whom the Note applies can be identified. At no point in the whole record of the case was the importance of these definitions squarely faced, so that the Commission's final report does not make it entirely clear whether evidence of authority was to be demanded of brokers signing as holders of record.

The Note lists various individuals as acting in a fiduciary or representative capacity when they execute an assent. For these, proper evidence of authority to act must be furnished. Here we are concerned only with how the depositary identi-

[22] 282 I.C.C. 750 at 760–762 (1953).

fies signers in such capacity; a later section considers what constitutes proper evidence of authority so to act.

The first problem for the depositary is to know who signs assents as fiduciaries or representatives. The answer comes from the stockholders' ledger cards. Those who sign as owners in their own names present no problem of authority.

A large group, known to the transfer agent (here also the depositary) as fiduciaries, sign in their fiduciary capacity: John Doe, Trustee, or Executor, Administrator, or other title named in a formal instrument of which the depositary is advised. These are the documents that constitute the evidence referred to in the Note. The ledger cards show on their face that the stock is held in the name of the fiduciary.

Still another class of signer comprises those who are not fiduciaries in the strict legal sense, but merely representatives in that they sign for the real owners. The officer of a corporation, mentioned first in the Note, "executes" the assent as the authorized signer for his company, which retains the power to vote the stock. So, also, various agents and attorneys on occasion are designated by the real owners to execute the letter of assent. These are not fiduciaries in the legal sense, in that they have no established relation as in a trust instrument, which names a trustee who acts for the beneficiaries. In these instances the ledger card does not show the name of the one who signs.

Although the distinction made here between fiduciaries and mere representative signers is not made in the briefs submitted in the case,[23] it helps to clear the discussion to read the note as referring to two classes: fiduciaries and those designated to represent real owners by signing.[24]

[23] An exchange recorded in the Deposition of Raymond A. McIntire, Boston, October 17, 1951, pp. 23–24, also illustrates this point. "Mr. Leonard, [Old Colony Counsel]: What is the language, representative or fiduciary? Mr. Gorman [Department of Justice]: I believe yesterday you tossed the word fiduciary around, I prefer representative. Mr. Leonard: Wait just a minute, so that we know what we are talking about, at the start of the hearing my understanding was the word fiduciary was to include brokers as well as the word representative which Mr. Donnelly put in. I think when I directed questions to Mr. Coulson I used fiduciary as a broker. . . ."

[24] Such a distinction is clearly established in the note (quoted later in this chapter) at the bottom of the ballot used in 1950 in the Missouri Pacific Rail-

The parties comprehended in the Note would appear in diagrammatic form as follows:

Signers of Assents who are acting for others

A

In a fiduciary capacity

| Administrators | Executors | Trustees | Guardians | "and others" |

The stockholder's ledger card reveals the fiduciary relationship; normally documents have been filed already to furnish authority for transfers and other acts of the fiduciary.

B

As representing the real owner

| Officers of corporation (or other body) | Agents | Attorneys | "and others" |

The stockholder's ledger card carries the name of the real owner; the signer of the assent has been authorized to sign for the real owner, i.e., as an officer of the company, a member of a firm, or an agent of the real owner; normally signature cards indicating the authorization have been filed already.

The Note made no mention of brokers. If the Commission had them in mind when it passed on the Note, they were included in the catch-all phrase "and others," or "as agent." Knowing, as it presumably did, that brokers' holdings were large, particularly of the speculative common stock, the Commission could have been expected to make brokers a special case if the question of their authority was of particular importance.

The relationship between brokers and their customers raises troublesome questions as regards "proof of authority." When, for example, Doe & Company is the record holder of 1,000 shares of Boston and Maine common stock, the whole lot may well be owned beneficially by many customers whose holdings are pooled or "commingled" in the broker's name, the street name, for convenience. By the rules of the exchanges, the broker must get its authority to assent from each of the beneficial owners. The broker is a representative

road Company reorganization, pursuant to section 77. Finance Docket No. 9918.

signer. It is not a fiduciary, holding Boston and Maine stock as part of a portfolio under a trust instrument, which would enable it to vote the stock as a part of a trustee's function. The assents in this case are merely incident to the fundamental broker relationship with customers.

This problem of broker classification — fiduciary or mere representative? — is decisive in the question raised about proof of authority to be demanded by the depositary. If the broker is a mere representative of its customers, it does what they say. It does not vote their stock independently.

In an additional sense, too, the signature may be considered representative. A partner in the brokerage firm signs for the firm. In the case of the broker, then, who holds stock in its street name for customers, there are really two separate steps in its role as representative: the broker represents the voting choice of the beneficial owners, and the partner signs the letter of assent as representative of the firm. There are not these two steps in the usual fiduciary relationship.

Proper Evidence of Authority: Timeliness

Vital questions in this analysis are concerned with what constitutes evidence and when evidence must be furnished. The note reads simply, "proper evidence" and "must be furnished," with no time designated. The Department's charge of the depositary's laxity was based on the interpretation that documentary evidence of authority must *accompany* the assent.

One essential issue is whether the depositary had the means of finding out the credentials of the signers if papers of authority did not accompany the letter of assent. It would seem that any reasonable interpretation of the words would not require a contemporaneous show of authority if proper papers were already in the trust company's files. It could be assumed that the officers of the depositary, where fiduciary signatures passed the desks daily, would act in the usual way. It is inconceivable that they would call for repeated "show of authority" by a fiduciary who had several transactions over a period of time. In the ordinary proxy procedure, it was the usual practice to accept proxies signed by fiduciaries as valid if evidence of authority was already on file.

It is helpful further to examine the use of a similar foot-note on ballots sent out by the Commission in its supervision of voting in section 77 cases. This would seem an obvious topic for research by the brief-writers concerned with this phase of the dispute. It is hard to explain why the antecedents of the Note were not studied by any of the parties to the litigation. Inasmuch as the Note on the Boston and Maine letter of assent was modeled after the Lehigh letter, which in turn traces back to the first letter of assent in a section 20b case, it is reasonable to suppose that the first note requiring authority of fiduciaries or representatives followed the form and purpose of a similar note on the ballots long used in the section 77 plans.

For example, ballots in the Missouri Pacific Railroad Company reorganization,[25] pursuant to section 77 of the Bankruptcy Act, were sent to the holders of record on December 1, 1950, of 15 classes of securities or claims. At the bottom of each ballot, the following note appeared:

> If the signature is by any person other than the owner of the claim, or by an owner in receivership or bankruptcy, he must attach hereto a copy of his power of attorney or other appropriate authorization. If the person executing this ballot holds said claim as receiver, administrator, executor, or trustee, he must furnish documentary evidence of his authority to execute the ballot.

The phrase, "he must attach hereto," obviously demands contemporaneous show of authority; and "he must furnish documentary evidence of his authority to execute the ballot" implies an action contemporaneous with the execution of the ballot, which is not expressed by the phrase in the Boston and Maine letter, "proper evidence . . . must be furnished." One cannot say whether this distinction in the precise wording had purpose or was an accidental variance. There is a significant difference, however, between the status of the Commission as the responsible party under section 77 for certifying the correct percentages of "accepts" and "rejects" of a plan, and the status of the official depositary of assents under section 20b proceedings. When the Commission acts

[25] Finance Docket No. 9918.

as depositary, it has had no previous connection with security holders, whether individual, institutional, corporate, or fiduciary, and therefore has no evidence of authority in its files. For this reason, when an "accept" or a "reject" is received, the authority of a fiduciary or representative must accompany the ballot to give the Commission a valid basis for recording the vote.

In section 20b proceedings, however, the most likely depositary would be the transfer agent, where the lists of holders are already held and where most holders, if fiduciaries or in like capacity, have previously filed evidence of authority. Such evidence is considered sufficient for recurring transactions, of which an assent on a section 20b plan would be only one.   A reasonable interpretation of full responsibility for certification in a section 20b case would seem not to require contemporaneous submission of authority in executing an assent.

An interesting variant in the section 20b proceedings of the Maryland & Pennsylvania Railroad Company [26] supports this conclusion quite pointedly.   The assents of the common stockholders were to be sent to the railroad company itself, while the assents for the bonds were to be sent to the trust department of the Baltimore National Bank, Depositary. At the bottom of the letter of assent for the stock was the note: "In all cases in which the Letter of Assent is executed by . . . or others acting in a fiduciary or representative capacity, proper evidence of authority to act in such capacity must be furnished *unless already on file with the Company.*" (italics added) The last phrase fully supports this analysis of the purpose of the Note: that the requirement is satisfied if the signatures of fiduciaries are validated by proper documents, sent along with the assent itself unless previously filed with the same depositary.

Old Colony's brief went further than this in the matter of time of filing, and argued that under the terms of the Note evidence of authority could be furnished at any time. "Typically in fact," it said, "in corporate elections the proof is furnished after the votes are all in and when some question is raised. The only purpose served by obtaining such proof is to establish that the apparent authority of the person sign-

[26] 275 I.C.C. 695 (1950), Finance Docket No. 17035.

ing existed in fact. Proof submitted after the vote has been received serves to establish the fact of real authority as well as proof submitted earlier." [27] It added later: "In this connection it is significant that at no time throughout the course of these proceedings to date has any specific assent signed by a person acting in a representative capacity been challenged." [28]

The majority of the Commission accepted Old Colony's position on this issue, finding that the latter "had in its possession or obtained proper evidence of authority" for all except a negligible number of shares.[29]

One Commissioner, however, dissenting, believed that those assents should be ruled out for which evidence was obtained after the close of voting.[30] He gave no reason for his dissent on this point. Let us suppose that the total vote failed to reach the statutory percentage in one or another class by the margin of those ballots the Commissioner would rule out because evidence of authority was not established before the voting closed. It is hard to believe that any court would uphold the failure of the plan on that account. The statute reads, "If the Commission shall find . . . the proposed . . . modification has been assented to by the holders of at least 75 per centum of the aggregate principal amount. . . ." If, in fact, such was here the case, even though certain ballots were not established as valid until after the period closed, on what basis could a court hold that the intention of the law was not met? If the court ruled against the plan, what part of the blame for the technical failure should lie with the Commission itself? Granted that the rules should be explicit in establishing the validity of ballots while the voting goes on, it would be clearly inequitable to the 75% who legally assented to have their vote on a fair plan nullified because of an irrelevant technicality.

Proper Evidence of Authority: Substance

The subject of proper evidence covers more than the matter of the time when the evidence is furnished; it also includes the type of evidence. In the words of the depositary's

27 Old Colony Brief, p. 32.
28 Ibid., p. 38.
29 282 I.C.C. 750 at 764 (1953).
30 Ibid., p. 800.

counsel: "To an extent perfectly amazing . . . it seems to have been assumed that 'proper evidence' can mean only formal documentary evidence." [31]

Fiduciary papers would be evidence that no one would question, whether presented with the letter of assent or already filed. An officer of the depositary testified that before stock could be transferred into the name of an executor, guardian, or administrator, the transfer department was obliged to examine certificates of appointment or similar fiduciary papers.[32] Therefore, all fiduciaries who were stockholders of record must already have made an adequate show of authority.

He admitted that in a few instances there were no papers. Such a case would be one where a successor trustee had not had the stock transferred into his name. The officer pointed out, however, that in such cases the solicitation material would have been mailed to the preceding trustee as the registered holder, who then passed it on, so that the form letter of assent would have come into the successor's hands only by legitimate channels.[33] It is not clear why in these cases the successor trustee did not promptly establish his authority and why the depositary did not insist that he do so.

A second category of evidence included signature cards already on file with the depositary, identifying the signatures of certain officers as authorized to sign for corporations and for brokerage firms, the registered owners of stock. All brokers who were members of the New York or Boston Stock Exchanges had filed such signature cards.

Another class of evidence also applied to representatives. Many corporations had filed with the depositary votes of the boards of directors authorizing certain officers to sell, assign, or transfer securities. In other cases, as with The Pennroad Corporation, the assent was accompanied by a vote of the Board of Directors authorizing the assent.

Beyond all these, the depositary accepted as evidence in other cases the fact that Mr. McIntire, the operating supervisor, knew the signature of the fiduciary or representative

---

[31] Old Colony Brief, p. 33.
[32] Hearing before the Examiner, August 25, 1952, p. 914.
[33] Ibid., p. 916.

signing and knew the person himself, either personally or through past dealings or both, and also his authority. The depositary argued that it had never been true either in the business world or in court that proper evidence meant only formal documentary evidence. Evidence of the authority of a person to act in a fiduciary or representative capacity could be found in the knowledge obtained through a long period of business dealings with the person, and found more reliably in this way than from documents provided with an immediate transaction.[34]

After the certification of assents had been challenged, counsel for the depositary supervised an extensive check of the assents by fiduciaries and representatives, obtaining papers for most of those not previously covered. Many of these cases, however, were in the category of persons known to the supervisor.

As for the evidence to be required of brokers, counsel for the depositary held that a broker was not a fiduciary and the Note had no application:

> An assent purporting to be signed by a holder of record who is not a fiduciary does not fall within any of the categories listed in the note. It would impose an unreasonable and indeed intolerable burden on the election judge to require him to seek to discover undisclosed beneficial interests represented by a holder of record. Established business practice recognized in the law dealing with corporate elections precludes the imposition of any such requirement. . . .
>
> This is especially important in the case of assents signed by brokers. The latter frequently hold stock as part of their own portfolio as well as beneficially for their customers. Where the broker is the record holder, there is no way to tell where the beneficial interest lies.[35]

The brief of other interveners held the same opinion.[36] Mr. L'Heureux also treated assents by brokers in a separate

[34] Old Colony Brief, p. 34.

[35] Ibid., p. 31.

[36] See brief of L. F. Rothschild & Co. and Goldman, Sachs & Co., p. 6. "Presumably the legend on the form of assent did not in any event refer to brokers assenting stock held for the account of customers since brokers in that category are not 'acting in a fiduciary or representative capacity' within the

category from fiduciaries, citing it to be the universal practice not to require them to show proof of authority.[37]

This discussion leads to one important conclusion to be held in mind when the phrase "acting in a representative capacity" is used. Stock assented by brokers for beneficial owners is a case in point. When the brokerage firm sends an assent on stock that it holds for its customers beneficially, but in its own name, it represents their expressed will as to the plan voted on but it is not compelled by business custom to disclose that fact.[38] Nor is the depositary obliged to look back of the fact that the stockholder of record, in this case a broker, has voted. The important thing for the depositary to check is the authority of the signer to represent the brokerage firm. This second meaning of signing in a representative capacity is the applicable one in the case of brokers' assents.

The Figures on Shares Assented by Fiduciaries and Representatives

Exhibit 8 summarizes figures compiled by a witness for the Commission's Bureau of Inquiry and by the depositary to present at the hearing in 1952 the number of shares assented by fiduciaries and representatives of stockholders. The Bureau's tabulation [39] amounted to a large percentage

---

ordinary meaning of those words. Neither Old Colony nor the Railroad could possibly tell whether an assent signed by a brokerage house represented stock owned by the brokerage house or stock owned by customers."

This is unquestionably true, because the broker is a stockholder of record and signs as such. The real question here is whether the Note on the letter of assent required the broker to do anything more to show that it had authority from its customers for whom it held the stock.

[37] L'Heureux, Opinion, p. 48.

[38] The fact that brokers generally in the Boston and Maine balloting assented part of their holdings and not all may be taken to indicate that they conformed to the Stock Exchange rules. Their reliance on instructions from the beneficial owners is also shown by the following excerpt from a letter dated October 9, 1950, to Mr. Everett W. Smith from Mr. Nye of Georgeson & Co. (quoted in the Department's Trial Brief, p. 23): ". . . So far we have only solicited brokers plus two or three larger stockholders where I had an entree. I think we sent up around 4,000 shares that we have gotten from brokers. I think we're going to get another 700 Common and 50 Preferred and I understand there are a few odd lots around the Street where the brokers are authorized to vote but probably not as much as 200 shares."

[39] Exhibit H–49 in the 1952 Hearings before the Examiner.

of the total shares assented, because it included all shares assented by dealers or brokers as well as those assented by such fiduciaries as executors or administrators. The depositary replied with figures [40] on the number of shares assented by fiduciaries for whom documents were contemporaneously presented or already on file and those assented by officers whose signature cards were on file. On this basis there was no question as to the adequacy of the number of assented shares in the prior preference and common classes, but there was a deficiency of 663.75 shares in the first preferred class and one of 643.26 shares in the plain preferred class.

The depositary contended that it had proper evidence of fiduciary authority on all but a minute number of the remaining assented shares. One large category, amply covering the deficiencies noted above, was made up of the shares assented by persons whose identity and authority were known to the operating supervisor through a long course of business dealings.[41] Beyond this large category, there was a group of shares for which documentary evidence was obtained after the close of the submission period. This evidence, said the depositary, was as valid as evidence on file during the period. An additional group was assented by registered owners, most of them brokers or nominees, called representatives in the Bureau's tabulation but not represented by signature cards or other papers. The depositary's position was that all assents by owners of record when not registered as fiduciaries were acceptable without further proof.

Although it seems reasonable to accept the adequacy of personal knowledge in this instance, as the Commission did, this decision should not be a precedent for exceptions to a rule on proper authority to sign. The validity of an assent in cases of fiduciaries or representatives should be a matter of documentary proof and not merely of personal identification. The aim of adequate regulations is to produce a dependable result regardless of the personal knowledge of the supervisor of the vote counting operation. An adequate procedure should be the same whether the supervisor is entirely new to the job or, as in this case, one whose personal knowledge of fiduciaries and signatures is extensive.

[40] Exhibit H–70 in the 1952 Hearings before the Examiner.
[41] Exhibit H–71 in the 1952 Hearings before the Examiner.

EXHIBIT 8. TABULATION OF ASSENTS BY FIDUCIARIES AND REPRESENTATIVES, SHOWING ALLEGED DEFICIENCY IN TWO CLASSES AND THE CATEGORIES OF ASSENTS AVAILABLE FOR MEETING THEM

	Prior Preference	First Preferred	Plain Preferred	Common
Total number of assented shares, as certified	198,665	308,445	27,674	302,430
Shares assented by fiduciaries or representatives, and brokers or registered owners *	138,550	174,877	24,142	246,370
Number of assented shares to meet the required percentages	172,060.5	290,874.75	27,403.26	296,046
Minus: shares not assented by fiduciaries, etc. †	60,115.0	133,568.00	3,532.00	56,060
Additional assented shares needed to meet percentages	111,945.5	157,306.75	23,871.26	239,986
Fiduciary, etc., assents for which documents or signatures were filed contemporaneously or previously ‡	126,885.0	156,643.00	23,228.00	244,581
Excess or (deficiency) of assented shares	14,939.5	(663.75)	(643.26)	4,595
Shares assented by persons known to supervisor §	7,000	8,033	775	1,119
Shares for which documents were obtained after the submission period ‖	112	2,738	125	370
Shares assented by registered owners, said to represent stockholders, without documents	4,542	7,407	14	272
Shares assented by fiduciaries, without documents	11	56	0	28

* From Exhibit H–49 of the Bureau of Inquiry in the 1952 Hearings before the Examiner.
† These figures were obtained by subtracting the shares assented by fiduciaries, etc. from the total assented shares.
‡ From Exhibit H–70 in the 1952 Hearings before the Examiner.
§ From Exhibit H–71 in the 1952 Hearings before the Examiner.
‖ The total number of shares for which papers were obtained after the close of the submission period was as follows: prior preference, 6,203; first preferred, 7,668; plain preferred, 871; common, 1,385. (From Hearing before the Examiner, 1952, p. 1728.) Most of these shares, however, have been included already in the tabulation under "Shares assented by persons known to supervisor."

Source: Compiled from Exhibits H–49, H–70, H–71, and the summary in the Commission's report, 282 I.C.C. 750 at 763 (April 21, 1953).

The Commission's final evaluation of the evidence on fiduciary assents, based upon its consideration of both the time of furnishing and the type of evidence, follows:

> It is apparent that, under a reasonable interpretation of the note on the letter of assent, Old Colony possessed or obtained "proper evidence" of authority of all persons who could logically be classified as fiduciaries or representatives of stockholders whose assents they signed. It is significant that . . . throughout the course of these proceedings no specific assent has been challenged upon the ground that it was signed by someone not properly authorized to do so.
>
> . . . We also conclude and find that Old Colony had in its possession or obtained proper evidence of authority of persons acting in a representative or fiduciary capacity to give their assents to stock owned by others, and that except for the negligible number of shares shown in item No. 11 of the table, none of the assents affected by the question of fiduciary authority should be excluded.[42]

INDEPENDENCE OF THE DEPOSITARY

The Department's charge that the depositary did not act independently was based on three situations in which its officers took highly important matters to the Railroad for advice, and on the fact that neither on these matters nor on any others did they consult the Commission.[43] The Department

---

[42] 282 I.C.C. 750 at 764 (1953). Item No. 11 was the "Shares assented by fiduciaries, without documents." Mr. L'Heureux's conclusions were (Opinion, p. 48) : "In the case of assents signed by brokers, it is the universal practice not to require proof of authority. . . . Old Colony was expected to follow the business custom in this instance. . . . It is inconceivable that the I.C.C. would not regard as valid, letters of assent that were simply not accompanied by proof of fiduciary authority although such evidence existed and was known to exist by officials of Old Colony Trust. Not one such case was challenged by the Justice Department nor anyone else on the ground that the authority to vote the stock was not actually possessed by the fiduciary."

[43] The Trial Brief also made some issue of the fact that Mr. T. J. Coolidge was a director of the Railroad, of Old Colony, and of the First National Bank of Boston; and that Mr. French, president of the Railroad until April 1952, was a director of both the Railroad and the First National Bank. Since the Railroad's board consisted of 19 members and the other two of 25 members each, it is difficult to argue that either Mr. Coolidge or Mr. French could control the boards. In addition, Mr. Coolidge testified that he had no conversa-

therefore drew the conclusion that the depositary was not in fact acting independently but was, on the contrary, "highly dependent upon the railroad management." [44]

Implicit in these charges is the assumption that the depositary had to be strictly independent of the Railroad in the recording operation.   The Trial Brief gives no authority for this assumption.   The statute makes no mention even of the depositary arrangement.   In the Commission's order submitting the plan to vote, as in all the section 20b orders, the depositary was not called an "independent depositary" but "the applicant's designated depositary."   A plausible explanation for the Department's making so much point of the "independence" of action by the depositary is that the word certificate perhaps suggested the auditor's certificate, and the idea of strict independence in the auditor's role was carried over in its concept of the depositary function.

The depositary's function is not described in the order in terms of strict independence.   The certificate for the total vote cast was made the responsibility of the applicant, supported by the depositary's certificate.   Every reference to the depositary in the order implied that it was acting as the Railroad's agent, selected by it as satisfactory to the Commission; it was selected presumably because a corporate trust department, being a specialist in proxy matters and with all records at hand, was better fitted than the applicant itself to do the job.   Although the Commission itself acted as depositary in section 77 cases, it decided to delegate this responsibility in the section 20b cases.

That the Railroad interpreted the relation of the depositary as one of a specialist acting as the Railroad's agent is indicated by the letter of instructions referred to previously. The letter outlined in detail the over-all procedure to give effect to the Commission's order.   The Railroad's officer would hardly write such a letter to its independent auditor with regard to a review of accounts.   This is not to say that the depositary should not be independent in the sense that it would assert its opinion on the validity of ballots.   Its in-

tions with the bank officers relative to the counting of assents.   (Hearing before the Examiner, August 27, 1952, p. 1254.)

[44] Department of Justice, Trial Brief, p. 37.

dependence would insist on honest performance, as would be expected of any operating officer within an organization. An accountant in a controller's office, for example, would be expected to assert his independence by resisting an order to misstate facts, but he is still not independent in the sense of being an outside auditor.

That the Commission itself did not think of the depositary as analogous to the independent auditor is shown by the fact that the order in one of the section 20b cases made the applicant itself the depositary for the common stock ballots.[45] Presumably, if independence were so important a consideration as regards the depositary function, the Commission would have made its orders explicit with a clear directive to the depositary that it was not an agent of the Railroad but was an outside auditor completely insulated from the influence of Railroad officers. Viewed in this light, the Department's charges that the depositary lacked independence were of the "straw man" variety.[46]

Of the three instances of alleged lack of independence, the first concerned the decisions on the handling of the fiduciary note. The depositary's officers agreed that they had consulted the officers of the Railroad, but they did not consider this a mandatory step. They maintained that they themselves made the final decision on policy. The second problem on which the depositary turned to the Railroad was presented in the troublesome situations where a broker assented less

[45] Maryland & Pennsylvania Railroad Company Securities Modification, 275 I.C.C. 695 at 721 (1950). Assents from holders of securities other than the capital stock were to be sent to a depositary satisfactory to the Commission and not connected with the applicant. Several other orders call for assents to be sent to the applicant, in care of the depositary. It might be noted that Maine Central Railroad Company, whose application was denied with the result that no order was ever issued, proposed that the depositary report and certify directly to the Commission. (275 I.C.C. 261 at 265 (1950)). None of the orders contains such a provision, however.

[46] The Department's intention to make its own study of balloting procedures, performance of the depositary, and other problems, without consultation with the Commission on any point, suggests that it believed that objective conclusions could best be reached by its own independent analysis. In this instance this isolated approach led it to establish a requirement not expressed in the law or rules and not known to be the intent of the Commission itself.

than his record holdings and then sold part of his holdings. Officers of the depositary talked this problem over with Railroad officers, but maintained again that they made their own decision.

The third instance was a small technical deviation from the letter of the Commission's order. The letter of assent stated that revocation could be effected on a form to be obtained from either the depositary or the Railroad. In fact, the depositary never was supplied with such forms. It referred requests to the Railroad management, which promptly supplied the forms to the stockholders. The particular complaint by the Department was that the Railroad management would learn of the intended revocation and thereby be "given an uncalled-for opportunity to renew its solicitation with respect to the subject stockholder." [47]   Of course, even if the depositary had kept a supply of revocation forms, the Railroad could still find out about any stockholder's request for the form and follow with a second solicitation. Even so, how this would offend the statute in either letter or spirit is not revealed. Railroad officials were permitted by the Commission's order to solicit assents; they were not forbidden to solicit the same person twice or even more. Of the three instances described by the Department as examples of the depositary's lack of independence, this last suggests straining to bolster a case.

A review of these three episodes can lead only to the conclusion reached by the Commission:

> In summary, there is no evidence that the railroad attempted to dominate Old Colony in the exercise of its functions as a depositary; nor is there any evidence that Old Colony was subjected to or yielded to any such influences. [48]

One incident, not mentioned by either the Department or the Commission in this connection, calls for comment. In spite of the letter of instructions that only revocations received within the period could be counted, the Railroad authorized that the Zucker revocation be honored, and the depositary did so, explaining that ". . . if the Railroad de-

[47] Department of Justice, Trial Brief, p. 37.
[48] 282 I.C.C. 750 at 797 (1953).

sired to 'lean over backwards,' [it] would go along with this desire." [49]   Was it not the duty of an independent depositary to determine for itself the voting status of such a revocation and to handle it accordingly?

The Trial Brief did make a significant observation in noting the lack of close communication between depositary, Railroad, *and* Commission on all procedural matters.   Obviously, if the order of the Commission could be expected to cover all possible situations, no questions would arise.   The fact that questions of procedure did come up shows that circumstances arose not anticipated by the order.   In this event it would seem to be natural for the Railroad and the depositary to go to the source of the order, the Commission, for clarification. Consultation between the Railroad and the depositary would not be foreclosed thereby; but the depositary's officers must have known that the Commission had long experience in balloting matters and recent experience in other section 20b cases.   On the other hand, can the depositary be held to have failed in a duty when the Commission did not provide for receiving prompt information on unexpected problems?

All this raises a basic question of the proper organizational relationship among the parties in the operation, in order to avoid the unilateral decisions that the Department here complains of.   When the statute reads: "the Commission shall cause the carrier, in such manner as it shall direct, to submit . . . to the holders of each class of its securities . . . for acceptance or rejection," the responsibility seems directly placed with the Commission to provide administrative devices for finding answers to problems when they first arise.

SUMMARY AND CONCLUSIONS

What conclusions derive from these two chapters on the Department's charges against the depositary?

The first conclusion is that the record reveals nothing to reflect against the full intention of the depositary to fulfill its responsibility as a fiduciary.   A clear distinction must emphatically be made, and one not always made in the Department's Trial Brief, between honest mistakes and "slipshod

[49] Old Colony Brief, p. 51.

operation." It is one thing to question the adequacy of a procedure and another to imply that all inadequacies are due to irresponsibility or incompetence.[50]

Mr. L'Heureux gave his opinion that ". . . the proof conclusively shows that Old Colony Trust acted with the greatest efficiency and according to the highest standards and traditions of the great financial institution which it unquestionably is." [51] One week later (April 21, 1953) the Commission itself, on the basis of the entire record, without exception cleared Old Colony of the charges brought against it by the Department. The system was adequate, even including the troublesome record-keeping when brokers assented less than their total holdings; Old Colony fulfilled the "reasonable" requirements of the Note on the letter of assent. The whole tenor of the Commission's report, as it concerned the depositary, attested to a performance above criticism.

Are we to conclude from these reports that if the Commission were to issue an order tomorrow for another section 20b procedure it would not change any part of the system for recording assents? Its final report implies as much. From the Commission's whole analysis, only one suggestion for change in the depositary arrangement comes out: "The record before us raises a question as to the propriety of permitting the debtor's transfer agent to act as a depositary under a program for obtaining assents." [52] This is a startling conclusion after everything had been found in order. Perhaps the welter of charges against the depositary, even though groundless, suggested a possibility of collusion and irregular procedure in other cases, which could be prevented if no previous relations existed between applicant and depositary. Mr. L'Heu-

[50] The following short extracts from the Trial Brief illustrate the distinction we are making:

"Nevertheless, in the face of all these considerations Old Colony declined to give proper significance to the time element! Old Colony's attitude, and actions thereunder point up the unreliability of its certificate." Trial Brief, p. 40. "It is hardly contestable that the Old Colony personnel was well aware of the impediments in the system." Ibid., p. 40. "This type of slipshod operation falls far short of the standard required of Old Colony in its status as the fiduciary which functioned as an independent depositary." Ibid., p. 44.

[51] L'Heureux, Opinion, p. 59.

[52] 282 I.C.C. 750 at 799 (1953).

reux picked up this "patent inconsistency in the I.C.C.'s report" and took special care to reiterate his finding that "the implication is totally unsubstantiated by the record. . . . Both the evidence on record and my personal investigation of this matter have proved that beyond peradventure." [53]

Can we accept the analysis of the last two chapters and still agree with the Commission's apparent judgment that the recording system was adequate? Or, an even harder question, can we admit that the system needs tightening, the rules need sharpening, and still accept the final tally in the Boston and Maine case as fulfilling statutory requirements?

The analysis of the last two chapters finds several places where the system as used requires tightening to assure strict accuracy. The satisfaction of the Commission with the depositary's procedure is consistent with its refusal, from the first petition of the Sakis group in January 1951, to reexamine the validity of assents. One can speculate as to when the working of the system would ever have been reviewed by the Commission had not the three-judge Court invited its inquiry.

Conclusions on the Recording System

The Commission found from all the evidence that the depositary's treatment was proper for assents where a broker assented less than his total holdings and later sold stock. This was the matter most in dispute; and the depositary admitted that the method of handling was chosen as the most nearly correct of more than one available alternative. One can agree that the solution was reasonable and in the circumstances of this case probably gave approximate accuracy, and still hold that it was not an accurate method. Our analysis shows that even the "best alternative" was a makeshift likely to minimize errors but never sure of excluding them.

The fact that the receiving date and not the mailing date was taken as the test of an executed assent had the effect of lowering the total of valid assents. The order was not rigorously followed as to the definition of an executed assent;

[53] Memorandum from Robert D. L'Heureux, Chief Counsel, to Chairman Tobey of the Senate Committee on Interstate and Foreign Commerce, April 24, 1953, p. 3.

"given by sending" was thus loosely translated into "counted when received." This interpretation when applied on the important cut-off date shut off assents not yet received. A substantial number of votes were mailed the last day, properly executed under the order but not counted. This treatment was later explained as sound because it did not *overcount* assents; but an accurate certificate demands that there be no *undercounting* either.

On balance, one can feel sure that at least 75% of each class were valid assents; but to say that enough votes were valid in this instance to meet statutory requirements is not to say that the system was a precision instrument. If our analysis is correct, (a) the system did not follow the definition that a ballot became executed when mailed; hence, some properly executed ballots were not counted at all; (b) anything short of relating the certificate numbers to assented shares transferred by brokers will not produce an accurate count of assents carried through to transferees.

Conclusions on the Note on the Letter of Assent

Some questions about the purpose of the Note and what constituted full compliance were settled: that evidence of authority "must be furnished" did not mean that it must accompany the assent. Documents previously filed were acceptable. In fact the Commission, with one dissent, accepted evidence received after the close of the period. Furthermore, evidence need not be formal documents but could be knowledge obtained through past dealings with the party.

The report supports the depositary in its decision not to require brokers to show authority of their beneficial owners for the assents they sign. Nevertheless, the Commission's argument on this point impresses one with the urgent need for further clarification of what a Note should require. The Commission could not have thought that the Note in this case demanded a show of authority by brokers to vote the shares of their beneficial interests; the depositary asked for no such authority and its practice was accepted as reasonable. Yet, when Old Colony in its brief defended its decision in this respect by citing proxy law to the effect that it is not incumbent on the election judge "to seek to discover undisclosed beneficial interests *represented* by a holder of record," [54] (italics supplied), the Commission denied the applicability of the principle without reservation to the "situation with which Old Colony was confronted." The Commission held that:

> . . . it was incumbent on Old Colony to have or to procure "proper evidence of authority" in those instances where it was apparent or there was reason to believe that a letter of assent was executed and submitted by a person acting in a representative capacity.[55]

A number of assents, which were necessary for an adequate percentage, were validated as "received from persons whose identity and authority were known to McIntire through a long course of business dealings." This raises a question of what would constitute good practice on the part of less responsible depositaries. The fact that later check found all these assents regular does not make the practice sound. Also, if authority and identity were known, what was to prevent obtaining the same documentary evidence? The Commission's regulations should be so drawn as to minimize the personal equation in carrying them out.

The Commission says the Note was intended and was directed by it in the order of April 19, 1950. After the record of misunderstanding in this case, it is clear that in the future the definition of "fiduciary or representative" should be so explicit that classification of signers would never be in doubt. Furthermore, the Note was addressed to the voting stockholder. If it had been intended to put the depositary on notice, it would better have been in the Commission's order. Then, doubtless, it would have reached the depositary directly by way of the Railroad's letter of instructions on procedural matters.[56]

---

[54] Old Colony Brief, p. 31.

[55] 282 I.C.C. 750 at 762 (1953).

[56] After this chapter was written, the Commission's order in the Western Maryland Railway case was explicit in avoiding issues raised by the Note in the Boston and Maine controversy. The order itself included the following provision:

". . . To be valid, an assent or revocation executed by a person other than the holder of record of the shares of stock respecting which the assent or revo-

Conclusions on Administrative Procedures

These conclusions relate to the effective organization of the three parties to the balloting operations rather than to questions of the techniques themselves.

The Railroad chose its depositary, confirmed by the Commission, and sent its own interpretation of the Commission's order. The Commission did not direct the proceedings actively. The depositary naturally looked to the Railroad. Again naturally, it viewed its own function in terms of its long experience in ordinary proxy matters. Anything apparently different, as the Note, was interpreted in the groove of customary action. It took questions to its principal, the Railroad, rather than to the Commission.

When one reviews the difficulties in this case, a central fact stands out: of the three parties to the operation, the Railroad and the depositary worked in their respective spheres, and at times between themselves, without ready reference of their problems to the Commission — the responsible agency of regulation under the statute. It was this situation that led the Department to allege lack of independence in the depositary. A necessary first step to forestall similar operational problems in the future is to make the three parties function as a unit, with the Commission as the head responsible for directing the vote. Then it will be clear that the depositary is but the lengthened arm of the Commission in a specialized function.

---

cation is given must be accompanied by documentary evidence of the authority of such person to execute the assent or revocation on behalf of the record owner; provided, however, that the foregoing shall not be construed as requiring such documentary evidence of authority for the execution of an assent or revocation by (a) a partner in behalf of the firm of which he is a member, or (b) an officer thereof in behalf of a corporation when such execution is attested under the seal of such corporation." 290 I.C.C. 445 at 473 (October 14, 1954).

CHAPTER IX

Charges Against the Railroad:
Solicitation Procedures

THE CHARGES against the Railroad ran still deeper than those against the depositary. Criticism of the latter was directed at details in the operational procedures. The Railroad was charged with failure to meet the basic requirements of the statute itself, first in the soliciting of assents, and second in counting votes given for stock that the Railroad could be said to control. In both these areas it is not easy to establish standards so that all cases are black or white; there is a large zone of gray. Where judgment plays so large a part it is natural for disputes to arise. Also, where lines of distinction are blurred it becomes easier to impute wrong motives for decisions that objectors do not like. This is particularly true in financial transactions where the techniques so often obscure the realities.

Here again, the Department's statement was more than the strictly factual account that would be expected of a government agency in an investigation. Apparently the writer of the brief was not content merely to establish the facts of illegality; the facts must be described in language that carried his opinion as to the motives of the Railroad management. A few illustrations will suffice:

> The railroad was careful not to make a disclosure to the Commission of its resort to the services performed by Nye and Greer [solicitors of assents]. (Trial Brief, p. 26)
> This is the crowning example of the extremes to which the railroad management resorted in order to put this plan through at any cost. (Ibid., p. 61)
> That the railroad acquired control of substantial blocks . . . through connivance with the director of another corporation. (Ibid., p. 21)

> Greer, in an attempt to give some color of credibility to his
> version, said that. . . .   (Ibid., p. 53)

These statements are not objective in tone; they reflect personal impressions of the brief-writer.   The Department presented no evidence that the Railroad deliberately kept the
Commission in the dark about hiring Nye and Greer; nor did
it adduce evidence that the Railroad "connived" to get control of stock to gain assents for the plan.   These implications
of low action and sinister purpose became particularly noteworthy in a Department of Justice document, which itself
was bringing charges of improper representations in the soliciting activity of the Railroad and its agents.

The Department's charges against the Railroad were:

> 1. That railroad solicitors in seeking to induce stockhold-
> ers to assent made representations exceeding the material
> approved by the Commission as to sufficiency and correct-
> ness.
>
> 2. That contracts of the railroad with paid solicitors were
> contrary to the terms and conditions approved by the Com-
> mission, and these solicitors were very active in obtaining
> *invalid* assents.

*   *   *   *   *

> 4. That the railroad acquired control of substantial blocks
> of stock through purchases by a railroad director, through
> borrowing by a paid railroad solicitor, and through con-
> nivance with the director of another corporation.[1]

Only the first two charges are taken up in this chapter.
Chapter X is given over to analysis of the fourth charge, in
terms of the statutory meaning of controlled stock.[2]

CONTRACTS WITH PAID SOLICITORS

The second charge in the list above is so bound up with
the first and the fourth that analysis of it clarifies the meaning of the others.

[1] Department of Justice, Trial Brief, p. 21.

[2] The third charge, directed primarily against the depositary although involving the Railroad to some extent, was the subject of the two preceding
chapters.

The Commission's order provided:

(5) That the directors, officers, and regular employees of the applicant may take part in soliciting assents, and the applicant may retain the services of one or more firms or persons specializing in such work to assist in the solicitation; that reasonable provision may be made for the compensation of such firms or persons; and that such solicitation may be carried on by personal interview, mail, advertising, telephone, and telegraph.

In accordance with this order, the Railroad obtained the Commission's approval in July 1950 for a form entitled "Compensation Claims for Letters of Assent," for use by banks, registered securities dealers, and brokers in claiming compensation for securing letters of assent. It was known that these institutions would be at some expense in connection with assents by their customers. It was decided to pay on the basis of assents received so as to compensate for the clerical and mailing expense of sending material to customers, and the expense and time of communicating with customers by telephone or in person. The compensation was intended to cover out-of-pocket costs.[3] The forms were used by brokers as expected during the submission period; and the Railroad reported $15,000 as the total claims for this type of compensation.[4]

Two Specialists in Solicitation Hired

When balloting had been under way for some time, the Railroad officers concluded that to rely on solicitation of assents by brokers and others, to whom solicitation was only an incidental activity, would not bring in the necessary assents from the common stockholders. The original plan to

[3] Hearing before the Examiner, August 27, 1952, pp. 1408–1409. The form provided for payment at the rate of 20 cents a share for the first 50 shares assented by each holder, 10 cents a share for the next 50 shares, and 5 cents a share for all thereafter, but in no case was compensation to exceed $100 for assents obtained from a single stockholder. Assents obtained from institutional investors, such as banks and investment companies, were not to be paid for. Furthermore, no payment was to be made to these solicitors until the plan actually had gone into effect.

[4] Supplemental Application No. 2, December 27, 1950.

use the Railroad's traffic representatives to talk with stock-holders had been abandoned because these traffic officials, not being financial men, would require a considerable amount of instruction to be effective. The result was that there was practically no solicitation by Railroad officers or employees except with personal friends.[5] At the public hear-ing in 1952 it was testified that at one time 400 to 500 stock-holders of record could not be located, and, in addition, there was stock standing in the names of brokers who had long since sold it.[6] The common stock, the only class listed on the New York Stock Exchange, was notoriously specula-tive. The need was for professional help to track down stockholders, particularly of the common stock, and to solicit their assents.

Accordingly, the Railroad hired two specialists in solicita-tion. The first was Mr. Joseph J. Greer, a salesman for a registered securities dealer in Boston. He was paid $100 a month for the remainder of the submission period, plus out-of-pocket expenses.[7] His compensation was not contingent on the success of his solicitation or the plan.

The second specialist, hired somewhat later, was George-son & Co., a leading firm in the preparation and presentation of corporate proposals and in solicitation. It was chosen not only for its prominence in the field but also because it had successfully handled the Railroad's solicitation in the bond reorganization in 1940. The contract provided for a flat fee of $5,000 plus expenses, which were expected to be something over $5,000; and the payment did not depend on the success of the plan.[8]

---

[5] Hearing before the Examiner, August 27, 1952, pp. 1330–1331.

[6] Ibid., pp. 1339–1440.

[7] His expenses were reimbursed in two different ways: the substantial items for out-of-town trips were itemized on an expense voucher, but the in-cidentals and smaller items in the metropolitan area were considered to be covered by the payments for assents reported on the regular brokers' compen-sation form.

[8] In January 1951 Mr. Nye, the managing partner of Georgeson & Co., ob-tained the Railroad's agreement to an increase in the fee to $6,000 on the ground that the campaign was longer and required more of the partners' time than had been anticipated. Expenses were listed at that time at $5,486. The bill was paid in full in January.

The Department's objection to hiring these specialists seems to rest on two grounds: first, that they were not paid according to the brokers' compensation form; and second, that they made improper representations, that unlike the brokers they were "willing to cut corners and engage in connivance in order to put the plan over," [9] and that they "far transcended normal solicitation activities." [10]

The first objection is similar to one made by the Sakis group that the Commission was wrong in not limiting the expense that the Railroad might incur in hiring agents, brokers, and employees as solicitors. The Court in February 1952 dealt with both these objections, holding that section 20b did not require the Commission to set maximum limits of expense and that it gave the Commission discretion as to the manner of solicitation. The statute, said the Court, contemplated oral solicitation. The Court concluded, also, that the Commission acted properly in authorizing reasonable expenses. The Railroad in due course had reported to the Commission the total compensation paid, and the Commission had approved.[11]

The Court's conclusion adequately disposes of the Department's charge that the contracts with the solicitors were contrary to the Commission's terms. When the Commission permitted the hiring and reasonable compensation of specialists in solicitation, it must have expected the terms to differ from those offered to brokers procuring assents primarily from their customers.

THE CHARGES OF IMPROPER REPRESENTATIONS
BY SOLICITORS

The dangers of improper representation in oral solicitation had long been emphasized by the Sakis group, which objected to personal solicitation as early as July 14, 1950. Its petition on February 20, 1951, for rehearing by the Commission, alleged that "The Committee, upon information and belief, believes that undue influence was exercised by per-

[9] Department of Justice, Trial Brief, p. 26.
[10] Ibid., p. 25.
[11] *Sakis* v. *United States*, 103 F. Supp. 292 at 306.

sons soliciting assents and that a thorough inquiry into the representations made by soliciting through telephone and personal contact, might reveal that the necessary assents were not freely given to support the plan."

Almost a year later the Sakis Committee made several further allegations.[12] The first and most important was that the Commission acted contrary to law when it permitted solicitation by telephone and personal interview. The basis for this charge was that the provision of section 20b requiring approval by the Commission of "all letters, circulars, advertisements, and other communications" included oral solicitation. The Court concluded, however, that in the context of the statute the meaning of "other communications" was restricted to written communication. The Court added:

> . . . The court is not unmindful of the danger of improper oral solicitation. There is a safeguard against this danger, however, in the written material which is approved by the Commission according to the provisions of the statute and sent to the stockholders. If doubt is created in the mind of a stockholder by some oral communication as to the true nature of a proposed plan of security modification, reference may be had to this approved written material.
>
> Of necessity, a certain amount of oral communication is vitally important. The percentage of assents of each class of stock required by the Mahaffie Act is high. It would no doubt be difficult, if not impossible, to ever obtain the required percentage of assents if oral communications were not permitted.[13]

At the same time the Committee challenged the written material used by the Railroad and approved by the Commission, contending that the material did not make a fair and proper disclosure of the plan. The Court found this allegation also to be without merit.[14]

[12] At a pretrial conference before the three-judge Court in October 1951 and again at the trial in January 1952.

[13] 103 F. Supp. 292 at 305.

[14] The Committee further alleged that a financial statement for the first five months of 1950 was included by the Railroad in solicitation material without the Commission's approval. The Court pointed out that the record showed that approval was given. The Committee also complained that the Commission refused to include certain information in the solicitation material

The charge that Railroad solicitors made representations beyond the material approved by the Commission was the first of the Department's three major charges against the Railroad. From the very nature of solicitation, it was the charge hardest to support with evidence that would stand up. Such evidence was personal testimony only. If the solicitors had prepared circulars with data and arguments not passed upon by the Commission, the charges could be checked against the substantive material. The only evidence supplied by the Department, however, consisted of affidavits of sundry small holders who reported that they were urged to assent for such and such reasons. Such evidence can be no stronger than the individual affiant's knowledge of the subject matter, his emotional reaction either to the plan itself or from his own position in the stock, or other factors affecting the dependability of his story. The affidavits were taken nearly a year after the assents had been made and in several cases the affiants were unable to identify the alleged solicitor.

We have in this situation opposite points of view about a necessary procedure called solicitation. The Commission, drawing from its long experience with section 77 cases and latterly with section 20b cases, had written an explicit order to deal with solicitation of assents or rejections from stockholders. The plaintiff was an objecting minority, the Sakis group, with no experience in such matters but with positive opinions about the right and wrong in solicitation method. The Department turned to these issues and after investigation presented charges and evidence. It is again important to get answers to basic questions: What is solicitation in terms of the Commission's order? What limits are imposed by statute and order? What regulation is feasible?

As for standards of proper representation in solicitation, probably all would agree that certain acts are improper —

---

as requested by the Committee. To this the Court replied that the record showed that substantially all the requested material was included, and that, anyway, the Committee itself had the right to submit the material to stockholders with the approval of the Commission. The Committee's final objection, that the Commission did not limit the expense that the Railroad might incur in hiring agents, brokers, and employees to solicit assents, has been discussed above.

deliberate misstatements, promises of favors in return for assents, and other trafficking in votes. At the other extreme, any statement made directly from Commission-approved material would surely be considered proper. The controversial areas lie between these two extremes. One should not be dogmatic about the proprieties of statements on matters that divide even the experts. And some statements are in fact misleading although made with no intention to mislead.[15]

THE ITEMS INCLUDED IN THE SOLICITATION MATERIAL

The packet of materials sent to holders of record at the beginning of the submission period included the Report and Order of the Commission, April 19, 1950, and those of July 10, 1950, issued after reconsideration and denial of the petition of the Sakis group. In addition there was a 4-page short description of the plan, with a paragraph on the procedural detail of assent and revocation. Included also was a comparative income statement for the 12 years ended December 31, 1949, and the five months ended May 31, 1950, together with a condensed balance sheet as of the latter date. The package was completed by the form letter of assent and a letter of transmittal dated July 28, 1950, from the president of the Railroad. The president's letter, in asking for support, emphasized the danger to the Railroad's credit in the large arrearages of the various preferred stocks. It pointed out that these encouraged market fluctuations by the operations of speculators rather than investors. The letter made a strong appeal to the two lowest layers of stock by referring to their "almost hopeless" outlook for dividends, which, if the plan succeeded, would turn into a "reasonable prospect of obtaining an immediate participation in earnings."

---

[15] Problems of proper representation were not confined to the Railroad solicitors in this case. We have those charging misrepresentation by solicitors and continuing at the same time to attack the plan because the allocation of the new stock among the classes was not based on "book values." Hardly a more discredited principle of allocation could be advanced, although the book-value basis has strong appeal to classes with little or no equity in earnings and can be demonstrated by the company's own last published balance sheet.

The statute with reference to solicitation material specifies "letters, circulars, advertisements, and other communications," and impliedly these would originate with the Railroad or objecting groups, to be submitted for Commission approval. In this sense would the Commission's reports be considered as solicitation material? By inference they constituted a strong argument for acceptance because they explained the opinion that the plan was necessary, just and reasonable, and in the public interest. They spelled out and defended the method of arriving at the allocation between classes, which was one of the sore points of the opposition. Even if the Commission had not required its reports to be sent to all holders, the Railroad certainly would have requested that it be done. No document prepared by the Railroad would carry so much weight with the stockholder as would the official opinion of the regulatory body charged with guarding his interest.

In the strict wording of the statute the Commission's reports would not be called solicitation material because they were not submitted for approval as such. They were official documents of the Commission, but the Commission was not a solicitor of votes. The Commission's reports, however, were the main part of the solicitor's kit. Although not addressed to the stockholders as purposive circulars in solicitation, they served as double-purpose documents — to put the full reasoning for the Commission's acceptance of the plan into the record, and also into the stockholder's hands when he was being asked to vote. When the stockholder opened the packet, it was all "solicitation material" to him under an official release.

UNDERSTANDING THE SOLICITATION PROCESS

In no area of the Department's charges is it so important to face squarely the realities of business practices. What does the Department mean by its charge that solicitors made "representations exceeding the material approved by the Commission as to sufficiency and correctness"? Does the Department imply that a solicitor shall say nothing that is not in the printed matter given to the stockholder? To take a likely example, suppose the earnings figures in the exhibits of comparative earnings over the past 20-odd years go only through the preceding May 31, and since that date the Railroad has published interim quarterly figures. Is the solicitor not to mention the later reports, nor answer any question the holder may put to him about them? One would expect more questions from holders of Boston and Maine stock than from the bondholders in the other section 20b cases, because of the type of security and the market history of the several classes, so largely in speculative hands and occasionally held by those who had long since forgotten their holdings. It would be expected that a solicitor would meet a barrage of questions on which any answer might be taken as a representation beyond the material in the hands (or in the wastebasket) of the stockholder facing him. Perhaps the Department really is saying that solicitation can hardly ever be strictly legal as it interprets legality.

Most of the stockholders would confess their inability to interpret much of the material, many would pay no attention to it, and both these groups would expect solicitors, especially their brokers, to advise them on what to do. In appraising the affidavits one must bear in mind that a holder who admits innocence in financial affairs is hardly a dependable source one year later for the verbatim statements of a solicitor.

The requirement of the statute for approval of solicitation materials is the first and largest step toward control of the solicitation process. Even though the Commission had, after public hearing and intensive study of its own, found the Boston and Maine plan to be fair and in the public interest, it was still obliged under the statute to pass upon the material to be put in each stockholder's hands as useful for his decision.

Although the statute made no mention of oral solicitation, one can assume that the Commission considered the solicitation process to be more than putting its own reports in the hands of the stockholders. The reports, in the usual practice of regulatory agencies, were written to present the Commission's own analysis of the plan. Those who actually wrote the documents were not thinking of them as solicitation material, but rather as a technical presentation of the reasons for the Commission's approval of the plan. It is one thing to write a report to complete the record, and quite another to provide the stockholder with information that will be useful for his decision.

The material distributed to stockholders was not in a real sense *solicitation* material, but more properly could be called useful matter for those with the rare financial ability to use it. It was not a sales document, but a reasoned presentation of the facts from which a stockholder could come to his own decision.

If the Commission had thought a personal appeal to stockholders was forbidden, it is reasonable to suppose that additional and simplified material would have been supplied to stockholders. The Commission could hardly have contemplated complete insulation of the stockholder, left to puzzle out his attitude toward the plan without further help.

We can be sure that the framers of the statute had a very realistic conception of the solicitation process. They knew that solicitors are salesmen, in this instance not of a product but of a plan that would change the rights of all stockholders. The Commission was well aware that the sales effort by solicitors would not be of standard pattern; and so the statute provided for a core of basic reference material to be approved by the Commission and then placed in each stockholder's hands for him to refer to as he saw or heard comments on the plan. No realist can believe that the "official" printed material solves all solicitation problems. Stockholders will be in a cross fire of arguments, specious and otherwise, and no regulations have ever been devised that will screen out truth from distortions of truth.

When the Sakis group argued that oral solicitation was forbidden by the statute because in the nature of the case it could not be supervised (the statute giving the Commission the responsibility of passing on solicitation material), it strained over words rather than meanings. If the statute intended to bar personal contact with holders after a packet of condensed and technical financial literature was supplied to them, it would do something that no other such statute has ever done. The Court had no doubt that the order permitting oral solicitation was in accordance with the statute; after all, it said, the holder always has his "written material" to fall back on.[16] Even the full disclosure objectives of the Securities Act of 1933 and its sequels are chiefly concerned with careful rules about the Registration Statement and the Prospectus. These acts do not forbid oral solicitation as the documents are being used.

There is a difference, however, between the prospectus under the Securities Act and the solicitation material in this case. In the former there is an emphatic disclaimer that the Securities and Exchange Commission passes on the merits of the security; in a section 20b modification plan, on the contrary, there is the explicit opinion of the Commission that

---

[16] A commentary that deals directly with this point is a Note in *The Yale Law Journal*, "Solicitation of Assents to Railroad Reorganization Plans under Section 20b of the Interstate Commerce Act" (Vol. 62, April 1953, p. 806). As to the opinion of the Court on this point, the author says (pp. 811–812): "Though the Sakis Court [the three-judge Court] was quite correct in finding no specific statutory prohibition of oral solicitation — Congress, in fact, never considered the matter — there is good reason to justify judicial interpolation of such a ban. The only assurance of a full and fair presentation of 20b plans to security holders lies in the provision for a prior ICC check over both the 'correctness and sufficiency' of solicitation communications. . . . Yet oral solicitation, so conducive to misleading argument and innuendo, can nullify the sole check Congress imposed. Solicitors, particularly when paid on a sliding scale correlated to the number of assents they acquire, can be expected to exercise every possible wile of oral persuasion. This expectancy is borne out by the Justice Department investigation of the Boston & Maine campaign which revealed startling instances of oral misrepresentation of the value of Boston & Maine stock and the carrier's financial position." (Footnotes omitted)

There are some startling implications in this commentary on the place of oral solicitation in campaigns for recapitalization. The commentator admits the statute is silent. But predecessor statutes have been controlling reorganization procedures for 20 years, and oral solicitation has been accepted all the while. The writer comes near to saying that what a statute does not spell out as required, it forbids, and the omission here could justifiably be rectified by the Court. If the Court's duty is to interpret a statute in terms of the intent of Congress, it would be reasonable to suppose it would give decisive weight to the Commission, which looks upon this statute as one of a long line in which oral solicitation was taken as standard practice. Inasmuch as one of the Commissioners, Mr. Mahaffie, sponsored the bill, it can be presumed that the regulations of the Commission on which he sat were framed in full accord with the statute.

the plan is fair and equitable between classes.   Oral solicitation in this latter case at least starts with a favorable opinion
of a government agency and can be checked against its own
published report.[17]

In this case the solicitor of assents has his sales manual
prescribed in the kit of materials approved by the Commission, but he obviously is not limited except by implication
that the materials are always his reference point. By its very
nature, solicitation is an active effort at persuasion.   The
Commission's order covers the permissible devices of solicitation: personal interview, mail, advertising, telephone and
telegraph.   It is unrealistic to expect direct supervision by
the Commission over any of these devices except the mail and
advertising.

The order specified that solicitors were those in the Railroad's own organization who had been assigned to such work
and those with whom the management had entered into special contracts to solicit.   The Commission foresaw that to get
the attention and assent of holders more needed to be done
than to mail them a packet of condensed financial exhibits
on the plan and the financial condition of the Railroad.   It
doubtless understood that the solicitation included a request
for an assent, some replies to questions perhaps, some argument, and in many cases an appeal.   The Commission would
know that the officers and directors, who had been working
on the plan for seven years or more, would have positive
views which they would support with evangelistic fervor; yet
they were named first as appropriate solicitors.   The Com-

---

[17] In spite of its explicit opinion, the Commission required that the usual
disclaimer be included in the solicitation material.   The Railroad printed it
at the top of the president's letter to stockholders.

NOTE: This note is to advise you that, pursuant to the requirements of
paragraph (2) of Section 20b of the Interstate Commerce Act, as amended,
this letter of transmittal and the documents accompanying it have been approved by the Interstate Commerce Commission as to the correctness and sufficiency of the material facts stated therein; but such approval should not be
construed or represented as advocacy by the Commission of either assent or
opposition by the stockholders to the submitted plan of modification.

Hand and Cummings (63 *Harvard Law Review* 957 at 964, footnote 30)
have commented that ". . . it seems unreal to suggest, as such a legend undoubtedly does, that the Commission has taken no position as to the merits of
a plan. . . ."

mission could also expect the usual stockholder lethargy in recapitalizations. The rules therefore permitted the retaining of specialists to apply their skills in locating stockholders and persuading them to assent.

Others who performed the soliciting function were not engaged to do so by specific agreement. This distinction must be emphasized because there has been confusion on the point by some writers on the case. Brokers, as required by exchange rules and by reason of their market function, became intermediaries for passing out the official solicitation materials to their customers, and were reimbursed for this service. They also were entitled to compensation according to the assents they could be credited with, payable only after the plan had gone through. These brokers were not solicitors in the sense of being official appointees of the Railroad within the meaning of the Commission's order, but they were solicitors in the broad sense and were paid on a preannounced scale with the Commission's approval.

Actually, many brokers were known to be active in supporting the plan with their own customers. Customers asked advice on how to vote, and brokers gave it. It was through the brokers that customers with beneficial ownership got their information about the plan in the first place. It was natural for them to turn to brokers for comment. If one considers advice to stockholders as the essential of the solicitation process, then brokers were in fact solicitors.

From the very beginning of the activity toward the formulation of a plan, the brokerage houses were looked upon as important intermediaries for enlisting the support of the stockholders, especially the stock held in street names. Brokers were invited to make suggestions on plans, and over a four-year span scores of such plans came to the Railroad. One New York broker,[18] after offering several plans of his

---

[18] A. J. McNeal of Price, McNeal & Co. early began circularizing his customers with plans for recapitalization. He objected strongly to the all-common plan first suggested by the Railroad and promptly withdrawn. Although his own plan differed somewhat from the Railroad's amended plan, he supported the latter and collected compensation for a large number of assents, as did many other brokers.

own, met with Railroad officers and others to work out a compromise between the Railroad's proposal and that of opposing stockholders. Although the effort to compromise failed, he decided to go along with the plan finally submitted and advised his customers to assent. This is illustrative of the participation of many brokers.

If one took a poll of all assenting stockholders on the extent to which their assents were influenced either by the official materials or by the advice of a broker, the latter group would probably be much larger. The long history of recapitalizations, particularly of the type represented here, indicates that the solicitation material, so shielded by statute and by official prescription and release, plays a relatively small part in the voting process. This is not to say that it is not better to have certified releases to stockholders, even if studied by few, than to give free rein to managements to use data as they please. Granted the necessity of such approved releases, however, their positive effect must be small relative to the oral appeals from various sources, notably brokers, who may offer to inquiring customers reasons that have little relation to the contents of the 50 pages of "solicitation material." If opinions cannot be given when asked of brokers, unless all comments are mere echoes of officially released materials (in this case released several months previously), then censorship is implied to an extent that would make recapitalization of this sort impossible.

The right and wrong of solicitation methods are easier to visualize when one makes a clear distinction between the brokers, who solicited assents from their customers, and the paid agents of the Railroad under special agreement, who were expected to locate stockholders and solicit assents from them everywhere possible. The criticisms in the Department's brief do not apply equally to both these groups, each of which was active in a different way in obtaining assents from stockholders.

We have seen that there is no basis for the charge that the Railroad erred in not paying the special solicitors according to the brokers' compensation scale. Their work in solicitation was not the same and their relation to the Railroad was

different.   Furthermore, the scale of payment correlated to
the number of assents, which has been criticized as conducive to high-pressure methods,[19] was actually designed only to
cover brokers' out-of-pocket expenses.   The special agents,
not being brokers with a customer list, solicited assents
wherever they found them and were paid a set fee regardless
of the success of their solicitation.   The temptation to use
high-pressure methods was thereby reduced at the same time
that the fee was sufficient to make it worth the agent's while
to give the matter more attention than the average broker
would.

Again, visualizing these two groups separately emphasizes
how unrealistic it would be to forbid oral solicitation entirely.   Even if paid solicitors were not permitted, there
would still be oral solicitation resulting from the broker-
customer relationship.   Would brokers be expected to clear
with the Commission all comments on the plan put out in
their market letters to customers?

Recognition of brokers as solicitors, although of a type
different from the paid agents, is helpful in an analysis of the
extent to which the agents made improper representations.
The Department's charges were directed almost entirely at
the special solicitors, in spite of occasional confusion of the
two types of solicitor.   The Sakis group's objections were
aimed wholly at the officers, employees, and agents of the
Railroad.   Did the agents go further from the approved material in their comments than brokers did?   Did the Department investigate the solicitation methods of brokers for pos-

[19] The Note in *The Yale Law Journal* (Vol. 62, April 1953, p. 806), ex-
cerpted in footnote 16 of this chapter, does not make the distinction between
official paid solicitors and those who may do the same thing but are not special appointees for the purpose.   In fact, the Note reads as if the writer considers brokers as paid solicitors because it speaks of solicitors (particularly
when paid on a sliding scale correlated to the number of assents they acquire)
as being especially inclined to high-pressure methods.   In the Boston and
Maine case, only brokers were to be paid on this basis, and they were not official solicitors.   If the writer has here thought of brokers as solicitors, then his
conclusion (p. 814), "Ideally, oral solicitation should be forbidden," takes no
account of the realism of the broker-customer relationship.   Furthermore, if
oral persuasion is to be prohibited, then oral *dissuasion* should be as carefully
protected against.

sible infractions of proper methods? Perhaps it would be found that the statements that struck the Department as so improper when made by the agents were not different from those made every day by many brokers.

Nevertheless, there is a significant difference between brokers on the one hand and paid solicitors on the other. The brokers were not retained by the Railroad to solicit. The confidence of their customers in their good judgment was more important to them than the success of the plan or the small compensation for assents. It can be assumed that misrepresentation would be counter to their long-run interests. Paid agents, however, were temporarily employees of the Railroad, vitally and primarily interested in the success of the plan while the campaign lasted. They would be more likely to have an intensive approach in solicitation, which would naturally lead to "sales talk."

Even with the specialists in proxy matters, however, there is a professional attitude which in itself forces attention to standards in representations. Professional solicitors have their own reputations to protect. Mr. Nye, of Georgeson & Co., pointed out that he and his employees knew that their firm would not stay in business long if they made improper statements in solicitation. "We have handled 175 campaigns in the past 12 months," said Mr. Nye, "and no one campaign is worth the risk that you would subject yourself to by making improper statements." [20]

THE AFFIDAVITS TO SUPPORT THE CHARGES

The Department presented to the three-judge Court in January 1952 some 19 affidavits and 15 depositions taken in the fall of 1951. Many of these, the affidavits in particular, related to alleged representations and inducements by solicitors for the Railroad. They were said by the Department to be a spot-check [21] of a small number of the assenting share-

[20] Hearing before the Examiner, September 10, 1952, p. 1771.

[21] It would be helpful in weighing the importance of this evidence to know more about the methods in the "spot check." If these affidavits are the results of 100 interviews taken at random by the Department, they indicate that about one out of five of all individual holders would allege improper

holders to ascertain whether solicitors had confined themselves to the approved material.[22]   Other commentators, however, have indicated that lawyers of the Department spent several months on the case, with two to four months of concentrated investigation aided by FBI agents throughout the country.[23]

Of eight affidavits placed in the record of the public hearing, six referred primarily to representations by solicitors. Six affidavits had been discarded by stipulation at the prehearing conference on April 29, 1952.   At that time another affidavit, to the effect that the stockholder's signature had been forged on an assent for 100 shares, was accepted by all parties without further argument and his assent was recognized as invalid.   Two affiants were called as witnesses and their affidavits were not used.   One affiant, whose interest was that his father was a stockholder, and who had made damaging assertions concerning the solicitation, did not answer a subpoena to testify.   As it turned out, this type of evidence added up to little or nothing.

Alleged Improper Representations as to Value of the Common Stock

The alleged misrepresentation most frequently described in the affidavits, and the one that has received the most attention from analysts of the case, related to the value of the common stock.   One affidavit stated that two solicitors said the stock was going down to 75 cents a share; another gave a figure of 90 cents; and a third named 12 cents as the likely

---

representations.   If the spot-check was not a statistical sample but merely followed up leads by objectors to the plan, however, it has quite a different significance.

The emotional setting is always important in evaluation of the testimony of the small stockholder.   For example, in the case of Boston and Maine Railroad, he holds a few shares of nondividend-paying stock, perhaps bought without knowledge or interest in the basic values; and he is disappointed that quick profits have escaped him.   There may be the general bias against the large corporations, railroads in particular.   In this state of mind, any bias or distrust he may have had is heightened by a call from an FBI agent, whose very inquiry signifies that officially the whole procedure is suspect.

[22] Department of Justice, Trial Brief, pp. 65–66.

[23] L'Heureux, Opinion, p. 61.

bottom figure. One stockholder said that she was told that if the plan failed the stock would be practically worthless. Another said a solicitor told him that the value of the stock would probably decrease after the plan went through. A third stated that he was told that unless he signed, the stock might become practically worthless; and a fourth, that the stock was practically worthless and was "under water." [24] Market prices of the common stock during this period ranged from $2\frac{1}{2}$ to $3\frac{7}{8}$ on the New York Stock Exchange.

The criticism by the few small stockholders and the Department seems to be based on an assumption that the value of the stock should be measured only by market prices. The emphasis on this meaning of value shows in the Department's comments on one affidavit:

> [This stockholder] was told by another railroad solicitor that his 100 shares of common stock would be worthless if he did not assent it, and that he did assent acting on this improper representation. The fact is that his stock would become practically worthless if the plan were to be put into effect. The new common stock is selling for approximately $12 a share, whereas the outstanding common stock was last quoted at a low of $1\frac{1}{2}$ and a high of 5 on the Boston Stock Exchange on February 21, 1951 (when it was withdrawn by the railroad). Under the plan [this stockholder] would receive only five shares of new common for his 100 shares of old. The 5 new shares would be worth $60, whereas 100 shares of the old common were worth at least $150. [25]

We have here confusion between market value and investment value. The latter is a concept unrelated to short-term market movements. If one took the Department's statement literally, no common stockholder would have reason to assent because "the fact is that his stock would become practically worthless if the plan were to be put into effect," and his old common stock was then selling at $2\frac{1}{2}$ times ($150:$60 for 100 shares and 5 shares, respectively) what it would be given in new common stock under the plan. This focus on market value caused confused thinking when the modifica-

---

[24] Several of the affidavits not put into the record were along these same lines.

[25] Department of Justice, Trial Brief, p. 66.

tion plan was being considered at the first public hearing in
March 1949 and here again when the Department alleged
misrepresentation by solicitors.

It should be obvious that recapitalization plans are not and
cannot be drawn on the basis of market values. For the
Boston and Maine common stock in particular, the market
price in 1950 could not reflect income possibilities, because
on the existing capital structure and the earnings forecast
used for the plan, with the huge preferred arrearages, the
common stockholders could not hope for dividends until far
beyond the year 2000. What, then, gave the stock a market
value? It had market value because there were enough trad-
ers on the market who were playing for the short movements
in its price. Furthermore, as long as the success of the plan
was uncertain, there would be chance variances in the market
between the old stock and the new "when issued." Would
the Department think it "proper representation" to advise
the aforementioned stockholder not to assent because his old
stock at market ($1\frac{1}{2}$) represented $2\frac{1}{2}$ times the market value
of the new stock he would get under the plan? Does this
prove that the plan is not equitable? One might with reason
advise the stockholder to sell his stock if he thinks $12 will
be about right for the new stock; and such advice is not inconsistent with an argument to assent on the grounds that
the plan is fair and equitable. The disparity in the market
prices has no relevance to the question of assenting, however
much it may have to the question of selling.

The solicitors, on the other hand, might have been talking
about intrinsic investment values or perhaps giving their
opinions of what the market price would be if unaffected by
the speculative activity caused by submission of the modification plan.

When the Railroad presented the plan to the Commission
in 1949, both in public hearing and by brief, it stressed the
impossibility of assessing in rational terms the reasons for the
current market quotations of its several classes of stock, or
for the fluctuations in those quotations. Consequently, market values were rejected as having little bearing on the problem of allocation of new stock to the old classes of stock.[26]

[26] Railroad Brief, May 31, 1949, p. 30.

The Railroad explained that the determining principle for the allocation of stock among the various classes and series of stock was "earnings and the relative claims of the several classes to future earnings." [27]   Using this basis, the officers concluded that the noncumulative preferred and common stocks defied value analysis. "There are informed people," said the brief, "who consider those stocks worthless (R. 489), since there would be no possibility of dividends on such stocks for at least seventy-four years." [28]

The Commission accepted the arguments of the Railroad justifying the exchange of stock proposed for the noncumulative preferred and common stocks.   The report in April 1950 said:

> . . . In view of the long period necessary to pay off these arrears, it appears that the plain preferred-stock holders have little to hope for under the present capital-stock structure, whereas under the proposed plan they would have some reasonable prospect of an equity in the future earning power of the company. . . .
>
> Thus, for all practical purposes, as stated by witnesses for the applicant, both the plain preferred and the common stocks are worthless, since they represent no more than a call upon future earning power many years hence — approximately 75 years under the applicant's estimate — and in this respect there is little distinction between the two classes of stock. . . .
>
> Thus, while under the present capital-stock structure there is practically no equity left for the common stock, it appears that under the proposed modifications there is at least some chance of participation in the company's earnings.[29]

Again, in July 1950, the Commission referred to "the present noncumulative preferred stock, which, according to the evidence, is practically worthless from the standpoint of any equity in prospective earnings . . ." and to "the present common stock, which is of even less value from an earnings standpoint than the plain [noncumulative] preferred. . . ." [30]

The failure of the Department to see any other meaning

[27] Ibid., p. 33.

[28] Ibid., p. 36.

[29] 275 I.C.C. 397 at 445–446 (1950).

[30] 275 I.C.C. 527 at 544 (1950).

to value than that of market value made it entirely blind at this point to the investment value concept which lay at the very heart of the plan. Its interpretation of value led it to the easy conclusion of misrepresentation when any alleged statements by solicitors differed from the then market quotations.

No financial concept is harder to define in terms of "true representation" than that of value of stock. Quite obviously, if the stockholder asked, "What is my stock worth?" having in mind the current market (which ranged from $2\frac{1}{2}$ to $3\frac{7}{8}$), and the reply was "12 cents a share," either there was not a meeting of minds, or there was misrepresentation if the solicitor knew that the question referred to the market price of the day. But why assume that the questioner meant market price? If the solicitor had said "practically worthless," he would have been repeating what the Commission itself had been saying. There is no doubt but that one buying stocks for their *investment* worth in the fall of 1950 would have said Boston and Maine common stock was practically worthless even with the market at $2\frac{1}{2}$ a share.

Another seeming paradox in the question of values in this case is the disparity between the markets for the old common stock and the new stock to be issued in the ratio of one new share for 20 old shares. If an old share sells currently for $2\frac{1}{2}$, what convincing argument can be advanced for anyone to assent to a plan that will give him something worth perhaps only $2.50/20 or $12\frac{1}{2}$ cents? Mr. Nye mentioned this in a letter to the Railroad as a serious obstacle to getting the smart holders of common stock to assent; the best prospects, he thought, were the small scattered ones over the country.

There is a clear answer to the holder who refuses to assent to the plan on such market facts. The solicitor might well put the following questions:

(1) If the plan does not go through, is your stock likely to stay at $2\frac{1}{2}$?

(2) If it does go through, and the new common stock becomes dividend paying, will the price of the new stock be likely to stay at $12\frac{1}{2}$ cents? If a year's dividends on the new common stock start at $1 a share,[31] then will not a new share

[31] This was the year's dividend declared conditionally on the new common stock by the directors early in 1951.

giving $1 a year be worth more than the 20 old shares, which have paid nothing since 1931 and offer no hope of dividends for 74 years?

When one sees lawyers and expert witnesses spar for hours in cases where the valuation of stock is in dispute and where there is no meeting of minds because different concepts of value are involved, it is no surprise that an innocent holder of stock might think he was misled by a solicitor calling his stock worthless when $2\frac{1}{2}$ was the market.[32] Further analysis could have saved the Department from its conclusion that there was misrepresentation on this point.

The same reasoning applies to a stock being called "under water." How could stock be under water, the charge ran, when market value was something, even if low? In the true sense of that much used financial expression, the Boston and Maine common stock was decidedly "under water." The values assigned to the entire property under the "fair" plan passed by the Commission left nothing for the old common stock, and not the full amount for some layers of stock ahead of it. To conclude that it is misrepresentation to call old Boston and Maine common stock "under water" shows that the basic principle of the modification plan is not understood.[33]

[32] Even informed students of the subject fall into loose statements at times. Mr. L'Heureux, who rightly emphasizes the distinction between intrinsic (what we have called investment) and market values, says (p. 26 of the Opinion) : "Whether Greer was discussing the market value or the intrinsic worth of the present stock, it was a correct prediction that the value of the old stock would decrease after the plan went into effect."

If the exchange proposed by the plan was fair, would not the intrinsic worth of the new stock given in exchange for the old common stock be equal to the intrinsic worth of the old stock? Writers who overlook these distinctions in meaning, as did the author of the Note in *The Yale Law Journal,* are likely to add confusion rather than clarity. This note assumes throughout that "value" means only "market value," and on this basis refers to "startling instances of oral misrepresentation of the value of Boston & Maine stock." 62 *Yale Law Journal* 806 at 812 (1953) .

[33] It is not for this book on balloting procedures to consider fully the many points in which the interveners apparently failed to use financial terms in their accepted meaning. For instance, the Sakis group often used "book value" and "liquidating value" as synonymous. See, for example, the Commission's first report (275 I.C.C. 397 at 437) : "This intervener's [Sakis] proposed capitalization . . . was predicated on the applicant's present capital

The essential concept in this area of stock values is that "speculative value" and "investment value" are things apart. Would an *investor* buy Russian Imperial Bonds in 1945? Would a trustee fulfill his responsibility for prudent management if he bought some? They sold for 22 in 1945. There are long-shot takers in finance as at the race tracks.

Other Allegedly Improper Representations

Three stockholders declared that they had been urged to sell their stock. One of these had received two telephone calls, one from an unidentified man and one from a brokerage house, urging her to sell her stock on the grounds that it was worth about 75 cents a share. She refused either to sell or to assent. The other two stockholders did finally decide to sell, one within two weeks, and the other in the spring of 1951, when he sold at $2\frac{1}{2}$ stock that he had bought in 1946 at 10. Both assented their stock before selling. Testimony by Railroad officers was to the effect that they had never authorized giving stockholders advice to sell.[34] Furthermore, the Railroad was not interested in buying the stock itself, and these sales were in no way related to the purchases by one of the Railroad's directors, to be discussed later.

Two affidavits charged solicitors with saying that the plan was going through anyway and that almost enough assents had been received. An optimistic statement of this type had been deleted by the Commission from the first draft of a letter mailed by the Railroad to stockholders in September 1950. Neither of these affidavits was placed in the final proceedings, however.

Two affidavits specifically charged Mr. Greer, a special solicitor, with promising favors in return for assents (a job

stock liability plus surplus as shown on its books, resulting in a total new stock capitalization of $148,696,431, designated otherwise as the 'liquidation value' of the present stock or, also, as 'the book value of the total assets minus the total liabilities.' "

[34] The Railroad's Brief, dated October 20, 1952, said on page 21: "Advice to sell out would have been prejudicial to the Railroad, since such advice would have been the counsel of despair — certainly greatly at variance with the only possible philosophy which could motivate the promulgation of the Plan. Such advice would hardly conduce to an attitude favorable to the Plan."

with the Railroad, a directorship, low shipping rates). But one of these affiants was shown in the 1952 hearings to be an unreliable witness; and the other did not answer a subpoena to testify at the hearings. Furthermore, the former stockholder in his deposition of November 1951 admitted that he had not been misled by the alleged promises.

COMMISSION CONTROL INCLUDES THE SOLICITATION OF REJECTIONS

In all the charges and argument over the abuses in solicitation by those seeking assents it seems to have been completely overlooked that the statute was also careful to provide protection for the stockholder against high-pressure salesmanship from those who urged him to dissent. Nowhere in the briefs or testimony is there any reference to the possibility that objectors to the plan might be as interested in getting holders to dissent as the Railroad and its solicitors were in obtaining assents. In the argument over the proprieties in these solicitation matters, particularly oral solicitation, one would expect some reference to the possibility that the alleged misrepresentations in soliciting assents might be matched by the adverse statements of those who were rounding up the objectors. The statutory responsibility of the Commission for control of solicitation is as great for one as for the other.

The activity of objecting groups would seem of necessity usually applied more in oral solicitation than through specially prepared documents approved by the Commission. First, their arguments would be so diametrically opposed to the reasoning in the Commission's own report that it would seem hard to phrase objections that would pass its scrutiny. Next, the expense of circularizing would be an obstacle to small minority groups. The Department apparently never considered the possibility that those who were bending every effort to defeat the plan might be as guilty of misrepresentation as those urging its acceptance.

The underlying assumption of those who made a big issue of the alleged misrepresentations seemed to be that small holders are easy prey for unscrupulous solicitors. The Railroad, they said or implied, had power on its side, particularly in money for solicitation expense. This point of view apparently leaves out of account the power already given minorities by the high percentage of assents required, and the application of the percentage to the total outstanding securities rather than those voting. In the face of such power, there certainly is no warrant for giving sole attention to the misrepresentations of those soliciting assents to the entire neglect of possible like abuses by the opposition.[35]

It would seem logical for the Commission to worry as much or more about pressure tactics of those who solicit opposition to a "fair" plan as about the tactics of those who are trying to gain assents.[36] These questions become somewhat academic in modification plans where the securities concerned are bonds, and where the 75% assents may be obtained easily by no more effort than mere publication of the plan. But in closely fought contests, as wholly stock modifications are likely to be, the solicitation problem does not arise altogether on the side of the applicant itself.

THE COMMISSION'S FINDINGS AS TO IMPROPER REPRESENTATIONS

The Commission gave special consideration to these particular charges of the Department, the more so because they came after extensive investigation and were supported by affidavits and depositions. In themselves, the legal formalities and the costly effort to marshal the evidence supported a

[35] This one-sided treatment of misrepresentations, particularly in oral solicitation, carries throughout the Note in *The Yale Law Journal* (Vol. 62, April 1953, particularly pages 810 ff.). The author of this Note carries his whole discussion in terms of solicitors of the Railroad, with no implication that there may be equal inducements for those on the opposite side. It is unrealistic to assume that a solicitor of assents would stoop to "every possible wile" mainly because he is given some compensation, and that those who solicit for the opposition typically operate on the highest ethical plane even though their motives may be inspired by their nuisance value.

[36] The Commission does recognize the problem when it decries methods that would encourage "strikers" to withhold their assents to meritorious plans unless they secure "better treatment than they deserve." Query: Is a stockholder who himself is holding out against assent in order to sell out at a price above the market, and urges a fellow stockholder to do the same, a solicitor using improper methods?

presumption that the Department thought it was constructing a tight case as to illegal solicitation methods. Nevertheless, the Commission concluded:

> We find no support in the facts disclosed in the above-described affidavits for charges of misrepresentation which would justify invalidation of the assents in question. In this connection, it should be noted that none of the stockholders who gave assents under these circumstances has attempted to withdraw his assent or is urging that the Commission's order approving the plan be set aside.[37]

The implication here is that "where there was smoke there must be fire" in the tactics of solicitors, but not enough to justify invalidation of the assents. In general, the Commission concluded that personal solicitation presents important problems, that it is necessary for a successful campaign where securities are widely distributed,[38] and that "It may be impracticable to attempt to eliminate all pressure tactics of the solicitors." [39] The Commission adds, finally, that "Correction of improper methods which might be used in personal solicitation can best be accomplished by closer supervision of the solicitors." [40] This general observation gives no criterion of propriety in solicitation methods, or of the effective devices for supervision of solicitors.

In all the appeals to stockholders for assents, a fact to keep in mind is that the Commission itself issued the initial strong appeal by accepting the plan as just, reasonable, in the public interest, and in the best interests of the Railroad and each class of its stockholders. Nevertheless, in controlling solici-

[37] 282 I.C.C. 750 at 773 (1953).

[38] And it might be added, when they are highly speculative and in some cases lost and forgotten because of a long history of no dividends and low value as in this case.

[39] 282 I.C.C. 750 at 800.

[40] The report on the Western Maryland Railway securities modification (290 I.C.C. 445 (1954)) incorporated the conclusions drawn from the Boston and Maine case. It said, at pp. 471–472: "Applicant is cautioned to exercise close supervision over any solicitors employed for the purpose of procuring assents and over any of its regular employees soliciting such assents to assure, insofar as possible, the avoidance of false or misleading representations and undue pressure tactics. . . ." The order in the Western Maryland case followed the Boston and Maine order very closely as to solicitation practices.

tation methods, the Commission is really saying that the end, a fair plan, does not justify every means for getting it accepted. A stockholder should be protected even in making a wrong choice — his dissent from a fair plan.

The Commission's suggestion that the remedy for improper solicitation methods might lie in closer supervision of solicitors leads naturally to the question of how best to achieve it. The first requisite for a good salesman is to know his product. The thing sold here is a plan; the solicitor for assents is really asking a holder to buy a new security. High-pressure salesmanship, if it means only enthusiasm expressed in repeated telephone calls, is harmless if based on honest description of the product. The major obstacle to proper representation in soliciting assents or dissents to recapitalization plans is the difficulty both the solicitor and the holder have in understanding the plan. In contrast, there would be little danger that an engineer-salesman of a machine tool would succeed in misrepresenting his product to an equally informed plant manager of a workshop.

Perhaps the most feasible method for accomplishing closer supervision of solicitors is to find some administrative device for making the solicitation material more useful to the stockholders. The analysis in this chapter supports the view that personal solicitation is necessary for successful campaigns, especially for wholly stock plans. The ideal is for all assents to represent a reasoned conviction; intelligent voting depends on informed opinion. The solicitation material should throw clear light on the essence of the problem; the solicitor should be able to face the stockholder with effective analytical material to support and explain the plan.

The prospectus requirements written into the securities legislation in the 1930's present at least a partial analogy to the problem at hand. The prospectus is a device for simplifying the more elaborate registration statement, and is meant to be a specialized piece of sales literature. The purpose and content of the legislation on prospectuses as it was included in the Securities Act of 1933 have a direct bearing on the official solicitation material in the section 20b cases. We carry the analogy only so far as to observe that new securities are put out in both situations; there is need for information before an intelligent decision can be made; and the statutes, section 20b and the Securities Act of 1933, provide specifically for certain official materials — "solicitation material" and the "prospectus," respectively.

It is also true that the ICC's functions under section 20b are distinctly different from the SEC's functions under the Securities Act. The SEC disclaims directly that it expresses an opinion on the merits of the security. Indeed, it is a criminal offense under the Securities Act to represent that the effectiveness of the registration statement is an indication that the information is true and complete. In a section 20b case, however, the ICC has the statutory responsibility for passing on the merits of the plan, a function more analogous to that of the SEC under the Public Utility Holding Company Act.

The main part of the so-called "solicitation material" sent to stockholders in all the section 20b cases has been the Commission's closely reasoned report (58 pages in the Boston and Maine case), together with the order covering submission procedure. The typical stockholder, however, is not interested in such refinements, for example, as the technical explanation of why the Examiner's recommendations as to allocation among the lettered preferred stocks were modified slightly in the final plan. The Report of April 19, 1950, is an admirable example of orderly presentation of conflicting views in the evolution of a plan. But the Commission itself would deny that its report was written to "sell" the plan, although it would not have found the plan fair and in the public interest unless it thought its report supported such finding. Relatively few of the many stockholders would have any interest in careful study of the Commission's report or could understand it thoroughly. Such documents are not for popular consumption. Detailed analysis and fine distinctions in reasoning are important for the record but they do not make potent sales literature. This is not to argue for omitting the Commission's report from the solicitation material; but there would be point in adding a simplified abstract to emphasize the gist of the proposal.

With reference again to the analogy of the sale of a new security, if a prospectus is thought so necessary where the active market agents are dealers, how much more is a simplified document essential for a complicated plan (providing for a new security) being offered to 8,000 stockholders. The principal questions for the Boston and Maine stockholders were: What are prospective earnings in which my present holdings have rights to share? How do my rights under the plan compare with what I have now? A proper sales document could provide answers for these essential questions in simple and direct statements without the confusing details and technical explanations. Such a document might well follow the methods used by many corporations when they propose plans involving stockholders' interests; they list a series of significant questions likely to be raised, with concise answers to each.

It would not be the responsibility of the Commission to produce such a document but only to scrutinize it as sales literature. The Railroad started the plan, prepared argument for the public hearing, and could be required to prepare an effective appeal for assents. The problem is how to get helpful representation of facts and to minimize the opportunity for misrepresentation.

CHAPTER X

Charges of Controlled Assents

THESE charges were particularly important because they involved interpretation of the statute. Of the many charges brought by the Department, they were the only ones that the Commission found to require disqualification of assents. The framers of the statute took special care that assents to a section 20b modification should come only from holders of securities not controlled by the carrier itself or by those controlling the carrier. The three episodes in the Boston and Maine case that were finally held to result in invalid assents raise fundamental questions of principle and procedure. For necessary background we first turn to the statute.

THE STATUTORY BAN ON CONTROLLED ASSENTS

The statute provided that:

. . . For the purposes of this section [20b] a security or an evidence of indebtedness shall not be deemed to be outstanding if in the determination of the Commission the assent of the holder thereof to any proposed alteration or modification is within the control of the carrier or of any person or persons controlling the carrier.[1]

In its final report in this case the Commission found its definition of control in section 1 (3) (b) of the Interstate Commerce Act, which construes control for purposes of specified sections of the act [2] as

. . . *actual* as well as legal control, whether maintained or exercised through or by reason *of the method of or circum-*

[1] From section 20b (3).
[2] Sections 5, 12 (1), 20, 304 (a) (7), 310, 320, 904 (b), 910, and 913. When section 20b was added, it was not specified as one of this list.

247

stances surrounding organization or *operation,* through or by common directors, officers, . . . *or through or by any other direct or indirect means.* . . . [Italics added by the Commission.]

Although these tests of control were made applicable to certain named sections of the act, of which section 20b was not then a part, the Commission believed that it should be guided by them in determining the questions of control under section 20b.[3]

Certain questions are decisive in understanding the statutory restriction on controlled assents in section 20b. First, when are assents "within the control of the carrier or of any person or persons controlling the carrier"? Second, whose responsibility is it to decide this question, on what principle, and at what stage in the proceedings?

The Meaning of the Provision Against Controlled Assents

The best authority as to the original purpose and meaning of the "control" clause (section 20b (3)) in the statute is that of the Commission itself:

> The purpose . . . is to prevent a company which controls or is controlled by an applicant from voting the applicant's security for an alteration or modification thereof proposed by the applicant. It was intended to protect the holders of the publicly-held securities which it proposed to alter or modify, and to prevent situations similar to that which arose in the Chesapeake & Ohio–Pere Marquette merger, where the controlling company was accused of proposing terms which the dissenting stockholders of the controlled company, including holders of common stock of the company, alleged were adverse to the controlled company and not just and reasonable from the standpoint of the publicly-held stock of the controlled company, including the common stock.
>
> It is obviously undesirable that a carrier, or a holding company or parent company, be permitted to vote its bonds on a question affecting bondholder rights, inasmuch as it may have a conflicting interest. . . .[4]

---

[3] 282 I.C.C. 750 at 787 (1953).

[4] Letter from the Committee on Legislation and Rules, Interstate Commerce Commission, to Senator Charles W. Tobey, Chairman, Senate Committee on Interstate and Foreign Commerce, March 6, 1953 (mimeo.), p. 3.

The reference here is altogether to securities held and voted by the carrier itself, or a holding or parent company. Legal writers [5] have explained that those drafting the bill had in mind the inequity when a carrier, which was the author of a plan of bond modification, or its controlling stockholders voted bonds owned by them. When the bill was changed before enactment to permit stock modifications, the clause on controlled assents was adapted to include stock, seemingly through inadvertence. This produced the illogical result that "in a readjustment plan involving voting stock, the shareholders controlling the carrier are disenfranchised, despite the fact that they are seriously affected by the proposal and have no conflicting interests." [6]

None of the discussion of the clause has applied to the purchases of voting securities during the voting period by individuals connected with the carrier's management. It is noteworthy, also, that the amendments proposed in a 1953 Senate bill would rewrite the clause so as to retain the voting power of all stock in a modification plan.[7] The Commission favored the amendment provided it could retain power to increase the percentage of assents required in a class if it appeared there were definite conflicts of interests between the controlling stockholders and the minority stock interest. It is in the light of the legislative intent of the clause and also of the suggested amendment that one must view the Department's charges and the Commission's decision to invalidate certain assents as being controlled by the Railroad in this case.

As an illustration of "persons controlling the carrier" we have, in the recent case of the Central Railroad Company of New Jersey, the Reading Company as holder of $57\frac{1}{2}\%$ of the

---

[5] Chauncey H. Hand, Jr., and G. Clark Cummings, "Consensual Securities Modification," 63 *Harvard Law Review*, 957 (1950).

[6] Ibid., p. 966. Billyou also has commented on the problem of securities controlled by the applicant (39 *Virginia Law Review*, 490–491 (1953)).

[7] Hearing before the Committee on Interstate and Foreign Commerce, U.S. Senate, 83d Congress, 1st Session, on S. 978, March 23, 1953, p. 2. The last sentence of 20b (3), quoted above, would be changed to read: "For the purposes of this section a security (other than a security entitled to vote for the election of directors of the carrier). . . ." Further discussion of these proposed amendments is left for Chapter XII.

applicant's outstanding common stock and also some of its general mortgage bonds. As the Commission's report stated, Reading Company controlled the applicant and had power to have the application for the section 20b action withdrawn. Therefore the ensuing order withheld the vote from the stock held by Reading Company.[8]

The Reading Company decision suggests a further aspect of the control question. Does control of a carrier mean the control of enough of its voting stock to dictate all management decisions, or of just enough to be able to exercise negative control through veto of a specific act of management, in this case a recapitalization plan? For instance, when one holder votes over 25% of the outstanding amount in a class, being enough to veto a plan, it can be said that control of plan-making resides in that one holder.[9] This was the actual position of The Pennroad Corporation in the Boston and Maine case.

If one considers the lineage of the control clause in the statute, and the former section 20b cases where it has been applied, it is clear that the concept of control is not broad enough to include control in a special area only, as through a veto power of a modification plan. The Reading Company's control of Central of New Jersey was an instance of absolute control of voting stock. Such instances have been regulated since the 1920 Transportation Act, which in sec-

---

[8] 271 I.C.C. 501 and 692 (1949). It is interesting to note that the holding of Reading Company constituted almost the whole of the assurances of assent (59½% of the common stock) filed. With regard to the provision in the statute giving the Commission power to raise the required percentage above 75% if fewer than 25 holders held 75% of any class, the order in this instance stated "omitting the shares held by the Reading Company, not more than 75 percent of the remainder is held by fewer than 25 holders."

The fact that the assurances of assent of the Reading Company were reported on the application to the Commission shows that at this point in the proceedings there was apparently no thought of the disfranchisement of the Reading holdings under the control clause.

[9] Realistically, it would take a concentrated holding of less than this theoretical figure because of the normal expectancy that much less than 100% would be likely to vote. Thus, if only 90% of the outstanding stock in a class returned an assent or refused to do so, one holder of 15%+ would hold an effective veto. This percentage would decrease as those who did not take a stand either way increased.

tion 5 gave the Commission powers over applications of railroads for acquiring control of other carriers. Applications
that involved consolidations into systems were not allowable
because such objectives must await a comprehensive plan to
be formulated by the Commission. For our purpose, it is
sufficient to note that the machinery of control described in
section 5 comprised not only the contractual relations between carriers in pooling arrangements and use of joint facilities, but the control of one carrier over another through
acquisition of stock interest.[10] Nothing is found in the history of Commission action in the cases under section 5 to support the conclusion that the phrase in section 20b — "persons
controlling the carrier" — would apply to the veto power of
Pennroad through its holdings of over 25% of one class of
Boston and Maine stock.[11]

A further question, however, arises in Pennroad's power in
this case to veto the plan: should not the statute provide for
such a contingency in some such manner as it does for a class
of security when 75% is held by less than 25 holders? It
would seem inescapable logic that if concentrated holdings
in a class should be examined to prevent their domination of
the decision of the class, the veto power of a single holder of
25%+ would be a still greater threat to the broader interests
of the scattered holdings of the remaining percentage.[12]

There is evidence in the Commission's initial report of
April 19, 1950, that its conception of controlled assents at the
time related only to control through stock ownership as in
the Reading case. The report included the facts and the de-

[10] A thorough account of Commission decisions on applications for approval of such plans for acquisition of control is found in I. L. Sharfman,
The Interstate Commerce Commission, Part III, Volume A (1935), pp. 430–
474.

[11] The decision of Division 4 in Western Maryland Railway Company
Securities Modification, 290 I.C.C. 445, confirms this view. That decision
stated (p. 470) : "The fact that LaGrange and Johnson may control enough
of the applicant's stock to defeat any plan under section 20b for alteration or
modification of its stock, as argued by intervener, does not constitute 'control
of the carrier' as that term is used in the last sentence of paragraph (3) of
section 20b."

[12] The implications of such questions were more fully discussed in Chapter V, in which the decision of the Commission to require 87% to assent in
the plain preferred class was considered.

cision on charges that Pennroad Corporation and Boston Railroad Holding Company in fact controlled the Railroad. The two together held 42.91% of the shares of all classes and the Holding Company 55.53% of the common stock. Officers of the Railroad denied any exercise of control by these two holders, and the Commission so found. Presumably, if the Commission had expected other "control" situations to arise during the submission period like the three later identified as such in its final report, its regulations for certification of the final vote would have provided for the exclusion of assents of such origin.

This report concluded that ". . . with the exception of shares held in the applicant's treasury and which are to be canceled, none of the affected securities of any class is held by any holders whose assent to the proposed alterations and modifications is within the control of the applicant or any person controlling the applicant." [13]   Even if there had been no reference to treasury stock, it would not thereby have become voting stock nor would it be considered to be outstanding.[14]

All precedents lead to the conclusion that "control" as used in the statute refers to ownership of securities by either the carrier itself or a company controlling it.   Furthermore, "control" should be considered in its absolute sense as denoting full power to direct action, rather than a limited power, or influence.

Questions of Controlled Stock in This Case

There were three instances in this case where control of assents by the carrier was charged by the Department and found to exist by the Commission.   These were instances, the Commission explained, where common stock held by individuals was assented by the holders in circumstances that amounted to virtual assents by the Railroad itself.   This was a new interpretation of control, but inasmuch as the ballots

[13] 275 I.C.C. 397 at 424 (1950).

[14] It is established in corporation law that treasury stock may be reissued until canceled, but has no dividend or voting rights and is not held to be outstanding.   See Henry Winthrop Ballantine, *Ballantine on Corporations* (Chicago, Callaghan and Company, rev. ed., 1946), pp. 614–618.

disallowed on this basis were not needed after the outstanding stock was refigured, the broader interpretation has not been tested in the courts.

With respect to controlled assents, as with other charges in the Trial Brief, the Department asserted illegality by its own interpretation of the statute. The Trial Brief stated:

> That the railroad acquired control of substantial blocks of stock through purchases by a railroad director, through borrowing by a paid railroad solicitor, and through connivance with the director of another corporation.[15]

Beyond this, the Trial Brief opened up still broader questions on controlled stock when it raised the "substantial legal question" of whether the Commission should not have excluded all directors' stock from voting. Although facts on directors' holdings were available to the Commission, it had raised no question of control with reference to them. Nowhere has the Commission indicated that it would consider directors' stock in the category of controlled stock. With regard to the purchases by a director referred to in the Trial Brief, the Department went on to say that ". . . the railroad at no time made a disclosure to the Commission of the assents over which it with its director had acquired control. The railroad defaulted in this respect even though [two supplemental applications were filed]." The brief continued, "Thus there is brought into sharp focus the demand by the plaintiffs [the Sakis group] that the Commission afford . . . access to the ballots and related voting documents, and this was refused by the Commission."[16]

The Procedure for Designating Controlled Stock

It is clearly shown in the section 20b reports and orders that the Commission itself takes the responsibility for designating controlled or controlling stock, and does so at the time it issues its order of submission. This was the case, for example, in the order for Central Railroad Company of New Jersey just referred to. Again, in the bond modification plan of Macon, Dublin & Savannah Railroad Company, $5,000

---

[15] Department of Justice, Trial Brief, p. 21.
[16] Ibid., p. 29.

principal amount of bonds held by Seaboard Air Line Railroad Company, which controlled the Macon Railroad, were "not to be deemed to be outstanding" for voting.[17] In other cases the Commission has specifically found no controlled or controlling stock.

A further question is how to find out about controlled assents that develop during the period. Unless the Commission asks the carrier for its certificate as to controlled stock at the close of the period, whose responsibility is it to check on situations that have developed meanwhile? Certainly it is not that of the depositary, which recognizes only stockholders of record. In the Boston and Maine case, for example, the Railroad certified the vote on the basis of the depositary's certificate. Impliedly, having the official finding that there was no controlled stock at the beginning of the period, the Railroad would be under the obligation to report situations of controlled assents that had developed during the voting, and then to subtract the ballots so outlawed. This obligation, however, requires that the Railroad's officers have been advised as to what constitutes controlled stock.

The Commission has the positive duty to implement the statute with rules supplying clear definition of controlled stock. In voting contests, whether in politics or in finance, the two essential steps to a valid poll are, first, the list of eligible voters, and second, proper voting by those on the list. This sequence is significant. The official list is a *prevoting* matter; then the rules of procedure should protect against irregularities in voting from that list. The matter of determining controlled assents is a part of making the official voters' list. In this view, after voting starts there are no controlled assents in the statutory sense unless changes have occurred that would have classified the stock as "controlled" at the beginning of the vote. The only basis for disqualification after the submission period is under way is for patent illegality or a breach of an existing rule. These were never alleged by any party to this dispute.

Effective administration in any area of government regulation presupposes enough supervision of procedure to permit the regulatory body to be sure that the statutory require-

[17] 271 I.C.C. 376 at 387 (1948).

ments have been met. The Commission had notice of alleged controlled assents in the charges of the Sakis group and the Department after the balloting period closed, yet it made no independent study of them. The fact that 18 months after voting closed the Commission ruled out the three blocks of assents as being controlled by the Railroad suggests that its own mechanism for reviewing the whole procedure was inadequate. Only on the reopening of the case following the litigation pressed by the Sakis group and the Department did it review all the evidence and disfranchise the three blocks of stock. If the Sakis group had not brought civil suit, the modification plan would have gone into effect in regular course, and we never should have had the Commission ruling on the charge of controlled assents.

Unless the Commission can say when the balloting is over that its own close supervision shows no controlled stock has been voted, it clearly puts the burden on minorities to prove otherwise. The passive role of studying only alleged illegal procedures leaves the way open to possible abuse unless a zealous minority, at risk of an expensive legal action, is successful in accomplishing a rehearing of evidence. This places the responsibility for observance of the statute in the wrong place. Full compliance with the statute is not to be assumed until proved otherwise; it is to be assumed because the rules under which voting is conducted are framed to guard against invalid assents.

It is in the setting of the statutory disfranchisement of controlled stock that we turn to the three episodes cited by the Department and the Commission as control situations in the Boston and Maine case. There would be no need of tracing the detail of the episodes except to see how tenuous was the thread of the alleged control, and especially to find how the rules for future cases can be drawn to establish better balloting practices.

In determining the merit of the charges of invalidity of the assents in these transactions, we should keep three tests in mind: (a) does the transaction make the assents invalid under a provision in section 20b; (b) is any part of the transaction illegal in itself, quite apart from section 20b; (c) do the transactions violate in any way the Commission's rules for balloting? Although the Department's brief used words at times implying a planned maneuver to obtain assents, the Department, and finally the Commission, found the invalidity wholly that of assents controlled by the Railroad. One can assume that if the Department had found a trace of illegality other than under section 20b, it would have fully argued the point in its brief.

THE PENNROAD-PIZZINI TRANSACTION

The facts in the arrangement between The Pennroad Corporation and B. W. Pizzini & Co. were never in dispute. The following account is based largely upon the deposition of Mr. Pizzini, the briefs in the proceedings, and Mr. L'Heureux's report of his personal inquiry.

Pennroad had long held substantial amounts of the various classes of Boston and Maine stock and had assented all its holdings for the plan. Following their usual procedure toward the year end, in the fall of 1951 the officers were preparing for tax reasons to sell certain of the company's holdings where substantial losses would be taken. A block of 21,000 shares of Boston and Maine stock fell in this category. Mr. B. F. Pepper, Pennroad president, called Mr. Pizzini about the proposed sale, after talking the matter over with Mr. F. C. Dumaine, a Pennroad director who had recently been on the Boston and Maine board. The Pennroad officials wanted the assents to remain effective until the plan was consummated. Mr. Pizzini assured them that the sale could be made so as to maintain the assents even if he should sell interests in the purchased block to his customers.[18] He

[18] Each purchaser signed the following agreement with B. W. Pizzini & Co.:

In consideration of the sale to me of ___ shares of Boston and Maine A 1st pfd. stock at ___ per share, I hereby agree said stock may stand in the name of B. W. Pizzini & Co., Inc., who shall have full voting rights therein and will deposit same in a special account at the Trust Company of North America, 115 Broadway, New York 6, N.Y., until

1. The plan is approved.
2. The plan is disapproved.
3. If at the end of six (6) months neither Number 1 or Number 2 has materialized and I wish to dispose of my holding, I agree to offer same to you for the group account at the then fair market value.

had customers who would feel highly favored to participate in a purchase that looked profitable over the short turn; they had no interest in the voting rights.

If Mr. Pepper could have foreseen that the voting would end by December 14, the sale might well have been postponed and still have accomplished its purpose for his company. It was agreed that the stock would stand in Mr. Pizzini's name until the voting was over, and that the voting control of the block would be vested in Messrs. Pizzini, Dumaine, and French, the president of Boston and Maine Railroad. At this time Mr. French knew nothing of the arrangement. Mr. Pizzini, whose firm had long been a dealer in Boston and Maine securities and who had come to know Mr. French personally, suggested him as the third member of the voting group. In explaining this aspect of the arrangement, he said that it was not necessary that Mr. French even know about it, much less be made a voting trustee; but in view of their long association, the gesture was a natural business courtesy and would show the good intent of the parties to do nothing to jeopardize the plan. Mr. French's only official act was to verify the end of the voting period as of December 14, 1950, which freed the block of stock from the voting restriction.

The Department in its Amended Answer of November 1, 1951, described the incident and drew conclusions in one short paragraph, as follows:

> The railroad president on November 15, 1950 acquired joint control of the voting rights to a large block of railroad stock which had previously been assented, and by said joint control he was able to and did thereby foreclose the right of subsequent holders of said stock to revoke said prior assents, if they chose to do so, whereas the railroad did not declare the submission period closed until 5.05 P.M. on December 14, 1950 and thereby terminate for the first time the right of revocation. The railroad failed and neglected to disclose these circumstances to Old Colony or to the Commission. Said assents were improperly included in the certificates of Old Colony and of the railroad.[19]

[19] Amended Answer of United States of America, Defendant in Civil Action No. 763-51, in the District Court for the District of Columbia, November 1, 1951, p. 7.

The Trial Brief added a further argument. Referring to the terms of the Commission's order, the Department concluded that "any stockholder who had assented his stock, and his transferee, had the right at any time up to the close of the voting period to revoke the previous assent. By virtue of the conditions on the sale to Pizzini, his transferees were denied the opportunity to determine for themselves. . . ."[20]

The Department thus found that the Pennroad-Pizzini transaction invalidated the assents in two respects: the Railroad through its president acquired voting control, and the restrictive agreement on revocations was forbidden by the Commission's order.

With regard to the charge that the Railroad's president acquired joint control of the voting rights, the description of the transactions shows that Mr. French's participation was unnecessary and entirely passive. One must conclude that he did not foreclose the right to revoke; it was the contract between Mr. Pizzini and his willing customers that surrendered the right.[21]

[20] Department of Justice, Trial Brief, p. 64.

[21] Mr. L'Heureux gave special attention to the legal connotation in the Department's language. His criticism follows:

"When 3 trustees are named, the law is to the effect that all decisions are made by a unanimous vote, except in the case of a charitable trust. In this case, the purpose of the trust was to insure that the shares already assented would remain assented. It is totally unrealistic to contemplate a situation where Mr. French would want to rescind the assent and the other two would want to maintain the assents. However, if that unlikely situation developed, Mr. French could not veto the other two trustees, as they could get a court order to make him carry out the plain purpose of the trust. If the reverse were true, and the other two trustees decided to rescind the assents, Mr. French could make them adhere to the clear intent of the trust through a court order but this can hardly be construed to be a veto. The fact is that only those who created the trust could change the purpose of the trust during the submission period. It is hard to understand how the Railroad can be held to be in control of these shares under the circumstances." (Opinion, p. 41.)

In addition to this legal point of trust law, Mr. L'Heureux commented on another angle of the situation:

". . . Furthermore, there is no proof that the Boston and Maine Railroad, as distinguished from Mr. French, had knowledge of the existence of the agreement or had approved or authorized its President to represent the Railroad as a trustee. This can hardly be considered a matter within the usual scope of a railroad president's authority. Mr. French accepted to be a trustee

As to the second charge, that the agreement was forbidden by order, nowhere does the Department show that the order banned any contracts that stockholders might make regarding voting rights. In this instance the purchasers signed their rights away in a voluntary agreement and with full knowledge.[22] They were sheer speculators for profit, not purchasers with reasoned attitudes toward the merits of the plan.[23]

The Department's statement that "The railroad failed and neglected to disclose these circumstances to Old Colony or to the Commission," implies that Mr. French had a duty he did not fulfill. Nowhere in the regulations is such duty spelled out. If Mr. French had had any notion that his figurehead position under the agreement would invalidate ballots, he certainly would have refused to serve. Moreover, why should the depositary or the Commission be notified of an arrangement only designed to hold assents already recorded?

The Commission, in describing the incident, stressed that "At the time of the agreement, there had been no conversations with French on the subject and he was not a party to such agreement. However, he testified that, when later informed about it, he was agreeable to the arrangement, although it was made without his knowledge and upon no suggestion from him."[24] The Commission made no mention of the Department's charge that the agreement itself was illegal. Indeed, the implication was that the agreement served a purpose not objectionable in itself. The Commission said:

---

as an individual. The fact that he undoubtedly thought it benefited the Railroad does not vitiate his participation as a private individual trustee in this matter." (Ibid.)

[22] The Railroad's Brief of October 20, 1952 (p. 23) comments on the point: "There is some suggestion in the record that Pizzini's customers should have had the unrestricted right to vote the shares. But the customers when purchasing the stock from Pizzini entered into arms' length contracts with him, and any contract restricts the activities of the parties thereto *pro tanto*. Responsible people were bargaining at all times with full knowledge of all the facts." See also L'Heureux's Opinion, p. 41.

[23] At least it can be said that they were willing not to take a stand against it. As Railroad counsel put it: "By accepting the conditions of purchase they were in effect expressing their approval of the Plan." Railroad Brief, October 20, 1952, p. 23.

[24] 282 I.C.C. 750 at 789 (1953).

. . . his [Mr. French's] subsequent acquiescence in the arrangement made him a party to it, and gave *him* [italics supplied] the power to veto any attempted revocation of the assent, thereby giving him control over it. As president of the railroad, it was his duty to carry out the purpose of the railroad to obtain approval of its proposals. He was the railroad's representative and through him the railroad had the power to control the assent of the 21,000 shares. Since the assenting of these shares was within the control of the railroad, they cannot be classed as outstanding under the provisions of paragraph (3) of section 20b. . . .[25]

To rule that Mr. French was in control of these assents is to give serious meaning to a descriptive term, "voting trustee," which loses significance when the real factual situation is analyzed. The trust arrangement was an unnecessary formality, and Mr. French played no necessary part. The agreement to forego the right of revocation was the essence of the transaction. To call these assents controlled by the Railroad is a surprising decision.

This is an instance where a close operational setup between Commission, Railroad, and the depositary would have provided the means of ready communication on balloting matters, so that the Pennroad-Pizzini arrangement would have come up naturally in discussion, and as a result the only thing found objectionable — Mr. French's acceptance of a sinecure — could have been avoided. The mistake, if any, was in giving grounds for the suspicion that any such transaction touched by an officer, particularly a president, must be a maneuver for control.

STOCK PURCHASES BY A DIRECTOR

Here also, as in the Pennroad-Pizzini transaction, the essential facts were never in dispute. Mr. Coolidge, a director of the Railroad and a member of the committee to work out the plan of recapitalization, decided late in November 1950 to purchase blocks of unassented common stock and assent them.[26] He knew that assents for the common stock were

---

[25] Ibid., p. 790.
[26] An illustration of somewhat similar action and intent by an officer of

coming in slowly. He had already assented his own and his family's substantial holdings of prior preference stock, and he stood ready to go still further by purchasing common stock, if necessary, up to $30,000 from his brokerage account. As came out at the hearing, any losses that might result could be offset against capital gains. A director of long standing, he wished to see the plan succeed. His plans for an extended absence required that he leave the purchases to his broker, with instructions that if the president of the Railroad confirmed the continuing need for assents in the common class, the broker was to buy unassented common shares for his account.

Obviously, Mr. Coolidge could not be sure that additional assents would result from purchases in the market; his purpose was to get *new* assents. Probably a premium would have to be paid for unassented blocks. How much was warranted? Presumably, if votes were coming in rapidly, a small premium would be sufficient. If a large block turned up, the broker might make a higher offer in order to make a quick purchase. Mr. Coolidge and his broker agreed that the Railroad's officers, who were keeping score on assent to-

---

another railroad was given in a statement of James M. Hood, president of the American Short Line Railroad Association, before a House Committee in 1947. Mr. Hood said:

"To digress a moment, I recall before the enactment of the Chandler Act an attempt by one of our railroads to compose a mortgage securing 1.5 million dollars of 6-percent bonds which had become burdensome and on which the maturity day was only a few months distant. We finally succeeded in securing the assent of all but $3,000 of the 1.5 million dollar issue to a 10-year extension of the maturity date and a reduction of the interest rate from 6 to 4 percent.

"As stated before, there was no provision in the law at that time to require the owners of those $3,000 in bonds to assent. It would have been a preferment of creditors to use corporate funds to retire those $3,000 of bonds, and the president of the railroad personally acquired them at a considerable premium.

"In other words, he paid well over $1,000 for each bond. I have forgotten the exact figure, but it was something like $3,600 in accrued interest that he paid for $3,000 of bonds, which, in effect, were facing reorganization. He used his personal funds to do that, and then after acquiring them, assented." Hearings before the Committee on Interstate and Foreign Commerce, House of Representatives, 80th Congress, 1st Session, on H.R. 2298, May 19, 1947 (Washington, Government Printing Office, 1947), p. 41.

tals, were the natural source of information. Mr. Everett W. Smith, in the Railroad's financial office, was on the lookout for unassented stock and could gauge the need for assents and a reasonable price for available blocks. All the participants in the discussions testified that the actual decision to purchase in each case was to be the broker's.[27]

Early in December the Railroad president, who knew of the plan, sent his financial officers to confer with the broker. The officers knew of unassented stock that could be bought. The broker was ready to buy at a satisfactory price. It was also agreed that time would be saved if the broker asked the sellers to execute an assent before the sale.

All told, the broker bought 8,500 shares of assented common stock in three blocks. The simplest transaction was the purchase on December 12 from one of the broker's customers of 800 shares at $3\frac{1}{8}$, which was $\frac{3}{8}$ of a point over the market bid price. The Railroad officers' only part in this sale was to assure the broker, when asked, that assents were still needed and that the price seemed reasonable.

Another transaction was the purchase on December 13 by the broker's New York office of a block of 2,700 shares at 4, a price $1\frac{3}{8}$ points above the market bid. Georgeson & Co. had made unsuccessful attempts by telephone to obtain the assent for these shares. The stockholder was willing to assent and sell if it was made worth his while, and finally said he would sell at $4 a share. When this information reached the broker through the Railroad officers, he decided to make the purchase. Only 2,400 shares were assented, 300 still being in the names of brokers who had formerly owned them.

The largest purchase, and the one particularly involved in charges of improper solicitation and recording, was that of 5,000 shares belonging to Mr. Harry Zucker. This block was located by Mr. Greer, a special solicitor, and Mr. Everett Smith.[28] Mr. Zucker was persuaded to lower his asking price

[27] Hearing before the Examiner, August 26 and 27, 1952, pp. 1170, 1196, 1262, 1350.

[28] It happened that the three blocks of stock bought for Mr. Coolidge's account were all purchased from individuals who later signed affidavits related to improper representations by solicitors. These charges, which have been discussed in Chapter IX, raise questions distinct from the basic one in

from a substantial premium, and on December 15 the broker bought at $3\frac{1}{4}$, which was $\frac{7}{8}$ of a point above the market bid.

The net result of Mr. Coolidge's purchases, after subtraction of shares previously assented, was to add 7,500 assents in the common stock class. This total was reduced to 6,200 with the honoring of Mr. Zucker's revocation of the assent for 1,300 shares. In late December 1950 and early January 1951 Mr. Coolidge instructed his broker to sell his Boston and Maine common stock. The record shows that his loss on the sale before tax adjustments was about $9,000, for which he was not, and did not expect to be, reimbursed by the Railroad.[29]

The Department's Charges

The Department summarized the transactions in its Amended Answer of November 1, 1951, as follows:

> During the submission period, the railroad expended its own money to negotiate the purchases by a railroad director, at a price in excess of the market price, of unassented blocks of railroad stock, and thereby procured for the railroad the control of the assents to said stock. The negotiators of these transactions were also paid solicitors of the railroad. The railroad failed and neglected to disclose to Old Colony or to the Commission its success in obtaining control of such assents. Said assents were improperly included in the certificates of Old Colony and of the railroad.

The Trial Brief made a longer story of it. Mention was made of Mr. Coolidge's directorship in Old Colony and also in the First National Bank, and of Mr. French's directorship in the latter. In this longer account, the direct participation of Railroad officials in the transactions was emphasized in detail.

The various ways in which the situation is described in the documents throughout the proceedings are significant for understanding what the objectors really thought was wrong.

---

the Coolidge purchases, namely, whether stock purchases by a director in the circumstances described should result in invalidating the assents given.

[29] Hearing before the Examiner, August 27, 1952, pp. 1259–1260.

The petition of the Sakis group in February 1952 read as follows:

* * * * *

(g) That officers and agents of the applicant improperly negotiated for and did purchase stock of the applicant at prices above market for the sole purpose of obtaining the stockholders' assents, that said improper negotiations for and purchase of stock at prices above market for a director of the applicant were supervised and financed by the applicant.

This clearly implies the essential evils complained of were: (1) that the stock was bought for the sole purpose of obtaining assents; (2) and at above-the-market prices; (3) and officers and agents of the Railroad were involved; and (4) that the purchases were supervised and *financed* by the Railroad.

More thorough examination of the facts eliminated the charge that the Railroad itself had financed the purchases. The Trial Brief clarified the origin of the funds by treating the episode under the heading "Railroad Control of 8,500 Assents Through the Negotiation of the Purchase of this Stock with a Railroad Director's Money."

The Department found the wrong to be control [30] of the assents by the Railroad because officers and agents were involved. For instance, on one transaction, its Brief concluded that "the railroad acquired control of the assent by negotiating its purchase by Mr. Coolidge, a railroad director. The assent . . . should be substracted from the certified total of common stock assents." [31]

---

[30] It relied upon the definition of control stated in section 1 (3) (b) of the Interstate Commerce Act, quoted at the beginning of this chapter.

[31] Department of Justice, Trial Brief, p. 56. Note that the Department did not subtract the shares also from the outstanding shares. The Railroad Brief (October 20, 1952, pp. 43–44) points to the mathematical result of section 20b (3), which requires that controlled securities shall be subtracted from the total outstanding. For this transaction, for example, 6,200 shares would be subtracted from the 394,728 outstanding common shares and from the 302,430 assented common shares, thereby lowering the assents from 76.61% to 76.24%. The Commission later followed the Railroad's method of calculating the percentage vote.

Mr. L'Heureux held that in the light of the circumstances the assents were valid. He said: [32]

> Again here, the I.C.C. has a simple legal question, whether a director of a railroad, who can unquestionably assent stock which he owns, can purchase other stock with his own funds and assent that or have it assented before he purchases it, for the purpose of helping the plan be adopted.
>
> There was no evidence that the railroad caused Coolidge to purchase the stock or controlled the purchase in any way. Simple discussions with railroad officials to locate unassented stock and with reference to the reasonableness of the price to be paid certainly do not constitute control.
>
> I know of no principle that would make the above transaction one of control by the railroad as a matter of law.
>
> Conceivably, the I.C.C. might place a different emphasis on the consultations between [the broker] and Railroad officials and hold . . . that there existed control in fact. . . . However, I do not think that is likely to occur in the light of the evidence adduced at the hearings. [33]

Nevertheless, he was concerned about the propriety of purchases and assents of stock by officers and directors during the voting period. There was a danger, he thought, that assents of such stock could be controlled by the company and the control would be hard to prove. The possibility of connivance struck him as strong enough to call for preventive action by the Commission. Therefore, he suggested that the Commission's regulations should flatly prohibit any officer or director of an applicant, or any member of their immediate families, from assenting stock purchased during the voting period or in expectation of a stock modification plan. He also proposed that certificates be required from all officers and directors of an applicant that they have not assented shares purchased during the submission period, and a further certificate be required from the applicant that it has

[32] After he had read the Commission's report, Mr. L'Heureux wrote to Senator Tobey on April 24, 1953, that there would be a good chance that a court would overrule the finding that the Railroad controlled Mr. Coolidge's assent "in fact" but not as a matter of law. His difference with the Commission was not in the facts, but in his interpretation of them.

[33] L'Heureux, Opinion, pp. 43–44.

not caused any person or company to purchase shares either
to assent them or to prevent their being assented.[34]

The Commission's Finding

The Commission placed a different emphasis on the con-
sultations between the broker and the Railroad officers, and
found that the Railroad controlled the assents in fact.   Its
reasons were stated as follows:

> . . . While the final judgment as to whether a purchase
> should be made and a price accepted lay with [the broker],
> who was acting as the agent of Coolidge, it is clear that none
> of the stock purchased for Coolidge would have been pur-
> chased except for the fact that officers of the railroad or their
> solicitors had located it, but were unable to persuade the
> holders to assent it, and indicated to [the broker] that it
> should be purchased.   In other words, the purchases were the
> result of active participation by the railroad pursuant to a
> prearranged plan with Coolidge.   The decision as to whether
> or not stock should be purchased lay in the first instance en-
> tirely with French and the officers of the railroad.
>
> . . . While the officers of the railroad had no power to
> force [the broker] to purchase any of the stock for Coolidge,
> they had in effect been given authority to cause [him],
> within the limits specified, to make the purchases required
> by the railroad for the purpose of obtaining the necessary
> assents.[35]

Thus the Commission found the same legal basis as the
Department for disqualifying the assents on shares bought for
Mr. Coolidge's account.   In addition, the Commission found
such practice objectionable because "If . . . followed generally, it would tend to defeat the apparent purpose of the
purchaser to effect what he might genuinely believe to be a
meritorious plan, since it would encourage 'strikers' to withhold their assents to meritorious plans unless they secure better treatment than they deserve, either through provision in
the plan or through the sale of their securities at unreasonable prices." [36]

We cannot assume from this that the Commission would

[34] L'Heureux, Opinion, pp. 67–68.

[35] 282 I.C.C. 750 at 787–788 (1953).

[36] Ibid., p. 799.

rule the Coolidge assents out because he paid more than the market price, if he alone had been concerned in the transaction with no assistance from Railroad officials. That the Railroad controlled the Coolidge assents was the reason for disqualifying them; then the Commission added an opinion on the dangers to plans if there is bidding for stock for its assent value alone.

One can easily agree with this attitude toward strikers and deplore their ability to fatten at the expense of the supporters of a fair plan. Nevertheless, there are strikers in every situation in business where a successful outcome depends on obtaining the last increment of a short supply — in this instance, votes. Paying a premium above the market for a block of stock is a rational decision by a purchaser who wants the block, just as selling a block below the market is a logical decision by a holder bent on selling. When a public purpose is to be served, the power of eminent domain is used to remove the strikers. This remedy is not available in reorganization procedures, whatever the public interest may be judged to be.[37] Strikers will find some reorganizations profitable. Who is to say that upholding the principle of "no purchase above the market price"[38] is more important than the success of a fair plan?

Conclusions on the Commission's Finding

The Commission's opinion extended the meaning of controlled stock beyond what it had held two years earlier on the same set of facts. The Commission was not shocked when it first heard of the circumstances of the Coolidge purchases. It even refused to permit further research by the Sakis group into the assent records. Finally, in April 1953, it found an element of control, enough to disqualify the assents. It had broadened the meaning of control to mean influence as well

[37] The "cram down" provision in section 77 is similar in effect to the use of the power of eminent domain; the court can force a class to accept a plan even if the vote does not meet the statutory percentage. This club over minorities is not available under section 20b.

[38] Even a sale at the market may be a premium in a sense. If Mr. Zucker wanted to sell his entire block of 5,000 shares, it would doubtless have depressed the market to unload such an amount in a quick sale. Hence, he would really be getting a premium if he sold the block at the market price.

as power, thereby including in this case those officers who merely participated in an action that resulted in assents.

Every part of the Coolidge purchases can be explained by the business circumstances of the transactions. There is no warrant for the implication of a collusive maneuver as expressed, for instance, in the Department's language, "the railroad expended its own money to negotiate the purchases by a railroad director. . . ."

To say that the broker's advisers, Mr. French and Mr. Smith, controlled the assents is extending "control" to mean having any part in a transaction, if only as a source of information. The broker would not have purchased except that he received answers from officers of the Railroad to two questions: Are these votes needed? What margin do I need to pay to get them? Mr. Smith was, in effect, an assistant bargainer. He was also empowered to solicit according to the Commission's order, which explicitly provided "That the directors, officers, and regular employees of the applicant may take part in soliciting assents. . . ." This provision would clearly cover instances where Railroad officers located unassented stock. Furthermore, nowhere is a director forbidden to buy and assent stock in his own account.

Looking after the event, with the briefs and opinions at hand, one can say that Mr. Coolidge should have done no more than give instructions to the broker and leave the decision to him to buy at not more than, say, a point premium. Nevertheless, the Coolidge purchases were of the kind that, standing by themselves, gave effect to no improper motive. A believer in the plan, one who helped fashion it and held substantial long-term interests in other classes of the Railroad's stock, he was prepared to commit further sums temporarily into a critical vote in order to get the plan through. His decision was not controlled by the carrier in the sense that he was, or could be, ordered to put $30,000 into such a venture. "Control" seems a strong word to describe the part the officers played in keeping Mr. Coolidge's broker advised.

On the evidence one can conclude that the Coolidge assents should not have been disqualified on any of the three tests set up earlier as criteria of validity. If the Commission considered that the circumstances of the purchases constituted bad practice, the remedy lay in new rules rather than retroactive application of a theory of control to transactions of which it had long had knowledge.

ASSENTS GIVEN BY A PROFESSIONAL SOLICITOR

No assents caused more confusion than those given by the managing partner of Georgeson & Co., the soliciting firm engaged by the Railroad to round up the lagging common vote. The solicitor's transactions in the common stock took two forms, one as outright purchases and the other the boring of stock through brokers. The Department's charges and the Commission's findings were related only to the assents on the borrowed stock. The borrowing transactions demand our careful attention because the Department characterized them with the strongest language in its whole brief.

> "This is the crowning example," it said, "of the extremes to which the railroad management resorted in order to put this [stock modification] plan through at any cost. Conduct of this sort cannot be countenanced." [39]

As it turned out, the disqualification of these assents by the Commission did not rest on the nature of the transactions but solely on the alleged control by the Railroad of its agent, the paid solicitor. He initiated the borrowing transactions that ended in the assents. The Commission found that in itself assenting borrowed stock was entirely proper, a finding that contrasts sharply with the impropriety implied by the Department. But the Commission did not go on to disqualify any assents on the stock purchased outright by the solicitor, as one would expect if control was the only taint. Unless the Department believed that something sinister lay

[39] Department of Justice, Trial Brief, p. 61. Although the implication here is one of sharp practice participated in knowingly by the Railroad, there is no evidence in the record that the Railroad officers knew anything about the borrowing transactions.

The Railroad brief found the assents to be valid on a strictly legal basis, and made no attempt to explain the proxy solicitor's dealings with the several brokers, although the Railroad had been flatly accused of connivance in cutting corners to get assents. The brief of counsel for the New York banking houses ignored the stock borrowing aspects and dismissed in a sentence the question whether the stock should be considered "controlled" stock. There was no evidence, it said, that the proxy solicitor was controlled by the Railroad or that the Railroad officers even knew about the assents.

in the "intricate brokerage transactions," it need not have spelled them out in such detail. It charged invalidity only on grounds that the assents were made by the Railroad solicitor, and not because the stock was borrowed.

In this matter, also, the SEC made its own investigation. No firm inference can be drawn from the fact that to date the investigation, whatever its direction and extent, has brought no special remedial action. Presumably, if any official body thinks there is anything to correct by law or rule, some action to find a remedy will be taken by the responsible agency in due course. The stock exchange authorities knew of the investigation, first by the Department and then by the SEC. In view of the vigilant concern of the stock exchanges over standards of good practice, one can assume that the existing rules were thought to be adequate or prompt changes would have ensued.

Description of the Transactions

As the submission period wore on, the Railroad faced difficulty in getting assents on the common stock. As usual, large amounts of common stock were being traded in street form, in names of brokers who had long since sold their stock and had no inkling where it had come to rest. Georgeson & Co. was engaged to track down these certificates and speed up the lagging votes. Mr. Richard S. Nye, the managing partner, directed the soliciting operations. The transactions that resulted in disputed assents related to two blocks of 1,200 and 2,000 shares, respectively, which were borrowed for the personal accounts of the Georgeson partner and eventually assented. Four brokerage firms were involved in one series of transactions, and three in the other.

The procedure of lending and borrowing stock in any case is complicated: the purpose for doing it, the relationship of the parties to it, the financial details as to interest, premium, and the like.[40] The ordinary complexities were compounded

[40] As typically used the arrangement serves a necessary financial function in that it supplies shares for regular delivery on short sales or when a seller otherwise does not have the shares in hand to deliver. This latter occurs when sales are made "against the box" (long securities owned and available for delivery at a later date). The loan contract may provide a premium on a daily basis payable by the borrower; it provides also that he put up cash equal to the market value of the stock, and additional cash on market rises.

in this case into what the Department's brief described as "a number of intricate brokerage transactions." The depositions and the extended public hearing together did not produce all the facts necessary to a full explanation. This incident, because it occurred in the setting of a contest, was like so many others in finance where the very intricacies of the transaction suggested to some that dubious purpose was being implemented by clever methods in order to make the steps hard to trace.

The paid solicitor during the same period bought and sold some 3,400 shares of common stock, exclusive of the borrowed shares.[41] The record does not say how many assents he mustered from these. It is important to note that the whole discussion about disqualification of the solicitor's assents centered on the borrowed stock and ignored the large block of his regular market transactions.

The itineraries of the two blocks of borrowed common stock can be shown in simple diagrams: [42]

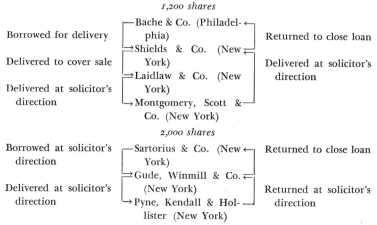

1,200 shares

Borrowed for delivery — Bache & Co. (Philadelphia) — Returned to close loan

Delivered to cover sale — Shields & Co. (New York) — Delivered at solicitor's direction

Delivered at solicitor's direction — Laidlaw & Co. (New York) — Montgomery, Scott & Co. (New York)

2,000 shares

Borrowed at solicitor's direction — Sartorius & Co. (New York) — Returned to close loan

Delivered at solicitor's direction — Gude, Winmill & Co. (New York) — Pyne, Kendall & Hollister (New York) — Returned at solicitor's direction

Note: Although each broker could transfer the certificates to his own name, it was not necessary for him to do so. Certificates in street names are "good delivery" through the stock clearing house. The record shows that when the shares were transferred to the last broker in each series, these brokers were instructed to become the record holders and assent.

[41] Figure derived from description of transactions in letter of Georgeson & Co., dated November 1, 1951, in the Railroad files.

[42] Information regarding these transactions is included in testimony given in the Hearing before the Examiner, September 10, 1952, pp. 1701–1718, 1739–1762, 1804–1813.

The essentials of the first sequence of transactions by the paid solicitor start with his purchase of 1,200 shares through Laidlaw & Co. and the sale of 1,200 shares through Shields & Co. November 22, 1950, was the settlement date for both these transactions. His accounts were to be *in* and *out* of 1,200 shares the same day. The testimony establishes that when receipts and deliveries were matched in the clearing house, Laidlaw & Co. being due 1,200 shares and Shields & Co. to deliver 1,200 shares, the solicitor as principal on both sides asked Shields & Co. to borrow the shares. This it did from Bache & Co. on November 27, paying the premium and putting up the market value in cash. The solicitor testified that he had no knowledge of where Shields & Co. borrowed.

In the next few days Shields & Co. delivered the 1,200 borrowed shares to Laidlaw & Co. to cover the sale, and Laidlaw & Co. delivered them to Montgomery, Scott & Co. Acting on standing instructions by the solicitor, Montgomery, Scott & Co. transferred the shares to its name, to be held for the customer beneficially, and assented them. The record is not explicit, but probably Montgomery, Scott & Co. soon sold most of these shares on the solicitor's order. In any case, the solicitor delivered enough additional shares to Montgomery, Scott & Co. to enable it to return 1,200 shares to Shields & Co. on December 12, and the latter closed the loan from Bache & Co. on December 18.

The second series of transactions involving borrowed stock can be explained more briefly. The record states that early in December the solicitor learned from the cashier of Gude, Winmill & Co. that the latter firm had recently borrowed Boston and Maine common stock from Sartorius & Co. to deliver on a short sale. The stock at that time was "very tight." Sartorius & Co. had made known that it had additional shares to lend. The solicitor thereupon arranged to have Gude, Winmill & Co. borrow 2,000 shares on December 12, and deliver them to Pyne, Kendall & Hollister. On the next day the latter, also as directed by the solicitor, had the shares transferred to its own name and assented them. On December 18, Pyne, Kendall & Hollister returned 2,000 shares to Gude, Winmill & Co., which then returned them to the lending broker. It should be noted that here the borrowing was not a financial device to provide good delivery, but the solicitor borrowed for the purpose of achieving the power to vote.

The solicitor said in a deposition [43] that he had a double purpose in the transactions, one to assent the stock and another to find out who the buyers and sellers were. Although the stock was very active in November and December 1950, few shares were transferred to new names. Furthermore, he reported, there were rumors that certain interests were buying stock to block the plan. Through his own purchases he could locate the sellers, and through the selling brokers he hoped to find out the buyers. The more he knew about the market, the more effective his solicitation could be.

The Charge that Through the Borrowing Process a Dissent Became an Assent

There was a special circumstance connected with the stock loan by Bache & Co. that highlighted the problems connected with protecting the voting interests of a beneficial owner when his broker lends the stock in which he has an interest. There was testimony that a customer of Bache & Co. in the first transaction above had emphatically dissented, but also had permitted the broker to lend his stock, which later through Montgomery, Scott & Co. was assented.[44] His dissent thus became an assent through the borrowing process. The Trial Brief referred to him as an owner who —

> did everything in his power to cast a vote against the plan. Although not required to do so, he returned the form letter of assent to Old Colony with the notation that he dissented to the plan. The railroad management immediately was notified of this and a railroad official wrote him a personal letter seeking to induce him to change his position which he refused to do.
>
> Of the 1,300 [sic] shares of common stock which Nye borrowed from Bache & Co., 1,000 of those shares were owned by [this stockholder], held in the street name of Bache & Co.

[43] Taken October 19, 1951, pp. 31–32.

[44] It should be noted that the Commission's conclusion on these facts was as follows: "Since it does not appear from the evidence of record that the . . . shares were included among any of the borrowed stock voted in favor of the plan, we conclude and find that the charge with respect to the voting of his stock is not sustained." 282 I.C.C. 750, at 795–796.

As stated above, Nye had these shares of stock moved from broker to broker until they were finally included in the assent of Montgomery Scott for 1,300 [sic] shares which was counted by Old Colony in the final voting.[45]

The customer said in his affidavit dated December 6, 1951:

> Sometime in November, 1950 . . . it was suggested that someone in New York desired to borrow Boston and Maine common stock and was willing to pay a premium therefor. . . . I understood that while stock was out on a borrow basis . . . the borrower had no right to vote borrowed stock. . . . I felt that my stock could be lent without placing in jeopardy the position which I had taken. . . .

The customer received half the premium paid for the loan of the stock. By mid-December, he said, he became disturbed about the situation, so much so that on December 14 he asked his broker to call back the stock and transfer it to his name. The transfer was made on December 22, after the close of the voting. It turned out, in later investigation, that the shares transferred into the customer's name were assented shares.

The decisive point in the charge that the dissent was willfully changed to an assent after the shares were borrowed rests with some unknown facts about the customer's stated understanding that he had "frozen" his dissent in the borrowing broker's hands. It is highly unlikely that a broker would borrow stock carrying a restriction that would make it different from any other block of common shares. Stock encumbered with a "frozen" dissent would not be the fungible commodity bargained for. We have to assume either that the customer was misinformed or that, in his later disappointment about his dissent's being nullified, he rationalized a misunderstanding.

As regards the part of the dissenting stockholder in this transaction, Mr. L'Heureux's Opinion commented that he "can blame only his ignorance or his imprudence for the consequences." His filing of a dissent was not effective because

---

[45] Department of Justice, Trial Brief, p. 61. The confusion between 1,300 and 1,200 shares is explained by the fact that the assent given by Montgomery, Scott & Co. was for 1,300 shares, including the borrowed 1,200 shares.

dissents were not counted. Moreover, he could have guarded himself by refusing to lend the stock or by lending it "with the reservation that it could not be assented, if that were acceptable to the borrower." [46]

On this same point, the Commission was constructive in its recommendations that security holders be better informed as to what their brokers may legally do with street-name stock unless specifically restricted by agreement.[47]

The Charges and the Commission's Finding

In the Department's charges that the solicitor's assents were invalid, the emphasis is on the borrowing. The charges also point up the plight of the broker's customer who "did everything in his power to cast a vote against the plan," but was thwarted when his shares "moved from broker to broker until they were finally included in the assent . . . for 1,300 shares which was counted . . . in the final voting." [48] The Trial Brief concluded with its interpretation that the whole series of transactions was resorted to by the Railroad management "in order to put this plan through at any cost." [49]

From these charges, full of inferences of intentional wrongdoing, we find little to define what the specific wrong is. Is it illegal to vote borrowed stock? Was it the intricate transactions themselves or the part taken in them by the Railroad's proxy solicitor that was wrong? If a broker has a customer who has expressed his intention *not* to assent, how can the broker as a fiduciary holder of stock for his customer lend stock and still protect his customer's intention as to vote?

The Commission did not question the validity of the assents on the ground that the stock was borrowed. It dismissed this question of legality in as lucid a short explanation as one can find:

It appears that the practice among brokers of borrowing stock is and has been common practice for such length of

[46] L'Heureux, Opinion, p. 33. Stock with such a restriction would be of no use to the borrowing broker; one share to him must be as usable as another.

[47] 282 I.C.C. 750 at 799.

[48] Department of Justice, Trial Brief, p. 61.

[49] Ibid.

time as to create a body of custom to govern its operation and in connection therewith certain legal principles have been developed. Among the legal incidents of stock borrowing it seems to be established that when the loan is made legal title to the stock passes to the borrower or his transferee; that the borrower is not a trustee, bailor or pledgee, his only obligation to the lender being a contractual one to return to the lender, on demand, stock of the kind and in the amount borrowed, at which time there is returned to the borrower the amount of money deposited by him as security, with necessary adjustments to reflect any fluctuation in the market value of the stock in the interim and credit to the lender for any dividends paid on the stock or charges against him for any assessments levied thereon, so that both parties are restored to the financial positions which they would have maintained had the loan not been made (except for interest or premiums).[50]

From the foregoing, it is clear that the borrower of the stock in question acquired legal title thereto, and would have been entitled to vote the stock for the election of directors. However, there is a further question whether, during the period the stock was beneficially owned . . . the assent of the holder thereof was within the control of the railroad.[51]

The questions of propriety raised by the Department as to the borrowing transactions themselves were passed over by the Commission. It went on, however, to disqualify the assents on the grounds that the Railroad's solicitor caused the assents; he was its agent, and the stock was in the control of the Railroad and under the statute was to be considered as not outstanding. There was no evidence, said the Commission, that the solicitor assented in response to the Railroad's suggestion, or that the officers of the Railroad had knowledge of the circumstances surrounding the giving of the assents.

. . . Nevertheless, when the assents were given, Georgeson & Co. . . . was acting as agent for the railroad for the purpose of procuring assents, and one of the admitted purposes of borrowing the stock was to assent it. The assenting of the

[50] Meyer, *The Law of Stock Brokers and Stock Exchanges,* pp. 186–188, 356–357; Dos Passos, *Stockbrokers and Stock Exchanges* (1905), p. 327 et seq; *Provost* v. *United States,* 269 U.S. 443. [Footnote quoted].

[51] 282 I.C.C. 750 at 794 (1953).

stock was within the control of the railroad's agent, and even though, in acquiring the stock, the agent may have acted beyond the limits of its express authority, we believe the conclusion is justified that the assenting of the stock was within the control of the railroad within the meaning of paragraph (3) of section 20b and that such stock, and the assents in respect thereto, should be excluded from consideration in determining whether the requisite percentage of common stock was assented.[52]

The record does not show that the agency of the solicitor extended beyond the soliciting duties. Unless it can be shown that his personal operations were specifically covered by the agreement to solicit, the charge of direct control can hardly be sustained. The stock-borrowing was not a part of the soliciting process. These legal aspects of agency, however, raise questions for the lawyer. The conclusion is that, in any case, the paid solicitor was not directed to borrow, buy, and assent. It is a severely technical approach to call his assents controlled by the Railroad. But the question remains, should the practice be ruled against?

Some Questions of Principle Raised in the Stock-Borrowing Episode

The case ended without resolving some central questions of principle. Two questions must be clearly separated. The one is whether a paid solicitor should give assents for any stock, borrowed or not. It will be further considered in the concluding section of this chapter.

The second question relates to what further regulation, if any, is needed over stock-borrowing procedure. First, how can customers' rights as beneficial owners be protected during a voting contest? Next, how can the borrowing device be restricted to the financial purpose of providing good delivery? These questions are particularly important in the submission-period procedure with assents remaining with transferred stock until revoked.

The finding of the Commission does not reach to these issues. If the borrowing procedure, a routine device to implement good delivery where necessary, can be used either

[52] Ibid.

purposely or inadvertently for producing votes, there is what can be called a perversion of use. Attention should be given to means for insuring the strict financial use of the procedure.

The protection of customers' voting rights during contests can be left to the existing rules and the continuous surveillance by exchange authorities and the SEC. On the other hand, the use of borrowed stock to produce votes poses a special problem. Admittedly this is a difficult area where, for instance, there is only a fine distinction between the votes on borrowed stock and those on stock purchased, voted, and promptly sold. Nevertheless, it would seem to be a sound rule of brokerage practice to limit stock borrowings to strictly financial purposes. The objective should be clear, namely, to prevent misuse of the necessary device of stock loans. The matter cannot be left to the lending broker, who cannot be expected to determine the intentions of the borrowing broker. Perhaps the exchanges can find a way of putting borrowing brokers on notice that the procedure of borrowing stock is to be used for financial purposes only. There remains the administrative question of whether these matters of regulation are for the stock exchanges themselves or for the SEC.[53]

COMMENTARY ON THE COMMISSION'S FINDING OF CONTROLLED ASSENTS

The analysis in this chapter has found no statutory basis for disqualifying the assents allegedly controlled by the Railroad. No other illegality was cited, nor was there any breach of an existing rule. The question remains as to whether the disqualified assents were given under circumstances that call for a preventive rule.

The Commission's decision interpreted the part played by

[53] The SEC, redrafting its rules during 1955, proposed to adopt Rule X–14 B–1 under the Securities Exchange Act of 1934. This rule related to the circumstances under which certain brokers or dealers might give proxies, consents, or authorizations in respect of securities carried for the account of a customer. The purpose of the rule would seem to embrace the kind of situation just described in the Boston and Maine case. See Sec. Exch. Act Release No. 5166, May 5, 1955.

the Railroad officers, however indirect and incidental the part, as establishing an official connection between the management and certain assents. The statute forbade the carrier to give assents that were under its absolute control; here were instances where officers were in the act that ended in assents, although they did not initiate or direct the assents. So the argument ran.

The influence of management over assents was thus made to cover more than absolute control, a determinable fact as implied in the statute. The Department questioned the propriety of directors' assents. There were also to be considered the personal holdings of stock by officers, as well as the participation of officers in the assents held invalid in this case. Included also as a form of official influence on assents is solicitation by officers, which was accepted as good practice and authorized by rule of the Commission. How far is it proper for management to influence assents? The importance of judgment in this area of regulation is manifest.

An argument could be made for the unlimited right of officers to vote all their holdings and to buy more shares to assent, as well as to urge assents by others as they were authorized to do. What group would be better informed on the merits of the plan than those serving the Railroad as officers? Furthermore, if their existing holdings could be assented, it would seem to follow that assents could be counted on new purchases. Their assents would be personal transactions only, quite apart from their position as officers.

Both the Department and the Commission drew a sharp distinction in disqualifying the assents; in each case the particular taint was the active part taken by the Railroad officials in joining with others to muster up votes for the plan. In one instance, the Railroad's president had a nominal connection with a trust device to retain assents already given; in another a director arranged for a liaison between the Railroad's officers and his broker; in the third a paid solicitor, the Railroad's agent, was using the financial mechanism of borrowed stock to obtain the assents. In the latter two instances, the *other* assents given by the same individuals were counted; only those resulting from the "arrangement" were barred. Apparently, assents by the same people were valid enough if made independent of the *ad hoc* arrangement for the purpose of assenting. This is a fine line indeed. It poses a basic question of proper standards for assents and feasible rules for their enforcement.

Considerations in Determining Proper Assenting Practice

In discussing the circumstances of these disqualified assents, one does not need to judge the motives of the persons who assented. Rules can deal only with facts, not motives. The decisive questions are: Is there anything about these transactions that is not good practice? If so, what is the wrong and how can it be prevented?

One can generalize about good practice in elections — political or financial — by saying that the returns should accurately record the preference of those entitled to vote. This axiomatic statement begs the essential question, namely, who are entitled to vote? What circumstances beyond patent illegalities should disqualify the assents of a record holder? The issue of controlled assents in this case could readily be broadened to the question of whether any assents by officers or agents should be allowed on securities acquired during the voting period or a stated time previous to it.

The question seems to be primarily one of protection against possible adverse interests of officers. Recapitalizations furnish only one of the areas in finance where an officer's personal interests and his official role often come into conflict. Such conflict is frequently found in plans for clearing up preferred stock arrearages. The Railroad officers here framed the plan and presumably would favor its acceptance. If it failed, they could expect the continuance of an obsolete financial structure, with its low-priced stocks an invitation to continued speculation that might jeopardize the whole management. Faced with this outlook, an officer would work for added votes in any class where needed for the 75% majority. Or an officer might already have holdings in classes that objectors might claim were favored by the plan. For him personally to buy stock for assents would appear to mix official responsibility with his own personal interests.

In framing the plan for adjusting the capital interests, the officers were representing, presumably, the company rather than particular stockholders. They should be just as objective during the voting period and leave the outcome to other holders. Otherwise, a public holder could well feel that the officers of his company were buying and assenting stock against his interests. It is not consonant with the theory of an officer's fiduciary responsibility for him to be buying and voting shares in certain classes in a way that other classes may feel is unfair to them.

There is something about the mad rush for votes that attends these vital contests in corporate affairs that does not square with the concept of corporate elections as being a reasoned expression of opinion by owners as investors. Questions may be raised about any transactions in stock with an eye to the voting right only. By and large, stock is bought for the whole of its rights and not for the voting right alone.

Votes go with ownership and, in general, eligibility to vote cannot be determined by the motives of the legal owner in obtaining his stock. A stock operator may buy just to become a record-holder for the vote. There are no grounds on which he can be disfranchised as a mere trafficker in votes, as much as we may deplore the purchase of a transitory right to vote.

It becomes important, however, that management act as fiduciaries for all owners and that all who play a part professionally, such as paid solicitors, conform as closely as possible to the principles of a fair vote held within a closely knit stockholder group. In corporate elections, even under official proxy regulation, there is a limit to what laws can do, but under a statute empowering the Commission to direct the vote there is opportunity and responsibility for enforcing good practice.

Questions commonly arise in capital readjustments as to how far those in the management have personal interests at stake in the outcome. It seems a sound principle to expect those connected with the management, including paid solicitors, to keep their own personal resources outside the contest. When "insiders," such as officers or directors or agents, get a transitory right to vote by buying or borrowing stock for the sole purpose of adding to the assent total, they can be said to create an artificial atmosphere for voting. Those connected with the carrier should not extend their position in its securities admittedly "to put the plan over." True, disqualification in such instances takes away temporarily the privilege and opportunity of a director or officer, presumably the most informed voter, for purchasing a stock he believes in and voting for a plan he thinks will benefit his company. But the larger good, the *public interest,* would be served and a better climate for voting would be maintained if assents by insiders were limited to their existing holdings.

The role of the professional solicitor presents a special case. He is hired for his ability to round up assents, and his success is measured by the assents he brings in. There is a flavor of buying a vote when a paid solicitor gets a transitory right for the vote only. The professional solicitor is hired to get holders to vote, and not to tip the scales by adding his own assents, which may be based entirely on temporary ownership with an eye to his own prestige as a vote-getter.

These are not the only situations in corporate management where officers are required to forego the opportunity for using their private resources as they see fit. "Insider trading" in company shares has long been a matter for restrictive legislation; this is only one variant. It would be entirely consistent with this proposed rule to permit assents for securities already owned by the officers before the plan was under way and voting started.

Effects of Disqualified Ballots on the Required Percentage

There were two views as to how the disqualified assents affected the official count. The Department gave full effect to the invalid ballots by subtracting them from the assent total. The Railroad argued that by statute the outstanding stock also must be reduced by the amount of stock controlled by the carrier. When the Commission decided that the illegality was statutory (controlled assents) it reduced the stock outstanding, thereby lowering the amount necessary for a 75% majority. This was the same as reducing the valid assent total by only 25% of the total number disqualified. Because the invalidity was one of "control" under the statute, the effect of the disqualifications was reduced to one-fourth what it would be if the taint were called other than control.[54]

The widely different effects of invalidity on the assent count, according as the particular defect is diagnosed as control or as something else, put great responsibility on those who determine the cause of the invalidity. Those who framed the statute could hardly have realized that the clause on controlled assents could have this result.

A Problem for the Statute or for Rules?

In sum, the end result was that the Commission brought a finding of invalid assents on a broad interpretation of the statutory clause on controlled assents, the clause that it was proposing to amend as unfair when applied to voting stock. The finding could be interpreted as disapproval of certain voting practices but with no existing means of nullifying them except to hold that the control clause applied. The result was to extend the meaning of control into an area where a clear factual determination is difficult.

It is one thing to rule against such assents in future cases and quite another to invalidate them, even though no present rule is violated. An existing clause — "the Commission shall cause . . . in such manner as it shall direct . . ." — seems to give leeway enough for rules to prevent directors,

---

[54] A simple example will illustrate:

Shares

Total stock	110,000	("outstanding" on company books)
Eligible to vote	100,000	(because 10,000 were found "con-
Required assents (75%)	75,000	trolled" by the carrier)
Actual assents	76,100	

$$\% \text{ of assents certified} \qquad \frac{76,100}{100,000} = 76.1\%$$

After the balloting is over, it is alleged that assents for 2,000 shares are invalid. The Commission investigates and finds all 2,000 are invalid because of "control" under section 20b (3)'. It then reduces the amount outstanding by 2,000, thereby reducing the percentage of valid assents to 74,100/98,000 or 75.61+ %. This percentage is still above the minimum required. If the invalidity had been found other than "control," the plan would fail, the percentage being 74.1%.

officers, and agents of the carrier from assenting securities acquired during a stated period. Such rules would handle the problem without interpretation of the statute to include an imputed control, thereby inviting possible attack in the courts.

CHAPTER XI

Policies in Retrospect

UP TO THIS point the study has dealt with the many charges brought against those directly concerned with the balloting operations. The method was to find the meaning of each charge to test its validity, and to suggest means for avoiding the difficulty. Back of operations, however, there is the policy-making that sets the pattern within which operations are carried on. Although the immediate cause of trouble may lie in the defective operations themselves, the fundamental cause of the difficulties may be explained in terms of over-all policy — or lack of it. It is in the broader framework of policy that we now consider, in retrospect, the relationship and the action of the parties in this case.

The first cases to come under a regulatory statute are of necessity "test runs." The Boston and Maine stock modification was different in many respects from others under section 20b. It was a *first* in many significant ways: the first all-stock modification; the first challenge to the validity of the assent count; the first in which the Department of Justice became a critic of procedure; the first that included a court action; and so on.

This chapter takes a backward look at events and decisions to determine the points where a different policy would have been better. To be critical of policies from this vantage point is not to say that the parties making the decisions should have foreseen all the ensuing troubles. One must bear in mind that decisions made along the way but reviewed after the event were made when all the factors were not in view. This notable case carries the lesson that the crucial problem in administration is to develop a procedure that will produce valid balloting and, if challenged at any point, will avoid costly litigation.

One approach to a review of the policy aspects of the case would be to ask the parties what they would do differently if they could start again. The answers to such inquiry could be expected to relate to events within each party's responsibility and not to deal with the biggest question of all: did the welter of troubles about the balloting stem from some basic defect in the over-all system of balloting, from which the subsidiary mistakes were just unfortunate incidents?

An instance in the Boston and Maine balloting illustrates this difference. There were various ways to handle assent procedures under the broad direction of the statute to vote by classes. One was a record-day system as in ordinary proxies, another a submission period with assented shares deposited and deposit certificates given therefor, another the system finally adopted. The method selected should be the best, on balance; but once it is selected the *operation* should be set up to withstand any challenge. Indeed, the choice of method may well hinge on the difficulty of the operational procedures. This particular policy decision will be recognized as the source of much difficulty in operation.

From the extended litigation in this case over a process usually routine and from the record of many recapitalizations, the quick assumption is that the cause of the trouble lay in the tactics of interveners, adept at taking advantage of all legal opportunities for delay. The skill of the plaintiffs' counsel so impressed the defendants that a settlement was reached to purchase withdrawal of the Sakis group so as to avoid a further delay estimated at two years. The fact, however, that at the end of three years the Commission found three blocks of votes invalid suggests that the delay caused by persistent interveners did force a re-examination of a procedure previously considered adequate, and did give the opportunity to study basic principles of the balloting process.

In reviewing the case at the policy level, we propose to designate areas of procedure in which the experience of administrators has established certain principles of action. These principles are not abstractions, but have been proved essential in those situations when many parties, each with its own responsibilities, play a part in reaching a joint objective — in this case a regulated ballot correctly certified.

COORDINATION A PRIMARY NEED

In the Boston and Maine balloting situation there were three parties joined in the common purpose of speedy accomplishment of a proper vote. The Commission was responsible for observance of the statute; the depositary was designated to count assents within prescribed rules; and the Railroad was watchful of voting progress and was authorized to solicit assents and hire agents to do so. The accepted practice in business management, when a new project is undertaken, calls for complete understanding by department heads as to how the operation of each department is affected. If a new production program concerns plant operation, sales, finance, and accounts, the officers of all these departments meet to exchange ideas and to agree upon the part of each. A higher executive views the project as a whole. All are aware that interim adjustments are likely when unforeseen developments occur. In military language, there are first the over-all strategy, then the campaign plans, then finally the orders for separate units. The important principle is to start with objectives and clear procedure, so that as unexpected problems arise they are immediately brought to the attention of the group, and answers found.

Sound administration requires coordinated organization. Organization implies clear definition and understanding of the relations between individuals combining for a common objective. Coordination implies that the parties understand their mutual relationship from the beginning; it also implies flexibility and lines of communication to make prompt adjustments to unforeseen developments. Any person in administrative levels of any business or activity — military, governmental, or institutional — can see this principle as it applies in actual instances of his own experience.

The necessity for coordinated action, so generally accepted in company administration, is just as applicable to the joint effort of Railroad, depositary, and Commission. The fact that the three parties were separate entities with only a temporary common purpose does not impair the analogy. A syndicate of investment bankers is an association for a specific purpose only; but the arrangements are drawn in detail, the venture is under a manager with powers, and each banker has known relations to the group. Section 20b leaves no doubt as to the responsible party in balloting; "the Commission shall cause" implies direction, control, awareness of unforeseen problems, and ready communication. The Commission had long been assuming this responsibility under section 77 proceedings.

With responsibility thus centered, the essential step in organization for the job would be clearance of ideas among the three operating parties. There would first be a preliminary conference of Railroad and depositary with the Commission's Bureau of Finance. Representatives of the Railroad and the depositary would come with ideas and questions to be tested against the wide experience of the Commission in such matters. This conference would achieve common understanding of each party's function. The Commission would insist that problems be brought promptly to its attention. Such understanding, for example, would have forestalled in this case the unilateral decision of the depositary, after advising with officers of the Railroad, not to follow the literal meaning of the fiduciary note.

Effective coordination would certainly have gone far to lay bare the recording problems later examined by the Department. If this emphasis on a coordinating organization appears to add work to an already burdened Commission, the record supplies an answer. One need only compare the extra time for establishing a coordinated setup at the start with the time later taken up by all parties in the litigation and the subsequent investigation by the Commission.

One cannot be sure that even the most closely knit organization would have halted the action by objectors. One can be reasonably sure, however, that if the Commission had been kept informed of recording problems, the decision on these matters at the time would have taken the force out of charges of slipshod practices so exploited in the Trial Brief. If the Commission had shown the Court at a pretrial hearing that it had thoroughly studied the alleged improprieties so loosely described in the Trial Brief, the Court might have been so impressed that its opinion of the following February would not have urged the Commission to proceed further with an investigation of its own. The knowledge that a competent Commission was keeping informed at all points would be a strong deterrent to innuendo by interveners, and especially by another government agency.

NECESSITY FOR PRESTUDY OF PROCEDURES

Coordination further requires that each party analyze his own function as it relates to the joint effort. Each operator must know the part the others play, if only to avoid misunderstandings over jurisdiction. Several troublesome aspects of this case involving the depositary and the Railroad illustrate the importance of thorough prestudy.

The depositary was chosen as agent of the Railroad to record assents. Officers of the depositary set up the recording system with great care, but they did not provide for certain peculiarities in the Commission's rules in section 20b cases. The depositary never had a supply of revocation forms, although stockholders were told to request forms from it. Its officers learned of the troublesome "fiduciary note" after assents had come from fiduciaries. There came the sudden realization that this was not an ordinary record-day proxy routine but a submission period of six months, with the added complication that assents were binding on transferees until revoked. Then attention fell upon the intricate problem of brokers' votes; the brokers' failure to report certificate numbers required assumptions and careful checking to avoid double-counting when transfers were later made. In the military analogy, the unit was advancing without definite orders over unfamiliar terrain and without thorough reconnaissance; nor were there established lines of communication with headquarters.

The Railroad also had its own reconnaissance to make. Its officers did prestudy the problem in many areas and well in advance, for example, in selecting the letter-of-assent method from alternatives and in planning the material to be sent to stockholders. They never foresaw, however, that the fiduciary note was destined to draw fire from the Department. The note was taken verbatim from that used in the Lehigh case, the officers making the very natural assumption that the note was standard practice, accepted and understood by the Commission.

As we have suggested, a conference of Railroad and depositary with the Commission's Bureau of Finance could well have cleared up all such procedural questions. Instead, it was necessary to await the Commission's final report of April 21, 1953, to get an official explanation of what the fiduciary note required. It can be presumed that the Commission knew its own requirement, made standard on each assent form. What principle of procedure makes it inappropriate for the Commission to carry out its responsibility by an official ruling to its functioning agent, the depositary, *at the time the problem comes up,* or, preferably, in anticipation of the problem?

Another area where prestudy was important for the Railroad was the difficult problem created by lost stockholders. This problem was known to be heavy in the two lowest classes, and even substantial in the first preferred class. It was especially crucial in view of the requirement of assents from 75% of each class. Money and effort would have been well spent in repetitive inquiries, or even employment of professionals in the search, in advance of the submission period. Advantage could have been taken of the rule of the New York Stock Exchange [1] that brokers could be required to transfer "street" names to their own on reimbursement of transfer expenses. This would have helped with the problem of voting by brokers, which was thorny enough on many counts. It would have made solicitation of unassented stock much more direct.

---

[1] Rule 874. Member firms when so requested by the Exchange are required to transfer shares held for their own accounts or others into their own names prior to the record day. This is to facilitate convenient solicitation of proxies. The Exchange will request this action if asked by the issuer or a holder of 10% of such stock.

Although, as in other rules, the reference is to proxies, there is no reason to suppose that the same rule would not apply to the assents in a special vote such as this case provided.

Under this rule the Department of Stock List issued special circulars to members of the Exchange, requesting transfer of stock into their own names, in number by years as follows: 101 in 1953, 109 in 1954, and 89 through Oct. 24, 1955.

An intensive study of lost stock, especially in the two lowest levels, would probably have drawn attention to the plain preferred stock, 75% of which was held by less than 25 holders. The concentrated holding gave the Commission discretion to raise the percentage required for acceptance. The facts about lost stockholders in the class, and especially of the cross-holdings between classes, were crucial to the Commission's decision. Such facts might have flagged the serious threat of a veto by a small percentage of nuisance-value speculators playing on the margin between the 87% required vote and the actual percentage of holders that could be located at all.

Sometimes good policy fails for operating reasons. When an operation expected to be routine turned into a major battle rather than a skirmish, in retrospect all the participants could well regret something. The Railroad, for example, if the power and tactics of interveners had been foreseen, could have settled down for a "cold war" of nerves and planned its moves with an eye to a sure defense. The Sakis counsel had given every evidence of resourcefulness as a challenger. The Railroad might earlier have made systematic inquiry from other carriers in recent modification campaigns to learn where troubles can arise. Events in other cases often showed unexpected pressures added to the usual tasks of a railroad's legal work.

These are obviously areas in which the backward look sharpens the vision. To point out mistakes only draws attention away from the careful study and effective work of the parties in other directions. One is impressed, for instance, with the generally fine analysis of Railroad officers and consultants in preparation of the plan itself. Their decision to make four voting classes was supported by one of the clearest expositions in the whole case.

Decisions made in the course of a proceeding with so many unexpected turns are likely to offer occasional illustrations of mistaken policy. An example in the Railroad's area of responsibility was the decision to close the polls at the very instant the depositary reported that 75% of the common stockholders — the last class to accept — had assented. It was a natural reaction of the management, eager to get the job finished, not to risk revocations; but the decision added the risk that later contests might nullify the fractional margin of assents.   Moreover, it encouraged interveners to hunt for invalid ballots; for only a few would be needed.   The publicity given to the fact that professional solicitors had been hired to get out the vote encouraged the opposition of those who felt that oral solicitation was a banned practice.   Looking back, one can now see that a week or two more might have supplied margin enough to discourage those who were ready to challenge the validity of particular votes.

POLICY QUESTIONS FOR GOVERNMENT AGENCIES

There are many reasons for expecting government agencies to recognize the importance of well-conceived policy to effective operation.   Agencies are parts of one government, their functions are defined by statute and usually by long experience, their single objective is the public interest.   Coordinated effort is implicit in the very nature of agencies of a government.

It was in the area of coordination, however, that the Department of Justice fell short of its most effective contribution in appraising the charges being brought against the Railroad and the depositary.   The full story of the Department's participation is not available, but enough is known to say that in the search for corroborating evidence on the Sakis charges the Department neglected completely an obvious first step in understanding what responsibilities the Commission had and its rules for fulfilling them.   One might assume that the Department, responsible for justice under law, would not switch suddenly from defending the United States to leading the attack of the plaintiffs without carefully checking the charges with the regulatory authority directly responsible.

Should not any investigation have included the most accessible information the Department could get, namely, the records and explanation of the Commission itself as to what the procedures meant in terms of other section 20b cases and the Commission's own long experience?   Although the Department was not a party to the proceedings before the civil suit was begun, it could have found in conferences with the

Commission's Bureau of Finance and the Examiner an effective substitute for early participation. From the administrative angle, it would seem of paramount importance, particularly for the evaluation of charges involving not only the interpretation of the law but also the good faith of a railroad and a trust company, to be sure that the evidence included the Commission's knowledge of the particular case.

Instead, we see the Department launching its own investigation and using its regional offices to commandeer records, conduct depositions, and assemble affidavits and other data for its Trial Brief. Its whole effort supports the judgment that an objective search for facts, oriented and aided by the Commission's staff, would have resulted in a more constructive result, free from the innuendoes of the Trial Brief. It should be noted that the Department drew a sharp line as to how far it was willing to accept the Commission's expertness and administrative judgment. It would do so on the stock allocation under the plan but was ready to pit its own opinion against that of the Commission on the legal question of whether there were only four classes of affected stock outstanding.

It is difficult to comment on Department procedure in terms of operating and policy decisions because an outsider cannot know what moves were directed at top level. For example, who decided that Commission personnel would not be interviewed in order to clarify technical matters that the Department was not familiar with? Was the Trial Brief passed upon as adequate in substance and tone by the head of a Division, or perhaps someone still higher up? Also, on what basis was it decided to drop out of the case, which was held so important until the three-judge Court refused to admit the Department's evidence? If the matter was too serious to be left to the Commission when the Department first came into the case, then for the same reason should the Department not stay with the proceedings until its charges were proved or disproved? These are really questions for the administrative lawyers, especially those responsible for making the Department of Justice an effective force in cases that involve other government agencies.

Mr. L'Heureux held strongly to the opinion that the Department "should have remained in the case to see that the issues of fraud and irregularity were properly presented, if they felt that there was probable cause to believe that such fraud and irregularity existed. They should not have relied upon the Sakis Committee to protect the interest of the public." [2] If this is a sound conclusion, the Department's continued participation in the case, at least as an observer, became still more important when the Sakis group's withdrawal left no plaintiff at the final hearing. The Department could say that, once it had presented and supported the charges in its Trial Brief, the Commission then became the proper agency to follow them up. This explanation of its withdrawal, however, would not square with its decision to make its own full investigation entirely apart from the Commission, and to become a plaintiff in fact during most of 1951.

An appraisal of the methods of the complainants must necessarily be based on the documents they presented in the case, particularly the brief filed by the Sakis Committee in the civil suit and the Trial Brief prepared by the Department. Both were written with statements and implications of purposeful wrongdoing by Railroad and depositary officials in obtaining the necessary assents. The objecting parties not only cited numerous specific errors but by emphatic assertions, and often by innuendo, conveyed their opinion that the sum of numerous separate actions amounted to planned flouting of the law.

[2] L'Heureux, Opinion, p. 57. Mr. L'Heureux said also (pp. 17–18) that the Department represented the United States, the defendant in the Civil Suit, but once the case was out of the courts, there was no legal position imposed on the Department. His argument for continued participation is one of fulfilling a continuing duty to carry on with evidence of fraud that was considered so compelling by the Trial Brief.

In seeking for a plausible explanation of the Department's withdrawal, Mr. L'Heureux concluded (pp. 19–20) that ". . . it more likely would attempt to hide behind the cloak of so-called independent spheres of jurisdiction between Government agencies. They might say that it was up to the I.C.C. to ferret out the proof of the charges contained in the Justice Department's affidavits and depositions. It is true that the I.C.C. was intensely interested in the charges. . . . However, they did not possess the intimate knowledge of the conditions under which these documents were obtained. They were not in a position to meet the objections of the adverse parties . . . as the Justice Department was."

That the three-judge Court also got this meaning from the Department's documents appears in the final paragraph of its Opinion:

> The affidavits and depositions submitted by the Justice Department . . . *contain serious charges of irregularity and fraud on the part of the Railroad, its officers, agents and employees in the obtaining of assents to the modification plan and of the depository, the Old Colony Trust Co.* These documents offer evidence which if credible and true charge that a grave and serious fraud has been perpetrated upon the Interstate Commerce Commission. *If the facts alleged in these documents were established by competent evidence and were not explained and dissolved by other competent evidence, the gravity of the perpetrated fraud would shock the conscience of a Court or Commission.* . . . The Court believes that the Commission is the proper forum to sift, hear, evaluate and act upon the matters charged by the Justice Department. . . .[3] [Italics added]

This significant paragraph highlights the responsibility of both agencies of the government; first, as regards the charges of the complainants and, second, toward each other. If the Court calls the Commission the proper forum to "sift, hear, evaluate and act upon" the matters charged, it was just as much the Commission's responsibility to do so at the same time, or even before, the Department began its own sifting and evaluating. Furthermore, if the Commission is named the proper forum, by implication the Department is not.

Once the Department decided to investigate, in the Court's words, it had a responsibility for making sure that any evidence submitted would be fully supported as "credible and true." One would think that the basic policy of the Department would permit no document to be issued unless its attorneys were sure that the evidence offered could be classed as credible. The only question remaining for the Commission would be whether the credible evidence was relevant to the question of validity of ballots.

It should be noted also that the Court refers to the Department's offered evidence, and not to mere assertions as to motives of Railroad and depositary officials. We can assume

[3] 103 F. Supp. 292 (1952), pp. 313–314.

that the Court would exclude assertion from credible evidence on issues of irregularity and fraud. The preceding six chapters show notable instances where the official documents of both the Sakis group and the Department reach conclusions, or include damaging inferences, without the support of evidence. Unless one can believe this pattern of presenting the case was accidental, or caused by haste, its purpose must be weighed merely as a technique in litigation.

The official body in this case to receive the briefs and decide the issues was either a court (here the three-judge Court) or the Commission. In either case, those who would decide were trained and competent to recognize credible evidence, to screen out assertion, particularly charges of bad faith, unethical practices, and even collusion to by-pass a law. If only by standards of effective presentation, it would seem that any appearance of skillful exposition to create overtones of maneuvers to defraud, when the evidence was insubstantial or absent, could only detract from the parts of the brief with real merit.

Beyond these practical tests of sheer effectiveness, there are more sober considerations relating to the responsibility of the Department's brief writers. In this respect, the Justice Department was in a different category from the Sakis group. Sakis counsel were representing a private interest. The plaintiffs were shareholders, for one reason or another objectors to a plan, risking somebody's money and time to fight, presumably, for stockholders' rights. In the frustration of the long stand against the Commission, the skill of the Sakis Committee's counsel was applied to tactics as they saw them. Even so, personal attacks,[4] with inference of fraud, were a questionable

---

[4] After the Railroad certified that enough assents had been received, Sakis counsel asked permission to examine original assents and revocations. Having no specific instances of invalidity but relying on "information and belief," they supported the request in part by saying, in a petition to the Commission on February 20, 1951, ". . . The fact that the applicant refused to permit the intervenors to inspect the original assents and revocations, or to make available a list of stockholders, created an inference that warranted a demand for the best evidence. . . ." The inference was clear: The Railroad refused because there was something to hide. The petition containing this derogatory statement was filed a month after the Commission had given its reasons for denying the request to inspect.

expedient in a document written to impress a court or Commission.

The Department, however, was in a different position. This is a government agency at work to see that justice prevails. Its investigations should create an atmosphere of competent inquiry, and certainly avoid any appearance of seeking out facts to buttress an opinion that something is wrong. If the end result of its inquiry is to be presented to a court, as in this case, its function is analogous to a special Master to the court, specifically appointed to supply technical analysis and objective opinion. It would be astonishing and alarming to see a Master's report with even a trace of bias or unsupported assertions. Rather, one would expect full study and exposition, tight argument, and conclusions to serve as a solid base for a court's opinion.

Technically, of course, the Department was not serving at a court's direction; but when its representative came with a Trial Brief to the pretrial conference, the document should have been as meticulously drawn as the findings offered by a Master for the court. Otherwise, the Department was not serving the cause of justice.

On the other hand, the question also appears of why the Commission, when informed of the Department's investigation, did not assume the responsibility of rechecking the Boston and Maine voting experience, if only to reassure itself that its rules had been followed.[5] We have here the anomaly

---

A still stronger slur on the veracity of a Railroad officer was a later statement that the Railroad's Supplemental Application No. 1, supported by the affidavit of the financial vice president, "misrepresented" facts regarding assurances of assent. Although the basis for reporting assurances was fully explained and had no bearing on the final voting, it was still used to discredit any affidavit signed by the same individual (Brief for Plaintiffs in Civil Action No. 763-51, January 1952, p. 14).

[5] The three-judge Court wrote:

"If the Commission were required to independently examine the assents and revocations received by the appointed depository when it has no reason to suspect that the depository did not perform its function properly, a wasteful and unnecessary burden would be imposed on it." 103 F. Supp. 292 (1952) at 308–309.

This statement describes sound administration. The implication is that examination is desirable when questions do arise. If the problems of recording had been brought to the Commission's attention when they first arose, or

of two government agencies located only two blocks apart, each with responsibilities for finding facts to test the validity of serious charges, but with no apparent cooperation in doing so.

Other policy questions for administrative agencies in government are raised here. When an agency has made rules that it considers adequate to fulfill its responsibility under the statute, should it then maintain a passive role in proceedings, thereby placing the burden on objectors to make their case? In the ordinary case a passive role may be enough, when the Commission through experience has developed a procedure to assure dependable results. If its procedures then stand up under criticism in public hearings, it has fulfilled its responsibility. This conclusion assumes, however, that the procedure has been long tested and the Commission has an adequate internal check as a case proceeds. The principle of constant vigilance as the work progresses is an axiom in business management, especially in the first runs of a new product. The Boston and Maine case was a first run, in which the burden of proof should not lie wholly with the interveners.

If the management of an applicant carrier expects advice on procedure and does not get it, that management begins to wonder what the obligations of regulatory responsibility really are. If the depositary arrangement is a device to save an already overworked staff from the burdensome task of ballot-counting, then the depositary is essentially an agent of the Commission. Agency is a device to carry out a principal's purpose; it follows that the purpose should be ascertainable. In other business relationships the agent comes to his principal for instruction; the same thing would seem to hold true here. In processing ballots under a section 77 proceeding, which the Commission handles itself, a Bureau of Finance official is directly responsible. The depositary arrangement in a section 20b case extends the arm of the Commission by taking the ballots physically off the premises; it

---

if the Commission had made its own inquiry when the Department was investigating, the whole dispute might well have been settled a full year earlier.

does not thereby relieve the Commission of responsibility to advise and regulate.

The Value of the Examiner's Report

At the end of the final public hearing in August and September 1952 the Railroad and the depositary waived the Examiner's Proposed Report. Their impatience to expedite the expected favorable action of the Commission led them to forego the right to argue the Examiner's opinion. Their request was natural enough; the litigation had been dragging along for a year and a half and another year-end was near. The Sakis group having withdrawn, the only purpose remaining for the hearing was for the Commission to "sift, hear, evaluate . . . ," as the Court had said. The managements of depositary and Railroad, confident of the result, were anxious for a quick decision. They and the banking houses wanted the litigation over; they would waive anything that would cause delay. As events turned out, they had to wait until April 1953 for the Commission's order making the plan effective on its finding enough valid votes to supply the legal percentage.

The effect of the waiver of a Proposed Report is to keep the Examiner's opinions out of the public record, along with the exceptions to the Report. For those interested in the development of regulatory procedures this is unfortunate. An Examiner's close attention to these cases always makes his views of particular significance. Since the Examiner's Proposed Report, as separate from his part in the preparation of a report for approval and issuance by the Commission (or Division), is distinctively his own independent analysis and recommendation, the result in this case could be expected to be a document of great significance in the formulation of principles of procedure under statute. The most revealing steps in the evolution of a final document are the transformations between the first draft and the last. The reasons for changes are necessary for full understanding of the final draft.

Because of the attempt to save a little time by eliminating the Proposed Report and exceptions to it by the parties, the record lost the much broader basis of views and argument

against which the Commission's final decision could be measured. The charges put a challenge to the procedures, thereby
giving the case particular significance in establishing principles of balloting. The waiver of the Proposed Report was
a high price to pay for the hope of saving a few weeks.

POLICY QUESTIONS ON THE SETTLEMENT

Another decision, hard to defend from the Railroad's point
of view although easily explained from the point of view of
the banking houses, was the settlement that removed the
Sakis group from the proceedings. The Railroad wanted an
end to the dragging proceedings. It looked like a good bar-
gain cashwise, even at a cost of $65,000, to avoid added ex-
pense of perhaps double or triple that amount, in view of
some still untapped tactics of delay. Officers of the Railroad
did not believe that the Sakis group had any other evidence
to support the charges.[6] There was the fact that the Department had withdrawn from the case, from which the inference
could be made that everything the Department had, or at
least its best, was in its Trial Brief. The speed and energy
with which the Department prepared its argument and
fought the case through the Court proceedings would hardly
leave any reserve of evidence or argument still available to
counsel for the Sakis group.

It was no concern of the Railroad what the banking group
might do to persuade opposition to withdraw in order to
expedite a plan, make their when-issued contracts fulfillable,
and thus liquidate their large holdings of old stocks. These
arbitrageurs were interested only in early consummation of
the plan; the Railroad and the depositary were interested in
disproving what they had called unfair and untrue charges.

> The Railroad has stood ready to tell its story for over a
> year and a half. When the door of the proper forum was
> opened, it told that story fully — a story that the Railroad
> desired to tell in order to repel the innuendoes raised by the
> Trial Brief.[7]

[6] Railroad Brief, October 20, 1952, p. 8.
[7] Ibid.

Administratively the alternatives seemed clear. A settlement had been in the wind since May 1952. The first price being too high, the Railroad withdrew until brought in again by an intermediary who was still hopeful that a settlement could be made. This situation could well give a basis for thinking that the plaintiffs were just bargainers, and might be content with what the arbitrageurs might do by themselves to purchase the plaintiffs' withdrawal. The Railroad and the depositary both had their good names at stake, particularly the depositary, and the presence of the plaintiffs at open hearing would only make the defense that had been prepared to demolish the Trial Brief more effective. If the settlement had not been made, the result could be either

(a) the withdrawal of the Sakis group on the payment by the arbitrageurs only; or
(b) the attendance of the Sakis group's counsel at the hearing.

If the first result came about, the Railroad would have accomplished, without involvement, the same result that it actually did by agreement. If the second, the Railroad and the depositary could face those who had fought the case with the Department's help and at long last were forced to show *all* that they had by way of evidence and argument.

In other words, the settlement of August 21, 1952, precluded the Sakis group's participation in the climactic hearings soon to start, where all defendants would learn the whole strength of the opposition and where the issues would be sharpened to make a fuller record. The Railroad and depositary stood ready to disprove all charges; the presence of the accuser would presumably have made their task easier. If the defendants were successful, the plaintiffs would have the handicap of starting out in a new direction. Two things in particular about the settlement remain doubtful policy: the timing, with nothing apparently to lose and everything to gain by keeping the plaintiffs in until after the hearing; and the Railroad management's decision to settle without discussion with the depositary, which had identical objectives in a full hearing and record.

Strategically viewed, therefore, the settlement removed the

opportunity for public display of what the defendants considered as the weak case of the plaintiffs. If the Sakis group's
withdrawal could be arranged on August 21, it would be still
easier to arrange after the hearing and probably at a lower
price. So it could reasonably be argued. In addition, defer-
ment of the settlement until after the hearings would avoid
any basis for the inference that the settlement was possibly
for the purpose of removing a threat to the defense case.

There are also broader interests here than those of the immediate parties concerned. By repeated allegations in a score
of petitions and briefs, the Sakis group was apparently leading a veritable crusade to annul a Commission order which,
if made effective, would result in "irreparable and immeasurable injury and damage to the plaintiffs herein, the Boston
and Maine Railroad and the stockholders. . . ."[8] In the
face of these dire consequences, its withdrawal would still
leave the Railroad and stockholders and the public interest
to suffer if its absence kept from the record additional testimony, which might have carried the day for the plaintiffs and
brought a reversal of the order.

Other policy matters involved in the settlement perhaps
got too little attention in the rush of events. The Commission had been kept informed of the pending negotiations by
the Railroad, the plaintiffs, and the banking houses. In
fact, all the parties wanted assurance that the payment would
not be considered as a modification of the plan;[9] otherwise
the settlement would defeat its own purpose. The fact that
the nature of the settlement was known within the Commission raises the question whether the Commission should have
directed its Examiner to take any particular action when the

[8] Affidavit attached to Amended and Supplemental Complaint, February 28,
1951, in Civil Action No. 763-51.

[9] By the Commission's final order of April 21, 1953, further payments on
the settlement were prohibited until further hearings were held on the matter. At the hearing in New York on March 12, 1954, partners in both
L. F. Rothschild & Co. and Goldman, Sachs & Co. testified of their concern
for keeping the Commission informed as to the nature of the proposed settlement. They drew no inference that the Commission as a body committed itself; they said only that their counsel had discussed the terms so as to assure
the principals that the settlement would not jeopardize the plan itself.

settlement was announced at the opening of the hearing. The hearing was very important to the Commission. The Sakis Committee, an original intervener and later the plaintiff in the suit to annul the order, by withdrawing as the Department had already done would reduce the hearing to the clarification of an existing record. Would it not have been useful to keep the Committee's counsel in the proceedings, since they had worked with the Department as plaintiffs? Was it within the Commission's power to subpoena them in case an invitation by the Examiner was not enough? If the Commission considered these questions, it does not appear that the Examiner was officially advised, although he might well have known that negotiations for settlement were proceeding.[10]

An aspect of the settlement raises questions about its being a modification of the plan. Any part of the settlement so construed would be grounds for reversal of the Commission's order. The Railroad agreed to buy $2,000,000 of the new preferred stock within a year if conditions so warranted. This was not made a firm commitment because counsel for both the Railroad and the bankers were of the opinion that, if firm, it would be held to be a modification. Query: Would not a contingent agreement also be a modification if entered in good faith? If this part of the agreement was not in good faith, it would be palpably unethical; if it was in good faith — that is, if the Railroad's directors had the intention to perform and there was some chance that the purchase would take place — then the contingent aspect should not be the test of the modification question. If the conditions that would warrant purchase were clearly in the minds of both

[10] Mr. L'Heureux wrongly charged the Examiner with a procedural error in granting the motion of the Sakis Committee to withdraw from the case. The record (letter, dated June 2, 1953, to Senator C. W. Tobey from Chairman Alldredge of the Commission, Finance Docket No. 16250, Vol. 1–c) shows that the Committee's counsel made no such motion; the Examiner was careful that the record was explicit on the point. The Examiner was alert to the procedural implications of this unusual situation and expressly refrained from making any ruling that might have the effect of deciding a motion to dismiss the proceeding or in any way of prejudicing a final determination on the merits.

parties, and such conditions came about, then the commitment would become an ethical imperative or the agreement was not serious in the beginning.[11]

In summary, this is an instance where there was time to plan a way to use the plaintiffs, who presumably could amplify the record. The reason for not getting the benefit of a zealous plaintiff is not manifest. Nor is it clear why the Railroad did not keep the depositary advised on the status of the negotiations for settlement with the Sakis group. If a settlement was in the wind, although the depositary had no reason for aiding and a strong reason for resisting, it would have been good policy to keep an associated defendant fully informed. Of all parties, the depositary had the most at stake — its reputation as a fiduciary.

In retrospect, also, the Commission might now be disposed to reconsider other policy decisions in connection with the settlement. On the record it had no part in the settlement; certainly it made no commitments of any kind. The staff did, however, hold informal talks with several individuals during the negotiation. Since such a settlement, particularly with the committee that had been so long an objector, always carries a suggestion of a buy-out, it is questionable whether members of the Commission individually, or staff officials, should even be in a position of interested listeners.[12]

[11] The insistence of the Sakis group that the contingent purchase and retirement of a substantial amount of the new preferred stock be included in the settlement agreement has an interesting parallel in a proposal made at the hearing on the modification plan. At that time the same group urged that the Railroad use its available cash resources to buy and retire various classes of preferred stock instead of planning to use section 20b at all.

The Railroad took strong exception to the propriety and even the legality of purchasing such stock at the then large discount, thereby cancelling arrearages and improving the position of remaining holders and of subordinate classes. In the settlement agreement we see the Railroad sanctioning the contingent and limited purchase of the new preferred stock, which the plan gave entirely to the old prior preference stockholders — whose stock it had previously on principle refused to purchase.

[12] The Commission by order of May 1, 1953 (Docket No. 31257), upon its own motion instituted an inquiry into the legality and propriety of payments under the settlement by the Railroad. Its decision of March 7, 1955, permitted the Railroad to complete the payments. A strong dissent was entered by Chairman Mitchell, joined by Commissioner Johnson.

It is beyond the scope of this study to make a thorough analysis of the

All this suggests that the overpowering urge for speed caused quick decisions which more cautious consideration of the implications would have avoided or modified.

hearing record, the briefs, and the decision. The divided Commission and, particularly, the characterization of the settlement make it clear that the decision was not intended to open the way for such arrangements. "The railroad's willingness to commit itself to the payment of an admitted 'nuisance settlement,' while not unknown in bankruptcy and receivership history, should be given no encouragement by our action in this proceeding as establishing any kind of a precedent in section 20b proceedings. Despite some testimony concerning the great amount of work performed and time spent by counsel for the committee, and other efforts at rationalization of the amount of the payment, the fact remains that it was made primarily because of the nuisance value, present or potential, possessed or deemed to be possessed by the committee." (294 I.C.C. 549 at 565.) As a disclaimer of any support for the settlement in principle the Commission added as a final paragraph that "Neither the action herein taken nor anything herein stated should be considered or construed as constituting approval of the settlement agreement or the payments made or to be made thereunder."

CHAPTER XII

Recommended Changes in Statute and Procedure

EXPERIENCE with the eight cases that have come to final vote under section 20b has brought suggestions for changes in the statute and procedures. Bills amending the act have been filed in both Senate and House, and the Commission itself has proposed changes in the statute. The analysis in the preceding chapters furnishes a realistic background for appraising these various proposals. What further does this case study contribute by way of suggestions for changes in the law and the procedures under it?

PROPOSED AMENDMENTS TO SECTION 20B

Since not only the manner of voting but the majority required for acceptance of a plan under section 20b differed so widely from those of section 77, it would be expected that experience would bring some re-examination of these key matters.

Percentage of Assents Required

The phrase in section 77 — "two-thirds in amount . . . of such class . . . voting on said plan" — points up two issues: It sets no quorum [1] and it requires a record of pros and cons. Indeed, when no quorum is set the voting must be explicitly pro and con. Although the language of section 20b is identical with section 77 in submitting the proposed plan "for acceptance or rejection," apparently the Commission considered that rejection need not be explicit; it was implied in the

---

[1] "Quorum" is used here in the analogy of a deliberative body where a certain number is required for a legal vote.

absence of positive assent.   One should note that under section 20b the Commission could still require a pro and con type of ballot as under section 77, but the "quorum" in effect would have to be higher than the 75% of the securities outstanding in each class, to allow for the likely dissents.

Since section 20b was sponsored by the Commission itself, one can assume that the variance from the section 77 voting provisions was intended.   In some section 77 cases far less than 50% of a class have voted.   A certificate of vote returned in the Missouri Pacific case [2] recorded only 33.75% of the preferred stock voting, 26.58% of another claim, and only 65.8% of the first mortgage 5% bonds, the largest class voting.   The place of the court in section 77 procedure, the approval of the plan by the Commission, and the active participation of protective committees were doubtless held to be adequate protection for those who did not vote.

When the Mahaffie bill was framed, however, the wholly voluntary aspect of the procedure was thought to require special protection to minorities, even for those who for some reason do not vote.   The theory was that the plan should be accepted by a heavy majority of the outstanding amount of each class.   Section 20b thus gave special recognition to (a) those in each class of security who are lost holders in the sense that the voting forms never reached them, (b) those who have heard of the plan but do not vote, and (c) those who make a choice but a dissenting one.   These three groups together, if more than 25% of the outstanding securities, can block a plan.

The Commission's Committee on Legislation and Rules explained in 1953 that in the hearings on the bill there had been a difference of opinion on the matter of majority percentage.   It added that ". . . there is nothing sacrosanct about the 75-percent minimum . . ." but it is consistent with provisions of a number of mortgages approved in section 77 proceedings.[3]   These provisions apply to voluntary moves to

[2] Certificate dated May 18, 1951, in Finance Docket No. 9918; this vote was on the 1949 plan, which was never consummated.

[3] These were provisions whereby a railroad, with the approval of the Commission and the assent of holders of three-fourths of the bonds, could modify the time prescribed for payment of principal and interest.   Letter dated

modify bond indentures; by analogy the voluntary section 20b statute should put pressure on the applicant to frame a plan that would be acceptable to an equally large majority. The principle is sound, but the question remains: What minimum percentage of assents should be required for forcing a minority to accept a plan?

A bill introduced in both Houses of Congress in the first session of the Eighty-Third Congress [4] proposed an amendment to lower the percentage of assents necessary for acceptance. It would lower the present 75% to 66⅔%, and make the percentage base the principal amount or number of shares actually voted rather than the total outstanding in each class. It specified, however, that in each class of creditors' claims affected, at least one-half of the outstanding principal amount would have to vote.[5]

In a discussion of proposed amendments on the required percentage of assents it is well to keep the basic alternatives in mind:

1. To require assents from a certain percentage of the outstanding securities in each class (the present section 20b).
2. To require a vote explicitly *pro* and *con,* with a certain percentage of pro votes out of the total vote cast (the present section 77).
3. In a vote explicitly pro and con as in 2 above, to make the additional requirement that the total vote in each class reach a minimum percentage (proposal in the amending bill with respect to creditors' claims).

The Commission has taken a pragmatic approach to this question of the percentage of assents required. It has noted that where securities are widely distributed, 90% is about the

---

March 19, 1953, from Committee on Legislation and Rules of the Interstate Commerce Commission, recorded in Hearing before the Committee on Interstate and Foreign Commerce, U.S. Senate, 83rd Congress, 1st Section, on S. 978, Railroad Reorganization, March 23, 1953, p. 58.

[4] S. 978, which was introduced on February 13, 1953, by Senator Johnson of Colorado for himself and Senator Capehart, to supersede the shorter bill, S. 907, introduced a week earlier. The corresponding House bill was H.R. 3287.

[5] Note that this provision did not apply to stock. Nothing appeared in the hearings on the bill to explain the less solicitous attitude toward stock.

maximum in any class, either debt or stock, that can be expected to give attention to notices and to vote.[6] The remaining 10% presumably would include the apathetic holders and the ones not reached by notices. If, in fact, the lost-stock category is large in some classes, there is real danger that a scheming minority could block a good plan. Realistically, the Commission concludes that the present act requires in fact the positive assents to be 75 out of 90, or $83\frac{1}{3}\%$ of maximum voting expectancy. Its Committee on Legislation states that "it does not appear unreasonable that the 75-percent [in the present law] . . . be reduced to two-thirds, which is approximately equal to 75 percent of 90 percent." [7]

The Commission has been reluctant to go beyond the reduction from 75% to $66\frac{2}{3}\%$ of outstanding securities. The proposal to use $66\frac{2}{3}\%$ of those voting, with a 50% quorum (as in S. 978), would permit a plan to pass with an affirmative vote of $33\frac{1}{3}\%$ of the whole class. Such a marked easing of the law would change it in principle. In comparison with the situation before section 20b, when no security holder of a solvent railroad could be forced out of his contract, it would be a radical change to permit one-third of the total outstanding securities in a class to call the tune. At the Senate hearing on S. 978, representatives of holders of railroad obligations made strong protest to the proposed reduction.

The Commission has expressed opposition to pro and con voting in section 20b proceedings, giving reasons as follows:

Under the present [assent] procedure, the burden is placed upon the applicant railroad, where it should be, to obtain the requisite assents. With pro and con voting, ordinarily the carrier would be the only party with sufficient resources to wage an aggressive campaign. Naturally, the carrier would not be interested in seeing that votes be cast by se-

[6] Counsel for Boston and Maine Railroad reported in 1952 that 20% of the Railroad's common stock was believed to be lost. (Proceedings before a Three-Judge Court, Civil Action No. 763–51, January 21, 1952, p. 21.)

[7] Letter of March 19, 1953, op. cit., p. 58. In view of the fact that in the Boston and Maine case the narrowest margin was in the 76+ % assents of the outstanding common stock, this proposed change to $66\frac{2}{3}\%$ of the outstanding securities in a class would give considerable leeway. It would have relieved the pressure a great deal for the Railroad, and might have avoided the decision to employ special solicitors of assents.

curity holders who oppose a plan, and it is probable that the latter would not be represented as well in the voting as those who favor the plan. There are also procedural difficulties . . . which are not present where only assents are recorded.[8]

One must not let the phrase "pro and con" obscure the real issues in fixing the percentage of required favorable votes. In the present statute, with the 75% assent requirement, the "cons" are not explicit but they are there. They are included in the composite group that does not overtly assent — lost holders, the apathetic, as well as the dissenters. When negative votes are asked for on the ballot — as in section 77 and in the 1953 bill to amend — there is merely a sharper picture of the pro and con sentiment on the plan.

The crux of the problem in pro and con voting is not the technical method but the percentage of each class required to vote — the quorum. The basic objection to pro and con voting for section 20b proceedings comes down to the setting of a low quorum figure; for instance, the 50% proposed in the amending bill.

If the Commission recommends change from 75% to two-thirds of the outstanding securities, could it not also require a pro and con vote with a stated quorum of 90%, the maximum it has found likely to vote? This suggestion introduces other dangers. It would increase the incentive of a small opposing group to abstain from voting and thereby prevent a quorum, whereas its negative vote, if cast, would not be large enough to prevent attainment of the required percentage of assents. In reality, although not explicitly, the present section 20b sets a quorum of at least 75% of the total outstanding in a class, because that amount must assent. In fact, requiring minimum assents of 75%, with or without pro and con ballots, amounts to requiring a somewhat larger quorum than 75%, since a certain number of any class are sure to object.

The requirement of assents from a large percentage of the outstanding securities in each class, as in the present section 20b, seems much the wisest provision. It includes the essential elements of pro and con balloting and a minimum

8 Ibid., p. 59.

quorum, while avoiding the difficulties involved in setting an absolute quorum. There is justification for reduction of the 75% figure for required assents to perhaps 66⅔%; but, on the whole, the sanction of a heavy majority of assents is strong argument for the justice of a plan, in addition to approval by a government agency which also has the responsibility of seeing that solicitation is fair.

Holdings Disqualified from Voting

The Commission in the Boston and Maine case disqualified three blocks of stock which in its judgment were controlled by the Railroad. These were discussed in Chapter X with the conclusion that the Commission's ruling was a retroactive interpretation of a clause in the statute which had not previously been so construed.

The history of this case shows how the running tally of assents during a long submission period in which trading continued invited purchases for voting rights only. Stock purchases for the voting rights were made by a director in this case, and also by a paid solicitor. Is this objectionable practice? Existing statutes are drawn to prevent profit to insiders on sales of stock purchased within a certain period.[9] But the purchases by the Boston and Maine director were made not for personal gain but to add assents for the plan. There are fine lines of distinction here. One can feel certain that the Boston and Maine board, as a board, would not have held a special meeting to urge its members and other officers into large-scale purchases of common stock, even asking them to go the limit of personal resources to "put the plan over." If the practice would be unsound when aggressively promoted

---

[9] Sections 16 (a) and (b) of the Securities Exchange Act; also Section 17 of the Public Utility Holding Company Act and Section 30 (f) of the Investment Company Act. There was no allegation in the Department's brief that the Coolidge transactions in this case were illegal because of unfair use of inside information by those connected with company management. Its brief would disqualify the director's ballots on the purchased stock solely on grounds that they were controlled by the Railroad. We have seen that the purpose was not "trader's profits" in any direct sense.

For thorough discussion with case references on the subject of insider trading under SEC regulations, see Louis Loss, *Securities Regulation* (Boston, Little, Brown and Company, 1951 and 1955 Supplement) , pp. 561–598.

by the board, is it not equally unsound for individuals on their own initiative?

A record-day vote, the advantages of which are discussed below, would avoid much of this problem. Even with a record-day vote, however, there can always be stock purchases in anticipation of the vote, although there is not the running tally of votes to make it possible to gauge the purchases needed to give the final push.

There is good reason to do everything practicable to restrict votes to long-run investors who own stock for all its rights. Purchase of stock for only its vote smacks of buying an election. Granted that the validity of ballots cannot in general be tested by the motives of the buyers, are there particular buyers who should not vote stock bought during the submission period? If so, a new restriction is being introduced in recapitalization procedures. In a submission-period vote, ballots cast by directors, officers, or paid solicitors of the railroad for shares acquired after the vote has been ordered should be disqualified by rule. In a record-day vote also, such ballots should be disqualified on shares acquired after the plan is ordered to a vote by the Commission. Such a rule would defeat any charge that the required percentage had been attained through assents financed by those inside the company.

The principles governing curbs on the right of management and agents to acquire and vote stock on a modification plan are important enough to be set by Congress in the statute itself. Then the Commission would not be left to accomplish the same result by extension of the provision regarding controlled assents.

The voting of borrowed shares, as was done by a paid solicitor in this case, is a procedural matter more properly handled under exchange rules for brokers. The borrowing transaction, a financial device to implement delivery under rules of the exchanges, would come under the disqualification of the preceding paragraphs if carried out by an agent of the railroad. Whether the stock-borrowing transaction is initiated by an agent or any other party, there is reason for considering ways to limit its use to strict financial purposes.

Reference has already been made in Chapter X to the

Commission's own proposal, based on its experience in the Central Railroad of New Jersey case, to amend the provisions in section 20b regarding controlled securities. The proposed amendment would permit all securities entitled to vote for directors to vote on modification plans, with the restriction that if 25% of such stock is controlled by the applicant then the Commission could prescribe a higher assent percentage than the normal, as it "may determine to be just and reasonable and in the public interest." The amendment has met with favor, in agreement with the Commission's argument that the existing provisions would deny majority stockholders the right to vote in many cases and might result in the failure of a meritorious plan through the refusal or neglect of a small minority of holders to assent.

The amendment has the merit of permitting the Commission to review the circumstances to see if the advantage of the carrier in having a 25% head start in the class voting should be offset by giving the public holders a stronger voice in the decision. It presents a dilemma in administration, however. One cannot raise the total percentage of assents required for acceptance without increasing the power of a minority and thereby encouraging holdouts.

Furthermore, when one recalls the implications of the cross-holdings of Boston and Maine stock (Chapter VI), it is clear that as a procedural matter the Commission before setting the higher percentage should consider carefully the facts that bear on the question of whether all within a class would vote the interest of the class.

Clear Definition of the Commission's Powers and Responsibilities

Some questions about the Commission's powers under section 20b, as well as the limits of its responsibility, were dealt with in clarifying amendments in S. 907 and S. 978. They may be conveniently discussed under the following topics:

(a) *Assurances of Assent*. The discussion of this topic in Chapter V shows that confusion exists as to the purpose and handling of assurances of assent. The statute gives the Commission discretion in deciding whether to require assurances, except with regard to carriers applying for transfer from equity or section 77 proceedings, which must obtain assurances. But the regulations require that applications show any existing facts as to assurances. The Boston and Maine management, careful not to solicit assurances but only to test stockholder sentiment on an informal basis, had the initial problem of determining the precise amount of assurances obtained on such basis. The interveners at the first public hearing raised many questions about assurances. The informal proofs acceptable to the Commission were not accepted by the Sakis group.

The wide discretion given the Commission by the statute, all the way from complete waiver to requirement of a particular percentage of assurances from each class, suggests that the purpose was simply to provide the Commission with the means for finding out whether it was worthwhile to continue the proceedings in any particular case. It is common sense for a railroad to postpone application until it has come to some understanding with the more important security holders affected.

That the Commission itself was not rigorous in its application of the clause is shown by its acceptance of the first Boston and Maine application, which reported assurances of only 1% from the common class. Furthermore, there is no evidence that it saw, or asked for, any show of material used by the Railroad in its test of stockholder sentiment. Yet in these circumstances the first application was set for hearing, although later withdrawn. The speed with which opposition developed suggests that the assurances of assent in connection with this first application were rather meaningless as an administrative tool for both carrier and Commission. Probably the Commission knew of the in-between legal status of Boston Railroad Holding Company, which held over half of the Railroad's common stock and for technical reasons was not in a position to give assurance, but undoubtedly would go along.

When a matter is so much one of administrative decision, it would seem better either to leave it out of the statute altogether or to go in the other direction and spell out the administration in more detail. The word "assurances" seems too strong for the meaning intended. The procedure is one of sounding out sentiment so that the management is not presenting the plan as a shot in the dark or a trial balloon. If this is the intent, the statute could omit direct reference to assurances and simply read, "Upon presentation of any such application, the Commission shall, if satisfied that the plan is offered in good faith and with substantial support from the security classes affected, set such application for public hearing. . . ." A matter for such wide administrative discretion is more properly for the rules, not the statute. The statute provides the boundaries that must be observed in formulation of the rules to carry it into effect.

The Commission's rules and regulations then would implement the real purpose, perhaps prescribing alternative methods of handling assurances. At one extreme might be a postcard vote pro and con by all security holders on a general description of the proposed plan, such as was used on one M–K–T plan, with a formal report of results. Under such circumstances supervision by the Commission of the descriptive material would be necessary. There are disadvantages in this method. A security holder after giving his assurance may find himself in disagreement with the final plan, either because the Commission required amendments or because the general description omitted features objectionable to the security holder. Another point raised by the Commission in stressing the necessity for its supervision of the preliminary solicitation material is that a security holder giving assurance of assent as to the preliminary plan may thereby give too little attention to the material on the final plan.

At the other extreme would be an informal oral report on acceptance of a proposed plan by stockholders, made by the railroad's officers to the Commission or its staff. Such a step was all that was actually involved in the Boston and Maine situation.

(b) *Matters of Solicitation.* When one puts the charges of illegal solicitation against the Commission's final finding of no proved irregularities, there is a strong suggestion that the statute is not clear on all points. The Commission has proposed an amendment to clarify its authority and procedure.

The different interpretations of the statute relate to three questions:

1. Is oral solicitation forbidden?
2. What jurisdiction has the Commission over solicitation of assurances of assent?
3. What jurisdiction has the Commission over material used to solicit opposition of holders in either the assurance or the final voting stage?

The statute needs amendment unless it gives clear answer to these questions.

As regards oral solicitation, the statute certainly would not be silent about so important a part of the process if it were forbidden. But there would be no point in preventing so necessary and natural a part of solicitation, regardless of the difficulties in controlling it. The SEC, which has gone to great lengths in the regulation of proxy procedure, does not say that once a proxy letter has passed its scrutiny the letter can be handed out only in absolute silence. That would be preposterous. Furthermore, the law is adequate to handle fraudulent statements if evidence is established.

Certainly the Commission itself, which sponsored the statute, had no idea that oral solicitation was forbidden. The order submitting the Boston and Maine plan to vote authorized the hiring of special solicitors. It would hardly be expected that no comment, even as to the contents of the solicitation material, would be made by a solicitor to a stockholder. Nor is it likely that the Commission would prohibit a natural method of salesmanship, one it had long accepted in its section 77 practice.

As for the Commission's jurisdiction over solicitation of assurances of assent, the one reference to solicitation in the statute clearly refers to the voting when the plan itself is put to vote. Recognizing that there may be confusion, the Commission has recommended amendment to include control over material to solicit assurances. Its reasoning for making its jurisdiction clear is convincing: the purpose of the present statutory approval of material might be defeated if the carrier had already created a false impression in connection with its preliminary activity with assurances.[10]   The proposed amendment is a sound one.

The third question — what jurisdiction has the Commission over material used to solicit opposition to the plan — also points to the need for clarification and development of the directives.   If the purpose of any regulation of solicitation material is to prevent votes given upon the basis of erroneous or misleading information, it is clearly as desirable to regulate material asking for dissents.

The statute speaks of the solicitation of the opposition, but with reference only to the final plan:

> All [material] to be used in soliciting the assents *or the opposition* [italics added] of such holders shall, before being so used, be submitted to the Commission for its approval as to correctness and sufficiency of the material facts stated therein.

The Commission's rules are addressed entirely to the carrier's action regarding the application.   They repeat the clause in the statute and add "but this requirement shall not be construed to apply to normal and ordinary correspondence or other communications between the *carrier* and a creditor, stockholder, or other interested party."   [Italics added]   The rules do not cover assurances of assent; they do include approval of material proposed by the opposition; but the reference to normal communications, presumably including oral communications, is related to carriers only. The statute and the rules should be amended to cover all formal efforts of minority committees to encourage dissents at all stages of the proceedings.   The material prepared by them should be subject to the same Commission scrutiny as the material prepared by the carrier to encourage assents.

Clarification of all these matters of solicitation is provided by the following amendment proposed by the Commission as a substitute for the fifth sentence of paragraph (2):

[10] Letter from the Committee on Legislation and Rules, Interstate Commerce Commission, to the Chairman of the Senate Committee on Interstate and Foreign Commerce, March 6, 1953 (mimeo.), p. 8.

The Commission shall have the power to make such general rules and regulations and such special requirements in any particular case in respect of solicitation of assents, opposition, assurances of assent, approval or disapproval of such holders (whether such solicitation is made before or after approval of the proposed alteration or modification by the Commission), as it shall deem necessary or desirable; and no solicitation shall be made, and no letter, circular, advertisement, or other communication, or financial and statistical statements, or summaries thereof, shall be used in any such solicitation, in contravention of such rules, regulations, or special requirements.[11]

It is important to note that this amendment provides still other improvements over the existing statute. Specific authority would be granted to the Commission to issue rules and regulations to guide railroads in the preparation of solicitation material and the Commission's staff in the supervision of such material. In the opinion of the Committee on Legislation and Rules, such a provision would relieve the Commission of much burdensome detailed action on material submitted. The experience in the Boston and Maine case confirms the assistance that definite regulations would give to a railroad. Furthermore, within the rules set up, the railroad's officers would be in a position to turn more freely to the Commission's staff for advice, and helpful opinions could be expected in normal course from the staff.[12]

In addition, the Commission would no longer be required to approve the "correctness and sufficiency of the material facts" in solicitation material. It has been pointed out [13] that the statute places on the Commission a much more difficult task in this respect than that imposed on the SEC under its own extensive proxy rules. The SEC does not ordinarily in-

[11] Letter of March 19, 1953, from Committee on Legislation, recorded in Hearing on S. 978, p. 57.

[12] On the subject of solicitation, Chapter IX suggested that railroads, under the Commission's supervision, develop simplified prospectuses urging assents, similar to prospectuses for the sale of new securities. Such a document would aid unsophisticated investors to understand the more detailed Commission report and order.

[13] For further discussion, see Hand and Cummings, "Consensual Securities Modification," 63 *Harvard Law Review* 957 (1950), at p. 964.

vestigate to establish the correctness of the information furnished to security holders, but may do so as circumstances indicate.

(c) *The Use of a Depositary.*   We have noted that the original act made no mention of the depositary arrangement. Doubtless the litigation in the Boston and Maine case inspired the special attention given the depositary in the proposed amendments.   S. 978 provided that "The Commission may direct that the assents . . . shall be addressed to a bank or trust company, approved by it . . . ."   Further, "[such institution] shall certify to the Commission the result . . . and the Commission may, in its discretion, rely upon such certification as conclusive evidence in determining the result of such submission."   In the hearing on the amending bill it was stated that after comments by the Commission the sponsors were agreeable to changing the words "rely upon" to "accept," and "conclusive" was to be struck.[14]   These new words remove the note of finality in the depositary's certificate, and suggest that certain circumstances might warrant further evidence than the depositary's bare certificate.

The wording of this amendment — "the Commission may direct . . ." — gives effect to the conclusion of this study as to the Commission's direct responsibility in the count of assents.   If the Commission chooses not to use a depositary for counting, presumably it would undertake the count itself as in section 77 proceedings.   Furthermore, the way left to the Commission for considering the depositary's certificate only as evidence, but not necessarily the last word, suggests situations where it would want something more.   This points clearly to adequate direction at the beginning, so that the Commission can feel sure that, barring fraud, the certificate can be accepted.   This is not to say that the Commission should plan the depositary procedure in detail; but it must know whether the procedure fulfills the requirement of a valid certificate when voting is over.

The depositary arrangement so far used in section 20b proceedings is a natural projection of the Commission's function and internal organization in proceedings under section 77. The depositary is only its extended arm in the section 20b

14 Hearing on S. 978, op. cit., p. 3.

case. It is proper and sensible to have the railroad's own transfer agent as depositary, but that should end the relationship for operating purposes. Any assumption that the depositary is the railroad's agent is wrong administration; the statute imposes the responsibility otherwise. It could well be that arrangements with outside vote-counting specialists would be found useful also in other procedures which have been so long conducted on the Commission's own premises.

Another suggestion, not for the statute but for depositary procedure, comes from the form of the Commission's own certificates on the results of voting that it has itself conducted. For example, in the Missouri Pacific plan of 1949 the Commission in May 1951 reported the results of the ballot in eight separate tables, four of which were breakdowns of defective ballots according to types of deficiency. This carefully planned certificate in its very make-up shows completeness and demonstrates that thought was given to the earmarks of valid balloting. What the Commission finds useful for itself should be equally so for its agent. A complete statement with information readily available would leave less opening for charges about laxity and would lessen chances of petitions by objectors to review the records.[15]

(d) *Determination of Classes.* The dispute in the Boston and Maine case over the determination of classes for voting purposes has led the Commission to propose that the language of the statute explicitly give it power to prescribe classes.[16] Although determination of classes must precede the vote by holders in each class, and the three-judge Court clearly upheld the Commission's decision in the Boston and Maine controversy, there is point in making sure that no room is left for argument about the Commission's power in this respect. Because of the many complexities in the determination of a class, definition of a "class" in each particular situation is best left to the judgment of the Commission.

---

15 Mr. J. J. Donnelly, Jr., Special Assistant to the Attorney General, noted the omission of any such tabulation in the certificate of the depositary in this case. Proceedings of a Three-Judge Court, Civil Action No. 763–51, January 22, 1952, p. 139.

16 "The Commission shall, for the purposes of this section, divide the securities to be affected by any modification or alteration proposed into such classes as it shall determine to be just and reasonable." From Sec. 3 of S. 978.

(e) *Responsibility for Supervision.*   Of major importance is the location of responsibility in the matter of supervision of the whole procedure of voting.   The study has emphasized this as the key administrative problem and at various times referred to the statute, which says in paragraph (2) :

> . . . the Commission shall cause the carrier, in such manner as it shall direct, to submit the proposed alteration or modification . . . to the holders of each class. . . .

This is a definite statement which gives the Commission sole responsibility as the directing agency in the voting process. Some have held that the phrase "in such manner as *it* [emphasis added] shall direct" refers to the carrier.   Although grammatically the antecedent of *it* is not clear, the interpretation is hardly reasonable that a regulatory agency would be given the authority to cause a vote to be taken, but be left without the authority or responsibility to direct the manner.

How can a regulatory agency escape the ultimate responsibility for regulating?   Lest any confusion in responsibility be caused by mere language, an editorial change should be made in the above-quoted clause, so that it reads:

> . . . the Commission, in such manner as it shall direct, shall cause the carrier to submit the proposed alteration . . . to the holders of each class. . . .

There are enough difficulties in interpreting a statute without the further question raised by an ambiguity in an antecedent, particularly when the location of administrative responsibility is of paramount importance.

Clarification of the Status of Committees

A striking contrast between section 20b and section 77 is that the operation of committees, even their formal existence, is entirely ignored in the law covering voluntary security modifications.   One can assume that the omission was a studied one.

The contrast becomes more striking when the detailed attention to committees under section 77 is recalled.   The Commission's rules [17] cover in great detail its control over

[17] Code of Federal Regulations (1949 edition), Title 49, Part 58, Sections 1–12.

the operation of minority committees in reorganization procedures. Each individual or committee wishing to solicit or act under proxies must apply formally, give information for each security class for which it desires to act, give extensive information as to committee members and their occupations, special solicitors employed, compensation arrangements to the applicant and solicitors, and arrangements for financing until expenses are ultimately approved. All this information is required also for the secretary and counsel of a committee. The SEC has similar regulations over the operation of committees in reorganizations under the Public Utility Holding Company Act.

A notable distinction is thus presented between the administrative concepts found in section 77 and Holding Company Act proceedings and those found in section 20b procedures. The difference demands explanation.

One can be certain that the neglect of committees in section 20b is not a deliberate move to run roughshod over minorities. The statute recognizes the possibility of opposition in that the Commission is empowered to approve solicitation material for the opposition. When the percentage vote for acceptance by a class was put at 75% of the amount outstanding, the thought was that in a voluntary proposal there should be overwhelming acceptance. The implication seems to be that any opposition then would be desultory and not formally organized in committees. The mere size of the majority vote required, however, does not make it any less likely that sizable minorities may organize against a plan. On the contrary, the requirement of a high percentage of assents makes an objecting group more potent and thereby encourages committee organization.

A collateral question relates to the expenses and fees incident to committee opposition. One can sympathize with the Commission's purpose to avoid the high expenses common to reorganizations, as well as its reluctance to take on additional supervision in that troublesome area. The question cannot be solved, however, by assuming there will be little formal opposition and therefore no problem of expenses and fees.

It appears that there is a significant gap in regulation when the new statute ignores the problem of operation of committees and rightful payment to them, except for a vague reference to approval of solicitation in opposition.   The Boston and Maine case highlights this unregulated area.   Although the draft of Mrs. Sakis' original letter soliciting proxies was submitted to the Bureau of Finance, its staff officers did not pass upon the letter, giving the reason that it has no jurisdiction over the formation of protective committees.   As early as the first hearing the Sakis Committee gave testimony that it represented several different classes of stockholders, but it did not submit any definite list until December 1951 in connection with the civil action before the three-judge Court. By that time many of the stockholders had sold their stock, or had assented it during the submission period; and the two-year time limit of all the proxies had expired.   Nevertheless, the Commission did not investigate protests in which the Railroad, as well as interveners in the later proceedings, raised questions about the committee's authority.   On the other hand, the Commission denied the request that it authorize expenses and fees for the Sakis Committee, again on the grounds of no statutory power.

In a section 77 case but not in a section 20b case the Commission demands careful reports on committee arrangements with counsel.   In the Boston and Maine case the modifications had been in effect for a year before it was testified at a hearing on the settlement that Mr. George P. Sakis considered himself an associate counsel for the committee and for this service would get $37\frac{1}{2}\%$ of the fees, which amounted to almost the total settlement of $100,000.[18]   What the Commission so meticulously regulates in section 77 cases it throws outside of official supervision under section 20b and leaves to private settlements.   If the purpose of Commission supervision over expenses and fees in section 77 proceedings is to protect the railroad estate against unconscionable raids, it follows that the Commission avoids this responsibility in section 20b proceedings when opportunity is given for private settlements for alleged expenses because there is no statutory provision to authorize them.

[18] Proceedings before the Interstate Commerce Commission, Docket No. 31257, June 2, 1954, pp. 161–167.

The Boston and Maine case emphasizes the need for thorough review of the place of committees in a section 20b proceeding and their proper regulation. Admittedly, committees are less important in section 20b than in section 77 proceedings, because section 20b makes no provision for plans drawn up by protective committees and railroads are unlikely to propose plans without a good prospect of acceptance by 75% of each class. Nevertheless, some opposition is probable with respect to most plans, particularly stock modifications. The rights of minorities to organize in opposition need more protection than even the ample public hearings customary in section 20b cases; and it seems only fair also that such minorities should be reimbursed for any constructive contributions to a plan. On the other hand, inasmuch as one of the purposes of section 20b is to expedite recapitalizations, minority committees should be regulated to prevent such long delaying actions as those in the Boston and Maine litigation, particularly if they represent only a small percentage of the stockholders.

The amendment proposed on supervision of solicitation material goes a long way to give the Commission authority over committees opposing plans. Tightening the rules and regulations will complete the job. Mr. L'Heureux [19] has suggested that the Commission require every intervener or committee to give the following information at the start:

1. Each intervener must state whom he represents.
2. If he represents other security holders, he should have written proxies following a model form prepared by the Commission. The expense would be borne by the intervener.
3. Each intervener must state what class he represents, and should not represent security holders with conflicting interests.
4. Proxies should be limited to a period of one year. Then new proxies must be obtained.

Some such rules would enable the Commission to gauge the importance of the opposition. A further rule authorizing allowance for fees and expenses where the interveners

[19] L'Heureux, Opinion, p. 69.

make contributions to the development of a plan would insure the rights of minorities to voice their objections and counterproposals.   Certainly, close control will be necessary to prevent exorbitant claims.   Nevertheless, the additional burden of supervising opposition and allowing reimbursement seems to be one that the Commission should assume.

CHANGES IN PROCEDURES

Good procedures fail with poor operation, and good operatives are handicapped by poor procedures.   Without trying to be precise about the mixture of these two that brought the results described in the foregoing chapters, this study has pointed to some conclusions as to procedural changes that promise some benefits.

Importance of Initial Organization for the Balloting Job

An administrative structure for managing a continuing organization, whether a business or other institution, is an assumed necessity.   The same is true for a temporary operation for a specific purpose, such as the voting arrangement for the Boston and Maine modification.

At previous points reference has been made to the lack of contact between the responsible head and its operating associates in the solicitation and voting process.   The record shows almost no communication between the Commission and the other two parties, the depositary and the Railroad, while voting was in progress.   Yet problems were continually arising, many of which were at the center of the subsequent litigation.   It is not necessary that the Commission should follow all operating detail as it goes on; but, as in a plant, the operating head must learn promptly of difficulties that may ruin the final product if not properly handled.   There should be no unilateral decisions on a team effort.

Record-Day Procedure Recommended [20]

The analysis in Chapter VII has emphasized that assents must be identifiable by certificate number for accurate recording in a submission period when assents are made to

[20] Note that this discussion relates specifically to stock.

carry through to transferees until revoked. We have noted that it was unusual for brokers to attach certificate numbers to assents and that it would entail substantial costs to do so.

The choice of method lies between the record-day type, as in section 77, and the submission-period type with assents and also the right to assent or revoke to follow the transfers. Record-day practice, where only owners as of a specified record day may assent and revoke assents, limits the voters to a fixed list. In section 20b procedures the Commission and the carriers have thought it advisable to depart from record-day practice and some writers have even thought it necessary to do so.[21] It would be theoretically possible, the argument runs, that with an actively traded security the necessary percentage might be unattainable "because more than twenty-five per cent of the class might be transferred after the record date without previously having been assented."[22]

This points to a significant criticism of the record-day method when there is a high percentage requirement for assents. The outcome rests with a fixed group of holders as of a given date, and the vote stands or falls on success with them. In a case involving securities with high market turnover, as the voting continues after the record day, there would be added a mounting number of record-day holders who have sold and are no longer interested. The number of holders who could be solicited would shrink as sales continued. This is an ominous development if the plan is to be accepted.

Quite understandably managements turned to an alternative that would not so foreclose continued solicitation: a long submission period and even its possible extension, assents to stay put on transferred stock until revoked, and the right to assent or revoke to go with transfers. One can be sympathetic with choice of a method to make the high hurdle of 75% assents easier to reach. The Boston and Maine management rejected the deposit-certificate method because it feared that sheer inertia would increase negative votes.

We have seen, however, that this favoring procedure has its

---

[21] Hand and Cummings, "Consensual Securities Modification," 63 *Harvard Law Review* 957 (1950), p. 963.
[22] Ibid.

problems too, not the least of which is that of accurate recording. In addition, this method compromises the strict meaning of an assent as a positive decision by the holder; for stock, once assented, may come to rest with a holder who has no notice of the assent status of the stock he has bought.[23]

The basic decisions on this matter of voting methods seem to be:

(a) to settle on the minimum percentage of acceptance that shows the preponderant judgment of each class — an acceptable consensus;

(b) to work out a method under which accurate recording will be ensured and the assents will be positive expressions by each voter rather than the mere absence of revocation. Assents would then signify active consideration of the plan.

The recommended lowering of the required assenting percentage from 75% to $66\frac{2}{3}\%$ fulfills the objective called for in (a). Present methods do not meet the requirements of (b).

This suggests a procedure that takes the best of both methods. To avoid complications in accurate recording when assents and the right to vote remain attached to transferred shares, the following method is proposed:

(a) Only holders of record on a named date would be eligible to assent or revoke. This date would be set by the Commission's order and placed well after the effective date of the order, say at least two months later in a situation like that of Boston and Maine Railroad.

(b) Promptly at the start of the period between the effective date of the Commission's order and the record day set by it, the railroad would distribute authorized material on the plan to the stockholder list, with appropriate directions to reach beneficial owners.

By the time of the record day, then, solicitation would be well advanced. The official list of record-day holders would on the whole be informed. The railroad would then send

---

[23] We leave it to the lawyers to follow the legal implications of the status of stock here described. Are there really two kinds of shares not discernible on their face, or in the contract with the issuer — one unassented, the other one assented but with no notice to the transferee? The stockholder must find out for himself which kind of stock he has.

solicitation material to all those on the record-day list who had not previously received it, and also assent forms to the entire list.

(c) The Commission's order would specify the voting period, which, as at present, could be ended earlier at the Railroad's direction when the statutory majority of assents had been received.

The result would be a fixed voters' list as a basis for accurate counting. The method approaches more nearly than alternative methods the ideal that assents should represent the considered opinion of the holders when the vote is certified. There is no reason to expect more manipulative market action than with the method used in this case. In fact, an adapted record-day vote would avoid the present running tally, which flags a close contest and encourages the hold-out for personal advantage.

Many of the procedural changes suggested in previous chapters would be desirable in a record-day vote.[24] Time and effort are well spent by a railroad management in bringing the stock list up to date before solicitation and voting start. A specialist in proxy solicitation might even be hired to trace lost stockholders at this early stage. The New York Stock Exchange Rule 874 can be used to request brokers, if reimbursed, to register in their own names their holdings of certificates in other street names.[25] The rules on counting assents should be clear as to whether an assent is countable when mailed or when received.

Fiduciary Signatures as in Usual Corporate Practice

The importance of trusteeship and other fiduciary relationships involving securities has made imperative a dependable procedure for validating transactions by those signing for beneficial interests. The emergence of a dispute in this

[24] Since my conclusion is that a record-day vote should be the method used, no summary is given here of the changes recommended to tighten up the method used in the Boston and Maine case. The reader can refer to previous chapters for discussion of specific places and means for revising the procedures in this case.

[25] Central Railroad of New Jersey in its solicitation asked banks, brokers, etc. to transfer into their own names the bonds or stock they held. Printed letter of June 22, 1949, in Finance Docket No. 16211.

case over the proper fulfillment of an instructional note to such signers was a startling development. The Department argued that the depositary had not observed the letter of the note, that the note was on a document passed on by the Commission, and the Commission presumably meant literally what it said.

This is clearly an administrative matter, on which the Commission's rules and orders should be explicit. Mr. L'Heureux has a remedy:

> . . . the I.C.C. to devise a form to be included at the bottom of the forms for letters of assent whereby a fiduciary certifies to the I.C.C. under the penalties of perjury that he has such authority. The depositary would then hold the letter of assent with the certification as the agent of the I.C.C. for that purpose. That would discourage an unauthorized person from assenting shares as a fiduciary and facilitate the task of the depositary.[26]

It would seem that anyone who signs purportedly as a fiduciary, but who is not one, would be subject to the same penalties for fraud, but inasmuch as the certificate flags the point it has merit.

There is nothing in this particular case that calls for other than the conventional practice with respect to fiduciary authority to sign ballots. If the Commission is not content with the accepted standards of trust company practice in the matter, however, it should spell out the additional requirement in directions to its agent, the depositary.

SOME GENERAL PROCEDURAL QUESTIONS

Corporate voting of any sort offers areas that call for reexamination. One of these is voting of street-name certificates by brokers. In present practice brokers' votes are accepted without show of authority from beneficial owners. Validity is assumed from the fact that stock exchange rules require the broker to report only votes he has authorization for. The corporation itself asks for no further evidence.

Practices followed occasionally in voting contests point the

---

[26] L'Heureux, Opinion, pp. 68–69.

way to more rigid requirements. For instance, in the Central Railroad of New Jersey proceedings, printed forms were distributed for brokers and similar record owners to use in requesting assents from beneficial owners. In the proxy battle for control of the New York Central Railroad in 1954 a large brokerage firm had an independent audit made of the votes of the beneficial owners whom it represented. To be sure, such practices in the ordinary corporate vote would be far too burdensome for brokers; but a vote of major significance, such as in a recapitalization, demands more formality in brokers' votes than it has received.

This is an area for study by both regulatory agencies and the exchanges to see whether present rules and practice of voting, particularly by brokers for beneficial owners, fully protect the integrity of the ballot. Contests for control on the scale of those recently carried on in several large corporations deluge brokers with added duties to their clients above those of the ordinary annual elections, and bring new problems perhaps not covered by existing rules. Certainly if section 20b proceedings continue to use the rule that assents follow transfers, there must be rigid requirements on record keeping, which must bring added costs to brokers.

This study has previously stressed the importance of the Hearing Examiner's Proposed Report in supplying a complete record for following the streams of evidence and opinion that converge into the Commission's final finding. The Proposed Report for the public record seems essential if a body of "case law" is to be fully developed in a line of decisions.

This recommendation to save the Examiner's opinions for the public is entirely consistent with the general point of view of a report made by the Attorney General's Committee on Administrative Procedure in 1941,[27] which recognized the importance of the Examiner in these quasi-judicial procedures by comparing his position to that of a trial judge. The report drew further from the analogy of the judicial system; the appellate court can reverse the trial judge's deci-

---

[27] U.S. Attorney General's Committee on Administrative Procedure, *Administrative Procedure in Government Agencies*. Part 11, Interstate Commerce Commission (Washington, Government Printing Office, 1941), p. 27.

sion, but the initial decision is still in the record. Even in Commission cases when the Examiner's opinion is reversed, his report has fully served its function in delineating the issues.[28] The recommendation of the Committee on Administrative Procedure included a statement that "The findings, conclusions, and recommendations of the hearing commissioner [a proposed change in title from "hearing examiner"] should be included in the record upon which any court review is sought." [29] My plea here does not relate to the formality of a court review, but only to the importance of the Proposed Report to an understanding of the Commission's final opinion.

CONCLUSIONS OF GENERAL APPLICATION TO ADMINISTRATIVE AGENCIES

This case is notable for the opportunity it presents for broad analysis of section 20b and the operating procedures under it. The foregoing recommendations are related closely to the issues raised in this particular episode. One cannot deal with such a many-sided problem, however, without forming opinions on administrative policies necessary for effective operation of regulatory agencies.

An important problem in every organization — business or government — is to get objective analysis of its own current policy and procedures. In their administrative aspects business and government are alike in that each requires a continuous and positive check on its performance. But there is a major difference between them. A business enterprise cannot survive mistakes for long. Competition forces alertness if its competitive position is to be maintained. A company cannot wait until it suffers from the better products of its

---

28 Ibid. Further aspects of the Proposed Report in agency practice are considered in Kenneth Culp Davis, "Official Notice," 62 *Harvard Law Review* 537 (1949).

29 U.S. Attorney General's Committee on Administrative Procedure, *Final Report* (Washington, Government Printing Office, 1941), Chapter IV, p. 51. See also Frank E. Cooper, *Administrative Agencies and the Courts* (Ann Arbor, University of Michigan Law School, 1951), pp. 176–179; and "The Status of the Trial Examiner in Administrative Agencies," a Note, 66 *Harvard Law Review* 1065 (1953).

competitors before it plans for improvement in its own. Within its organization there must be the means of keeping up a sustained offensive. It must ever be pushing toward the front rather than fighting rear-guard actions to keep in business.

For a government regulating agency, however, the tests of performance are not so precise or imposed by such compelling circumstances. A government agency, in the business analogy, has an absolute monopoly of operations in one area. Unlike the business monopolist, however, it has no urge from the profit motive. As it moves from case to case in its regulatory capacity, its record is judged satisfactory if it successfully deals with the challenges from those it regulates. The challenges may even extend to court action, which becomes a further test of agency policy.

These tests of administrative performance are not so objective as those in competitive business. In business the costs, profit figures, and trends are charted in the board room. No such records of performance face a Commission. In business organizations ways have been found for internal checks on performance, reappraisal of policies, planning for the future. A research division in business is frequently large and of necessity dynamic. A government regulating agency has similar problems, even more difficult because its product is that intangible something called administration.

The government agency's urge to better administration must come largely from within its organization, from policies directed to competency in operation and a professional attitude toward standards and objectives. Its product although intangible is as real as that of a manufacturer: first, to carry out the mandate of statutes; second, from its operating experience to find ways to improve the statutes and its administration of them. An administrative agency is thus a part of a national service organization to the business and social system on which our strength depends. Just as in a business organization, so each regulating agency must have developed within itself a system of self-criticism in the constructive sense, a positive method of treating each case as one of a continuing series from which advances in regulatory procedures are derived. In other words, close examination of methods should be a continuous practice, and not at all the sporadic result of a challenge by plaintiffs in a litigated case.

As problems come up during the course of a case, decisions are made until the case has moved along to its final disposition. At this point, there could then be what amounts to a clinical report by all those who had a part in the case. The report should be directed to two main questions: (a) What does this case bring up about the statute itself? Is the statute clear, complete, or does it need change? (b) Have any of the rules been inadequate, unrealistic, or otherwise unsuitable? Doubtless the essence of this suggestion is being carried out informally in government agencies, but there is advantage in making it a formality for internal records. There is tremendous gain to clear thinking when ideas are written for the record.

Further, there seems clearly to be a place for interagency communication in areas of overlapping subject matter such as technical financial procedures. The essential principles of many such problems are alike, only with different applications. This whole balloting matter is a case in point. The SEC has gone far into the regulation of proxies. It has staff members who have spent much of their time in this area since 1939, when extensive regulation started. One major salient of the attack in the Boston and Maine case related to solicitation; another to lack of evidence of brokers' authority to vote for beneficiaries. Although section 20b [30] directly excludes SEC supervision of any solicitation under it, there would be a great advantage if experience could be pooled on such technical matters as corporate voting. Interagency relationship could provide a basis for sharing ideas and information on many problems that come alike to both agencies. This procedure seems as logical as for the clinics in a concentrated hospital zone to have ready transfer of the results of research in an area of medicine.

This study has referred many times to the lack of liaison between the Department of Justice and the Commission throughout the greater part of this case. It should be impossible for those who make policy in a government agency to condone action by its own operating officials amounting to

[30] Section 20b (9).

a refusal to work with a sister agency, in this case with the one primarily responsible.

When one has had the opportunity, as has come in the preparation of this book, to assay even a small fraction of the materials that lie in the working files of regulatory agencies, progressively to be relegated to the archives, the question becomes insistent whether some systematic program of research is not an important need. Administrative tribunals were added to governmental machinery because the legislature and the courts could not deal with problems so complex and dynamic.

There is no clear answer on how best to achieve effective research in the case materials continuously flowing through our regulating agencies. Research must come in large part from within the agency as a necessary adjunct to its own operations. Occasionally a staff member [31] has started his own study, but such projects so far have not been planned by the agency itself. The success of such ventures suggests that some program [32] in this direction could be worked out to advantage. Also, there should be opportunity for those outside the agency to follow up lines of inquiry with access to the rich material of actual cases. A further advantage would come from discussions with those currently dealing with such business materials. It is not unlikely that some endowed

[31] A recent example is that of Edward T. McCormick's study, *Understanding the Securities Act and the S.E.C.* (New York, American Book Company, 1948). This authoritative study, written by a member of the operating staff of the Division of Corporation Finance of the S.E.C., deals with questions of principle that appear in the materials of day-to-day regulation.

A similar study is Louis Loss' *Securities Regulation,* published while he was Associate General Counsel of the S.E.C.

[32] This brings to mind a suggestion made by Mr. Justice Douglas in a talk to the S.E.C. staff in 1938: "Administrative agencies such as the S.E.C. require, not only in their early stages but during their later development, a continuous inflow of technically trained, competent, imaginative and adventuresome people. . . . I set about two years ago to try to work out on paper a scheme for a graduate school of finance within the S.E.C. . . . I believe if we can do something like that we shall have helped make administrative government increasingly attractive. . . ." William O. Douglas, *Democracy and Finance* (New Haven, Yale University Press, 1940), p. 277, footnote 2. Although Mr. Douglas' objective was a training program to nourish staff personnel, it suggests the possible extension into a research program of broader usefulness.

foundation interested in research in public administration or in the social sciences could see promise in a program of current studies of the source materials supplied by the production lines of government regulation.

The details of such a program are not our concern here. There are obvious problems: Should access be limited to the public records only? Are the results strictly for the internal use of the agency? If there is publication, under whose auspices should it come and with what restrictions and direction? Notwithstanding, wherever value is seen in doing something usually a way can be found.

One of Commissioner Eastman's points in "A Twelve Point Primer on the Subject of Administrative Tribunals" related to the important work of the staff. He said:

> In any large administrative tribunal, like the Interstate Commerce Commission, a vast amount of the real work must necessarily be done by the staff. It is a difficult problem to give the individual members of the staff proper recognition for work well done — recognition on the outside as well as the inside. It is very important that this problem be solved, but I am frank to say that its full solution has not yet been reached.[33]

As one means for formal recognition of contributions by staff officials, I suggest that they be given opportunity between the details of cases to stand back and view the process as a whole. This proposal holds considerable promise because it is a step toward the development of the agency's own research facilities. To take the Bureau of Finance of the Commission as an example, the staff members are close to the flow of agency work, first the details of the current case and then a new one close on its heels. There is little time for a broad view of the statute as an instrument of financial modifications, and the regulations as rules that must work. A cursory view of the docket in the Boston and Maine case is convincing enough of the prodigious effort necessary to process a case. True, expanded responsibilities and shortened personnel militate against suggestions that impose fur-

[33] *Selected Papers and Addresses of Joseph B. Eastman, 1942–1944,* edited by G. Lloyd Wilson. (New York, Simmons-Boardman Publishing Corporation, 1948), p. 377.

ther burdens. Nevertheless, it should be an important function of staff officials to summarize their experiences with a
case as it relates to the statute and procedure. The Examiner
and his superiors in the Bureau have lived and worked with
the details of the record on which the Commission bases its
decision. Those closest to operations would have further
usefulness to the Commission if they were requested to summarize in a formal report the lessons of the case for administration.

This suggestion of summary reports by the operatives on a
case is in line with the emphasis of the Attorney General's
Committee on Administrative Procedure on the function of
those who deal directly with the cases in process. It also
would help to achieve the objective expressed by Mr. Eastman: to recognize in a formal way the importance of those
whose work is the substance from which the final decisions
come.

APPENDIX A

Section 20b of the Interstate Commerce Act

AN ACT

To amend the Interstate Commerce Act, as amended,
and for other purposes.

*Be it enacted by the Senate and House of Representatives of
the United States of America in Congress assembled,* That it is
hereby declared to be in aid of the national transportation policy
of the Congress, as set forth in the preamble of the Interstate
Commerce Act, as amended, in order to promote the public interest in avoiding the deterioration of service and the interruption of employment which inevitably attend the threat of financial difficulties and which follow upon financial collapse and in
order to promote the public interest in increased stability of
values of railroad securities with resulting greater confidence
therein of investors, to assure, insofar as possible, continuity of
sound financial condition of common carriers subject to part I of
said Act, to enhance the marketability of railroad securities impaired by large and continuing accumulations of interest on income bonds and dividends on preferred stock and to enable said
common carriers, insofar as possible, to avoid prospective financial difficulties, inability to meet debts as they mature, and insolvency. To assist in accomplishing these ends and because certain classes of the securities of such carriers are in the usual case
held by a very large number of holders, and, further, to enable
modification and reformation of provisions of the aforesaid classes
of securities and of provisions of the instruments pursuant to
which they are issued or by which they are secured in cases where
such modification and reformation shall have become necessary or
desirable in the public interest in order to avoid obstruction to or

SOURCE: Preamble and section 2 of an Act to amend the Interstate Com-
merce Act, as amended, and for other purposes, approved April 9, 1948;
Public Law 478, 80th Congress, Chapter 180, 2d session, H.R. 2298. [Title 49
United States Code (1952 edition), Section 20b.]

interference with the economical, efficient, and orderly conduct by such carriers of their affairs, it is deemed necessary to provide means, in the manner and with the safeguards herein provided, for the alteration and modification, without the assent of every holder thereof, of the provisions of such classes of securities and of the instruments pursuant to which they are outstanding or by which they are secured.

Sec. 2.   Part I of the Interstate Commerce Act, as amended, is amended by adding after section 20a the following new section:

"Sec. 20b. (1) It shall be lawful (any express provision contained in any mortgage, indenture, deed of trust, corporate charter, stock certificate, or other instrument or any provision of State law to the contrary notwithstanding), with the approval and authorization of the Commission, as provided in paragraph (2) hereof, for a carrier as defined in section 20a (1) of this part to alter or modify (a) any provision of any class or classes of its securities as defined in section 20a (2) of this part being hereinafter in this section sometimes called 'securities'; or (b) any provision of any mortgage, indenture, deed of trust, corporate charter, or other instrument pursuant to which any class of its securities shall have been issued or by which any class of its obligations is secured (hereinafter referred to as instruments) : *Provided,* That the provisions of this section shall not apply to any equipment-trust certificates in respect of which a carrier is obligated, or to any evidences of indebtedness of a carrier the payment of which is secured in any manner solely by equipment, or to any instrument, whether an agreement, lease, conditional-sale agreement, or otherwise, pursuant to which such equipment-trust certificates or such evidences of indebtedness shall have been issued or by which they are secured.

" (2) Whenever an alteration or modification is proposed under paragraph (1) hereof, the carrier seeking authority therefor shall, pursuant to such rules and regulations as the Commission shall prescribe, present an application to the Commission.   Upon presentation of any such application, the Commission may, in its discretion, but need not, as a condition precedent to further consideration, require the applicant to secure assurances of assent to such alteration or modification by holders of such percentage of the aggregate principal amount or number of shares outstanding of the securities affected by such alteration or modification as the Commission shall in its discretion determine.   If the Commission shall not require the applicant to secure any such assurances, or when such assurances, as the Commission may require shall have

been secured, the Commission shall set such application for public hearing and the carrier shall give reasonable notice of such
hearing in such manner, by mail, advertisement, or otherwise, as
the Commission may find practicable and may direct, to holders
of such of its classes of securities and to such other persons in
interest as the Commission shall determine to be appropriate and
shall direct.   If the Commission, after hearing, in addition to
making (in any case where such alteration or modification involves an issuance of securities) the findings required by paragraph (2) of section 20a, not inconsistent with paragraph (1) of
this section shall find that, subject to such terms and conditions
and with such amendments as it shall determine to be just and
reasonable, the proposed alteration or modification —

" (a) is within the scope of paragraph (1) ;

" (b) will be in the public interest;

" (c) will be in the best interests of the carrier, of each class
        of its stockholders, and of the holders of each class of
        its obligations affected by such modification or altera-
        tion; and

" (d) will not be adverse to the interests of any creditor of
        the carrier not affected by such modification or altera-
        tion,

then (unless the applicant carrier shall withdraw its application) the Commission shall cause the carrier, in such manner as
it shall direct, to submit the proposed alteration or modification
(with such terms, conditions, and amendments, if any) to the
holders of each class of its securities affected thereby, for acceptance or rejection.   All letters, circulars, advertisements, and other
communications, and all financial and statistical statements, or
summaries thereof, to be used in soliciting the assents or the opposition of such holders shall, before being so used, be submitted
to the Commission for its approval as to correctness and sufficiency of the material facts stated therein.   If the Commission
shall find that as result of such submission the proposed alteration or modification has been assented to by the holders of at
least 75 per centum of the aggregate principal amount or number of shares outstanding of each class of securities affected
thereby (or in any case where 75 per centum thereof is held by
fewer than twenty-five holders, such larger percentage, if any, as
the Commission may determine to be just and reasonable and in
the public interest), the Commission shall enter an order approving and authorizing the proposed alteration or modification upon
the terms and conditions and with the amendments, if any, so

determined to be just and reasonable. Such order shall make provision as to the time when such alteration or modification shall become and be binding, which may be upon publication of a declaration to that effect by the carrier, or otherwise, as the Commission may determine. Any alteration or modification which shall become and be binding pursuant to the approval and authority of the Commission hereunder shall be binding upon each holder of any security of the carrier of each class affected by such alteration or modification, and upon any trustee or other party to any instrument under which any class of obligations shall have been issued or by which it is secured, and when any alteration or modification shall become and be binding the rights of each such holder and of any such trustee or other party shall be correspondingly altered or modified.

"(3) For the purposes of this section a class of securities shall be deemed to be affected by any modification or alteration proposed only (a) if a modification or alteration is proposed as to any provision of such class of securities, or (b) if any modification or alteration is proposed as to any provision of any instrument pursuant to which such class of securities shall have been issued or shall be secured: *Provided,* That in any case where more than one class of securities shall have been issued and be outstanding or shall be secured pursuant to any instrument, any alteration or modification proposed as to any provision of such instrument which does not relate to all of the classes of securities issued thereunder, shall be deemed to affect only the class or classes of securities to which such alteration or modification is related. For the purpose of the finding of the Commission referred to in paragraph (2) of this section as to whether the required percentage of the aggregate principal amount or number of shares outstanding of each class of securities affected by any proposed alteration or modification has assented to the making of such alteration or modification, any security which secures any evidence or evidences of indebtedness of the carrier or of any company controlling or controlled by the carrier shall be deemed to be outstanding unless the Commission in its discretion determines that the proposed alteration or modification does not materially affect the interests of the holder or holders of the evidence or evidences of indebtedness secured by such security. Whenever any such pledged security is, for said purposes, to be deemed outstanding, assent in respect of such security, as to any proposed alteration or modification, may be given only (any express or implied provision in any mortgage, indenture, deed of

trust, note, or other instrument to the contrary notwithstanding)
as follows: (a) Where such security is pledged as security under
a mortgage, indenture, deed of trust, or other instrument, pursuant to which any evidences of indebtedness are issued and outstanding, by the holders of a majority in principal amount of
such evidences of indebtedness, or (b) where such security secures an evidence or evidences of indebtedness not issued pursuant to such a mortgage, indenture, deed of trust, or other instrument, by the holder or holders of such evidence or evidences of
indebtedness; and in any such case the Commission, in addition
to the submission referred to in paragraph (2) of this section,
shall cause the carrier in such manner as it shall direct to submit
the proposed alteration or modification (with such terms, conditions, and amendments, if any, as the Commission shall have determined to be just and reasonable) for acceptance or rejection,
to the holders of the evidences of indebtedness issued and outstanding pursuant to such mortgage, indenture, deed of trust, or
other instrument, or to the holder or holders of such evidence or
evidences of indebtedness not so issued, and such proposed alteration or modification need not be submitted to the trustee of any
such mortgage, indenture, deed of trust, or other instrument, but
assent in respect of any such security shall be determined as here-
inbefore in this section provided. For the purposes of this section a security or an evidence of indebtedness shall not be
deemed to be outstanding if in the determination of the Commission the assent of the holder thereof to any proposed alteration or modification is within the control of the carrier or of any
person or persons controlling the carrier.

   "(4) (a) Any authorization and approval hereunder of any
alteration or modification of a provision of any class of securities
of a carrier or of a provision of any instrument pursuant to
which a class of securities has been issued, or by which it is secured, shall be deemed to constitute authorization and approval
of a corresponding alteration or modification of the obligation
of any other carrier which has assumed liability in respect of
such class of securities as guarantor, endorser, surety, or otherwise: *Provided,* That such other carrier consents in writing to
such alteration or modification of such class of securities in respect of which it has assumed liability or of the instrument pursuant to which such class of securities has been issued or by which
it is secured and, such consent having been given, any such corresponding alteration or modification shall become effective, without other action, when the alteration or modification of such

class of securities or of such instrument shall become and be binding.

" (b) Any person who is liable or obligated contingently or otherwise on any class or classes of securities issued by a carrier shall, with respect to such class or classes of securities, for the purposes of this section, be deemed a carrier.

" (5) The authority conferred by this section shall be exclusive and plenary and any carrier, in respect of any alteration or modification authorized and approved by the Commission hereunder, shall have full power to make any such alteration or modification and to take any actions incidental or appropriate thereto, and may make any such alteration or modification and take any such actions, and any such alteration or modification may be made without securing the approval of the Commission under any other section of this Act or other paragraph of this section, and without securing approval of any State authority, and any carrier and its officers and employees and any other persons, participating in the making of an alteration or modification approved and authorized under the provisions of this section or the taking of any such actions, shall be, and they hereby are, relieved from the operation of all restraints, limitations, and prohibitions of law, Federal, State, or municipal, insofar as may be necessary to enable them to make and carry into effect the alteration or modification so approved and authorized in accordance with the conditions and with the amendments, if any, imposed by the Commission. Any power granted by this section to any carrier shall be deemed to be in addition to and in modification of its powers under its corporate charter or under the laws of any State. The provisions of this section shall not affect in any way the negotiability of any security of any carrier or of the obligation of any carrier which has assumed liability in respect thereto.

" (6) The Commission shall require periodical or special reports from each carrier which shall hereafter secure from the Commission approval and authorization of any alteration or modification under this section, which shall show, in such detail as the Commission may require, the action taken by the carrier in the making of such alteration or modification.

" (7) The provisions of this section are permissive and not mandatory and shall not require any carrier to obtain authorization and approval of the Commission hereunder for the making of any alteration or modification of any provision of any of its securities or of any class thereof or of any provision of any mortgage, indenture, deed of trust, corporate charter, or other instrument, which it may be able lawfully to make in any other manner, whether by reason of provisions for the making of such alteration or modification in any such mortgage, indenture, deed of trust, corporate charter, or other instrument, or otherwise: *Provided,* That the provisions of paragraph (2) of section 20a, if applicable to such alteration or modification made otherwise than pursuant to the provisions of this section, shall continue to be so applicable.

"(8) The provisions of paragraph (6) of section 20a, except the provisions thereof in respect of hearings, shall apply to applications made under this section. In connection with any order entered by the Commission pursuant to paragraph (2) hereof, the Commission may from time to time, for good cause shown, make such supplemental orders in the premises as it may deem necessary or appropriate, and may by any such supplemental order modify the provisions of any such order, subject always to the requirements of said paragraph (2).

"(9) The provisions of subdivision (a) of section 14 of the Securities Exchange Act of 1934 shall not apply to any solicitation in connection with a proposed alteration or modification pursuant to this section.

"(10) The Commission shall have the power to make such rules and regulations appropriate to its administration of the provisions of this section as it shall deem necessary or desirable.

"(11) Any issuance of securities under this section which shall be found by the Commission to comply with the requirements of paragraph (2) of section 20a shall be deemed to be an issuance which is subject to the provisions of section 20a within the meaning of section 3 (a) (6) of the Securities Act of 1933, as amended. Section 5 of said Securities Act shall not apply to the issuance, sale, or exchange of certificates of deposit representing securities of, or claims against, any carrier which are issued by committees in proceedings under this section, and said certificates of deposit and transactions therein shall, for the purposes of said Securities Act, be deemed to be added to those exempted by sections 3 and 4, respectively, of said Securities Act.

"(12) The provisions of sections 1801, 1802, 3481, and 3482 of the Internal Revenue Code and any amendments thereto, unless specifically providing to the contrary, shall not apply to the issuance, transfer, or exchange of securities or the making or delivery of conveyances to make effective any alteration or modification effected pursuant to this section.

"(13) The Commission shall not approve an application filed

under this section by any carrier while in equity receivership or in process of reorganization under section 77 of the Bankruptcy Act, as amended, except that the Commission may approve an application filed by a carrier which, on the date of enactment of this Act, is in equity receivership and with respect to which no order confirming the sale of the carrier's property has been entered, or is in process of reorganization under section 77 and with respect to which no order confirming a plan shall have been entered, or, such an order having been entered, if an appeal from said order is pending on said date in a circuit court of appeals or the matter is pending in the Supreme Court on a petition to review any order of a circuit court of appeals dealing with said order of confirmation or the time within which to make such appeal or to file such petition has not expired, if prior to the filing of such application with the Commission such carrier shall have applied for and been granted permission to file such application by the district judge before whom the equity receivership or section 77 proceeding is pending. Any such carrier applying for permission to file such application shall file with the court as a prerequisite to the granting of such permission (1) a copy of the proposed application, (2) a copy of the proposed plan of alteration or modification of its securities, and (3) assurances satisfactory to the court of the acceptance of such plan from holders of at least 25 per centum of the aggregate amount of all securities, including not less than 25 per centum of the aggregate amount of all creditors' claims, affected by such plan. An order of a district judge granting or withholding such permission shall be final and shall not be subject to review. Upon granting of such permission, such proceeding, so far as it relates to a plan of reorganization, shall be suspended until the Commission shall have notified the court that (a) the application filed by such carrier under this section has been dismissed or denied by the Commission or withdrawn, (b) the Commission has approved and authorized an alteration or modification under this section with respect to the securities of such carrier, or (c) twelve months have elapsed since the filing of such application and no such alteration or modification has been approved and authorized by the Commission. Upon receipt by the court of notification that such application has been dismissed or denied or withdrawn or that twelve months have elapsed and no alteration or modification has been approved and authorized, the equity receivership or section 77 proceeding shall be resumed as though permission to file application under this section had not been granted.

Upon receipt by the court of notification that the Commission has authorized and approved such alteration or modification of the carrier's securities under this section as, in the judgment of the court, makes further receivership or section 77 proceeding unnecessary, the court shall enter an order restoring custody of the property to the debtor, and making such other provision as may be necessary to terminate the equity receivership or section 77 proceeding."

APPENDIX B

Rules Pertinent to Balloting Procedures, from Rules and Regulations of the Interstate Commerce Commission Governing Applications under Section 20b of the Interstate Commerce Act

Rules and regulations governing (A) applications under section 20b of the Interstate Commerce Act for authority to alter or modify any provision of any class of securities or any provision of any mortgage, indenture, deed of trust, corporate charter, or other instrument pursuant to which any class of securities shall have been issued or by which any class of obligations is secured; and (B) certificates of notification and reports relating to such alteration or modification of securities.

At a Session of the Interstate Commerce Commission, Division 4 held at its office in Washington, D.C., on the 25th day of May, A.D. 1948.

There being under consideration the above-entitled matter:

It is ordered, That the following rules and regulations be, and they are hereby, approved and prescribed; and that on and after May 31, 1948, all carriers making application under section 20b of the Interstate Commerce Act, as amended, observe and comply with these rules and regulations in making such application:

TITLE 49 — Transportation and Railroads
CHAPTER 1 — Interstate Commerce Commission
SUBCHAPTER A — General Rules and Regulations
PART 55 — Alteration or Modification of Securities and the Provisions of Instruments, and Filing of Certificates and Reports.

SECTION

55.1	Form and Contents of Application
55.2	Required Exhibits
55.3	Procedure
55.4	Certificates of Notification and Periodical Reports

SOURCE: Budget Bureau no. 60–R257, ICC, May 25, 1948. See Code of Federal Regulations (1949 edition) Title 49, Chapter I, Subchapter A, Part 55.

§ 55.1 Form and contents of application. The application and supporting exhibits shall conform to Rule 1.15 of the General Rules of Practice and shall show, in the order indicated, with the following paragraph designations, the following information:

. . . . .

(1) The outstanding principal amount, or the number of shares and par value per share, of each class of security affected by the proposed alteration or modification, and the percentage, if any, of the total of such principal amount and total number of shares for each such class as to which assurances of assent have been obtained from the holders, with a statement of the method of determining such percentage.

. . . . .

(n) Each class of securities affected, 75 percent of the aggregate principal amount, or number of shares outstanding of which is held by fewer than 25 holders.

(o) Amount, if any, of the securities affected which are pledged under a mortgage, indenture, deed of trust, or other instrument pursuant to which evidences of indebtedness of the applicant or of any company controlling or controlled by the applicant are outstanding, and the amount and description of such evidences of indebtedness; the name or names of any trustee or trustees under any such indenture or deed of trust; and the amount, if any, of the securities affected which are pledged to secure other evidences of indebtedness of the applicant or of any company controlling or controlled by the applicant not so issued under mortgage, indenture, deed of trust, or other instrument, and the amount and description of such other evidences of indebtedness so secured.

. . . . .

(q) Amount, if any, of securities affected by the proposed modification or alteration and of evidences of indebtedness secured by the pledge thereof as referred to in the foregoing paragraph (o), which are held by any holder whose assent to the proposed alteration or modification is within the control of the applicant or any person controlling the applicant.

. . . . .

(s) A statement of the procedures and methods which the applicant proposes to use in procuring and verifying the assents of the security holders affected by the proposed alteration or modification, and the character of the evidence which the applicant proposes to certify to the Commission in proof of such assents.

(t) Description and terms and conditions of any certificates of deposit that will be issued in connection with the proposed modification or alteration, by the applicant or committees representative of security holders.

. . . . .

§ 55.3 *Procedure.* The following procedure shall govern the execution, filing and disposition of the application:

. . . . .

(e) In connection with its findings required by paragraph (2) of section 20b the Commission will give direction (1) as to the manner in which the carrier shall submit the proposed alteration or modification (with such terms, conditions, and amendments, if any) to the holders of each class of its securities affected thereby, for acceptance or rejection, and (2) as to the manner of proof to be made by the carrier of the percentage of assents to the proposed alteration or modification by the holders of each class of securities affected thereby.

(f) All letters, circulars, advertisements, and other communications, and all financial and statistical statements, or summaries thereof, to be used in soliciting the assents or the opposition of holders of securities affected, shall, before being used, be submitted to the Commission for its approval as to correctness and sufficiency of the material facts stated therein; but this requirement shall not be construed to apply to normal and ordinary correspondence or other communication between the carrier and a creditor, stockholder, or other interested party.

§ 55.4 *Certificates of notification and periodical reports.* Sections 56.4, 56.5 and 56.6 of the Rules and Regulations governing applications under section 20a of the Interstate Commerce Act shall be followed as a guide.

And it is further ordered, That notice of these regulations be given to the general public by posting copies in the office of the Secretary of the Interstate Commerce Commission, Washington, D.C., and by filing with the Director of the Federal Register. 62 Stat. 162; 49 USC 20b

By the Commission, division 4.

W. P. BARTEL,
Secretary.

(SEAL)

APPENDIX C

Order

At a Session of the INTERSTATE COMMERCE COMMIS–
SION, division 4, held at its office in Washington, D.C., on the
19th day of April, A.D., 1950.

FINANCE DOCKET NO. 16250

BOSTON AND MAINE RAILROAD SECURITIES
MODIFICATION

Investigation having been made of the matters and things involved in the application of the Boston and Maine Railroad, filed
January 24, 1949, for approval and authorization, under section
20b of the Interstate Commerce Act, as amended, of the alteration and modification of its corporate charter and the provisions
of classes of stock issued thereunder, all as hereinafter specified, a
hearing having been held, and said division having, on the date
hereof, made and filed a report containing its findings of fact and
conclusions thereon, which report is hereby referred to and made
a part hereof; and

It appearing, That the classes of securities affected by the proposed alterations and modifications are (1) the said applicant's
prior preference 7-percent stock, (2) its first preferred stock, consisting of series A, 5-percent, series B, 8-percent, series C, 7-per-
cent, series D, 10-percent, and series E, $4\frac{1}{2}$-percent, (3) its noncumulative 6-percent preferred stock, and (4) its common stock:

It is ordered, That (1) the proposed alterations and modifications, subject to such terms and conditions and with such amendments as in said report are found to be just and reasonable, shall
be submitted by the applicant for acceptance or rejection, in the
manner hereinafter indicated, to the holders of securities of the
classes enumerated in the preceding paragraph of this order, except such securities as are held by the applicant in its treasury.

(2) That such submission shall be made by mailing, as soon as

practicable after the effective date of this order, (a) a copy of this order, (b) a copy of the report issued therewith, (c) a copy of the plan of alteration and modification, as amended, (d) a form of letter of assent, and (e) a letter of transmittal requesting the holder's assent.

(3) That the plan of alteration and modification, all letters, circulars, advertisements, and other communications, including written or printed instructions to solicitors, as well as all financial and statistical statements or summaries thereof, to be used by any party in soliciting acceptance or rejection of the plan by the holders of affected securities, before being so used, shall be submitted to the Commission for approval as to the correctness and sufficiency of the material facts stated therein, and, simultaneously, any such material so submitted to the Commission shall be distributed to all parties of record by the party seeking its approval.

(4) That notice of submission shall be promptly given by the applicant by publication, in a form to be approved by the Commission, once a week for two successive weeks in one newspaper of general circulation published in each of the cities of Boston, Mass., and New York, N.Y., and by such further publication of such notice at such other times and places as the applicant may determine.

(5) That the directors, officers, and regular employees of the applicant may take part in soliciting assents, and the applicant may retain the services of one or more firms or persons specializing in such work to assist in the solicitation; that reasonable provision may be made for the compensation of such firms or persons; and that such solicitation may be carried on by personal interview, mail, advertising, telephone, and telegraph.

(6) That the assent to the plan of alteration and modification by any holder of securities of the above-enumerated classes shall be given by sending his executed vote of assent, within the time specified in the next succeeding paragraph, to the Old Colony Trust Company, 45 Milk Street, Boston, Mass., the applicant's designated depositary, or, if for any reason, it is unable to act, such other depositary, satisfactory to the Commission, as may be selected by the applicant. Failure of any stockholder to act shall constitute a vote of rejection without execution of any ballot or return of the form of assent. An assent shall be revocable at any time up to the time of declaration of irrevocability as hereinafter provided, but, until notice of revocation is received by the depositary, an assent, once given, will bind the assenting holder, his heirs, successors, and assigns. Revocation may be made only by

the execution and delivery to the depositary of a letter of revocation in a form to be approved by the Commission, prior to one publication, as provided in the next succeeding paragraph hereof, in the same newspapers in which the notice of submission shall be published, of notice of the termination of the right of revocation, which publication shall be made only at a time when unrevoked assents of holders of 75 percent or more of the shares of each class of affected securities (other than the 6-percent noncumulative preferred stock, as to which the percentage shall be 87) are held by the depositary.

(7) That such assents shall be made on or before 6 months after the effective date of this order, or within such further time as the Commission may designate by subsequent order, provided that, if at any time prior to the expiration of such period or extension thereof, assents shall be received and remain unrevoked from the holders of 75 percent of the outstanding shares of each class of affected securities, except in the case of the 6-percent noncumulative preferred stock, as to which the percentage shall be 87, the applicant may declare the submission period closed as of such time, in which event it shall forthwith give notice thereof, and of the termination of the right of revocation, by one advertisement in the same newspapers in which the notice of submission shall be published.

(8) That the applicant, within 60 days after the closing of the submission period, shall submit to the Commission, in connection with a supplemental application, a certificate as to the total number of shares outstanding in each class of affected securities, the number of shares of each class of affected securities held by parties assenting to the proposed alterations and modifications, and the percentage thereof with respect to the total number of shares outstanding in the particular class. Such certificate shall be based upon and supported by certification by the depositary, as to the number of shares of each class of affected securities held by the parties assenting to the plan, such certificate also to be submitted to the Commission.

(9) That copies of the effectuation documents reflecting the plan of alteration and modification, as amended, shall be furnished to each intervener and shall be filed with the Commission for its review and approval prior to the issuance of its final order of approval of the plan of alteration and modification.

(10) That the applicant shall supply to any holder of stock of any class of affected securities, or to a duly authorized representative of such holder, upon request, or make available to such

holder or representative, under conditions reasonably convenient to their use, a current list of the names and addresses of the holders of record of such stock, or, in the alternative, if it so elects, the applicant shall mail, at the request and expense of such holder, copies of any material, the correctness and sufficiency of which have been approved by the Commission, proposed to be used by such holder in connection with the solicitation of assents or dissents to the plan of alteration and modification.

(11) That the effective date of this order shall be 30 days after the date thereof.

By the Commission, division 4.

W. P. BARTEL,
Secretary.

(SEAL)

APPENDIX D

Further Details on the Capital
Readjustments of 1926 and 1940

The Voluntary Capital Readjustment of 1926

The General Readjustment Committee's final plan, dated September 1, 1925, contained the following principal provisions:

1. A new 7% prior preference stock would be created to provide $13 million of funds for additions and improvements. The stock would be $100 par, cumulative, and callable as a whole but not in part at $110 and accrued dividends after January 1, 1930; it would have voting power share for share with all other classes of stock and priority over all other classes as to dividends and in liquidation.

   This new stock would be offered at par to all stockholders, and the amount not taken would be offered for sale at public auction at not less than par. Those assenting to the plan would have the choice of purchasing a certain par value of the new stock for each share they held, or of surrendering part of their old stock. These terms differed as between the series of the first preferred stock, and were made less favorable for the plain preferred and the common stock.

2. Holders of $43.5 million bonds due in the years 1925 to 1932 would be asked to extend maturities for 15 years by exchange for new refunding bonds. The new bonds would be convertible at par into 7% preference stock between 1930 and 1940. The Committee was to use its best endeavors to obtain concessions from the United States Government with reference to the latter's holdings of $48.7 million bonds due between 1929 and 1935.

3. Assenting first preferred holders, whether subscribing to the new stock or not, would agree to surrender the dividends already accrued from July 1, 1920, to July 1, 1925, and any further dividends accruing up to July 1, 1927.[1]

[1] The dividends from July, 1925, to July, 1927, were paid and did not accrue.

For this concession they would be given priority in liquidation over the assented plain preferred and common
shares for par value and for dividends accruing after
July 1, 1927. The Committee emphasized that these were
voluntary readjustments among those who consented, and
did not affect the rights of those holders who refused to
cooperate.

This surrender of accruals was qualified, however. If
in any year the common stock received a 6% dividend,
then one-half in amount of all dividends declared on the
common stock in excess of 6% would go to the several
first preferred series in proportion to their varying rates.
Such repayment would continue until half of the total
accumulation had been repaid.

4. Assenting common and plain preferred holders, whether
   subscribing or not, would agree to subordinate their rights
   in liquidation to the assented first preferred shares.
5. Stockholders were to assent by depositing their certificates
   and choosing to purchase or surrender stock. The certificates would then be stamped as assenting and returned
   either intact or reduced, according to the choice made by
   the holder. Assents were to carry over to successors and
   transferees, who would become bound to the plan.

By the middle of February, 1926, about 86% of the stockholders had assented, practically all as subscribers to the new preferred stock,[2] and their stock certificates were stamped as assenting. As soon as it was apparent that the bulk of the new prior
preference issue was subscribed, thus assuring substantial new
money, the bondholders were asked to exchange for the refunding
issue. The plan was made effective on September 1, 1926.

The entire issue of $13 million prior preference stock was sold;
about $11.7 million was subscribed by stockholders and $1.3 million was sold at public auction at an average price of $102\frac{3}{8}$.[3]

The old stock surrendered by the assenting but non-subscribing
stockholders was sold by the Committee.

The Voluntary Bond Adjustment of 1940

The 1940 bond adjustment may be summarized as follows:

[2] If a stockholder did not intend to subscribe, the alternative of keeping
all his stock by the simple expedient of refusing to assent was much to his advantage. Unassenting stockholders also had preemptive rights to subscribe to
the new stock.

[3] Boston and Maine Railroad, Annual Report for 1926.

The plan resulted in two new bond issues:
(a) $67,890,700 first mortgage 4% bonds, due July 1, 1960;
(b) $48,267,500 income mortgage $4\frac{1}{2}$% bonds, due July 1, 1970, interest payments to be contingent on earnings and to accumulate at 4%.

Some $7 million of the old funded debt was left outstanding, in addition to about 3\frac{1}{2}$ million in equipment obligations.

Alternative exchanges were offered to the old bondholders. They could exchange $1,000 face value of old bonds for either $500 face value of new first mortgage 4's and $500 face value of income $4\frac{1}{2}$'s or $300 in cash, $200 in first 4's, and $500 in income $4\frac{1}{2}$'s. Most assenting bondholders chose the second alternative, a natural preference if the first 4's would not sell at face.

By another provision of the plan, several banks and the RFC exchanged their holdings of nearly $20 million secured notes for the new first mortgage 4's in equal face amount. The RFC also took $26 million of first 4's in return for cash to be used to pay the bondholders who had selected the cash option of $300 a bond.[4]

The mortgage indenture included a formula for the application of available net income after fixed charges. The formula, which had a decisive bearing on the status of the entire stock equity, was as follows:

(1) from available net income, to the extent sufficient and at the discretion of the board of directors, there was to be set aside each year a capital fund of $1 million (less charges against income for depreciation of roadway and structures) to be used for property additions and betterments;

(2) from any remaining available net income a sinking fund for the first 4's was to be paid in an amount equal to 1% of the aggregate principal amount issued;

(3) from any then remaining income, interest was to be paid on the income $4\frac{1}{2}$'s in an amount up to $4\frac{1}{2}$% of the principal outstanding plus all accumulated interest;

(4) from any then remaining income, as a sinking fund for the income $4\frac{1}{2}$'s, an amount equal to 1% of the aggregate principal amount issued was to be paid;

(5) any balance might be applied in specified proportions to the purchase of funded debt, increase of capital fund,

[4] The RFC later was able to sell at a profit all its Boston and Maine bonds that had not been redeemed from the sinking funds. Hearings on H. R. 2298, op. cit., p. 56.

or other purposes chargeable to the property or investment account.

*Until $25 million principal amount of funded debt had been
retired, net income could not be used for any other purposes
than those specified.*

In sum, the 1940 plan immediately reduced fixed interest
charges by $2,630,659 annually.[5]   Furthermore, the provision that
additions and betterments were to be financed out of earnings
through the capital fund worked to check the growth of debt and
to increase the equity.

[5] Boston and Maine Railroad, Annual Report for 1940.

INDEX

Index